HEROINES AND HISTORY
Representations of Madeleine de Verchères and
Laura Secord

Heroines and History is a co-authored, comparative study of the images of Madeleine de Verchères and Laura Secord, symbols respectively of French-Canadian and English-Canadian loyalism and nationalism. The authors explore the roles of gender, race/ethnicity, and imperialism in defining national identity and shaping the past by looking at the role of local historical societies, the formation of narratives of Loyalism and the War of 1812 in school texts, and the use of historical figures in the service of twentieth-century consumer capitalism (e.g., the Secord chocolate company) and in the development of tourism.

This is a fascinating comparison of the histories of Ontario and Quebec as seen through the handling of their best-known heroines. Most Canadians are familiar with stories of Madeleine de Verchères defending Montreal against the Iroquois in 1692 and of Laura Secord and her cow bravely crossing the American lines to warn the British during the War of 1812. In both cases, the authors show how these heroines were used for nationalistic purposes in their respective provinces, and how their images changed down through the ages.

Heroines and History makes a significant contribution to the growing body of literature on commemoration, as well as to the literatures of gender, cultural, and Aboriginal studies. It will be of interest both to specialist academic readers and general readers of Canadian history and society.

COLIN M. COATES is the Director of the Centre for Canadian Studies at the University of Edinburgh.

CECILIA MORGAN is an assistant professor in the history program, Department of Theory and Policy Studies at the Ontario Institute for Studies in Education/University of Toronto.

Heroines and History
Representations of Madeleine de Verchères and Laura Secord

COLIN M. COATES and CECILIA MORGAN

UNIVERSITY OF TORONTO PRESS
Toronto Buffalo London

© University of Toronto Press Incorporated 2002
Toronto Buffalo London
Printed in Canada

ISBN 0-8020-4784-X (cloth)
ISBN 0-8020-8330-7 (paper)

Printed on acid-free paper

National Library of Canada Cataloguing in Publication Data

Coates, Colin MacMillan, 1960–
    Heroines and history : Madeleine de Verchères and Laura Secord

    Includes bibliographical references and index.
    ISBN 0-8020-4784-X (bound)   ISBN 0-8020-8330-7 (pbk.)

    1. Verchères, Madeleine de, 1678–1747.   2. Secord, Laura,
    1775–1868.   3. Women heroes – Canada – History.
    4. Nationalism – Canada – History.   5. Canada – History –
    Errors, inventions, etc.   I. Morgan, Cecilia Louise, 1958–   II. Title.

    FC267.W6C63 2002   305.4'092'271   C2001-901361-2
    F1005.C63 2002

University of Toronto Press acknowledges the financial assistance to its
publishing program of the Canada Council for the Arts and the Ontario
Arts Council.

This book has been published with the help of a grant from the Humanities
and Social Sciences Federation of Canada, using funds provided by the
Social Sciences and Humanities Research Council of Canada.

University of Toronto Press acknowledges the financial support for its
publishing activities of the Government of Canada through the Book
Publishing Industry Development Program (BPIDP).

To Mab and Bryn

To Paul

Contents

Preface

Most people remembered history in the same conceited yet evanescent fashion as they recalled their own childhood. It seemed to Dr Max positively unpatriotic to know so little about the origins and forging of your nation. And yet, therein lay the immediate paradox: that patriotism's most eager bedfellow was ignorance, not knowledge.

Julian Barnes, *England, England*

In Julian Barnes's dystopic future, the Isle of Wight is reconstructed as a tourists' reproduction England that supplants the attractions of the 'real England.' In a short space of time, the island's simulacra wield more drawing power than the original historic sites. Barnes's novel raises the issue of the tension between authenticity and historical memory that many historians have begun to address in their work in the past few decades. This book provides a contribution to a growing literature on the commemorative process, and offers a focus on perceptions of gender roles that is sometimes lacking in other works.

Like all published works, this volume has its own history which rests on elements of chance and opportunity. In part, this work stems directly from our previous publications: a study of the region of New France where the adult Madeleine de Verchères played an important role in managing her seigneury; and an examination of the discourse of gender in Upper Canada. Madeleine de Verchères and Laura Secord both figure in our previous books. But this volume stems from Colin's almost haphazard collection of references to Verchères in the course of researching a dissertation on another topic. Once this was completed, Colin thought he had enough material to construct into a larger argument. The first occasion for this was a Popular Culture conference in New Orleans which had as one of its themes 'Canadian women.' He contacted Cecilia to see if she wished to provide a companion paper at the conference on Laura Secord.

This book grew out of those initial conference papers. Colin has written the section on Verchères, Cecilia the section on Secord. We wrote the Introduction and the Epilogue together. This has been a truly collaborative venture, in which we shared research materials and maintained each other's enthusiasm for the project over the years it has taken to reach fruition. A number of clear parallels developed out of the comparison of Verchères and Secord, and this book develops the similarities and the differences in the treatment of the two heroines. In particular, it explores the desire to engage with the work of so many historical enthusiasts, since history is fortunately not only the province of the professional historian. We have striven to interpret in a fair manner the words and actions of the heroines and their commemorators. Both the women and subsequent enthusiasts chose certain words and genres to achieve their aims. These choices involved a search for the 'truth' at the same time that they suppressed certain themes which did not fit a desired picture. In this way, for instance, the commemorators attempted to inculcate certain images of patriotism that they thought responded to the needs of the day. But in turning the two heroines into icons, they sometimes neglected to see them as women who themselves participated in the creation of their own stories. In this book, we seek to uncover the ways in which the two women attempted to write their own lives, while at the same time we examine how others tried to reuse those narratives for different ends.

Along the way, we have incurred many debts. In particular, a number of friends and colleagues have shared research materials with us, just as we have had the pleasure of locating material for each other. Although we will acknowledge many of our debts individually, there are a few that we would like to refer to jointly. For years, Gerry Hallowell has supported the idea behind this work. He also was kind enough to send useful comments on the manuscript. Laura Macleod provided key encouragement at an early stage in the process. Three anonymous reviewers have been most helpful in pointing out inconsistencies and places for improvement. Our editor, Jill McConkey, and our copy editor, Ken Lewis, have both worked wonders.

Colin: My sincere thanks to Donald Wright, Kathleen Burke, Martin Massicotte of la Municipalité de Verchères, and Linda Blanshay for their help with research material. Mimi Cogliano kindly translated some Swedish research material for me. The librarians and archivists at the Archevêché de Montréal, the Diocèse St-Jean-Longueuil, and the Ottawa City Archives, Judith Nefsky of the Canadian Pacific Archives, Eileen Lim of the National Library of Canada, and D. John Turner of the National Archives, Film Division, all facilitated research for someone working at a considerable distance. Many thanks also to Thomas Wien, Megan J. Davies, and John S. Lutz for their help with and comments on versions of this material. The story of Madeleine de Verchères is in part a narrative about youth and courage. Mab and Bryn provided inspiration during the time I worked on this book, and as a result it is theirs as well. I dedicate this book with love to my wonderful children.

For assistance with research and conference grants, I would like to acknowledge the Département d'histoire de l'Université de Montréal and the Department of Foreign Affairs and External Trade in Ottawa (Canadian Studies Faculty Research Award), and ongoing support from the University of Edinburgh. I am grateful also for the help given by Grace Owens, Ged Martin, Nicole Chagnon, Paul Brisebois, Éric Daudelin, David McKnight, William Meredith, Catherine Annau, and Patrick Hill.

Cecilia: This book – along with my interest in historical memory – has grown considerably in scope since Colin's phone call on a dreary November day sparked my interest in narratives of Laura Secord. Although I had been very much interested in gender relations in Upper Canada, my own work on the War of 1812 dealt only slightly with Secord. From a solitary paper, written for a conference in New Orleans and focused on late-nineteenth-century historical societies' treatment of Secord, my research expanded to include textbooks, tourism, and – of course – confectionery.

In my search for stories of Secord, I've been fortunate to have had the help of numerous archivists and librarians. Thanks are due to the staff of the Archives of Ontario; Brant County Historical Museum; Queen's University Archives; National Archives; J.J. Talman Regional Collection, D.B. Weldon Library, University of Western Ontario; and Niagara-on-the-Lake Library. A number of individuals have also assisted me in my work: Winnie Jacobs, Woodland Cultural and Educational Centre, Brantford; Andrew C. Porteous, Niagara Falls Public Library; Roseanne Skoke, former librarian, Queenston Community Library, who helped me to locate the Jean Huggins Papers; Lynn Prunskus, Special Collections, Brock University Library; and Barbara Flewelling, Laura Secord

Candy Company, who generously assisted in gaining access to the Company's visual archives. I would also like to thank the Social Sciences and Humanities Research Council of Canada for providing me with a postdoctoral fellowship, without which it would have been impossible to conduct the research for this book. Thank you to Karen Dubinksy, Jane Errington, Sandra den Otter, Ian McKay, Robert Malcolmson, and Geoff Smith, Department of History, Queen's University, for their interest in and support of my work and career. Although he died long before this work reached completion, the late George Rawlyk provided much-appreciated encouragement and keen interest in my work. My colleagues in my new academic home, the History of Education Program in the Department of Theory and Policy Studies at OISE/UT, have provided me with the support and time I needed to write my portion of this book. Thanks to Glen Jones, David Levine, Ruth Roach Pierson, and Harold Troper for their generosity. Ai-ri Chung provided invaluable computer assistance to allow a 'Mac' person to speak to a PC user.

A number of other individuals have helped in numerous ways. Nancy and Ron Wood generously opened their home to me during my two years in Kingston, providing meals, wine, car lifts to both Queen's University and the train station, and, in particular, good company. I'd also like to thank Patti Borrowman, Brendan Morgan, Felicity Morgan, and Craig Oswald for their generosity in providing me with surrogate homes. I owe much to the following folks for their ongoing moral support, comments on portions of this work, and general good humour – not to mention patience with my obsession with Laura Secord: Karen Dubinsky, Paul Deslandes, Lykke de la Cour, Nancy Forestell, Franca Iacovetta (special thanks for the title), Patricia Jasen, Kathryn McPherson, Maureen McCarthy, Lynne Marks, Suzanne Morton, Ruth Roach Pierson, Ian Radforth, Tori Smith (my gratitude especially for the candy box), Steve Heathorn, and Mariana Valverde. Thanks also to Tina Davidson, Peggy Hooke, Kerrie Kennedy, Lorna McLean, Victoria Vasileski, Bay Ryley, and Nicole Woodman-Harvey for passing on various pieces of Secord memorabilia. My biggest thank-you is for Paul Jenkins, who has lived far longer than he'd probably anticipated or hoped with stories of the 'candy lady' and has done so with lots of patience and good humour. As a 'history groupie,' he has encouraged my work and has given up many fine summer days to be dragged around monuments, statues, and historic homes, in the process giving me the benefit of his much more acute appreciation of the visual world of the past. But he has also reminded me that historians must live in and make the most of the present.

HEROINES AND HISTORY
Representations of Madeleine de Verchères and
Laura Secord

Introduction: Why Heroines, Why History?

Laura Secord ... is to Upper Canada what Madeleine de Verchères is to Lower Canada.

W.J. Karr, *Explorers, Soldiers and Statesmen* (1937), p. 172

Captain Dominique Ducharme: *It is magnificent! Madam, I salute you. Our French heroine, Madeleine de Verchères now has a peer.*
Captain Fitzgibbon: *I never heard of her. And Mrs Secord, surely, will not be wanting to listen to our praise.*

Merrill Denison, 'Laura Secord' (1931), p. 142

The fourteen-year-old seigneur's daughter and the Queenston wife and mother, one defending the fort, the other warning the troops: such were the exploits of Madeleine de Verchères and Laura Secord, their characters and deeds memorialized in prose, poetry, drama, and other genres in French and English. From the late nineteenth to the early twentieth century, stories of these events and of the two women said to be their central characters were inscribed in narratives of Canadian nationalism. *Heroines and History* explores these processes of commemoration in their primary locations of Quebec and Ontario. We begin with their protagonists' first recounting of the events of 1692 and 1813 and then trace the ways in which their stories have been told by others: 'amateur' historians, authors of children's textbooks, monument builders, officials of the Canadian state, novelists and dramatists, film-makers, and the advertising department of the Laura Secord Candy Company. This book points to the similarities and the differences between the telling of these narratives and between their narrators. As well, it explores the variety of places where these specific forms of historical memory have been transmitted and transmuted in late nineteenth- and twentieth-century central Canada.

Heroines and History examines a number of related themes and questions that go beyond simply detailing the processes of historical commemoration. The study of these narratives tells us much about the complicated and complex 'histories' of competing national identities and imperialism in the Canadian context. A central concern is the place of women in popular and official histories for, as many scholars have shown, notions of the 'nation' and its 'history' have been gendered. Gender cannot be seen in isolation from other relationships: those of class, race and ethnicity, and sexuality. How was the memorialization of Verchères and Secord shaped by the interrelated dynamics of gender, race, and imperialism: was the inclusion of these women, for example, done at the cost of others' exclusion from the imagined community?[1] In a Western commemorative typology in which women have usually been archetypes and allegories, and not flesh-and-blood historical actors, Verchères and Secord are anomalous. *Heroines and History* explores the reasons why it was possible and, indeed, desirable for writers of popular and official history to use these 'real women' – but in ways that served particular aims and were shaped by particular historical contexts.

Historical Memory

When asked over the years of research and writing *Heroines and History* 'so what's it all about?' we have either responded eponymously, albeit narrowly – 'narratives of Verchères and Secord' – or grandiosely: 'historical memory in nineteenth- and twentieth-century Canada.' In a field in which the terms 'commemoration,' 'memory,' 'creation of heritage,' and, of course, 'the invention of tradition,' are common, the term we have chosen to use, 'historical memory,' warrants some definition.

Some scholars have seen the terms 'history' and 'memory' as antithetical. For French historian Pierre Nora, arguably one of the most influential scholars in the field of memory and commemoration, the two areas can be divided categorically. There is, Nora argues, an 'enormous distance that separates real memory – the kind of inviolate social memory that primitive and archaic societies embodied, and whose secret has died with them – from history, which is how modern societies organise a past they are condemned to forget because they are driven by change.'[2] For Nora, memory is life, always embodied in living societies and as such in permanent evolution, subject to the dialectic of remembering and forgetting, unconscious of the distortions to which it is subject, vulnerable in various ways to appropriation and manipulation, and capable of lying dormant for long periods only to be suddenly reawakened.

Nora also links memory to 'emotion and magic' – partial, ephemeral, subjective, and capricious, it is a process that 'thrives on vague, telescoping reminiscences,' that can be easily transferred and censored, and is the subject of multiple projections. It derives from multiple groups and can be summoned up only in concrete images and spaces, by gestures and objects. Memory is absolute, unlike history, which is relative and whose domain includes the abstract, the linear, the empirical, the analytical, and the objective. History, then, is the 'reconstruction, always problematic and incomplete, of what is no longer'; it is no special group's exclusive property and belongs to 'everyone and to no one.' And, in a distinction that is especially significant for our study, Nora argues that 'memory situates remembrance in a sacred context. History ferrets it out; it turns whatever it touches into prose.' For Nora, there is no longer any 'memory'; there is only now 'history' (and a surfeit of it at that), which, 'having renounced memory, now cries out for it.'[3]

Other scholars feel that such distinctions are overly rigid. For them, the relationship between 'memory' and 'history' is considerably more complex, as the two categories are fluid and intertwined. As British historian Raphael Samuel in his wide-ranging *Theatres of Memory* puts it, memory is dynamic and 'dialectically related to historical thought,' not its negative other. For Samuel, memory is 'historically conditioned, changing shape and colour according to the exigencies of the moment,' and, in turn, history 'involves a series of erasures, emendations and amalgamations ... it integrates what in the original may have been divergent ... and brings the half-forgotten back to life,' creating a 'consecutive narrative out of fragments, imposing order on chaos, and producing images far clearer than any reality could be.'[4]

In the context of this work, we have found neither that the distinctions between 'memory' or 'history' are clear-cut nor that 'history' simply operates as the default function of 'memory.' In studying the narratives of Verchères and Secord, and the historical actors who created them, the lines of such distinctions are blurred. When analysed historically, the labour of creating these stories can be seen as 'historically conditioned'; and it has encompassed 'erasures, emendations, and amalgamations.' The late-Victorian commemorators, for example, who were involved in shaping these narratives worked with archival sources (in Nora's view, the stuff of 'history') as well as what we might call 'oral histories.' They also sought to create sacred spaces, such as Secord's home in Queenston or Verchères's statue in the village that shares her name, in which 'memories' of the heroines would be brought to life. Historical pageants likewise revitalized the past. Yet these groups and individuals saw themselves, quite explicitly and self-consciously, as 'historians.' While it is possible to debate their claim in today's terms, it seems more useful to try to determine just what it meant in the context of the late nineteenth century, for these individuals found no contradiction in the wish to create both history and memory through their work.

These narratives were not the dominion of one, unanimous group. Neither Verchères nor Secord was created with the intent of being the sole property of either French-Canadian nationalists or English-Canadian imperialists, although certainly members of those communities were active in their heroines' commemorations. However, the images of these women and the meanings that were meant to be drawn from them were intended to transcend the local, particular, and regional. The images of Verchères and Secord were used both to invoke notions of 'the nation' and, simultaneously, to help create that very entity. If, as Nora argues, 'what we call memory today is ... not memory but already history,'[5] then perhaps we need to reconsider some of our definitions of history. Moreover, while the Laura Secord Candy Company appropriated her image as part of producing a 'history,' it did so in ways that also incorporated the vagaries of reminiscence. The result was a 'history' that was (almost) anyone's domain.

Canadian Memories

It is also worth pointing out the differences in studying history and memory in the Canadian context. Nora himself is scrupulous in making clear that, while there are parallels between the commemorative processes he examines and those in other national contexts, the specificities and particularities of the French context form a critical part of his analysis. While we would agree that certainly parallels between the European worlds of historical memory and that of Canada can be seen, there have also been some critical differences. Some of these are the result of historical timing and the heterogeneity of the societies whose notions of 'history' are being scrutinized.

For instance, the possibility of locating a living organic 'memory' of a 'traditional' peasant society in the Canadian context is remote. Unlike in

Europe, memory and local tradition had no legal status in a place where written deeds and contracts preceded most Euro-Canadian settlement.[6] Folkloric stories circulated, of course, acquiring layers of social commentary leading far away from the original 'facts' of the instance. The retellings of the fate of La Corriveau, a woman put to death in 1763 for the murder of her husband, is one important case in point. La Corriveau increasingly became a symbol of the mistreatment of French Canadians at the hands of the British conquerors after the fall of Quebec in 1759.[7] But it is not possible in the Canadian context, as in Nora's work, to construct a narrative of a 'pure' Euro-Canadian living memory being tainted and overcome by the work of the historians.

Furthermore, the colonial context of the deployment of both these narratives cannot be overlooked. Relationships with the 'national' histories of Britain and France have produced multi-layered Canadian historical memories.[8] These colonial contexts have meant that Aboriginal peoples' histories and memories have been both appropriated and forgotten. As *Heroines and History* shows, for many decades Aboriginal peoples were critically important to the writing of Canadian history as seen through the prism of these narratives, particularly in the process of forgetting and omitting. Simultaneously, the First Nations were denied their own history, being relegated to the realm of memory, fantasy, and desire.

From the growing literature on historical memories in the Canadian context, certain points of convergence have been delineated.[9] Conflicts between French and English speakers' views of history have provided one clear theme, as well as disputes between particular strains of Catholic or Protestant perspectives. The importance of social elites in the Canadian context, whether at the local or the national level, has been clearly demonstrated. More surprising, perhaps, is proof of a more widespread, popular desire to commemorate the country's past, at least during the late nineteenth and early twentieth centuries. Indeed, the anxious, integrative desire to create a common sense of destiny in the various sections of a disparate country remains one overriding theme of the studies of historical memory in Canada.

Despite the importance of social elites in encouraging popular support for the country's history, the distinction that John Bodnar draws for twentieth-century America between an 'authentic vernacular' memory and a 'manipulative official one' is not particularly useful in the Canadian context.[10] The nation-state was clearly involved in shaping and disseminating the Verchères and Secord narratives, but it would be misleading to argue for a simple imposition of the state's will to remember, or even for less direct and hegemonic control by the Dominion or provincial governments. Certainly such agencies, through their subsidies for monuments or their approval of certain textbooks, helped shape the stories of these women, but they often did so as a reaction to the demands of voluntary organizations or prominent individuals. In turn, the plays, poems, novels, pageants, and the candy company cannot be seen as having created an oppositional or popular memory distinct from that of the nation-state, for they shared many elements: most noticeably the belief in Verchères and Secord as emblems of the Canadian nation. Thus the categories of 'official' and 'vernacular,' while they help to remind us of the potential for conflicting memories and of the power relations embedded in these conflicts, are not entirely useful as organizing categories in these particular historical cases. The process by which Verchères and Secord were memorialized was more dialectical or even dialogical, with 'official' memory informing its 'vernacular' cousin – and vice-versa – so that the lines between the two are almost completely blurred and, at times, mutually reinforcing.

The cultural processes of memory and history cannot always be reduced to politics, for Verchères and Secord were created to provide unifying symbols for many groups of 'Canadians.' And there were particular historical moments when these symbols appear to have fulfilled this function. Yet it is no contradiction to argue that notions of 'the nation,' its 'history,' and 'memory' have frequently been constructs underpinned by the relations of class, imperialism, and race.[11] As historian John Gillis has argued, '"memory work" is, like any other kind of physical or mental labour, embedded in complex class, gender and power relations that determine what is remembered (or forgotten), by whom, and for what end.'[12] Jonathan Vance argues that people in commemorating the Great War responded to certain kinds of narratives simply to fulfil deep-seated needs and longings, and historians should not see them as being simply manipulated by the state and elites.[13] While we agree with the latter argument, we also believe that structuring our inquiries in order to find such 'needs' risks oversimplifying the circuitous, multi-layered, and often conflicted ways in which historical memories have been formed.[14] We also believe that such an approach tends to overlook an aspect of memory that the Verchères and Secord stories illustrate clearly: certain groups and individuals have, historically, responded to the same narratives and participated in the same commemorative processes – but for different, if at times overlapping, reasons.

The Gender of Heroism

In turn, Verchères's and Secord's stories also have been told and retold in ways that have created a plethora of similarities between the two women and the larger narratives that surround them. Both were, in the process of their commemorations, transformed into 'saviours' of the Canadian nation, their deeds seen as part of 'la survivance' in French Canada and, to no lesser extent, the 'survival' of English Canada. And the fact that both were women mattered to their commemorators. To be sure, it is possible that their stories might have been memorialized if they had had male protagonists at their centres. Yet the stories would have lost much of their force. As *Heroines and History* shows, the heroines' femininity was always placed in the foreground. For some, the fact that they were celebrating 'heroines' simply demonstrated the obvious: women were capable and willing to participate in the defence of the nation. As part of this more 'feminist' argument, women as historical actors set an uplifting and persuasive example for late-Victorian women's participation in the work of the nation. However, it could also be argued that the Canadian 'nation' and, particularly in Secord's case, the imperial tie were so compelling that their defence could be undertaken even by those who normally would be considered exempt from such responsibilities, those whose training and 'inclinations' would normally make them place home and family before the claims of patriotric duty. It could not be said that 'Canada' lacked important historical figures and national symbols: even women were part of its national pantheon of stirring and inspirational narratives.

Thus, 'women's' contribution to the tasks of national defence was rendered both natural and conspicuous. Their gender was mapped out in particular ways. Verchères's youth and virginity were predominant aspects of her femininity, while Secord was frequently celebrated as a wife and mother. To be sure, the circumstances differed: Verchères was defending the honour and property of her family, while Secord left her home to venture out into the wilderness of the Upper Canadian bush. Yet there were others points of juncture, for both women took on a masculine task and role in the absence or indisposition of adult males: circumstance, more than unwomanly ambition or aggression, was said to have forced them into such actions. Furthermore, the metaphorical use of 'family' also unites these stories. Verchères and Secord were not just acting to defend their immediate family; instead, the people in the fortress and the family of the Queenston homestead could also be read as representations of the 'families' of nation and empire. As scholars have shown, the use of familial metaphors in imperial and nationalistic discourse had particular symbolic significance and weight during the late-Victorian and Edwardian decades, years that saw the apotheosis of Verchères and Secord.[15] No matter the form in which the metaphor of family appeared – whether it was the isolation of the seigneury, a 'Castle Dangerous' that was an outpost of 'civilization,' or the cozy domesticity of the Queenston cottage that was left behind for the wilderness – the metaphorical defence of 'the national family' was firmly inscribed in these narratives.

As well as similarities between the 'facts' of the stories, there were also many points of comparison between the processes of commemoration. Despite their narratives being separated by one hundred and twenty-one years, the most concerted efforts to turn Verchères and Secord into 'hero-ines' and part of Canadian 'history' occurred from the 1890s to the 1920s. During those years, both English and French Canadians participated in vociferous debates over the meanings of nationalism and imperialism. Commemorations of Cartier, Champlain, Loyalists, pioneers, and the War of 1812 abounded in a number of locations. The 'historical profession' began, slowly, to take shape in Canadian universities, and challenges to Victorian gender relations were mounted by supporters of woman's rights both in Canada and abroad. Thus, Verchères and Secord became part of a panoply of 'national' historical figures in a context in which notions of 'history,' 'nation,' 'womanliness,' and 'manliness' were being contested and reshaped. This context also produced the very similar genres in which their commemorations were conveyed: the historical society report, the school text, the monument, the pageant, and – although this would be more successful in the case of Secord – the venue of commercial advertis-ing. Furthermore, those individuals and groups that worked assiduously to gain recognition for these women shared similar class origins, that is, the middle to upper-middle class of central Canada. Many were either francophone or Anglo-Celtic and, whether Catholic or Protestant, believed firmly that Christian churches and Christian morality had provided the backbone for the historical development of the Canadian nation. Moreover, whether they were obviously 'feminist' or even members of women's groups, the commemorators of Verchères and Secord shared a nationalistic and imperialistic narrative of Canadian history in which (cer-tain) women had a (certain) role to play.

The commemorative activities were wide-ranging and sometimes very expensive. It was almost as if the groups wishing to remember the country's history tried all methods, in the hope that one at least would protect the evanescent memory from disappearing. Verchères was first to get a 'film of her own' (in 1922) – Secord would not be so memorialized until 1974 (and even then, as we shall see, it was not primarily 'about' her). Although we have found many similarities in these commemorations, it would be disingenuous to overlook the number of significant distinctions, both in the narratives themselves and in the processes of creating them (the two things are, of course, interrelated). While both acts involved national duty and a degree of transgression of women's 'place' in both seventeenth- and nineteenth-century European society, in the lexicon of Victorian discourses about gender their actions might be interpreted in subtly, yet significantly, different fashions. Verchères had taken up arms and engaged in direct military conflict; Secord, on the other hand, had been a carrier of news and – although she was never identified explicitly thus – a spy. Verchères herself placed her actions within the 'woman warrior' tradition, a role that could be performed and then relinquished. No such configuration of Secord's walk was needed. While her commemorators insisted upon her bravery and courage, the absence of any kind of martial aggressiveness on her part made it easy to domesticate her deed of patriotism. Rather, the deed itself was open to a wide range of readings. It carried no 'essential' meaning other than that of patriotic duty – which could be interpreted in as conservative or as transgressive a fashion as desired.

Not only did certain key elements of these stories differ but so, too, did the success of the commemorations themselves. While much of the literature looks at commemorations that have been successful and long-lived, examining the decline in a historical figure's popularity should also be part of the historian's task. To be sure, both 'heroines' came under attack in the 1920s and early '30s, as those seeking to achieve a more sober and objective history attempted to rid national narratives both of such romantic feats and the female figures who had performed them. Both Verchères's and Secord's places in history underwent re-evaluation in light of these offensives. Verchères's story waned in popularity over the course of the twentieth century, while Secord's – although it did not regain the height of its popularity of the 1910s – continued to be told, particularly in books for children. Part of the continuing appeal of her narrative can be traced, of course, to the candy company, whose advertising kept Secord's name (if not her actual deed) in the public realm and public consciousness – albeit through the efforts of private enterprise.

Furthermore, while Verchères's story was itself part of a meta-narrative of the survival of French Canada, the fact that Secord's was set within the War of 1812 had different implications for its longevity. The success of historical commemorators in tying the War – and thus Canadian nationalism and the imperial bond – to the Niagara peninsula made it easier to identify Secord with a particular geographic location and with a specific historical event. While such a process was no guarantee of Secord's recognition, it did ensure her narrative an additional commemorative site. Yet even Secord's commemoration in the Niagara area was not a straightforward affair, for the work of the candy company was ultimately more important than that of the state.

Another critically important theme of these narratives is their reliance with respect to the heroines' interactions with Aboriginal peoples on the dynamics of colonial and imperial relations. Here, too, while there are certain important similarities, one particular aspect of Verchères's narrative makes it rather more difficult to recount today. The fact that she was engaged in direct military conflict with the Iroquois and that such conflict was essential to the narrative – and, indeed, to its past popularity – compromised late twentieth-century celebrations of Verchères as a straightforward 'heroine' (although attempts have been made to rewrite or contextualize this aspect of the confrontation). Secord's encounter with the Kahnawake Mohawks does not itself automatically rely on the theme of Native-European antagonisms. It will be shown how that meeting has been rewritten to accord with today's popular fantasies of those relationships. And thus, just as Secord's gender was domesticated by her late-Victorian commemorators, many of today's narrators have worked to domesticate her relationship with Canada's First Nations.

These women's encounters with Aboriginal peoples helped shape their own racial identity as white or Euro-Canadian women. As we will explore in the course of this book, particularly in the Epilogue, there was a relationship, albeit one little discussed, between 'white' women such as Verchères and Secord and Native peoples (specifically Native men), groups that have often represented 'others' in historical commemorations. While Native men and white women have not occupied the same position in either historical discourses or in Canadian society, their historical representations have often been used to shore up imperial and national hegemony. Particular individuals, such as Verchères or, in the case of Ontario, Tecumseh, might be venerated for their service to Crown and country. The antithesis of this veneration was the fear and unease that Native men and Euro-Canadian women might inspire, particularly through demands for political equality and autonomy. Women such as Verchères and Secord could be perceived as being threatened by Native men. This was a position which, given the historically formed parameters of 'white womanhood,' could not be reversed in the eyes of Euro-Canadian men and women. Furthermore, Euro-Canadian women could – and did – help shape this discourse of the nation's past. As we will discuss in the Epilogue, Native men and women did attempt to write histories of the 'Canadian' nation in which they were full-fledged historical actors whose narratives took centre stage. However, these narratives did not achieve much popular success, nor did the Canadian state bestow its stamp of approval on them.

While some historians may dismiss the narratives of Verchères and Secord as the work of earnest antiquarians or as stories told only for children, we believe that they have had a much greater significance and purchase in helping Canadians conceive of their history. By examining the 'histories' of these two 'heroines,' we are able to ask questions about the social role of history, in both past and present. So much of the commemoration of Verchères and Secord took place during an era when central Canada was undergoing 'modernization' that it is not, we feel, far-fetched to see a link between modernity and the creation of usable – and useful – pasts. We are hesitant to characterize the processes of commemoration and those who were responsible for them as being motivated strictly by antimodern sentiments, as much other literature about the shaping of 'tradition' or the use of the past in this period has argued.[16] It may be true that the price of early twentieth-century modernity was a continuous fear of the loss of 'history,' as a society that displayed keen self-consciousness of the changes it was experiencing – and had set in motion – scrambled to preserve those parts of the past that could be imagined in specific and useful ways. As Michael Kammen has noted, 'the more we read about memory, the more we also are reminded of amnesia.'[17] Constant change propelled constant commemoration in a society that had the material, social, and political resources to support such endeavours.[18] We have also found that history was used in a variety of ways to buttress and bolster modernity, not least as justification for change. The developments Canadian society was undergoing, historical commemorators argued, should be welcomed and their legitimacy guaranteed, as they were simply part of the progressive and linear pattern that the 'Canadian nation' had exhibited since the arrival of Europeans on the north-east coast of the Americas. Madeleine de Verchères and Laura Secord were part of this linear narrative of progress and advancement.

Heroines and History is divided into two sections. Part 1 is devoted to the commemoration of Verchères. It begins with her own narratives of the attack on the seigneury; then, in chapters 2 and 3, examines their translation into late nineteenth-century and early twentieth-century forms: the prose descriptions of Verchères as Joan of Arc; a large-scale 1913 statue; and the 1922 movie, the first French-Canadian feature-length film. The section ends with an analysis of Verchères's decline in popularity and her relegation to school texts aimed at children. Part 2 traces a similar route, starting with Secord's own accounts of her walk to Beaver Dams and then, in chapters 6 through 9, moving through the various kinds of locations and genres in which Secord was commemorated: the historical societies, children's textbooks, the candy company's advertising and other visual media, and historical tourism in the Niagara area. We end this book with an Epilogue, shifting our focus from the telling of these Euro-Canadian women's stories to those of Aboriginal peoples, whose presence was so essential to these narratives but who were seldom cast as historical actors, with their own motives and agency, in these scripts of the Canadian nation.

Both of us began our careers as scholars of the colonial periods in which Verchères and Secord lived; this project, then, was a chance for both of us to examine how those pasts were recreated in subsequent periods and constructed in national frameworks. As historians we share many concerns that we have sought to pursue in this research. What has been the relationship between 'the nation' and 'history'? How have the processes of creating national narratives been shaped by relations of gender, class, race, and ethnicity? Were there significant differences between 'French' and 'English' Canada in their remembering of the past? But in addition to the similarities of the questions that propelled this study, the sources pertaining to Verchères and Secord have sometimes led in different directions. The results of our investigations stand as a reminder that, as in the work of nineteenth-century commemorators, specificity and contingency have shaped the outcome of our historical inquiries.

Part One

Chapter One

Like Mother, like Daughter:
The Woman Warrior Tradition

On 22 October 1692, she would later claim, fourteen-year-old Madeleine de Verchères saved the occupants of her family's isolated fort to the east of Montreal from a surprise Iroquois raid. Caught unaware with other local settlers outside the small palisaded fort, she ran quickly back. She barely escaped the Iroquois warriors, unknotting her scarf from her neck just as one of the warriors grabbed it. She then slammed shut the gate of the fort and went about making hasty repairs to the palisades. As the eldest present child of the absent local lord, she assumed leadership and organized the defence. For as long as eight days, Madeleine maintained a constant vigil, rallied the occupants to maintain their courage, paraded with her brothers along the fort's palisades, and fired the cannon. Three times during the siege, she let the fort's gates be opened: to reclaim laundry that lay unattended on the riverbank, to rescue two visitors who had arrived by canoe, and to admit the cattle at night. Verchères opened the gates one last time, when she went out to greet the French troops who had arrived to relieve the inhabitants of the fort. These episodes provide the key elements of Verchères's two accounts of her own heroism, and they supplied much of the framework for subsequent retellings of her famous exploits.

By her actions, Verchères carved out for herself a position as the pre-eminent lay heroine of the period of French colonization in the New World. Her heroism would be retold time and again in verse and prose, and her imagined figure would be cast in bronze and depicted on paper, canvas, and celluloid. For many decades, Madeleine de Verchères would be celebrated as the primary heroine of French Canada.

Madeleine de Verchères's heroism was chronologically located in the seventeenth century, a time of hardy, embattled men and women, struggling to maintain their settlements and defend their faith on the frontier of European colonial society. Consequently, her actions could come to epitomize that period when the weak French colony successfully fended off its foes and laid the foundation of a future French-Canadian civilization. The seventeenth century would become a 'golden age' of sorts, which subsequent generations could remember for its factual and moral lessons. In Anthony Smith's theory of nationalism, this desire for a golden age is not at all unique to the French-Canadian context. Rather, all nations develop some version of it: 'the golden age must be able to act as a model and guide to [the nation's] destiny, demonstrating the capacity of the nation in the past to create a culture worthy of emulation, and highlighting the qualities – personal, political, intellectual and social – that can inspire national renewal and spur public emulation.'[1] Verchères provided a female icon who demanded emulation, at least in her heroic qualities, if not her military actions. Her glory stemmed not only from the successful defence, but also from the fact that she stepped into the shoes of the woman warrior figure of European culture.

Madeleine de Verchères was not the only woman in the history of French Canada to provide heroic armed defence: both Françoise-Marie Jacquelin de La Tour in Acadia and Marie-Anne de Saint-Ours in the St Lawrence Valley heroically wielded firearms during the period of French colonization. Verchères's descendant Agathe de Lanaudière[2] used a gun in defending her house against bandits. In the turmoil of the 1837 Rebellion, at least three women brandished arms in defiance of the Patriot rebels.[3] But Verchères, in part because her young age embellished the story even more, became and remains today the best-known of this group of warlike female figures.

Verchères's heroism fits comfortably alongside the other stories of pioneer bravery. The most obvious comparison is with Adam Dollard des Ormeaux, whose story achieved canonical form from the indefatigable efforts of the twentieth-century historian Abbé Lionel Groulx. In 1660, Dollard and his band of sixteen men set out from the struggling missionary village of Ville-Marie (Montreal) to canoe up the Ottawa River. Embarking on a fur trade expedition, they knew nonetheless that they were heading for danger. The long-standing conflicts between the Iroquois and the French were tipping strongly in favour of the Aboriginal nations, more numerous and very powerful, particularly since the dispersal in the late 1640s of the Huron Confederacy, who had been allies of the French. At Long-Sault (today Carillon) on the Ottawa River, Dollard and his companions, along with forty-four Huron and Algonquin allies, were attacked by a much larger group of some five hundred Iroquois. They heroically defended their position until most of the Aboriginal fighters abandoned them. The Frenchmen were slaughtered. But the expedition was not deemed a failure by subsequent historians. Rather, it represented for them a pre-emptive strike that convinced Iroquois forces of the indomitable courage of the settlers of Ville-Marie, and it staved off a fatal attack at a time when the colony was weak. Accounts of the Lachine Massacre of 1689 likewise present the danger of living in the sparsely settled countryside near Montreal, and the heroic approach of the French settlers to the adversity they faced.

Together, these stories form a meta-narrative of 'la survivance': small groups of French settlers, beginning the painstaking process of transforming the St Lawrence Valley into the agrarian landscapes of a seigneurial countryside, successfully fended off Anglo-American and Amerindian threats. Only steadfast resolve, unshaken Catholic faith, and the good fortune of the French army ensured their victory over their enemies. To tell the story of Dollard, of the early settlers of Montreal, or of Verchères was to provide an exegesis of the arduous civilizing mission of the French-Canadian people in North America. Much more was at stake than the mere facts, lively and bloody as they might be, of the stories themselves. The future of the French-Canadian nation was confirmed by these accounts, and generations of nationalists claimed inspiration from such stories.

Early Accounts

The earliest accounts of Verchères's actions are two letters she wrote and two published accounts by contemporary authors. It is highly probable that she did not compose the letters herself, and, indeed, the second letter departs rather far from verisimilitude at points. But she did send the letters and signed one of them – the first in 1699, and the second usually dated to 1722 (but, in fact, written after 1726) – and thus acquiesced in the construction of her story along lines that were deemed appropriate and acceptable to authority figures in the colony and in France.

She addressed the three-page 1699 letter to Madame de Maurepas, the wife of the Minister of the Marine, the French official responsible for the colony.[4] This was a direct petition for financial assistance. The letter begins by referring to the Count de Maurepas's benevolence towards New France, and mentions the cruel wars against the Iroquois.

Verchères then summarizes her heroic action. She was some four hundred paces from her father's ill-defended fort when the Iroquois appeared suddenly and captured twenty of the locals. Chased to the fort, Verchères herself barely escaped. Only her quick-witted action of undoing her scarf, then in the clutch of an Iroquois warrior, allowed her to enter the fort unscathed. She climbed up the bastion, placed a soldier's hat on her head, and shot the cannon. In so doing, she warned the nearby forts of the Iroquois danger. Having enumerated her feats of bravery, Verchères pleaded her family's circumstances. Despite her father's fifty years of service, his destiny was not a happy one. She requested a small pension of fifty écus, the same as that of many officers' wives in New France. Otherwise, she requested an ensign's commission for one of her brothers.

The second (unsigned) account was written at the behest of Charles de Beauharnois de La Boische, the governor of New France, who began his long period in office in 1726.[5] A much longer epistle, boldly entitled 'Relation of the heroic facts of Mademoiselle Marie Magdelaine de Verchére [*sic*] against the Iroquois, 14 years old, in the year 1696, 22 October, at 8.00 in the morning,' this version with all its exaggerations and embellishments provides most of the details taken up in subsequent accounts. Instead of being four hundred paces from the fort, Madeleine was five arpents (about three hundred metres) away in the second telling. The forty-five Iroquois chasing her did not manage to catch her; nor, when they stopped running and started shooting, did they hit her. Verchères made it to the fort, closed the gates, and repaired some of the breeches in the defences. She stopped a terrified soldier from blowing up the munitions and the fort. Then, throwing off her headdress and putting on a hat, she assumed command. Her younger brother and two frightened soldiers used their guns, but Madeleine fired the cannon. She marched down to the river to accompany Pierre Fontaine and his family back to the fort. She organized a defensive strategy that convinced the Iroquois that the fort was better defended than it was in actuality. At night, when the few surviving livestock bayed at the gate to be let in, she ensured that the Iroquois were not hiding among them and allowed the cattle to enter. Fontaine's wife begged to leave the fort for the safety of nearby Contrecoeur, but Fontaine refused to abandon Verchères. After eight days, Lieutenant de La Monnerie arrived to relieve the siege. Verchères added that on the day of the great battle she had led her brothers down to the shore to rescue the laundry that had been left there. This longer letter devotes five of its seven pages to the 1692 event (dated erroneously to 1696), then turns to a second act of heroism, which will be examined later.

These two manuscript accounts, contradictory in places, provide much – though by no means all – of the material for subsequent retellings of the story of Madeleine de Verchères. The first letter was explicitly a request for a pension, and therefore she had every reason to accentuate her personal heroism. The second letter was probably written to achieve an increase in her pension, though the letter does not make the purpose explicit.

In addition to the two manuscript letters, three other accounts were written during Verchères's lifetime, two of them published in books. Colonial government official Claude-Charles Le Roy de La Potherie wrote a lengthy account of the colony's military history, detailing the complicated encounters between the French and Aboriginal nations. He completed his book in 1702, making some additions in 1714, but did not publish it until 1722. In the book, La Potherie recounts the story twice. The first retelling is contained within a geographical and historical description of the Montreal government, the second in a chronological treatment of the military history of the colony.[6] The second version repeats almost verbatim Verchères's letter to Mme de Maurepas. Indeed, La Potherie claimed in the book to have helped her with the 1699 petition for a pension, an assertion supported by the resemblances between the manuscript and the printed versions.[7] Pensions for deserving military families were clearly on La Potherie's mind. He refers elsewhere in the book to the issue of pensions, particularly in the case of officers' widows: 'His Majesty helps a good part of the country to survive ... by pensions or premiums.'[8] He clearly considered the welfare of the families of military personnel worthy of mention and of support.

A second confirmation of Verchères's heroism appears in an official report in 1712. In his report on settlements in the St Lawrence Valley, royal surveyor Gédéon de Catalogne briefly mentioned her actions when he discussed the seigneury of Verchères: 'it was in this area that the daughter of the said seigneur repulsed the enemies who were ready to enter into this fort and she even discharged the cannon at them. Her action was rewarded by His Majesty.'[9] In this official report, Verchères's heroism was linked to the location that bore her family name and that witnessed her bravery.

The Jesuit priest and historian P.-F.-X. de Charlevoix includes a brief account of Verchères's heroism in his 1744 *Histoire et description générale de la Nouvelle France*.[10] This book, composed primarily in the 1740s, was based on extensive research of both manuscript and printed sources. Charlevoix used La Potherie's book, which he described as consisting of 'relatively undigested and poorly written memoirs.' However, he recognized that when dealing with the issues he himself witnessed, the earlier author appears 'sincere and without bias [*passion*].'[11] Charlevoix's retelling is situated within a description of a trip he undertook on the king's orders through the French territories in North America. He includes in this section of his work geographical descriptions, discussions of natural history, and occasional anecdotes. No mention was made of the defence of the fort in the chronological account of the colony's history, which comprises the first two volumes of the work. Like de Catalogne, Charlevoix firmly rooted Verchères's story in geography, not in history.

With these few exceptions, the historical evidence confirming Verchères's 1692 heroism is sparse. In that year's annual report to the Minister of the Marine (the French official responsible for the colony), the governor and the intendant did not comment directly on Verchères's bravery. It is difficult to imagine why the story would not have been worth telling in the letter to the Minister. The small-scale encounters that made up the drawn-out conflict with the Iroquois were a constant feature in the yearly accounts to the metropolitan authorities. But Governor Louis de Buade, Comte de Frontenac, and Intendant Jean Bochart de Champigny merely reported that a larger Iroquois raiding force had been frightened by the military precautions adopted by the French: 'there have been only on two different days, skirmishes and a few people killed on either side, after which they retreated, having seen that we were on our guard and resolved to receive them in force.'[12] In a letter the following year, they made passing reference to raids by the Mohawks (or Agniers, as the French called this Iroquois Nation) up the Richelieu River and the capture of French settlers at Verchères. The governor wrote laconically that 'the enemies killed and took prisoner some people at Vercheres, absconded with some livestock and scalped a soldier at St Ours.'[13] These accounts of military engagements in the region of the Richelieu River were brief, proffering no mention of the story that would much later come to typify many people's knowledge of late seventeenth-century New France.

Despite the limited contemporary confirmation of the military event that survives in the archival record to this day, Intendant Champigny later corroborated Verchères's story when asked to by the king. But his support was by no means effusive: 'What the daughter of the Sieur de Verchere claims in the letter that she gave herself the honour to write to Madame the Countess of Pontchartrain [de Maurepas] is true,' the intendant stated in 1700. As we shall see, he gave other members of her family much more prominence in his response.[14]

These are among the very few documents composed during Verchères's lifetime that refer to the exploit. The first version identifying Verchères as the heroic figure is dated seven years after the exploit. It is difficult to accept the accounts of her heroism at face value. Nonetheless, there does appear to be enough independent confirmation to assure us that some action along the lines indicated did take place. Given their chronological distance from the event itself, the versions rely on and exploit cultural and narrative themes that go beyond the mere recitation of the 'facts' of the story. The rest of this chapter evaluates these themes.[15]

Woman Warrior

Writers have long recognized that women in New France, especially in the seventeenth century, occupied a wide variety of public and private roles. Many of these would not be open to them in later periods. Nuns contributed extensively in educational, medical, and administrative functions. The names of Marie de l'Incarnation, Jeanne Mance, Marguerite Bourgeoys, and Marguerite d'Youville are remembered for their exceptional callings to service. Lay women also carried out significant economic activities in commerce: Marie-Anne Barbel in trade and Agathe de Saint-Père in the manufacture of textiles, for instance.

Twentieth-century historians have been attracted to these exceptional women, and many popular and academic studies relate their stories.[16] The explanations for the public prominence of these women vary, reflecting to a large extent the writers' perspectives on the expanding roles for women in twentieth-century Canadian society. Thus they may emphasize the women's pioneer status or focus rather on their class background. Yet it is arguable that the visibility of these women is as much a product of the early modern period itself, a time when gender roles were less bounded than they would become in the nineteenth century.[17] Certainly historians of France are able to point towards many women who fulfilled similar religious and economic functions. Catholic orders gave many women opportunities unavailable to the vast majority of their lay counterparts. But even among the latter, the various legal codes provided some protection of women's property that allowed them to take over their deceased husbands' enterprises. Clearly, class and fortune determined women's abilities to fulfil such roles, but these possibilities, however limited, existed nonetheless.

Whatever the margin of public manoeuvre for women of a certain class, Madeleine de Verchères clearly recognized that she was testing the boundaries of appropriate gender behaviour with her paramilitary heroism. Indeed, her actions were noteworthy precisely because they overstepped traditional gender roles. 'Although my sex does not allow me to have other inclinations than those demanded of me,' Verchères wrote to Mme de Maurepas in 1699, 'nonetheless, allow me, Madame, to tell you that I have feelings which draw me to glory as do many men.'[18] In appealing for a pension, she had to justify her military actions in a way permissible to women. A cultural figure was available to her: she could lay claim to the historical and literary tradition of woman warriors. To explain her defence of the seigneurial fort at Verchères against Iroquois attackers, she drew upon the long history of women warriors in the French and European traditions.

Madeleine de Verchères was following the honourable path laid out by key women from French history. Joan of Arc, the maid of Orléans, saved France by rejuvenating the French monarchy and leading a series of battles in 1429 and 1430 against the English army. Jeanne Hachette (Jeanne Laisné) led the defence of the city of Beauvais in 1472 against Burgundian attackers. Hachette captured a Burgundian standard and rallied the occupants of the city until the king's forces arrived. In 1588, Catherine-Marie de Lorraine, Duchess of Montpensier, wore a soldier's helmet and brandished a sword in leading the resistance to Henri IV.[19] These women provided a genealogy of women warriors in the French tradition. Even more immediately, Verchères referred explicitly to the actions of Philis de la Tour-du-Pin de La Charce, who in the same year (1692) had helped fend off an invasion by Savoyard troops in southern France. Significantly, the king awarded a pension to la Charce for her actions.[20] Verchères asserted that she had followed in the footsteps of other women: 'I know, madam, that there have been in France people of my sex during the last war who placed themselves at the head of their peasants to oppose the invasion of enemies entering their province.'[21] Claiming European precedents made sense of her actions. Since the time of the Greeks, the rhetorical device of the Amazon existed to explain and justify such women. Verchères's contemporaries agreed on her status as a woman warrior. La Potherie refers to Verchères as 'une véritable Amazone,' and Charlevoix agreed.[22]

In the last two decades, many scholars have shown interest in the phenomenon of women warriors. These women fascinate because they so clearly transgressed sexual categories. As historian Louise May argues, 'the equation of the military with masculinity and with men appears to be one of the most persistent of gender definitions, cross-culturally and throughout history.'[23] In specific circumstances, women could assume a military role and modify the link between maleness and warfare. For instance, the woman's rank or her religious beliefs could justify extraordinary actions. In revolution or rebellion, that is, during times of temporary but fundamental challenges to the status quo, women could act as warriors.[24] Verchères clearly fulfilled the criterion related to social class. She stepped into her father's role as defender of the seigneury during his absence. An ensign in the Carignan-Salières regiment that played such an important role in the defence and settlement of the St Lawrence Valley in the seventeenth century, François Jarret de Verchères chose to remain in New France in 1667. Marrying Marie Perrot in 1672, he received the grant of a seigneury to the east of Montreal Island two years later. Governor Frontenac requested letters of nobility for him in 1672, but he never received official confirmation.[25] Nonetheless, he lived in a noble fashion and had some recognition as enjoying that status. Certainly, Verchères judged it useful to point out her class in the second account of her defence of the fort, though interestingly enough not in the first. She encouraged her brothers to join her in fighting against the Iroquois: 'Remember the lessons that my father so often gave you, that gentlemen are born but to shed their blood for the service of God and the king!'[26] Other elements of the woman warrior tradition were also apparent in Verchères's case. Women became warriors in emergency situations,[27] and they generally returned to the domestic sphere after the exploit. Often, the woman disguised herself as a man in order to participate in military matters.[28]

Verchères was careful in both her accounts to distinguish her bravery from the fear manifested by the other women. In her 1699 letter, Verchères recounted that she was able to ignore the lamentations of the many women who had lost their husbands. In the later more detailed account, Verchères silenced the grieving women for the greater safety of the fort: 'I believed it prudent, while we fired on the enemy, to indicate to these distressed women and children the danger that the enemy might hear them despite the noise of the guns and the cannon. I ordered them to be quiet, so as not to allow the attackers to believe that we were without resources and hope.'[29] Alone, she rescued the Fontaine family when they arrived at the shore. After Verchères had safely ushered them into the fort and had successfully held off the Iroquois over the first night, Pierre Fontaine's wife, Marguerite Antoine, demanded to be taken to the sturdier fort at nearby Contrecoeur. Verchères commented that Antoine was 'extremely fearful, as is the custom of all Parisian women.'[30] Fontaine refused to accompany his wife, instead pledging to stay and assist Madeleine. Verchères had come to personify the defence and had surpassed her sex. She was able to act, she implied, beyond the bounds of typical female behaviour.

One particularly effective way to indicate that she had escaped the usual constraints of her sex was to refer to her adoption of male clothing. When she applied for a military pension in 1699, Madeleine de Verchères was careful to mention her change of apparel. She recounted that one of her first acts once she regained the seigneurial fort was to take off her headdress (coëffe) and don a soldier's cap. As she informed Mme de Maurepas, 'I then transformed myself by placing the soldier's helmet on my head.'[31] Not only did Verchères lock up all the frightened women, she displayed her full male courage by shooting a cannon. Verchères's second narrative is more circumspect about the cross-dressing, recounting only her 'throwing off her headdress and wearing a hat.'[32] In his 1744 version of the story, Charlevoix makes the transformation even more complete: she took off her headdress, knotted her hair, and donned a hat and a jerkin (juste-au-corps).[33] She changed clothes again and again in order to convince the Mohawks that the fort was well defended. Whether or not she actually donned male apparel (and she may have done so in order to allow herself to play the role she felt necessary), Madeleine de Verchères claimed that she disguised herself as a soldier.

Clothing had considerable symbolic value in an early modern society such as New France. As in many early modern settings, clothing revealed social standing – and sex, of course – at a glance. Religious and civil authorities policed apparel in New France. In attempting to assimilate the Iroquois, the Sulpicians were careful to inculcate gender-specific dress codes. 'We believe that they profit by living among us,' one member of the Sulpician order wrote in 1684, '... their women must wear skirts and their men hats and pants [i.e., trousers].'[34] In this, religious authorities echoed the biblical injunction in Deuteronomy 22:5: 'The woman shall not wear that which pertaineth unto a man, neither shall a man put on a woman's garment.'

In two cases, European women transgressing the boundaries of clothing were severely punished in New France. In 1696, a young habitant from Île d'Orléans borrowed or stole her brother's clothes in order to gain passage to Quebec and access to the governor's retinue. Anne Edmond then warned falsely of an impending English invasion. Judicial authorities seemed somewhat less concerned with the lie about the military threat than with the lie about the messenger's sexual identity. They presumed that a heterosexual affair explained her actions: Edmond had tried to stop militiamen, including her putative lover, from being sent to the West. She denied this interpretation, but her own version was suppressed by the court officials. In the end, she was punished by being stripped to the shoulders (perhaps enough to reveal that she was without doubt a woman) and beaten in public.[35] In a second case, in 1738, twenty-year-old Esther Brandeau arrived in New France disguised as Jacques Lafargue, though in her case her Jewish faith caused even more problems that her transvestism. Despite her willingness to convert to Catholicism, her 'flighty' character induced the officials to send her back to France.[36]

As scholars increasingly study the boundaries of gender roles, there is a growing literature about the phenomenon of cross-dressers. For some authors, cross-dressers reinforce gender roles by their transgression. The woman warrior generally had to dress as a man in order to accomplish an act considered unsuitable for her sex. Although she momentarily allowed herself new freedoms, she did not fundamentally challenge traditional gender roles. For these reasons, the female transvestite became a laughable stock figure in early modern European literature and theatre.[37] But it is nonetheless possible to see female cross-dressers as proto-feminists, as they fulfilled their own individualistic desires for freedom.[38] For some scholars, the phenomenon represents even larger threats to the status quo. Cross-dressing evokes the potential of sexual inversion and disorder.[39] Even more than inversion, transvestism subverts both genders at once.[40] What if the cross-dresser belongs fundamentally to neither sex? What if resuming the original clothing does not lead one fully back to one's previous sexual identity? Whatever the interpretative thrust, cross-dressing represents a challenge – temporary or more permanent – to the concept of gendered spheres of activity.

Contemporaries had few problems with Madeleine de Verchères's cross-dressing. As Charlevoix's and La Potherie's treatments indicate, despite the wider social anxiety in New France about cross-dressing, men could accept, even celebrate, temporary inversions such as Madeleine's. But this was because they could see Verchères as a unique, empirical case, not as a social icon. Two centuries later, as we shall see, men tended to react in a more hysterical fashion to the image of women cross-dressers, but they too could accept the story of Madeleine de Verchères as one of the key national narratives.

The Gates of the Fort

In Verchères's first account, the danger posed by the Iroquois ended after she fired the cannon, and there is no explicit mention of a continuing siege. In her later and longer version of the event, Verchères provides clearer indications of on-going suspense. As Verchères and her brothers held off what may have been a siege (though there is little precise indication of Iroquois activity after the initial firing), she permitted the gates to be opened on occasion. These openings and closings of the gates provide the remainder of the tension in the account, when there really was little to report. The danger of penetration implicit in the breech of the gates, resolved by Verchères's quick action in sealing up the damaged parts of the fortress walls, provides a subtle sexual subtext to the narratives. Verchères remained extremely cautious about the gates. Nonetheless, she allowed them to be opened, and she ventured outside on three occasions. Although the chronology is uncertain, the first instance was probably to rescue three sacks of linen and some quilts, which had been left outside the fort. Verchères then rescued Fontaine and his family when they arrived by canoe. Madeleine's solo sorties, she presumed, would be seen by the Iroquois as a trap, and she was successful in getting the Fontaines safely to the fort. At night, they opened the gates also to allow the domestic animals back in, ensuring that the Iroquois were not disguised under animal skins. When Lieutenant de La Monnerie (Thomas Crisafy, according to La Potherie and Charlevoix) arrived to relieve the fort eight days after the siege began, Madeleine left the fort to receive him at the bank of the river. The two engaged in gallant banter:

- Monsieur, you are indeed welcome. I surrender arms to you.
- Mademoiselle ... they are in good hands.
- Better than you can imagine.[41]

Thus, the closure to the tale is realized in two ways: Madeleine surrenders her arms to the 'real' soldiers; and La Monnerie, unlike the Iroquois, recognizes Verchères for what she is, a woman.

In this way, there was more to the story than the actions of a woman warrior. Verchères's accounts also hint at her virginity. There is no contradiction between these two propositions: a woman could resort to military action precisely to defend her virginity or, by extension, the integrity of her homeland. In early modern German accounts of women's bravery in defending their cities, writers stressed the virginal metaphor that the women represented. In beating back the challenge from attackers and refusing the penetration of the city, they maintained their virginity and their city remained intact. As German historian Ulinka Rublack has commented, 'women who resisted the capture of their cities and virgins who committed suicide after defeat in order to avoid being violated vouched for the city's virtue and willingness to fight.'[42]

In Verchères's case, the girl's age is a key to the story. Although some young women in seventeenth-century New France could be married by the age of fourteen, the experience was rare and towards the end of the century it was becoming less and less common. The metaphorical confirmation of Verchères's success in maintaining her virginity is provided in her first narrative with the episode of the scarf.[43] As Verchères runs for the fort, one Iroquois warrior manages to grab her scarf or *mouchoir de col.* Verchères deftly unknots the scarf and leaves it in the hands of her intended rapist/assassin. This melodramatic episode of the scarf would be repeated endlessly by subsequent authors, and would become a key element in many pictorial representations. The association of Madeleine with her scarf would be such that certain images would retain the apparel even after the narrative required her to leave it in the Iroquois warrior's hands (see fig. 1.1). Perhaps a literary connection can be drawn to the Palmyrnan warrior queen Zenobia, who rebelled against the Romans. Zenobia also wore a scarf, and the stories concerning her emphasized her chastity (despite her having given birth to three children).[44] Because of the rarity of women's military incidents, authors and painters depicting them tend to rely heavily on literary and pictorial stereotypes.

With her deft handling of her scarf and by controlling the gates, Verchères protected the inviolability of the French settlement under attack. The purity of seventeenth-century New France became a long-standing historical trope, the colony's genetic 'purity' used to confirm its moral essence in the ethnically diverse and materialistic North America. Subsequent writers stressed the small percentage of prenuptial conceptions and the presumed low rates of miscegenation, all proof of the morality and the homogeneity of the French-Canadian nation.[45] The image of Verchères's scarf, a seemingly inconsequential detail, fulfilled a larger narrative purpose. It is the rhetorical utility of the incident that made it useful for Verchères herself and for the many writers who found the story worth retelling.

1.1 Depiction of Verchères closing the gates to the fort. Her scarf is intact in this
image. (C.W. Jefferys)

Verchères's Mother

In Verchères's first version of her exploit, the cannon-shot ended the altercation with the Iroquois, raising the question of which frightened the Iroquois: her male disguise or the fire-power? Would the Iroquois have shared Europeans' views of gender roles in military affairs? In traditional Iroquois society, women in fact assumed influential economic and political roles and enjoyed a degree of freedom that shocked and titillated male European commentators. But they did not participate in warfare, an area where Iroquois men enacted and proved their masculinity. Warfare was largely, for both Europeans and Iroquois, a male affair. Yet the Verchères family provided the challenge to the rule.

In 1690, an apparently undisguised Madame de Verchères had herself defended the family fort. La Potherie covers this incident as a supplement to the daughter's story. On perceiving the attackers, Madame de Verchères escaped into the redoubt of the fort. She managed to reach her rifle and for over two days held off the Iroquois. 'She fought,' La Potherie wrote, 'with all the intrepidity of the most seasoned soldier.'[46] Charlevoix followed La Potherie's account in its principal points, but her act of bravery preceded Madeleine's in his version of events as indeed it did chronologically. Otherwise, even the wording is similar: 'She fought in that way for two days, with courage and with a presence of mind that would have honoured an old warrior.' Madame de Verchères was able to repulse the Iroquois, who were 'very ashamed of being obliged to flee by a woman.' In Charlevoix's explanation, the two Iroquois attacks on the fort in 1690 and 1692 served a providential purpose: 'only to let shine the valour and the intrepidity of the two Amazons.'[47]

If there is any reason to give credence to the versions published by Charlevoix and La Potherie, it is intriguing that in her own two accounts of her bravery, Madeleine de Verchères does not mention her mother's previous action. In the published stories, Madeleine was clearly acting in the footsteps of her mother, as well as those of her father. An important aspect of the story, therefore, is that it recounts an act that is not unduly innovative. Indeed, throughout the long hostilities with the Iroquois, Madeleine and other women of the 'Heroic Period' of the history of New France often had to act in such unforeseen circumstances.

Her mother's bravery did not occasion a petition for a pension, at least not one that survives in the archival record. A 1707 request to the French minister for assistance was merely appended to the plea of the widow de la Vallière that she had 'no wealth. Her husband died as a major of

Quebec having given great service in Canada.'[48] And Madame de Verchères requested the same favour, the intendant added. In 1700, Intendant Champigny endorsed Madeleine's account without referring to the mother's bravery. This is odd since it clearly would have enhanced the appeal for the pension, which was made in the mother's name as much as the daughter's. The mother's heroism therefore lacks any evidence independent of La Potherie's and Charlevoix's accounts.

Because of the juxtaposition by La Potherie and Charlevoix of the bravery of both Verchères women, subsequent accounts, up to the late nineteenth century, also often included them both. Basing himself on Charlevoix's account, the Scottish Enlightenment jurist and polymath Lord Kames used the heroism of the two women to analyse the lack of courage of the North American Amerindians. He discusses first the mother's intrepid defence, then that provided by 'a girl of fourteen, daughter of the proprietor,' to illustrate the faint-heartedness of the Iroquois. 'If the Americans [i.e., Amerindians] abound not with active courage, their passive courage [i.e., in the face of torture] is beyond conception.'[49] Another late eighteenth-century version even melds the two women warriors into one. British army officer Thomas Anburey conflates the two women in the guise of the mother. Madame de Verchères successfully defended the family fort in both 1690 and 1692 in this telling, aided in the second instance by 'a little girl' who escaped from the Iroquois and warned her of what was occurring. 'One would imagine,' Anburey concluded, 'that this spot of *Verchere* was destined for the trial of fortitude and bravery in the fair sex.'[50] Gustave Bossange's 1821 account provides equal billing to both Verchères and her mother.[51]

Accounts written in the mid-nineteenth century continued to place much emphasis on the mother. Philippe Aubert de Gaspé, although a descendant of Madeleine de Verchères, did not recognize his direct lineage from the heroine. He briefly compares his gun-wielding aunt Agathe de Lanaudière to his 'two great-aunts of Verchères, who at the head of other women in 1690 and 1692 defended a fort attacked by Indians and repulsed them.'[52] Early editions of François-Xavier Garneau's epic history of Canada make only brief reference to Madeleine de Verchères in the context of her mother's feat.[53] Abbé François Daniel's 1867 entry on Verchères in his *Histoire des grandes familles françaises du Canada* quotes extensively from La Potherie and Charlevoix to convey the heroism of the two women. It remained possible for other authors to mention only the mother during their brief accounts of women's heroism during the period of New France.[54] However, once her daughter's letters were rediscovered, Madame de Verchères generally disappeared from the litanies of heroic figures.

Only one longer late nineteenth-century account chose to concentrate exclusively on Mme Verchères's defence. This fictional story in the popular weekly *Le monde illustré* borrowed details from Madeleine de Verchères's accounts. 'Le Loup,' a Sokokis (Abenaki), stole a special dagger from Verchères's husband, and then swore revenge on him after the theft was discovered. He led a group of Iroquois to attack the Verchères fort, once M. de Verchères's men had left the area. Mme de Verchères valiantly defended the fort from the Iroquois, holding off their attack for two days until reinforcements arrived. Two years later, the story notes at its end, Le Loup would once again inspire the Iroquois to attack the fort.[55] With the exception of this story, by the late nineteenth century, the mother's heroism took a minor position in relation to Madeleine's, providing a pleasant gloss to the young girl's heroism, when the mother is mentioned at all. Nonetheless, Madeleine de Verchères's exploit fits into a tradition, both familial and cultural. She was a woman warrior by genealogy and by literary strategy. Yet she had to overcome a desire by others to suppress her story.

Silences

If the silence concerning Madame de Verchères is striking in the daughter's accounts, so is the general silence about Madeleine de Verchères's heroism. The first account dates from 1699, when Verchères submitted her petition for a pension to Mme de Maurepas. Why should this interval of seven years have passed before the first confirmation of the event, at least the first evidence that survives in the archival record? In transcribing the young woman's heroism for posterity, La Potherie's accounts openly struggle against the urge to stifle her story: 'I cannot let the heroic action of Miss de Vercheres pass in silence.' The second version in the same book repeats the line almost exactly: 'The action of Miss de Vercheres (the daughter of an Officer who has fifty years of service) appears to me to be too heroic to let pass in silence.'[56] La Potherie uses similar formulations elsewhere in the book in other contexts, but he implies that there was a concerted effort to suppress the heroine's story. He informs his fictitious correspondent that Madame de Pontchartrain (de Maurepas) granted a life pension to Madeleine de Verchères, although he did not wish to 'enter into the relation of all the details that it was necessary to give to the Court in order to confirm something that one had hidden until that time.'[57]

The reasons for hiding such an action are most obscure. Yet the official accounts of military events in 1692 had indeed made no mention of Verchères's heroism. What had changed by 15 October 1699, the date of Verchères's letter to Madame de Maurepas? The likely circumstance is the death of Governor Frontenac on 28 November 1698. Frontenac and Intendant Champigny had quarrelled endlessly in the last years they worked together, a not uncommon state of affairs in the history of the relationship of the two key representatives of royal authority in the colony. It is possible that Frontenac chose not to reveal news of Verchères's heroism to the royal court. Despite earlier benevolence, the governor bestowed few favours on the family. Though recently promoted to a lieutenancy, Verchères's father was reduced to half-pay status from 1694.

After the death of Frontenac, it was possible to record Verchères's heroism, and to inform metropolitan authorities about it. The colonial power structure was in flux, and perhaps Verchères and her allies believed that they would succeed in attracting attention at this specific time. By 1699, former governor of the Montreal district Louis-Hector de Callière had officially succeeded Frontenac as governor of New France. De Callière proved able to use his brother's standing as royal secretary at Louis xiv's court to acquire the position, besting his rival, Philippe de Rigaud de Vaudreuil, who himself had attempted to use his personal connections. At issue were the family ties that underpinned power at the elite level. The majority of governors and intendants throughout the history of the colony were linked by marriage to the Pontchartrain (Maurepas) family, the ministers of the Marine during much of the history of New France. De Callière was one of the few exceptions to this rule, and the supporters of Vaudreuil had reason to feel very displeased with de Callière's nomination. Intendant Champigny, the chief civil authority in the colony, had supported Rigaud de Vaudreuil's bid for the governorship. Connected to the Pontchartrains, Vaudreuil had married a Canadian noble, thus allying himself with the colony's chief families, such as the Verchères.[58] With de Callière acceding to the governorship, Verchères and her family may have felt excluded from the upper echelons of colonial decisions, but could a direct appeal to France achieve their aim of acquiring the appropriate recognition?

Verchères's petition to Mme de Maurepas in 1699 pointed out her father's fifty years of military service and requested either a pension of fifty écus or an ensign's commission for her brother. The government official La Potherie assisted in drafting Verchères's letter. In his book, he acknowledged that 'two years ago, I informed Monsieur le Comte de Pontchartrain [Maurepas], who is the Protector of Canadians, of the action of the young daughter.'[59] La Potherie himself moved in the same social circles as the Verchères family. In 1700, he married Elisabeth de Saint-Ours, a relative of Verchères. The power of the family connections that governed the political factions of the colony likely determined the moment for informing the king's minister about Verchères's feat. Intendant Champigny's restrained acknowledgment of Verchères's actions revealed more about her family than it did about the young heroine. His support for a pension rested more on her father's service than the daughter's (or the mother's) bravery. The fifty years' service of the father, 'who was a gentleman and the misfortune that the family has just experienced with his death' militated in favour of a royal act of charity. The pension would allow the family to escape 'from the greatest penury.'[60] In 1701, the intendant and Governor Callière welcomed the king's generosity in providing pensions to both the mother and daughter, giving assurance that they would see to it that the mother received the daughter's recompense.[61] Madeleine's actions as a woman warrior had achieved the same goal as her father's long military service. In this way, her sense of the cultural significance of her story was accurate. From the time the pension was granted to the 1720s, correspondence listing the recipients of the king's munificence described Madeleine as the 'daughter of the late Sieur Verchères lieutenant,' often suppressing her name.[62]

The intendant's support no doubt contributed to the award of the pension. But the family's loyalty was not necessarily won over to eternal gratitude towards the colonial authorities in office at the time of Verchères's windfall. It is possible to read Verchères's second account as an implicit criticism of de Callière. De Callière's name appears three times in the narrative. As governor of Montreal in 1692, de Callière had ordered Madeleine de Verchères's father to Quebec. De Callière thus was responsible for leaving the fort vulnerable. De Callière later learned directly from the Iroquois how they had planned to attack the fort during the first night but were fooled by Madeleine's sentinels. Finally, the relief of the fort came, not from de Callière himself, but from his lieutenant La Monnerie. The narrative concludes with a panegyric to Charles de Beauharnois, 'our illustrious Governor,' closely linked to the Pontchartrains. It also notes that Beauharnois's predecessor, Vaudreuil, who succeeded de Callière on his death in 1703, was particularly interested in evidence of Madeleine de Verchères's heroism. If the theory that

Governor Frontenac played an important role in suppressing the story is tenable, it is ironic that de Callière's name would be recorded in an implicitly negative fashion in Verchères's second narrative. After all, it was under de Callière's governorship that Verchères's heroism was duly recognized. But he may have had little personal desire to see this happen. Perhaps Verchères and La Potherie (who, as his book indicates, also disliked de Callière) had forced the case themselves with their direct petition to the minister's wife.

Echoes of Heroism

Perhaps those who situate their own history within a particular narrative structure are doomed to relive it. Verchères's heroism was not limited to her youthful episode of 1692. In 1706, at the age of twenty-eight, Verchères married Pierre-Thomas Tarieu de La Pérade. Tarieu was the second son, but his elder brother had never reappeared after a military episode, and he inherited the family seigneury of Sainte-Anne near Batiscan, about eighty kilometres southwest of Quebec. De La Pérade enjoyed an illustrious military career as lieutenant in the colonial troops, profiting on the side from the fur trade, as did many of his colleagues. Verchères thus married into a prominent military family, who owned a desirable seigneury, which she helped to manage. Verchères's activities placed her in contact with government officials who would record some of her actions for posterity. Although the people of New France are very well documented in so many ways, there are problems in discerning motivations and characters from the types of documents that remain. Much of the material related to Verchères deals with her relatively rare encounters with court officials. A series of court cases at the local and colonial level provides some of the best evidence, yet these cases can be read in a number of different ways.

One way to consider this material is to pursue the concept of appropriate gender roles, which seemed to stay with Verchères her whole life. As judicial archives reveal, Verchères fought a number of court cases against local priests, habitants, and seigneurs. According to legal custom, she could not act in her own right, but only in the guise of her husband. Which of the two initiated the various proceedings is impossible to determine. Pierre-Thomas Tarieu de La Pérade's military career would have kept him away from his seigneury and the law courts of Quebec. In any case, Verchères often appeared in court on their behalf. The most noteworthy case occurred in 1730, when the priest of Batiscan, Gervais

Lefebvre, took her to court to clear his name after she accused him of calling her a 'whore.' Lefebvre had, she claimed, publicly chanted a lewd litany which cast aspersions on her personal and sexual integrity.[63] This case set groups of supporters in the parishes of Batiscan and Sainte-Anne against each other, and allowed simmering hostilities to find their expression through calumny and innuendo.

This was a protracted case, with an initial decision against Lefebvre at the Provost Court level. The priest appealed to the Superior Court, which suppressed the proceedings of the first trial and condemned Verchères and her husband to pay expenses. Verchères then sailed to France to appeal this rather odd decision. She intended to confront the king's minister. The latter condemned the resolution and exhorted the local officials to conciliate the parties. In the end, Lefebvre lost his parish, as a result of accusations of 'impurity, drunkenness and impiety.'[64]

Through the lengthy testimonies that accompanied the two court cases, the social structure of the locality was laid bare, as priest and seigneur waged battle with their leagues of supporters and lackies. Among other issues, Verchères was attempting, it would appear, to see her social prominence acknowledged at a local level. The priest and the seigneur's wife both conspired to suppress some important knowledge, the priest only acknowledging in 1730 that the real author of the litanies had died in the course of the trial. This may have been Marguerite Dizy dit Montplaisir, against whom previous accusations of lewd behaviour had been made. In 1694, Marguerite Dizy had scandalized the colonial clergy by cohabiting with a man who was not her husband. In 1704, the intendant complained that she had slandered the parish priest of Batiscan. It is not difficult to imagine that she continued to have conflicts with the clergy some twenty years later. Whatever the actual origin of the calumnies that shook the local society of Batiscan and Sainte-Anne, the evidence in the court transcripts suggests indeed that the priest Lefebvre did have some role to play in denigrating Verchères.

At one point in the lengthy proceedings, the priest attempted to reassure himself and the court that 'God fears neither hero nor heroine,'[65] which indicates that Verchères had some popular acknowledgment in later life for her youthful heroism, in addition to the official recognition that she had received. Moreover, the 'whore' epithet suggested that she, like so many other women warriors and warrior queens, experienced the other implications of gender-crossing: attacks on their presumed wanton sexuality.[66] Such aspersions were easy accusations to formulate of an independent woman. It is possible that the 1730 court case revealed the ways in which Madeleine de Verchères continued to test prescriptive gender roles.

In other court cases, Verchères stood steadfastly for the rights of the seigneur over those of the local inhabitants. She successfully defended the seigneurial prerogative to force her tenants (*censitaires*) to use the banal gristmill. Likewise, when the parish priest of Sainte-Anne and other inhabitants attempted to make use of the forests on the common, she complained to the civil authorities. The priest was fined for having cut a sugar maple tree that the seigneurs claimed as theirs. In an even more striking case of seigneurial privilege, her family was accused of assault in reaction to a verbal insult. The Ricard family, including the pregnant Mme Ricard, were coming to cut the hay on their fields, when Mme Ricard commented that Verchères's son, Charles-François, was 'malicious' (*malin*) in beating a dog. On hearing this comment from a mere commoner, Verchères and her family beat the Ricards and threw them to the ground. Verchères herself attacked the pregnant Mme Ricard.[67] While physical violence was a part of everyday life in New France, it was still possible, class distinctions notwithstanding, for the Ricards to appeal to the court for retribution – the outcome of the case, and indeed Verchères's version of the incident, are not recounted in the archives. It would be difficult to avoid a characterization of Verchères's actions as strong-willed, though it may be more telling about nineteenth- and twentieth-century attitudes to the past to assume that women, in particular noble women, of the eighteenth century did not often exhibit such strength of character.

It seems clear from the court records and other evidence that Verchères conducted herself first and foremost as a noble, attempting to ensure her family's ascendancy over the local population. The very words chosen in the 1730 trial serve to illustrate this point. In discrediting one of her opponent's witnesses, she claimed that she was not interested in 'scum' (*canaille*) like him. Likewise, she referred to her family as 'people of standing' (*personnes de condition*).[68] Whether or not she had been born into a full-fledged noble family, Madeleine's marriage to de La Pérade solved that issue.

Verchères would claim another act of heroism in later life. She appended a two-page account of this event in her second narrative. In 1722, the letter went, she defended the family manor at Sainte-Anne against an attack by Amerindians. This was not an organized attack, but rather the work of a few angry Abenaki men and women, whose motivations are not clearly exposed. They exchanged angry words in

Iroquois with the ill-disposed de La Pérade and then attacked him with tomahawks. Verchères hit one of the men in the stomach and he fell to the floor. She was then surrounded by four women, who grabbed her hair and her headdress and prepared to throw her into the fireplace. Again, Verchères found it worthwhile to comment on how her dress had transformed her: 'At this moment, a painter seeing me could well have drawn a portrait of a Madeleine [Mary Magdalene]: my headdress off, my hair dishevelled, my clothes all torn, having nothing on me but rags, I resembled rather the saint, except for her tears, which never fell from my eyes.'[69] Having distinguished herself yet again from feminine imagery, Verchères nonetheless could not rely exclusively on the 'male' courage of her earlier exploit, as she required the assistance of her son and an unnamed Frenchman to fend off the attack. Her twelve-year-old son attacked the Abenaki women and expelled them from the house. Elements of the earlier act mark this narrative: the defence of the family hearth against a surprise attack, the Amerindian foe (even if this involved the Abenakis, who were traditional allies of the French), and the importance of the family's class standing.

In 1730, likely at the same time that her second letter was communicated to the French court, Madeleine de Verchères requested through the governor and the intendant an increase in her royal pension. Although she was not successful in this petition, a subsequent voyage to France afforded her the mark of the governor's and the minister's recognition, a minor recompense perhaps for the ignominy of the court case she had sustained against the priest Lefebvre.[70]

Conclusion

Madeleine de Verchères established much of the literary context within which her story would be commemorated and, latterly, denigrated. The cross-dressing and the exploit itself confused the issue of sex and sexuality in the person of Madeleine de Verchères during her lifetime and afterwards. After her death, her story was never forgotten, but authors dealt with it in summary fashion, usually basing themselves on the most accessible sources, La Potherie's and Charlevoix's accounts. The French archivist-historian Moreau de St-Méry clearly foresaw the interest in Verchères's accounts, as he, like a magpie, placed both letters in his files around 1800.[71] When others rediscovered these letters much later in the nineteenth century and published them, Madeleine fully entered the French-Canadian pantheon of heroes in her own right. One aspect of the appeal of Verchères's story lies in the fact that she expressed her own sentiments in documents that have survived. Whether or not she indeed constructed the stories as they appear, the documents explicitly carried her assent. For subsequent readers, these were first-hand documents, a direct connection to the past, and it was their apparent authenticity that imbued the stories with such force. Verchères herself concluded her second letter: 'Here is the simple and exact narrative of my adventure.'[72] Thus we face the apparently incontrovertible 'facts' attested in a first-hand account.

Verchères claimed in her second letter that it was of the utmost importance not to reveal to the Iroquois the weaknesses of the French defences; therefore, they must be kept out of the fort: 'it was infinitely important that they not enter any French fort, for they would judge the others by this one, if they captured it. Such knowledge could only serve to increase their pride and courage.'[73] Except in this defensive fashion, Verchères's heroism did not save the struggling colony from imminent defeat. Few are the enthusiasts who have made this claim. But surely her heroism should not suffer from the fact that her exploit was not a turning point in the history of the colony.

One of the key elements of Madeleine de Verchères's 'own' versions of her story was her insertion of the narrative into the tradition of cross-dressing women warriors. Although she did not herself refer to her mother's exploit in her letters, she was following in her mother's footsteps, as well as those trodden by medieval and early modern women in occupying a male sphere of activity in a moment of danger and opportunity. Like many of her predecessors, she relinquished her role as soon as practical – or, at least, she claimed that she did.

Chapter Two

Images of Heroism and Nationalism: The Canadian Joan of Arc

For over a century following her death in 1747, the story of Madeleine de Verchères almost disappeared. A handful of writers covered her exploit, usually in abbreviated fashion. Once her manuscript letters were rediscovered in the 1860s, she attracted much more attention. From the 1880s to the 1920s, she reappeared, not only as a historical figure, but also as a nationalist icon, a heroic symbol of the 'golden age' of French Canada. Her importance henceforth lay not merely in her act of heroism, but also in the larger meta-narrative that could be used to infuse the story with meaning and purpose. She was the principal lay heroine at a time of the growth of popular nationalist sentiment in French Canada, and the comparison to Joan of Arc allowed her to become a significant nationalist symbol. In order to use her as an appropriate emblem, writers and artists had to transform her from a woman warrior into a domesticated, if brave, young woman.

In one striking work, Frère Marie-Victorin, the renowned botanist and author, captured what Verchères came to signify for some three generations of French Canadians. In the midst of the conscription crisis that deepened the linguistic fault-line in Canada more than any previous issue had done, Frère Marie-Victorin's short play was first performed in January 1918. This play gives Madeleine de Verchères a major role in vindicating the worthiness of Quebec's past. The setting of *Peuple sans histoire* is in Quebec City shortly after the failed rebellion of 1837. Lord Durham resides in Haldimand's Castle while he writes his report on the causes of the rebellion. He pens his infamous phrase about French Canadians having 'no history' and then falls asleep. His young servant Thérèse Bédard reads his report, and is appalled by the portentous words. She takes the page and writes in large letters,

'THOU LIEST, DURHAM!' and signs the post-scriptum, 'Madeleine de Verchères.'

On awakening, Durham wishes to return to his important idea and is shocked to read the addition to his manuscript. When the servant returns, Durham asks her who was Madeleine de Verchères. After her rendition, he exclaims, 'This story makes one think of a canto of the Iliad! ... I did not know that this new country already had such glorious annals.' Thérèse replies, 'I was pleading a case in fact, your Excellency, that of my people, that of French heroism and its right to respect, to space, to survival, to liberty!' Having thus discovered the identity of the person who wrote on his report, Durham surrenders the page to Bédard, in recognition of the survival of the French in the New World: 'I can see indeed that the fort of Verchères is still French, and that, despite the passing of a hundred years, the shadow of the small Madeleine still returns sometimes during the night to the Castle to stand guard!'[1] Frère Marie-Victorin's account is explicit, whereas many treatments of Verchères's heroism were merely implicit: the contribution of Madeleine de Verchères (along with other members of the French-Canadian pantheon of heroes and heroines) was to demonstrate that the history of the French colony was worthy and worth remembering. She provided a heroic substance to the past. The proud history of French Canadians justified their existence and their future.

Symbols of Nationhood

There can be little doubt of the importance of a shared history to the construction of national identity. Certain attributes are often considered to adhere to cultural or political nations. Taking a prime place among these attributes is the attitude towards the past. While nations are objectively very recent, they are considered by their inhabitants to be subjectively ancient. As a corollary, nations require heroes and heroines, emblems of a worthy history, so that the 'people' can consider themselves full-fledged members of a distinct national entity. The appeal of national heroes, like nationalism in general, is at once specific and commonplace. Though eminently comparable to other locations, each national example must be *sui generis*. In the Canadian context, nationalism has often been experienced in contradistinction to other countries, and national heroes suffer and benefit from their comparison to other countries' figures.

In the late nineteenth and early twentieth century, there was a concerted effort to recognize the heroes and heroines of Canada's and Quebec's past. The great period of commemorative activity in both English and French Canada has been dated from the 1850s,[2] but Madeleine de Verchères did not fully enter the pantheon of heroes until the rediscovery and publication of her own narratives. French-Canadian historians had located Verchères's narratives by the 1860s, but their integral publication waited a number of decades. The national historian of French Canada, F.-X. Garneau, quoted from Verchères's second narrative in a 1864 companion volume to his earlier *Histoire du Canada*. In answer to his rhetorical request 'Give an idea of the *military* courage of women in New France,' he focused primarily on Madeleine de Verchères, citing her second account.[3] In 1869, Narcisse Faucher de Saint-Maurice wrote to a fellow historian to ask for a copy of the same letter.[4] When her accounts were published at the end of the century, editors announced them with a sense of breathless discovery. In 1897, Rodolphe Brunet reprinted both of Verchères's letters in *Le monde illustré*, claiming that they had only been discovered a few days previously. There was no doubt for Brunet that these letters constituted '[un] document très national.'[5] Archivist Édouard Richard's publication of the documents in the annual report of the Public Archives of Canada waxed eloquent about the greater significance of Verchères's heroism:

> Tragic, and in a higher degree still, heroic deeds when invested with a national interest, are calculated to make a deep impression on our minds, and to strike the most sensitive chords of our nature. And should the object of our admiration be a woman, her name, borne on the wings of fame, is stamped in letters of gold upon the heart of the nation and becomes the object of a cultus at once tender and patriotic. The facts themselves, reproduced and magnified in romance and legend, those willing helpers of that craving for the marvellous, to which we are all in greater or less degree inclined, become glorified in our eyes, nourish patriotism, and impart to history the vivid light which fixes the mind and captivates the imagination. We are as yet but in the infancy of our career as a nation.'[6]

Like Verchères, other figures of the French-Canadian nationalist pantheon were selected almost entirely from the period of New France. Governors and military figures like Count Louis de Buade de Frontenac and Pierre Le Moyne d'Iberville and explorers like René-Robert Cavalier de La Salle and Pierre Gaultier de La Vérendrye were celebrated alongside women like Marie de l'Incarnation, Jeanne Mance, Marguerite

Bourgeoys, and Marguerite d'Youville.[7] No particularly memorable characters from the history of the post-Conquest period ever commanded the respect and admiration accorded to the figures of New France. Despite some attempts to elevate the military figure Charles-Michel Irumberry de Salaberry, victor of the Battle of Chateauguay during the War of 1812, few heroes emerged from the hundred years of British domination of the colony. The celebration of Salaberry had much to do with one particular fan, J.-O. Dion, who solicited funds for a statue to the military hero.[8] The rebels against British rule in 1837–8 also had some supporters, yet they presented clear difficulties as unifying icons. Such reminders of the armed uprising were difficult symbols of unity, and unlike the case of countries such as France, the overarching search for political and social unity generally prevailed over the desire to advance one group's political philosophy.

In contrast, the series of heroic figures from the period of French domination more easily affirmed the legitimacy and strength of both French-Canadian and pan-Canadian nationalist sentiment. French-Canadian nationalists drew on the historical figures in order to provide evidence of the longevity of the 'national' struggle. English Canadians used the same figures in a similar fashion, though their use of the figures represented an attempt to appropriate the past of French Canada in order to provide a longer genealogy to the Canadian nation and to imply a continuous record of progress that linked French and English Canadians. In their reading, the history of the French colony was a prelude to British domination and Canada's evolution within the British Empire – a romantic preface, as it were, to the most significant part of the Canadian past from their perspective. The military antagonism between British and French that led to the conquest of New France could be subverted by the rather banal act of perceiving both sides as comprising 'heroes' who laid the foundations for Canadian greatness. It is telling that the English-Canadian attempt to appropriate French-Canadian heroes did not occur in reverse. French-language school history textbooks provide little discussion of the standard heroes and heroines outside of French Canada. Knowledge of Laura Secord in Quebec, for instance, has always been mediated through the advertising of the candy company.

For French Canadians, the key icon was unquestionably Dollard des Ormeaux. As told by Lionel Groulx, the story achieved a canonical form in which Dollard's sacrificial military sortie at Carillon saved struggling Ville-Marie from a large-scale Iroquois attack. Like the Greek defence at Thermopylae, the sacrifice of the few protected the many. Dollard thus became a symbol of the French-Canadian nation in his bravery and daring, a literary flourish the more necessary in light of the accusations hurled at French Canadians during the debates over conscription in the First World War. The perception of a lower rate of enlistment in the armed services among French Canadians led to increasing antipathies between the two main linguistic groups. For their part, French-Canadian leaders proclaimed the willingness to fight, but only in the direct defence of their own country. Historical figures such as Dollard des Ormeaux and Madeleine de Verchères confirmed this rhetorical stance as they epitomized the courage French Canadians could reveal in the face of imminent danger. The reverberations of the split between English and French Canadians over the issue of conscription contributed to Dollard's great popularity in the post-war years. The 'rose de Dollard,' a boutonnière which demonstrated the wearer's allegiance to the story and to French-Canadian nationalism, attained great popularity. Over one hundred thousand were sold in 1920 alone. Annual pilgrimages, beginning in 1919 and continuing through the 1920s, led hundreds of the faithful to the scene of his sacrifice.[9]

The larger cultural significance of Dollard's story placed it firmly in the mainstream of late nineteenth- and early twentieth-century French-Canadian nationalism. This nationalism focused on 'la survivance': the survival of a small French-speaking and Catholic island in a wider English-speaking, Protestant, and increasingly materialistic sea. This survival was clearly against all the odds – a hostile British imperial government, the loss of a sustaining link to the mother country (not just because of change of empire, but because of the radical and republican changes in France itself in the nineteenth century), the examples of antagonism from Protestant compatriots, and so on. On the side of survival was the basic fact of demography. French-Canadian women still tended to bear large numbers of children, a fact that gave a large, if circumscribed, role to women in nationalist thought. Moreover, until the beginning of the twentieth century, Canada generally failed to attract and keep the immigrants who might have overwhelmed the French-Canadian position in the overall population. When net migration began to have a positive effect, concern grew over the increasing marginality of French Canadians. Much of the 'survivance' nationalism which epitomized French-Canadian ideology during the late nineteenth and early twentieth centuries was specific to that part of the country, and the assumed audience remained within that linguistic group. The 'nous' employed was an exclusive, not an inclusive, pronoun. Nonetheless, the same themes resonated strongly with English-Canadian elites, who also faced the daunting task of surviving in the face of external threats.[10]

Comparing Verchères

While there is no question that Madeleine de Verchères occupied an important place in the pantheon of historic figures, her appeal never approached that of Dollard des Ormeaux. But her sex established her as a key figure in French-Canadian and pan-Canadian nationalism. Other more influential women of the New France period were members of religious orders or had close ties with the Church. Their manifold virtues could not be summed up by a single heroic incident in the manner of Verchères. The hagiographers of these saintly women were often to be found within their own religious orders, and they provided the serious biographies – preludes often to petitions for canonization – of these key women.[11] The theme of sacrifice dominated their stories, as well. But they lacked the narrative panache of the defence of the family fort. Verchères, as a lay woman, had greater appeal to the public at large. A great part of her attraction was her comparability to other key heroines and figureheads from other countries.

Many countries have found a certain utility in having a woman fulfil the role of national figurehead. The image of Marianne in republican France, for instance, is a prime example, where the anonymous and mutable icon could serve as an emblem for the nation. However, through the nineteenth century, her figure did not inspire unanimity. As historian Maurice Agulhon concludes, 'for some Marianne is a saint or a new goddess but for others she is the "trollop."' But because Marianne was an entirely invented symbol, she had no personal history for which to account.[12] In the United Kingdom, the anonymous icon of Britannia represented an analogous figure, a benevolent and mute symbol of imperialism and military might.

In the case of historical icons such as Joan of Arc, the personage became more of a symbol than a human being. French historian Jules Michelet penned an enduring portrayal of the heroine in 1841, in which she came to symbolize the nation: 'My French compatriots, let us always remember that our homeland is born of a woman's heart, of her tenderness, of her tears, of the blood she shed for us.'[13] The icon of Joan of Arc crossed many political chasms in France, appealing to political supporters of both the left and the right who struggled to appropriate her potent imagery. On the one hand, she defended her country's national and religious integrity, the eternal values of the French people, but she was also a woman 'of the people' who revealed the weaknesses of the ruling classes.[14] At the end of the nineteenth century, the French minister of public instruction, Raymond Poincaré, called for a truce in the historiographical battle between right and left: 'Joan can unite all the French people through all the fundamental values of patriotism, above party considerations, because she represents the passionate desire for the independence and greatness of the nation.'[15] But such appeals for unity in commemoration did not mask the ideological interpretations, and the commemoration of Joan of Arc remained yet another field upon which French ideological battles were waged. Whatever the attempts to portray Joan of Arc as a symbol of national identity, as historian Michel Winock has shown, Joan's image often provided a staunchly Catholic cover for anti-Semitic sentiment. Most recently, Jean-Marie Le Pen's right-wing and anti-immigrant party Le Front National has tried to appropriate the symbol of the pure and patriotic Joan of Arc.[16]

In the late nineteenth and early twentieth centuries, Joan of Arc's popularity extended far beyond France. In Britain and the United States, as in her own country, her heroism appealed to feminists and socialists as much as to conservatives.[17] In Quebec, her cult also had resonances. Statues were raised to her memory, and streets and hospitals were named after her.[18] French-Canadian nationalists made pilgrimages to the sites associated with her heroism. In 1907, Lionel Groulx visited Orléans, a city 'filled to overflowing with the memory of Joan of Arc.'[19] French-Canadian Jesuit priest and nationalist activist Joseph-P. Archambault (Pierre Homier of the nationalist publication *L'Action française*) wrote to a friend in Montreal in 1913 on his pilgrimage to Joan of Arc's birthplace: 'I prayed this morning to blessed and valiant Joan, for those in Canada who fight like her for French and Catholic traditions.'[20]

Other countries boasted their own equivalent heroines. For the English, Boudicca, the rebel Iceni queen who fought against Roman invaders in A.D. 60–1, provided a counterpart to Joan of Arc. It is no coincidence that her Victorian-era statue was placed prominently on Westminster Bridge near the rebuilt Houses of Parliament. As one historian's analysis of the commemoration of Boudicca points out, 'devoid of her sexual specificity, she has represented the more general and abstract ideas of Britain and national struggle.' Nonetheless, in many accounts, especially those written by men, she emerges as a mother figure, a model for British womanhood.[21] The emphasis on 'womanly' virtues rendered the image of the warrior queen much more palatable.

The persona of Madeleine de Verchères would also embody womanly attributes as she came to occupy the position of female figurehead in Quebec. There were different shades of opinion concerning her significance, as we shall see, but Verchères's image largely appealed to the nationalist right, if only because the left side of the political spectrum was relatively weak during this period in Quebec and was limited in its access to publication outlets. Although her similarities to Dollard des Ormeaux could also be used to accentuate her virtues, without question the key attraction of Madeleine de Verchères was the comparison one could make to Joan of Arc. Both in their teens at the time of their famous exploits, the two women presented themselves as virgins, and cross-dressed to achieve their aims. But there were also some important differences between them. Unlike Verchères, Joan apparently never used her weapons. Unlike the exploits of Joan of Arc (and Dollard des Ormeaux), Verchères's actions were primarily defensive. Verchères led the defence of the family fort; she did not initiate the military confrontation.

Verchères's comparability to Joan and Dollard allowed her to assume an important place in the nationalist pantheon. As early as 1859, lawyer Maximilien Bibaud noted the comparison of Verchères to Joan of Arc.[22] In 1902, a writer in the popular magazine *Le monde illustré* called her 'la Jeanne d'Arc du Canada.'[23] Writing in the pages of the nationalist journal *L'Action française* in 1926, Marie-Louise d'Auteuil proposed a 'Journée de Madeleine de Verchères' for schoolgirls, to accompany the increasingly popular Dollard Day, which was becoming the accepted name in Quebec for the holiday celebrated as Victoria Day elsewhere in Canada.[24] A few writers retelling Verchères's story preferred the comparison with Jeanne Hachette, defender of Beauvais. Given Hachette's successful rallying of her city's defenders in 1472, she offered a better analogy, even if it lacked some of the resonance of Joan of Arc.[25] The comparisons legitimized Verchères's heroism and, by extension, French-Canadian and Canadian history: 'It was done,' wrote journalist P. de la Chatre in a Trois-Rivières newspaper in 1929. 'Canada had the right to compare itself to France in this way: it now had its own heroine.'[26] Just as the 1867 and 1884 translations into French of Joan's trial contributed to her growing force as a heroine, so did the publication of Verchères's two narratives provide the authentic proof of her importance.

But authenticity was not always required of heroic national symbols. Evangeline, the semi-fictitious Acadian heroine, provides a further useful comparison, even if Verchères herself was never contrasted with this character. The creation of the American poet Henry Longfellow in 1847, she came to symbolize the sufferings of the Acadian people, deported from their homeland in the 1740s and scattered around the Atlantic world. Evangeline searched throughout North America for her deported fiancé, locating him only as he lay dying. Longfellow's poem was phenomenally popular in the English-speaking world and in Acadia, and it created a heroine who provided a romantic impulse for the surge of Acadian nationalism in the late nineteenth century. As French professor Ernest Martin wrote in 1936, her story inspired 'the moral rehabilitation of an entire race, hope and pride brought back to the heart of a million people.'[27] Although there was indeed a woman whose story can be said to resemble that of Evangeline, the problem with the character is her literary nature: useful for tourists as an attraction, she was nonetheless fictitious – not that she did not 'exist,' but that she did not have the ring of authenticity of flesh-and-blood heroines. Nonetheless, she came to represent the key motif in Acadian nationalist history, a figurehead for identity. Like Secord and Verchères, she too could become a focus for commercial advertising and tourist attractions both in Acadia and in Louisiana, an increasingly banal representation of national identity. Like them, she could also become the butt of ironic jokes: 'Evangeline, the Acadian Queen,' Acadian songwriter Angèle Arsenault sings – partly in English – with tongue in cheek.[28]

Where Verchères differed most strongly from Evangeline was the nature of her feat. Evangeline strove to find domestic bliss in her search for her true love. Verchères could not easily be cast as the romantic victim. She was a forceful protagonist, one whose very actions challenged strict gendered roles. Given the ideological constraints of the late nineteenth and early twentieth centuries, her heroism had to lead eventually, for narrative purposes, to domestic bliss.

Depicting Virtue

Between the 1860s and 1920s, dozens of published accounts commemorated Verchères's heroism. Writers dedicated poems, full narratives, or chapters in larger works to Madeleine's memory. Versions of Verchères's story cast her as a patriotic icon, with specific feminine attributes and virtues. While the emphasis varied to a small degree from author to author, the vast majority of the retellings of the tale of Madeleine de Verchères did not distinguish themselves by inventiveness. Most follow standard forms, with minor differences in wording and the choice of anecdotes, often depending on the ultimate source: one of the two narratives signed by Verchères, or the other accounts by Charlevoix or La Potherie. The attempts at commemoration feed upon each other, to the point of lacking originality. Very few of the accounts reflect in-depth research; this was not the strength of popular history. Rather, the defining trait of popular history seems to have been the retelling of a familiar story in a way that imbued it with moral values which surpassed the mere details of the narrative.[29] Protestants and Catholics, French Canadians and English Canadians, men and women, all placed their emphasis somewhat differently, although the versions generally had much in common with one another. The very familiarity of the story made it an appropriate inspiration for quick adaptations on a nationalist theme. Two participants in a 1918 literary contest run by the nationalist Société St-Jean-Baptiste de Montréal chose as their theme the story of the girl's heroism, even if the authors produced submissions strikingly similar to the usual accounts.[30]

In his 1877 volume on the history of New France, the American historian Francis Parkman introduced the term 'Castle Dangerous' for the fort of Verchères, an exaggeration of the scale of the settlement, but one with a nice literary ring nonetheless.[31] There is otherwise little to distinguish his story from the many others. Still, it is a testimony to the influence of Parkman's work over many later popular historians that the phrase 'Castle Dangerous' crops up so often in the accounts, particularly those destined for children. The inclusion of an excerpt from Parkman in the fourth reader for Ontario elementary school students meant that thousands of young English-speaking Canadians would be exposed to Verchères's story.

Many authors quote Verchères's own words for their resonance and authenticity. Both Catholic and Protestant authors laid emphasis on Verchères's religiosity, as did Verchères herself. Verchères's second letter recounts her prayers to the Virgin as she raced for the fort: 'Holy Virgin, mother of my God, you know that I have always honoured and loved you like my dear mother; do not abandon me in the danger I am in! I would a thousand times more rather perish than fall into the hands of a people that does not know you.'[32] Catholics were much more likely to include the prayer to the Virgin, but all were agreed that Verchères was a strong daughter of the Church. For Abbé F.-A. Baillairgé, the adult life of Verchères was that of a woman 'strengthened by the Gospel.'[33] A 1727 letter from the bishop indicating that Verchères later sponsored the construction of a new church in her seigneury served to prove her deep religiosity. For their part, Protestants acknowledged Verchères's deference to God, but they tended to bypass the saintly intermediary: for poet John Reade, 'God gave courage to a maid to act the man.'[34] Alan Sullivan agreed with Reade's emphasis: 'the Lord is God of battle – He will help us to defend ...'[35]

Writers also liked to quote Verchères's exhortation to her brothers: 'Let us fight to the death. We are fighting for our fatherland [*patrie*] and for religion.'[36] The fact that Verchères's concept of 'patrie' had little relation to the recognizable boundaries of the late nineteenth and early twentieth centuries was of little import. As Diane Gervais and Serge Lusignan demonstrate, Verchères may have described her country (*pays*) as being 'Canada,' that is, the St Lawrence Valley settlements of New France, but her fatherland was France, a country of many regions. Her loyal actions, as she described them, only made sense within the context of her allegiance to the French king.[37] Nonetheless, both English- and French-language writers liked to interpret her heroism as an act of valiant nationalist defence against a foreign enemy. Her defence could serve as an example for contemporary readers.

In this fashion, a range of contemporary nationalistic concerns were grafted onto Verchères's narrative. In 1916, Dominion Archivist Arthur Doughty published his study of Verchères in order to raise money for the Imperial Order Daughters of the Empire, drawing a parallel between Iroquois and Germans that wartime readers could not miss: 'Savage tribes who had lorded over the continent for centuries were challenging the advance of European civilization.'[38] Verchères could also be cast as a defender of French language rights. Nationalist writer Pierre Homier applauded the French-Canadian youths who refused to answer a train conductor until he spoke to them in French. According to Homier, 'it was their only response, but what a clear echo of the voice of the child of the fort of Verchères.'[39] Albert Larrieu's patriotic song showed the contemporary lessons that the heroine proffered:

Ton souvenir, Madelon de Verchères,
Ne nous a pas quittés!
La Canadienne, encor [*sic*] sous ta bannière,
Sait comme il faut lutter!
S'il fallait, pour defendre sa race,
Et sa langue et sa foi,
Sans hésiter, elle suivrait ta trace
Et vaincrait comme toi![40]

[Your memory, Madelon de Verchères
Has not left us!
The Canadian woman, still under your banner
Knows how she must fight!
If necessary, to defend her race,
And her language and her faith,
Without hesitating, she would follow your path
And would conquer as you did!]

Thus Verchères, like other heroic figures, fulfilled a mnemonic purpose: her image provided the means to remember and inculcate normative values. Verchères showed the way to defend specific attributes such as the French-Canadian language, or civilization in the case of the threat of wartime. The nation could be French Canada or it could be all of Canada.

One of the most successful treatments of the Madeleine de Verchères story was a short poem by William Henry Drummond. Irish-born Drummond had trained as a doctor in Canada, but he achieved international fame with his poetry. His earlier publication *The Habitant* had sold, one newspaper reported, over ten thousand copies. To sensibilities a hundred years later, the cloying rhymes of Drummond's poetry and the attempts to capture the French-Canadian accent in English do not stand up well. But Drummond was very popular in his own lifetime, achieving substantial critical acclaim and high honours.[41]

In 1898, Drummond published 'Madeleine Vercheres' in a chapbook with 'Phil-o-Rum's Canoe.'[42] 'Madeleine Vercheres' was recounted in orthodox English, although Drummond had attempted earlier versions in dialect, and the other poem in the chapbook attempted to capture French-Canadian English. One draft of 'Madeleine Vercheres' begins, 'She has pass down by de reever / She has pass down by de shore.'[43] Though the published version of the poem is in standard English, French words appear that make clear the provenance of the story. Drummond's poem is a tale told to a child:

I've told you many a tale, my child, of the old heroic days
Of Indian wars and massacre, of villages ablaze
With savage torch, from Ville Marie to the Mission of Trois Rivieres;
But never have I told you yet, of Madeleine Vercheres.

Erupting into the bucolic setting of French-Canadian farmers working happily in their fields, the Iroquois attack the habitants. Verchères, like a mountain deer, escapes back to the fort and rallies her small garrison to the successful defence by blowing the war-bugle: ''T was a soldier of France's challenge, from the young Madeleine Vercheres!' Twice the poet reminds the readers that Verchères fought 'for God and country.' She awakened her compatriots' Norman blood, an important element in the attempt at the turn of the century to locate a pan-Canadian nationalism in the specious Norman origins of both English and French Canadians,[44] and they fought off the Iroquois foe. The weather reflects and punctuates the conflict: 'And they say the black clouds gathered, and a tempest swept the sky, / And the roar of the thunder mingled with the forest tiger's cry, / But still the garrison fought on ...' When De la Monnière (*sic*) arrives to relieve the fort, 'he stood for a moment speechless, and marvelled at woman's ways.' The poem ends with the poet's hope that no such frightful sights should ever be experienced again: 'God grant that we in Canada may never see again / Such cruel wars and massacre ...' In the context of the Indian wars in the United States and the rapid settlement of western Canada, such concerns represented a way of linking the contemporary national narrative of westward expansionism to historical struggles.[45]

Despite the standard English of this poem, Drummond's effort was well received. His international reputation meant that his work was reviewed in a variety of American newspapers from Chicago to Pittsburgh. The *Chicago Chronicle* commented that 'it is a thrilling, heroic story ... and Dr. Drummond has embalmed it in swift, rhythmic, throbbing, heroic verse that will hardly fail to carry it far into the future.'[46] Drummond sent a copy of his work to the governor general Lord Minto, whose secretary responded that His Excellency looked forward to learning about French Canada from the poems.[47] Fellow poet Louis Fréchette wrote to congratulate Drummond on his work, and to invite him to visit him in Varennes, whence they could make the short trip to Verchères.[48] With its forceful language and its ability to capture the contemporary narrative of national expansion, this 'story of the maiden Madeleine' was one of the most successful English-language portrayals of the Verchères legend. It mixed patriotism, European expansionism, and a young woman's courage.

'Dangerous Women'

With the exception of the emphasis on her religious devotion, French and English Canadians tended to use Verchères as a symbol in similar ways. Unlike Joan of Arc, Madeleine de Verchères did not inspire writers to take widely divergent stances. It would be extremely difficult, for instance, to cast her as a woman of the 'people' given the class background she claimed for herself. The principal divergences did not occur between English and French Canadians or between right and left, but between men and women.

Verchères's icon raised issues of gender, ethnicity, and religion that could be used to fend off modernity. It is ironic, but by no means contradictory, that Verchères's popularity peaked during a time when women were beginning to occupy new roles in Canadian society. This was a period when men and women were faced with challenges to gendered spheres of activity, as married and unmarried women participated in the paid workforce outside of the family home, and they increasingly demanded political recognition of their contributions to society. Such trends enhanced fears about the nature of gendered social roles.

The late nineteenth century was, in the major metropolises of the Western world, a period of gender anxiety and sexual experimentation.[49] While Montreal was not London or New York, and certainly provincial Quebec (or Canada, for that matter) was not in these same cultural networks, the influences were spreading. Important figures in this cultural ferment such as Sarah Bernhardt and Oscar Wilde visited Montreal. Bernhardt's tour created consternation among the Catholic clergy, while at the same time her performances enjoyed packed houses.[50] Alongside this cultural ferment, women's organizations were demanding new rights, in particular the vote, and this blurring of public space frightened many men.[51]

This fear of changes in women's roles was true of Quebec as much as elsewhere in Canada. Leading male social commentators of the time fulminated against this 'problem.' Influential nationalist writer Henri Bourassa, editor of *Le Devoir*, reprinted under the title *Femmes-hommes ou hommes et femmes?* a series of articles in which he attacked feminism. Describing the likely results of women's suffrage, he poured out his invective on 'the woman-man, the hybrid and repugnant monster that will kill the woman-mother and the woman-*woman*.'[52] Bourassa was not alone in wishing to limit women's encroachments on the public sphere. As a quick illustration, we can take the views of two men who themselves played important roles in commemorating Madeleine de Verchères. In 1918, Liberal politician Rodolphe Lemieux rejected women's suffrage because elected female representatives would have to vote on military matters, an untenable position given his belief that 'women ... are unfitted for military service.'[53] And Abbé F.-A. Baillairgé wrote a pamphlet in 1925 warning of the dangers of North American modernity, among which was the confusion that would result if women dressed as men: 'The idea, for a woman, to become a man acts against nature ... Why make only one [sex], when God desires that there should be two?'[54] Gender anxiety had reached Quebec as well.

In such a context, one might have expected that a heroine who transgressed gender roles like Madeleine de Verchères would pose a problem for such men. Yet, as we have seen, even in the most conservative circles, another cross-dresser was having her second day in the sun. The image of Joan of Arc underwent a renaissance that culminated in her canonization in 1920 by the same Church that had burnt her at the stake.

Most authors and artists of this period chose not to emphasize the ways in which Verchères by her very actions tested gender boundaries. It was extremely rare for authors to acknowledge the 'woman warrior' element in her depiction of herself. In a lengthy article in *Le Devoir*, Marc de Germiny returned to La Potherie's characterization as 'a fourteen-year-old Amazon,'[55] a metaphor surprisingly missing in most of the early twentieth-century works on Verchères. Only one other author during this period of widespread popularity explicitly interpreted Madeleine de Verchères's story as the narrative of a woman warrior. Frédéric de Kastner emphasized Verchères's noble lineage, an ancestry that the author was quick to point out he shared, and recognized Verchères as one in a line of 'femmes guerrières.' Indeed, he complained that most depictions portrayed her as too slight and wispish. He was clear, however, that she should not be seen as a burly, working-class woman.[56] His intervention is interesting, if only because it went unheeded by artists of the period. The pictorial images of Madeleine de Verchères emphasize her femininity, downplaying her military actions and presenting her as an innocent, young child. Gerald Hayward's 1912 illustration depicts her in a pink dress with her scarf intact, the fort of Verchères visible in the distance behind her (fig. 2.1). Artists like Louis-Philippe Hébert, who sculpted an image of Verchères in the first decades of the twentieth century, expressed his difficulty in executing her figure. His inspiration was suspended between the image of a young female hunter, weighed down by her oversized rifle, and that of a 'virago.' Both representations seemed inappropriate to him.[57] Given that no contemporary pictures of Verchères existed, artists could use their imagination to invent her as they wished.[58] The femininity of the illustrations is all the more striking.

2.1 The young, innocent Madeleine de Verchères. (Gerald Hayward)

Authors and artists, both men and women, suppressed or downplayed Verchères's challenge to normative gender roles. Though many mentioned that she took off her headdress and donned a hat, few accentuated the maleness of the apparel. Indeed, many did not suggest that Verchères changed her clothes, or indeed even fired any weapons. None of the visual imagery in the least disguised her femininity, as artists were always careful to show her long dress. Some authors and artists placed emphasis on Verchères's virginity, a fundamental element of the Joan of Arc figure. The scarf incident, with its virgin imagery, was often repeated, even though most writers relied on Verchères's second letter, which did not include this detail.

Images of Verchères's defence depicted particular moments in the episode: her flight to the fort, her grasp of the oversized rifle, or her firing of the cannon. The least awkward images emphasize Verchères's femininity – those which depict her in the midst of military action lack fluidity, as if the artist could not contain his difficulty with the concept of a woman's military prowess (see figs. 2.2, 2.3). One of the most prolific producers of historical images in this period, C.W. Jefferys, provided two images of Verchères, neither of which depicted her involved in military actions (fig. 2.4). None of the pictures created in the period up to the 1920s was designed by a female artist.

Even with the woman warrior imagery suppressed, Verchères represented a potentially unruly female figure, which male writers wished to tame. One way to do so was to associate her with the innocence and peacefulness of nature that existed before the Iroquois attack. Rev. Aen. McD. Dawson's poem situates her in the pastoral landscape to which she will eventually restore order:

Where grandly flows St. Lawrence tide
A maiden fair was seen to guide
Her lonely steps. 'Mid sweetest flowers
Her pleasure found and shady bowers.[59]

More directly, authors attributed specific feminine traits to Verchères. Abbé F.-A. Baillairgé assured the reader, 'Yes, Madeleine, who was strong, was nonetheless soft and sensitive.'[60] In a collection of stories of heroism in New France, Thomas Marquis was able to picture the young woman: 'Her delicate, active figure, soft, *spirituelle* face – intelligent forehead, brilliant eyes and well-cut lips – all bespoke gentle breeding'[61] (fig. 2.5). Whatever courage she may have shown, she did not lose any of her femininity.

Another way in which the narratives resolve the issue of the challenge to gender roles was to ensure closure, the return to the status quo. As her second narrative had done, they ended their story with Verchères surrendering arms to La Monnerie (or Crisafy). Lionel Groulx, after attributing to his niece the comment that 'Madeleine was a little girl, and ... a little girl is not a little boy,' emphasized how Dollard's heroism surpassed that of Verchères. Women's active roles could only be fortuitous: 'They must sometimes fill in for men, but they must render them the arms for the battles that are more appropriate to them.'[62] Other male writers shifted the narrative to the soldiers' pursuit of the Iroquois and rescue of French prisoners.[63] Some added the apocryphal story, first raised by Abbé François Daniel, that Madeleine saved her future husband's life, and thus (illogically) 'she became, in turn, the conquest of the man

2.2 An awkward Madeleine de Verchères prepares the cannon. (James McIsaac)

2.3 A school poster illustrating a regal Verchères lighting the cannon. (J.-B. La-gacé)

2.4 Verchères welcomes the French troops. (C.W. Jefferys)

whose life she had saved.'[64] And men and women emphasized that Verchères resumed her proper gender role following the incident. One journalist wrote in 1912 that 'Magdelon was a perfect woman, as good a housekeeper as a mother.'[65] For Raoul Renault, Verchères was 'the perfect example of a model wife, of the true companion that God should give to all truly good and sincerely Christian men.'[66] The editor of James LeMoine's version pointed out that the heroines of New France represented appropriate symbols for the youth of the day: 'like so many stars, like so many beacons destined to lead us through the twisting paths of our existence, like so many patterns for our young French-Canadian women, like so many models of conjugal fidelity.'[67] These designations rely on the story of Verchères's protection of her husband from the Abenaki attack, but they also represent appropriate completions to the story of her youthful heroism. How more appropriately could a woman have fulfilled the promise of her early bravery?

As a rule, authors felt constrained by Verchères's own words. One of the few exceptional treatments of her story, Rodolphe Girard's 1902 play

2.5 The noble, demure Madeleine de Verchères. (E.-Z. Massicotte)

Madeleine de Verchères or *Fleur de Lys*, turned it into a romance. Unlike the legion of historical enthusiasts and commemorators who were responsible for most of the versions of the heroine's story, the twenty-three-year-old Girard approached the narrative with a great deal of licence and situated the story far outside the boundaries of historical accuracy.

Girard introduces a romantic drama into the story: the Chevalier de Briac is in love with Verchères; Jeanne de Brémont competes for de Briac's attention; and the Baron de Meules, a cowardly traitor, wishes to dispose of de Briac. De Briac is condemned to die for the offence of having treacherously conspired with the Iroquois attackers, while he was really trying to chase after them. In good romantic style, as he faces the firing squad, de Briac states, 'I die for having loved Madeleine de Verchères too much, she who loved me as well.' Madeleine pleads for de Briac's life and throws herself in front of him: 'If you fire, our two bodies will fall at the same time, our blood will mix together, we will be united in death and in eternity, since we have not been able to be so in life ...'[68]

Verchères's defence of the fort is not the focus of the play. At one point, Verchères informs her mother that she had escaped some thirty Iroquois. 'You know the rest,' she adds laconically.[69] The play uses the Iroquois attack as a means of allowing the romantic machinations to take their course. Once de Meules's treachery is revealed, all ends well. The play finishes with Verchères's betrothal to the Chevalier de Briac, although Madeleine apparently has little to say in this development. Her father determines the end: 'Forgive me, chevalier de Briac. I also must make reparation to you. Take my daughter, captain, take her, and may you have sons worthy of you and daughters worthy of her.'[70]

One critic commented on Girard's use of the romantic genre, 'the most popular genre today.' Others mentioned their pleasure that the play adopted a Canadian theme. The play enjoyed a week's run at the Théâtre national in Montreal, after which the author expressed his pleasure at the public's response and the financial results of the presentations.[71] The play was sent to the United States to be translated and adapted to the American stage, but it does not appear that it was ever produced there.

Girard's play provides the main exception to the rule: the retellings of Madeleine de Verchères's story often remain strikingly standard, limited by the words (if not necessarily the meaning) of the heroine herself. While some introduce the romantic element through fictitious connections with her future husband, most accounts stem more from the gothic tradition of a damsel in distress finding the courage to save herself and her companions. For most audiences, at least, the apparent authenticity of Verchères's account explained its appeal. Even Girard felt it useful to make the genealogical link between Verchères and contemporary society by dedicating his play to Charles Tarieu de Lanaudière, her direct descendant.

Women's Attitudes

Women as well as men commented on the closure to her story that Verchères's marriage to M. de La Pérade represented. In a period when maternal feminism was the dominant discourse of those in favour of women's rights, female writers wanted their subjects to fulfil the important aspects of the 'standard' woman's biography, in which women, regardless of their desire to live differently, ultimately placed men at the centre of their lives.[72] Nonetheless, women's versions sometimes had a different purpose than those of men. They used the story to stake out a feminist claim on Canadian history, and in some cases to justify the contemporary shifts in gender roles.[73] Thus, Mary Sifton Pepper wrote in 1902, 'Many of them [the women of New France] would even nowadays be looked upon as "emancipated" and "advanced."'[74] Teresa Costigan Armstrong begins her account of Verchères's heroism by examining a number of heroic women: 'The pioneer women of Canada have left behind them on the pages of history a long line of notable characters distinguished for their heroism, self-sacrifice and nobility of soul ...'[75] In Marie-Claire Daveluy's short play, young girls at a convent school complain that 'history is mostly for boys ... because of battles and soldiers.' An older girl rebukes them, saying, 'And Madeleine de Verchères? She was not a boy ... And they talk her in history.'[76] Franco-American Corinne Rocheleau makes a similar point in her play illustrating the roles of women in New France: 'It is said that happy people have no history. If this epigram applies to individuals, then the first French women settlers in America were happy women, because one never speaks about them ... or so little that it is the same thing!'[77]

Members of women's historical societies were drawn to the biography of Madeleine de Verchères: Bellelle Guérin in Montreal, Emma Currie in St Catharines, Teresa Costigan-Armstrong in Ottawa. Asked to deliver an address to the Women's Historical Society of Montreal, Louyse de Bienville (Mme Donat Brodeur) declared that she had thought of talking about early Canadian heroes, but turned her attention to heroines: 'Since I am a woman, my sympathy turns first to women.'[78] Emma Curie, in a chapter of a book focusing on Laura Secord, discussed Verchères's exploits, regretting (incorrectly) that her heroism too had been unjustly ignored when it came to the request for a pension because she was 'only a woman.'[79]

Some women writers found it easier than their male colleagues to acknowledge the limitations on gender roles that Verchères had tested. Mary Sifton Pepper judged Verchères's actions in this way: 'With a thoughtfulness that seems almost incredible in one so young, she tossed aside her woman's head-gear and placed a man's hat upon her head, so that if the Indians saw her they would take her for a man and therefore a more formidable opponent.'[80] Ethel Raymond supposed that Verchères 'often wished that she had been born a boy ...'[81] Mary Constance Du Bois, writing in the *St. Nicholas Magazine*, supplied Verchères's rallying words: 'Do not lose sight of my soldier hat! You will always find it in the path of honor!'[82]

By expanding the scope of Canadian history to include women, it was not such a long step to desire to extend the purview beyond the history of elites. Robert Glasgow, publisher of the Chronicles of Canada series, commissioned Isabel Skelton before 1914 to write a book on Canadian heroines. Skelton wished to extend the range of the study to include ordinary women. Glasgow concurred in the modification of the early project to go beyond 'the stereotyped heroines of the French period ...'[83] In the end, Skelton's volume included sections on Verchères, Marie Rollet, the first female settler in New France, and Marie de l'Incarnation. Skelton acknowledged the ways in which Verchères had tested the limits of women's actions and recognized her uniqueness: 'Marie Madeleine confessed that she herself entertained sentiments which urged her on "to aspire to fame as eagerly as many men." Not to many girls or women has fortune been so kind in appeasing such a desire.'[84] Skelton's study also covered the social history of early settlement in Upper Canada by looking at pioneer women. In the long run, the increasing interest in the social history of the common people would reduce the emphasis on the small number of heroes and heroines who occupied the historic pantheon.

Foreign Interest

While much of Verchères's appeal was specific to French Canada, other elements held more universal appeal. The reference to classical and literary traditions was important. John Reade wrote that 'Grecian poet, had he seen her, would have deemed her race divine.'[85] Mme Boissonault compared Verchères to the Greek hero Patrocles.[86] For Charles Colby, 'she remains a bright, alluring figure, perennially young, like the maidens on Keats' Grecian Urn.'[87] Despite her status as a national heroine, a general interest in heroic tales gave value to Verchères's virtues.

Beyond her nationalist appeal for French- and English-speaking Canadians, an interest that exemplifies the clash in the attempts to write the history of two nations, Verchères also attracted the interest of people from other countries. Initially the appeal of Verchères was as genealogical as it was in Canada, describing an ethnic nation that did not fit comfortably within state boundaries. Thus, a few Franco-Americans wrote stories about her, consciously attempting to transmit the values of French-Canadian culture. They reminded their audience of their ethnic allegiances at a time when American culture threatened to swamp the colonies of industrial workers in the New England states. The restrictions

on educational freedom in the United States in the context of the Great
War frightened many Franco-American elites. In 1918, Congress voted
that only English be used in primary schools throughout the country.
The application of the law varied from state to state, but the desire for
Americanization represented a challenge to the survival of Franco-Ameri-
can distinctiveness.[88]

For different reasons, writers from France retold her story, sometimes
from the perspective of genealogical connections between the old me-
tropolis and the colony. The fact that her lineage apparently came from
the Dauphiné district of France led a couple of authors to her story. For
Marie X. Drevet, Verchères was following in the footsteps of her
Dauphinois compatriot Philis de la Tour-du-Pin de La Charce: 'Daughter
of a Dauphinois man, the Canadian imitator of Philis merited this mention
to our compatriots. Good blood never lies.'[89] A correspondent of Abbé
F.-A. Baillairgé commented on the interest that two of Verchères's distant
relatives, the French Comtesse de Verchères and her sister the Countess
of Madrid, showed towards her.[90] Thérèse de Ferron justified her interest by literary and patriotic reasons, and spoke of having encountered
someone from the Verchères family in France. 'We maintain, amongst
our ancient French families, a very tender feeling and we are full of
admiration towards our Canadian brothers who have remained so faithful to us ...' Ferron was seemingly unaware of the deep chasms that had
been driven into Canadian society by the experience of the Great War.
She wished to re-establish ethnic ties that had lapsed over the decades.[91]

Other French authors have been attracted to the story for its sense of
adventure and the possibility of presenting the heroism of a teenager for
an adolescent audience. In his 1928 novel, Léon Ville laments the lost
heroic values of the *ancien régime*: 'Hum! I can barely imagine our young
French girls today in such a situation.'[92] French authors like Ville, Georges
Cerbelaud-Salagnac, and, more recently, Nicole Vidal mention that the
English were behind the actions of the Iroquois, implying that the
Aboriginal people lacked the independence to pursue their own military
strategies, and managing to score a point against the traditional antago-
nists of the French people.[93]

Likewise, a few Americans have also been interested in relating her
tale, mostly from the perspective of young and adolescent readers. Perhaps the most intriguing of all the foreign contributions to the Verchères
corpus is a series of three books aimed at adolescents by the Swedish
author Helmer Linderholm. These books used the heroic story as a

pretext for relatively standard Wild West novels in which the focus is more on the Aboriginal characters ('the warlike Iroquois') than on the young girl.[94]

This interest in a foreign national figure is in some ways surprising, yet the very specificity of Verchères also contributed to her universal character. Could she not be compared to heroines in other countries? Is not her fortitude in such adverse circumstances recognizable whatever the (Western) culture? Just as national figures are often in an odd way international in their appeal, so is nationalist sentiment an international belief, despite the specific culture to which it applies.

In this sense, the appeal of Madeleine de Verchères had much to do with the fact that she fit a international mould: she was the Canadian Joan of Arc, or the Canadian Jeanne Hachette. As such, she and Canadian or French-Canadian history, by extension, deserved respect and commemoration. For those reasons, when the list of historical figures was being drawn up for a historical procession to mark the 1908 Tercentenary Celebrations of Champlain's establishment of Quebec, there was no question but that Madeleine de Verchères would be invited. Beginning with François I and Marguerite d'Angoulême, a pageant of historical figures paraded through Quebec to demonstrate the compelling history of the colony. After the early explorers and the founders of the towns, 'then followed Frontenac, whose striking personality dominates one of the best scenes in the Pageant. Then the female counterpart of him and Dollard, Mlle de Verchères, who held the Iroquois at bay with a courage as undaunted as that shown at Rorke's Drift against an equally pitiless foe.'[95] As photographs of the procession show, she was placed along with her two brothers in front of Iroquois warriors (fig. 2.6). Verchères wore a man's hat, but her long dress reassured spectators that they had nothing to fear from the woman warrior.

Conclusion

In his long poem covering the heroic scope of the French-Canadian past, Louis Fréchette described the importance of the various heroes:

Ô France, ces héros qui creusaient si profonde,
Au prix de tant d'efforts, ta trace au nouveau monde,
Ne méritaient-ils un peu mieux, réponds-moi,
Qu'un crachat de Voltaire et le mépris d'un roi! [96]

2.6 Verchères and her brothers in public procession, followed by Iroquois warriors. Scene from the Quebec Tercentenary celebrations, 1908.

[O France, these heroes that inscribed your trace so deeply,
At such a high price, in the New World
Did they not deserve a bit better, tell me,
Than Voltaire's spit and the king's disdain!]

Much of the appeal of Madeleine de Verchères's story was wrapped up with the increase in Joan of Arc's popularity. Verchères became a national figure, primarily for French Canadians, but to a lesser degree for English Canadians as well. The ways in which the story was told reflected the particular class, religious, and gender politics of the artists. But the Canadian-ness of Verchères's story was also inevitably caught up in its international comparability.

The key purpose of retelling Verchères's story was to provide a peg upon which to hang particular traits deemed useful for the population at large. In her own petitions, she provided some of the phrases that enhanced her appeal in the nationalistic period that lasted from the 1880s to the 1920s. But her strength also lay in the similarities between her story and Joan of Arc's. Canadian history was worthy precisely because it contained figures like Madeleine de Verchères. Still, specific elements of her narrative were not deemed useful by many in the same period: thus her challenge of gendered spheres was strongly downplayed. Nonetheless, she emerged as one of the key heroic figures from the past for French Canadians, and when English Canadians learned about the history of French Canada, its heroes and heroines were the embodiment of that story.

Yet despite the efforts of enthusiasts for a historiographical rapprochement between French and English Canadians, Verchères ultimately remained for most English Canadians a distant character. As prime minister and historian Lester B. Pearson recalled in his memoirs, his school-boy knowledge of Quebec was limited to a few key figures and events: 'Quebec was virtually a foreign part which we read about in our school-books in terms of Madeleine de Verchères and the Battle of the Plains of Abraham.'[97] For the francophile Canadian historian Arthur Lower, Verchères's heroism clearly proved the national mettle of French Canadians. Writing about the late seventeenth century, he commented: 'It was the period of heroines like Madeleine de Verchères (1692), a period rich in the stuff of tradition, still vividly remembered by Canadians of French speech and the source of much of their spiritual strength today. English-speaking Canadians are the weaker for not possessing this trial-by-fire tradition.'[98] As the major attempts to commemorate Verchères illustrate, she primarily became an emblem of French-Canadian national history.

Chapter Three

Representing History: The Statue and Film of Madeleine de Verchères

Time and again, the prose retellings of Verchères's story indicated the desire to provide a solid commemoration of the story. As if to reassure themselves, the authors wrote of how her story would never be forgotten – despite the apparent necessity to retell it. William Chapman ends his poem to her memory, 'the centuries will never be able, as they rasp the years away, to erase her name from history.'[1] The chorus to I.S. Henri's 'Patriotic Song,' dedicated to Madeleine de Verchères, goes: 'Till Earth and Heaven grow hoary / Who dare forget thy story? / Memory of thee, shall ever be / While life and love yield glory.'[2] Teresa Costigan Armstrong asserted that 'the pen of the historian has done its duty and paid high tribute to her glorious achievement, making it impossible for her name to ever pass into oblivion.'[3] This is one of the ironies of commemorative exercises: the retelling of the key events nonetheless elicits the concern that people may soon forget if not constantly reminded.

While there was broad consensus in the late nineteenth and early twentieth centuries on the appropriateness of recognizing Madeleine de Verchères as a key heroic figure, there was some disagreement concerning the most effective way of doing so. While taking the time to produce such works, poets and historians nonetheless bemoaned the ephemeral nature of their publications. Surely Verchères deserved, as did other members of the pantheon of French-Canadian heroes, a more permanent monument than the printed page. In 1892, at the time of the bicentennial of Verchères's heroism, historian and librarian of the Legislative Assembly N.E. Dionne wrote, 'The Romans would not have forgotten to erect a monument or a statue to the memory of a heroine so young and so brave.'[4] In 1903, editor Henry James Morgan stated, 'Singularly enough ... no public statue has yet been erected by Canada to this the greatest of her heroines.'[5] Yet how could one accurately portray the heroic deed of someone who had left no visual evidence? How could one tell her story, and which was the most appropriate, the most permanent, way of doing so?

Fear of Ephemerality

It is possible that the writers who feared that the public would forget Verchères were correct. In 1916, the English-born Arthur Doughty, the Dominion archivist, wrote a short book, published in both English and French, ostensibly on Madeleine de Verchères, but really only including one main chapter on her exploits. Rather, like some of the more recent juvenile literature (see chapter 4), this work uses Verchères as a pretext to cover many important aspects of early French Canada: the land-holding system, the military realities, the nature of government in the colony. In this way, Doughty provided an accessible account of the social and political history of New France – for the time, one of the most accessible in English. The book was also intended to be a worthy cause – Doughty planned to donate all the proceeds of the volume to the Magdeleine de Verchères chapter of the Imperial Order Daughters of the Empire (IODE), an Ottawa chapter that included both French- and English-Canadian women and in which his wife played an important part. The book draws historical parallels between Madeleine de Verchères's bravery and sacrifices and the duties demanded of men and women in wartime: 'Surely the words of Magdelaine, embodying the loftiest sentiments of loyalty and devotion, should be cherished by every true Canadian, for happy is the country, in time of peace and in time of war, whose honour and whose safety are confided to loyal souls.' The people of New France faced an enemy implicitly comparable to the enemies of the Great War.[6] But other battles also had to be engaged at home.

Doughty's work is part of a concerted effort in the late nineteenth and early twentieth centuries to create a sense of national purpose in the diverse and dispersed Canadian population. Such grandiose endeavours as the Quebec Tercentenary Celebrations in 1908, stage-managed by Governor General Lord Grey with the assistance of a small group of enthusiasts including Doughty, represent other examples of this tendency.[7] Doughty made his aims clear in his book on Verchères: 'Some day, perhaps far distant, we shall enter into the full status of our national life. Then we shall appreciate the value of those treasures which are as yet a sealed book. Then also, as of old in other climes, poet, painter, sculptor, the writer of history and the writer of romance, will put forth their efforts to create an art and a literature worthy of the Canadian people.'[8] The irony of a relatively recent immigrant from the old country lecturing his Canadian readership on their sense of nationalism is inescapable, but through much of this period, some of the strongest Canadian nationalists had barely arrived on this side of the Atlantic. Two of the members of the nationalist Group of Seven painters, for instance, Arthur Lismer and F.H. Varley, immigrated from Sheffield in the 1910s. British journalist Richard Jebb toured the Dominions in the early twentieth century, commenting on and encouraging indigenous colonial nationalisms,[9] a project even more striking in view of the massive numbers of British immigrants arriving in the Dominions at precisely that time.

It is not at all clear that such endeavours were successful. One author from France commented that Doughty's book had had great success in Canada.[10] However, the accounts of the Ottawa-based IODE chapter suggest the contrary. According to these records, sales of the book did not cover the costs of production. The accounts list costs of production of some $3,228, yet only have returns for some $2,000 during 1917–18, with relatively limited sales thereafter.[11] It is likely that much more money was raised through the subscriptions to the volume, which are listed at the end of the volume and indicate both the widespread support for such nationalist Canadian narratives, and the author's good contacts with high society in his native Britain. A copy of the book with gold ornaments and bound by Tiffany of New York, containing an inscription and a portrait signed by HRH Princess Patricia, was advertised for auction with the comment '$1000 Has Been Offered For This Book in New York.' The funds would go to the coffers of the Canadian Red Cross.[12] The apparently limited returns to the book undoubtedly say more about the precarious state of Canadian publishing than they do about Doughty's intentions. They nonetheless provide a useful context for such commemorative endeavours: the fervour of nationalists was not always rewarded by popular acclaim. There were indeed reasons why artists and authors felt it necessary to inculcate a sense of nationalism in both English- and French-speaking Canada. Their efforts to do so were not always rewarded with the sustained attention they so desired.

The urgency of commemoration arose during a period of massive immigration and fundamental socio-economic change. A desire to create a stable national culture in a time of flux underpinned the efforts of commemorators in the early twentieth century, although financial concerns also played an inevitable role. In the early twentieth century, alongside the dozens of prose and poetic accounts of Verchères's story, two attempts at commemoration stand out for their sheer scale and cost: the statue raised to her memory in 1913 and the film (the first feature-length French-Canadian movie) of 1922. Both of these endeavours were initiated privately but ultimately led to appeals to the state. Such attempts at reaching a broad public, and one not exclusively literate, were considered appropriate strategies to adopt during this time of 'invented traditions.' Yet the irony of such definitively 'national' endeavours is that they often were undertaken in direct competition with, and imitation of, other countries. Many countries felt the need to erect commemorative monuments in an attempt to render history concrete and seemingly immutable. Likewise, the desire to establish national film styles to convey the essence of national cultures was by no means unique to French Canadians. Other nations were equally concerned about the influence of the American film industry, and attempted to establish policies to promote indigenous versions of the art form.

Commemorative Statues

The work of history in Canada as elsewhere in the early twentieth century was closely tied up with the desire to inculcate perceived national values. It was necessary to overcome the potential loss of history, the forgetting of the important roles played by heroes and heroines of the past. In the context of French Canada, Bishop Alexandre-Antonin Taché provides an eloquent, if perhaps unconvincing, explanation of the importance of statues: 'Men have the ability to remain silent, and even often enjoy the sad privilege of forgetfulness. Stones, on the contrary, cannot remain silent, and monuments render memories imperishable.'[13] Such attitudes lay behind this brief period of statue mania in Quebec.

In the late nineteenth and early twentieth centuries, there was a population boom of commemorative statues in Quebec. Fully part of the desire to remember the high points of French-Canadian history, this movement also reflected a general Western emphasis on bronze and granite monuments.[14] The investment in statues as commemorative devices is noteworthy because of the significant sums involved. Historian Benjamin Sulte recounted how a branch of the Royal Society had encouraged Quebec to join the statue movement: 'depositing a commemorative plaque, a column or other sort of marker, in a place where the passer-by sees nothing today to attract his attention, this will activate patriotic feelings.'[15] Statues were erected in an attempt to catch up with other Western countries, the various levels of the Canadian state playing a significant role in this process. Established in 1919, following decades of small-scale and localized commemorative efforts, the Historical Sites and Monuments Board aimed to demarcate the appropriate locations and personages of the Canadian past. Dominated by English-speakers, the board wrangled with the appropriate recognition of French-Canadian history, often to the chagrin and protests of the French-Canadian members. Although their definitions of the 'national' community might differ, both French and English Canadians saw writing history and erecting statues of figures from the past as ways of enforcing a sense of civic belonging.[16]

In the Quebec context, commemorative projects sometimes involve a struggle over which 'national' narrative – French-Canadian or Canadian – should best subsume the historical figure.[17] The erection of a statue commemorating the key French-Canadian hero Dollard des Ormeaux is a case in point. Concerning the proposal to raise a monument to Dollard des Ormeaux, federal politician Charles A. Doherty congratulated in French the committee on its work in commemorating 'an act of heroism whose glory belongs to the French-Canadian race, but one of which all Canadians have the right to feel proud.'[18] Not all correspondents agreed on this pan-Canadian purpose. One writer wanted to see the statue raised with only French-Canadian contributions, 'as a primary glorification of these heroes by those who share in their religion and their nationality.'[19] Meanwhile, the publisher of the *Montreal Herald* congratulated himself on having had the idea in the first place.[20]

Other statues by their very existence testified to the gaps between French and English Canadians. The difficulty in erecting statues to the Patriot leader Jean-Olivier Chénier and other heroes of the 1837 rebellions provides instances of such divisions. Some French Canadians tried to raise money for the endeavours, while others opposed the commemoration of figures who would remind onlookers of past divisive struggles.[21] On a more empirical level, one Great War monument in Saint-Hilaire was blown up in 1922 because its inscription failed to list the names of all the local combatants.[22]

But these examples were the exceptions. Statues were not overtly intended to antagonize sections of the population. They represented attempts to create a sense of community and communal public space, primarily in the larger urban centres. Later, with the erection of Great War memorials, the geographical scope expanded to smaller towns and villages. They had the obvious didactic purpose to inculcate pride in the history and development of the country. But the financial limitations of late nineteenth- and early twentieth-century Quebec must be kept in mind. Monuments in Quebec were local phenomena – intended to commemorate a figure of local prominence, to symbolize that person's connection to his or her locality. Unlike nineteenth-century France, for instance, where statues of the same French political figures proliferated throughout the country,[23] most of the statues in Quebec were unique. Up to the early 1920s, prominent French-Canadian politician George-Étienne Cartier might have three statues in his honour, Prime Minister Sir Wilfrid Laurier two, Queen Victoria three, Joan of Arc two, and Dollard des Ormeaux two, but other dedicated monuments were the only remembrances of specific individuals. These figures were almost exclusively Quebeckers. There was little commemoration of people from the history of other parts of Canada: the only exceptions being Ontario politicians Robert Baldwin and Prime Minister Sir John A. Macdonald. Only a few foreigners with no particular connection to the province, such as Joan of Arc or Dante, inspired statues.

These were primarily statues celebrating famous men. Very few of the statues represented women, even if some of the religious monuments used women as allegorical figures (if one can indeed assign a sex to angels). Joan of Arc and Queen Victoria had more statues between them than all the women of Quebec's history combined: the Mohawk saint Catherine Tekatwitha, heroine Madeleine de Verchères, early nurse Jeanne Mance, and wife of the Governor General, Lady Head. Perhaps this desire to commemorate men so much more than women reflected the restrictions on women's access to public space; or, rather, it implicitly revealed the concerns about maintaining the limitations on women's public roles at a time when these were increasingly under challenge.[24] Such restrictions, when applied to statuary, did not pass without debate. In 1916, historian and librarian Marie-Claire Daveluy protested the depiction of the first female pioneer of the colony of New France in a monument dedicated to her husband. Marie Rollet, she complained, was placed at her husband's, Louis Hébert's, feet, and not accorded her proper role by his side as the first *canadienne*.[25]

To a certain degree, the government of Quebec considered the commemorative movement a success. Requesting of the provincial archivist a list of all the monuments erected up to 1923, the Quebec government discovered that indeed there were a healthy number of statues in the province. The calumnious suggestion that Quebec lagged behind an unnamed

'neighbouring province' in its commemoration of its past could be satisfactorily dismissed.[26] But the provincial government had not itself populated the landscape with statues. Rather, the statues had largely been
erected through private subscriptions, and had depended on the actions
and financial support of relatively small groups of individuals.

Verchères's Monument

The erection of a statue to the memory of Madeleine de Verchères was
undertaken in the spirit of this wave of historical commemoration. In
this case, two separate initiatives – one led by the priest of Verchères and
the other by the governor general of Canada, Lord Grey – attempted to
remedy the problem of providing a visual recognition of Madeleine de
Verchères and her heroism. Abbé F.-A. Baillairgé wanted to raise the
statue to Verchères as much as a way of putting the parish of Verchères
on the map as paying tribute to the heroine's memory. A nationalist
activist in his own right and a prolific author on a variety of subjects,
Baillairgé led a protest in 1912 demanding that the local government
post office in the predominantly French-speaking area have a French
sign. He attracted attention across Quebec and in Ottawa with a public
procession and pamphlet. Undoubtedly, Baillairgé saw the erection of a
statue to Verchères in a similar nationalist framework. The cost of raising
a statue was far beyond the means of even a relatively prosperous agricultural parish. Baillairgé held tombolas (lotteries) to raise funds, and by
July 1912 had raised only some $2,250 towards the statue.[27]

By 1908 the Montreal artist Louis-Philippe Hébert, sculptor of a number
of other heroic statues, had crafted a bronze statuette in her honour. He
made some twenty-four copies of the statuette.[28] It was, he recalled, a
difficult figure to model, since he was afraid of turning her into a woman
warrior: 'Sometimes I felt that trying to translate all her beautiful energy,
I would turn my young heroine into a virago.' Ultimately, the inspiration
came from Louis Fréchette's poem, in which Verchères is compared to
Jeanne Hachette. (In his letter accepting the commission, Hébert used
Fréchette's epithet: Jeanne de Verchères.)[29] Coiffed by the soldier's hat,
which appears to be a soft, leather cowboy hat, she clutches her large
gun nervously, if heroically, her skirts swirling in the wind (fig. 3.1). The
statue, Hébert commented, showed a young woman 'transfigured by
the idea of saving her people and defending the home of her birth.'[30]
J.-Edmond Roy agreed that Hébert had succeeded in striking the right
note in the design of Verchères: 'She is neither virago nor amazon, even

3.1 Louis-Philippe Hébert's statuette of Madeleine de Verchères.

less a musketeer in a skirt – she is a very feminine personality, vibrant, with a special mark, which the artist offers to capture our eyes.'[31]

Lord Grey purchased a copy of the statuette for Rideau Hall and enthusiastically promoted a larger public statue of Verchères. In 1909 he informed Lord Strathcona, railroad magnate and Canadian High Commissioner in London, of his daughter's desire 'to interest the Schools and the women of Canada' in the project.[32] But public, not private, subscription ensured success. In 1910 he gave federal cabinet minister Rodolphe Lemieux the mission to inspire his political colleagues in Quebec City. He hoped that Lemieux would place the statuette on the supper table of a politicians' meeting, and 'fire [Premier Lomer] Gouin with the desire to find such money as may be required to signify the great entrance to Canada by the erection on Verchères bluff of a figure which will tell the immigrant that the heroic virtues are the bedrock foundation of Canadian greatness.'[33] Lemieux's action apparently failed to win over the premier of Quebec, but more success was to be found with the federal prime minister Sir Wilfrid Laurier.[34]

Lord Grey, like other governors general, was a key figure in the attempt to create a sense of wider national purpose in Canada.[35] Much of his energy had been channelled into the three-hundredth anniversary celebrations of Champlain's establishment of Quebec in 1608. He enlisted politicians, church leaders, foreign dignitaries, and the citizens of Quebec City in a skilful attempt to overcome some of the divergent historical narratives that he felt divided Canadians.[36] At the same time as he assisted in the celebration of a broader Canadian unity, Lord Grey also emphasized the need to distinguish Canadian history from American. To this end, he suggested establishing a massive monument on the Plains of Abraham, so that people sailing up the St Lawrence to arrive at Quebec would not focus on the imposing building in their vista: 'The present entry to Canada, via Quebec, is not creditable to Canada, for people who look up to the Plains of Abraham from their steamer see no inspiring monument, but only the Provincial gaol ... I should like to see [a statue] taking the form of a great Goddess of Peace, on the extreme point of Quebec, so that it may be the first thing visible to the vessels coming from across the seas.'[37]

Lord Grey's Goddess of Peace never graced the skyline of the provincial capital. But he was not to be discouraged from the grand concept. If Grey could not have a Goddess of Peace at Quebec, the St Lawrence River at least offered other potential vantage points that could serve a similar purpose. Once he had settled on the idea of a commemorative monument for the young heroine, he compared the approach to Montreal as one passed Verchères parish to the typical immigrant's perspective on New York City:

> The contrast between the message conveyed by the statue of Madeleine de Vercheres on the St Lawrence, and the statue of Liberty at the entrance to New York Harbour, will be wholly in favour of the Dominion. In too many cases the statue of Liberty suggests only license and the freedom to pursue individual, at the expense of the public interest; while the history of Madeleine de Vercheres will suggest the highest ideals of citizenship.[38]

Lord Grey's enthusiasm succeeded in convincing the federal government to commemorate the heroine. Laurier could only ignore the indefatigable Grey's entreaties so often. Moreover, the promise of a statue to the Liberal constituency of Chambly-Verchères surely offered some political advantages. Laurier's Liberal government agreed to support the project, earmarking $25,000 for the statue.

In the end, Laurier's candidate was defeated in the raucous 1911 election by Henri Bourassa's acolyte, J.H. Rainville. The prospect of the Nationaliste MP reaping the benefits of the Liberal government's generosity must have rankled with Laurier, but the timing of the change in allegiances was perfect. In their odd alliance with Borden's Conservative administration, the Nationalistes now controlled the constituency, and the incoming government kept the promise of paying for the statue. In 1913, former postmaster general Rodolphe Lemieux remarked caustically in the House of Commons on the federal government's generosity in light of Baillairgé's complaints about the post office sign: 'I am happy to see that this worthy curé will have a superb statue of Madeleine de Verchères to contemplate in his own parish ... This is the response of the Laurier government to the agitation created by Abbé Baillairgé.'[39]

The monument would not be located on the bluff as Lord Grey had desired. Instead, Arthur Boyer, member of the Advisory Art Council, local MP V. Geoffrion, and Pierre Hébert visited Verchères in the summer of 1911 to compare potential emplacements. The high ground in front of the parish church was not deemed acceptable. Poorly visible from the river, the impact of the statue would be reduced by its setting: 'its standing in front of the Church would hide part of its beauty as it could and would be taken as part of it and thus lose a great deal of effect, the church front acting as a background would be most ineffective.' Instead the committee recommended a flat bit of land close to the shore, near a windmill, one of the oldest buildings in the village. This windmill, lacking any connection to the story of Verchères, nonetheless would provide an aura of aged authenticity to the statue. A small lot of land was purchased from the Richelieu and Ontario Navigation Company. Although susceptible to springtime flooding, this location, the committee provided assurances, was the most appropriate of the statue. The monument would itself be raised into the air by a stone wall, built 'to imitate an old French Fort; both ends of this wall could be left unfinished so as to appear in ruins; the old mill at one end (though thirty feet from this wall) would appear from the river as a bastion of the old Fort, part of it having fallen with age.' Invented and accidental historical authenticity thus provided a novel effect.[40]

Although Abbé Baillairgé had been swept aside in the planning for the statue, he was the president of the inauguration committee. Despite his own ill health – he would be hospitalized only a few days later – the day represented a victory for his nationalist perspective on Madeleine de Verchères. Now having completed his term of office, Lord Grey and his vision of heroic inspiration for all Canadians were absent from the ceremony. Special trains and boats were leased from Montreal for the pilgrimage to the statue on 20 September 1913. After numerous speeches by men, the mayor's wife (the one woman with a public role in the ceremony) unveiled the statue before the almost five thousand people in attendance.[41] A twenty-five-foot version of the statuette, this Madeleine de Verchères stands firmly atop a tall crenellated battlement.

The speeches reflected many of the themes apparent in the male literature on Verchères. Speaking first, the Nationaliste Member of Parliament, J.H. Rainville, praised the actions of the heroes and heroines of the French-Canadian past, stating that Verchères, the Canadian Jeanne Hachette, 'has lived our own lives.' Without having to be any more precise about which nation he referred to, he stated that he offered the statue on behalf of the Canadian government to 'the nation.' The auxiliary bishop of Montreal, Mgr G. Gauthier, wished that other French-Canadian women could become Madeleine de Verchères, but he was quick to specify what kind of woman this represented: 'There have been other Madeleines de Verchères lately, when French-Canadian [female] teachers preferred to lose their salaries rather than stop teaching French to their pupils.' For his part, House of Commons translator Wilfrid Larose compared Verchères with Joan of Arc: 'If the kingdom of France was delivered and regenerated by Joan of Arc, this colony, then French in its cradle, was exemplified by Madeleine de Verchères.' Montreal judge Amédée Geoffrion believed that the statue was the most effective way to ensure the perpetuation of Verchères's memory: 'She enjoyed the admiration of the elite, but her image had not been engraved in the imagination of the people.'[42] The curator of Fort Chambly, J.-O. Dion, expressed his wish that mothers would produce more women like Madeleine de Verchères.

Perhaps the key figures at the unveiling of the statue were Lieutenant-colonel Charles de Lanaudière and his sister Mme Norman R. Neilson, direct descendants of Madeleine de Verchères. By their presence, they provided a genealogical link and legitimated the tie between the present and the past. They incarnated, as did all French Canadians, the noble traits exhibited by Madeleine de Verchères over two hundred years previously. This was not the only time that Lanaudière's social and military standing allowed him to fulfil such a role. In 1922, he also unveiled a war memorial in the family village of Terrebonne to the north of Montreal.[43]

This statue and the statuette that preceded it are perhaps the most effective of all the different commemorations of Madeleine de Verchères, infusing imagined details with poetry and capturing some of the bravery and contingency of the act of heroism. But this was not a statue of a woman warrior, even a young one. Gazing upon the statue (fig. 3.2), no one would mistake her for a man: the swirling dress, the feminine facial features, the long braids dangling down her back, the pubescent breasts, all precluded misinterpretation. Only her man's hat and massive gun hinted otherwise. For Maurice Hodent, who saw the statue in Paris, where it was cast, there was no question whatsoever concerning Verchères's sex: 'More than one Canadian seeing it as he sails up the St. Lawrence will say that there is no prettier girl under the blue sky.'[44] The feminine icon cloaked all traces of the woman warrior. The statue, more than any other single depiction, would serve to illustrate subsequent articles and books.

The specific location of the statue would ultimately disappoint its federal supporters. It did not become the improved Canadian version of the Statue of Liberty. Even though located close to the shore, it was visible only to ships which passed very close,[45] or to pedestrians or car drivers who took the twisting road down to look at it. Nonetheless, Abbé Baillairgé still maintained his vigilant interest in the statue, cleaning it on occasion, and petitioning the federal government to install floodlights in order that nocturnal meetings not occur at its base.[46]

There are other difficulties with investing historical memory in monuments. Soon after a statue is raised, it ceases to attract attention. Rather, it becomes a permanent part of the built environment, a fixture in an

3.2 Postcard photograph of the statue of Madeleine de Verchères in the village of Verchères.

urban landscape. 'The most striking feature of monuments,' writes one European commentator, 'is that you do not notice them. There is nothing in the world as invisible as monuments.'[47] As if he recognized this point, Baillairgé wanted to continue placing metaphorical, as well as real, spotlights on the statue.

In 1923, Baillairgé importuned General Cruikshank, the head of the Historical Sites and Monuments Board of Canada, to provide a historic plaque for the statue. The members of the board were consulted concerning the wording, the British Columbian judge F.W. Howay suggesting that part of John Reade's poem be added to the inscription. 'Such quotations give a scholarly and finished air to an inscription,' he maintained, 'and incidentally show to the stranger that the incident has caught the fancy of a poet and therefore must be worth further investigation.'[48] Difficulty finding a French-language equivalent precluded this poetic addition, although the board members did not appear to look very hard for a French poem. Commissioner J.B. Harkin wished that Verchères's historical achievement be made explicit: 'I would suggest something like the following, "This heroic act stemmed the Indian onslaught and saved the colony," or any other phraseology which would render the idea sought for.'[49] The divisions between French- and

English-speaking members of the board, a frequent problem of its early years, were clear in this episode, as successive Quebec representatives argued in favour of limiting the inscription to the accepted facts. Pointing out the two different versions of Verchères's narratives, librarian Aegidius Fauteux argued that 'we shall probably never know which is the truest and it would be as useless as dangerous to show the variations between the two.'[50] In the end, the plaque eschewed poetry and dramatic conclusions about the import of Verchères's feat.

For his part, Baillairgé desired a second unveiling at the time of the placing of the commemorative plaque in 1926 as a way to sustain public interest in the statue. Baillairgé's interest in the statue provides evidence of the way in which a public monument commemorates those who supported it as much as it remembers those depicted in it. More than a decade after the erection of the monument, the Commissioner of the Canadian National Parks continued to rely on Baillairgé's enthusiasm so as to ensure the proper attention was being paid to the upkeep of the statue.[51] At Baillairgé's funeral in 1929, the officiating priest commented on the curé's enthusiasm: 'Few monuments have been erected with so much love, so much conviction, so much faith in the future of our race. M. Baillairgé was, in a word, devoted to Mademoiselle de Verchères, whom he called the Joan of Arc of New France.'[52] Over time, such devotion remained limited in geographical scope, for the statue rooted the memory of Madeleine de Verchères firmly in the locality.

The statue was intended to place Verchères on the tourist map, and to a certain extent it did so. Tour guides and travel books used the monument as a pretext and an illustration for a discussion of the actions of the young heroine. Through the 1920s and 1930s, historical pilgrims flocked past the statue. In 1930 the caretaker estimated that as many as one thousand people came by per month from June to September; by the 1950s, this number had dropped to around two thousand per year.[53] Such figures, estimated by the part-time caretaker, must be approached with caution, but they do demonstrate a certain initial degree of popularity, which experienced a decline afterwards. Local tourist brochures today still emphasize Verchères's statue, but these are not part of a larger strategy to entice visitors and provide the gift shops and other commercial paraphernalia that often appear on such sites. Part of the problem is that the statue of Madeleine de Verchères remains federal property, while the interpretation has essentially been subsumed into a Québécois nationalist framework, and, as the next chapter will show, one that takes an ironic stance on her heroism.

In 1992 the three hundredth anniversary of her feat, which coincided with the occasion of Canada's 125th anniversary, would be celebrated, primarily by locals, at the foot of her statue – and nowhere else. The numbers attending the official speeches were not legion, although the corn roast a short distance away did a booming business. Despite the enthusiasm and the money invested in the endeavour, the promise of anchoring Verchères's memory in stone was illusory. Interest in the statue could not be sustained without a good deal of public awareness of the heroine herself. The bronze monument remains a silent reference to a belief that a shared past could be forged for all Canadians, a focus for local tourism brochures to be sure, but little else. Perhaps celluloid film could have provided a more effective way of commemorating her.

The Verchères Film

As a form of popular entertainment, cinema in the early twentieth century offered a tremendous challenge to nationalist thinkers throughout the world. Cinema presents the same stories in myriad unconnected settings, with no regard for the context in which the films are shown. The actual location of the projections was important as well: a dark room where class and other distinctions were momentarily obscured. Although some intellectuals feared the viewers' passivity, during the first few decades, screenings could be raucous affairs, as the audience shuffled in and out of their seats and hurled comments and laughter at the actors on screen.[54]

As Hollywood producers and distributors came to dominate the types of films shown, increasing anxiety arose in many countries about the nefarious influence of American ideologies on unsuspecting national cultures. Great Britain and France, among other countries, responded to these concerns in the 1920s by imposing quotas in order to enhance local production of films.[55] To a certain extent, the same concerns were apparent in English Canada as well, but they were perhaps most virulent in French Canada. In Quebec, Church leaders and Catholic intellectuals criticized the American influences in often anti-Semitic tones. In 1918, Abbé Lionel Groulx bemoaned the public enthusiasm for the American films: 'Never before in our history have our people been so unconsciously force-fed with the worst forms of exoticism. Cinema has become the first and only book, novel, serial, theatre, and catechism of popular deformation.'[56] American films did not recognize the distinctiveness of French Canada: 'Our little people, our children, our last reserve, who themselves ignore the heroes and the nobility of our history, are impassioned throughout the year by famous bandits, by low-level ham actors, by dramas of pistols and law courts, by a vulgar and bufoonish art, by the sad heroes of American magazines or of foreign melodramas.' Furthermore, the mocking of authority, one of the popular themes of early films, was of immense concern to conservative critics. Their complaints sometimes involved a request for a total ban on film projections. The provincial government responded with strict censorship laws, as in other provinces, and promulgated stern regulations concerning attendance, which were ignored by theatre owners and audiences alike. From 1911, children under fifteen years of age (sixteen years in 1919) were not allowed to attend the cinema without accompaniment, although this rule was often ignored.[57]

While these concerns were sometimes expressed in the hope of outlawing the cinema altogether, a small number of people wished instead to foster a cinema more responsive to French and Catholic values. How better to do this than to begin with those distinctive traits of French Canadian culture, the values that were represented by the heroes and heroines of French Canada's past? It is not surprising, perhaps, that French-Canadian film entrepreneurs should turn to Verchères (and by extension to history) for the first feature-length French-Canadian film. The equally compelling Dollard des Ormeaux story had already been filmed in 1913 by the British American Film Company, an English-Canadian firm. This film, *The Battle of the Long Sault*, restaged the conflict between the French soldiers and the Iroquois to thrilling effect.[58] Likewise, the Verchères story could marry action and drama. It could also, by bending the story a bit, include a romance and give a starring role to a young woman at a time when the film industry relied so much on female characters. As one newspaper commented, 'of all stories in the Canadian epic, the life of Madeleine de Verchères lends itself the best to the screen.'[59]

Situated on the margins of such nationalist groups as the publishers of *L'Action française*, Le Bon Cinéma Limitée (later Le Cinéma Canadien Limitée) appealed for funds from subscribers to the nationalist journal. Their purpose, they stated, was to make Catholic and moral films, addressing a fear of the cinema that the Catholic clergy and intellectuals shared widely. 'The cinema in Canada today, an American import,' wrote a contributor to *L'Action française* in 1921, 'is fatal to our language, our morals, and our traditions.'[60] Appealing in the pages of the same periodical for investors, the company claimed to be involved in 'essentially moralizing work, and productive in the national sense of the word.'[61] A flyer soliciting investment was even clearer on the aims of the company: 'it is urgent to begin fighting against the so often inept American cinema and its generally corrupting and fatally anglicizing tendencies with films based on a Catholic perspective, therefore honest and clean, and essentially French-Canadian in direction and tone.' With the support of some sixty parish halls, attractive dividends would flow easily: American film companies achieved returns of 1000 per cent: 'at least the 95% of film producers who are Jewish achieve those results. Cannot a Canadian company, which has nothing to fear – given the quality of its films – from the impressive Jewish-American competition, obtain easily such strong results?'[62]

J.-A. Homier supplied the practical expertise for the film. An experienced photographer and cameraman, he had filmed the burlesque comedy *Oh! Oh! Jean!* in 1922.[63] Later that year, he joined forces with the young writer and publicist Emma Gendron, who wrote the screenplay based on Baillairgé's pamphlet on Madeleine de Verchères. Most of the actors were from the Montreal stage. Men from Kahnawake, the Mohawk village to the south of Montreal Island, filled the Aboriginal roles. The production was filmed amid unusual September wind and snowstorms[64] in a specially built fort in Kahnawake. The film involved significant production expenses: some $4,400 (one-fifth the cost of the statue, and a third more than Doughty's book).[65] The film was submitted to the Bureau of the Censor on 6 December 1922, and was passed without alteration the following day.[66] Two weeks later, *Madeleine de Verchères* premiered in Montreal, alongside a documentary on the Eucharistic Congress at Lourdes and two short comedies.[67]

In many ways, the scenario follows the standard recapitulations of the story, though sources do not permit a total reconstruction of the plot – the nitrate-based films were destroyed by order of the Fire Department in the 1950s.[68] Using newspaper accounts, Abbé Baillairgé's notes in his personal journal, and the collection of photographic stills, it is possible to recreate the main lines of the screenplay. The film begins with the departure of the French troops, summoned elsewhere in the colony, including Verchères's love interest, Pierre-Thomas Tarieu de Lanaudière (her future husband). Verchères hangs a cross around his neck as he departs for Quebec. The introduction of this romance was characterized by one newspaper in a mild reproach: 'The small – and very naïve – sentimental intrigue that the writer has grafted onto the film doesn't harm the drama in the least.'[69] Perhaps because of the insertion of a love story into the narrative, the producers chose a visibly more mature actress, nineteen-year-old Estelle Bélanger, to play the fourteen-year-old Madeleine (fig. 3.3). With only a few Frenchmen left in the area, the Iroquois attack and then lay siege to the fort. Verchères escapes the Iroquois warriors, leaving her kerchief in an attacker's hand. She organizes the defence, in doing so, according to the film's publicity, 'anticipating by two centuries the heroic feat of Verdun: "They shall not pass."'[70] Verchères fires the cannon to scare away the foe. She is more than a soldier in this film; she also takes care of the wounded and encourages the defenders. She rescues the linen drying by the river, and later ventures out to save Fontaine. Leading a group of French troops, La Monnerie finally relieves her, saying: 'You have saved the country.' 'I have only performed my duty,'[71] replies Verchères (fig. 3.4). Just before La Monnerie rescues their prisoners, the Indians perform a dance around them. The episode finishes with prayers of thanksgiving in the fort (fig. 3.5). 'It is truly a page from the life of our fathers,' concluded Baillairgé after seeing the film.[72]

The promoters of the film used the historical content of their production as its primary selling point. The 'truth' of such accounts provides a key to their popularity. Indeed, one of the main attractions of historical films is their claim to accuracy. Lucy Hughes-Hallett reports that one of the early Cleopatra films went so far as to paint the stars in the same place they would have appeared in 20 B.C. Yet, as she adds, such 'historical' films can still 'be dated to within five years by anyone with even the most cursory knowledge of the history of twentieth-century design.'[73] Likewise, the strongest praise for *Madeleine de Verchères* was indeed its 'accurate' portrayal of the historical events. The Quebec City newspaper *L'Action catholique* commented on the lack of typical American 'tricks' in the film, praising the producers for making it 'by conforming scrupulously to historical truth.'[74]

But historical accuracy does not always lend itself to great film-making.[75] Although its greatest asset, the film's reliance on history received rather ambiguous critical acclaim. 'It is a good picture,' one critic wrote, 'which should be seen as much as possible for its good history lesson.'[76] The historical lustre of the film could not compare with Hollywood products, and indeed the sets were spartan to say to least, which one newspaper commented was an appropriate reflection of the history of New France: 'They are poor people, in poor houses in a poor country. No sumptuous uniforms, no flattery for the eye.' Commentaries also focused on the pioneering, but somewhat rude, production values. According to a critic in *Le Devoir*, who nonetheless encouraged the devel-

3.3 Madeleine de Verchères bids farewell to M. de La Pérade. Still from the film *Madeleine de Verchères*, 1922.

3.4 Madeleine de Verchères welcomes the French troops. Still from the film *Madeleine de Verchères*, 1922.

3.5 Prayer of thanksgiving inside the Verchères fort. Still from the film *Madeleine de Verchères*, 1922.

opment of a French-Canadian film industry, 'one could describe it as a man admiring an amateurish portrait of his ancestors. It is more a patriotic than an aesthetic emotion.'[77] Gustave Comte, writing in *La Patrie*, complained that few attended the matinee presentation of the film.[78] Still, all journalists, French or English speaking, commended the desire to produce French-Canadian films, and hoped that the company would produce more such features.[79]

After a week in Montreal, the film toured a series of parish halls, beginning of course in Verchères itself. On 22 December 1922, the film company (S.T. Grenier, J.-A. Homier, Estelle Bélanger, and Emma Gendron) came in force to the church hall. Abbé Baillairgé was relatively pleased with the spectacle: 'The film about Madeleine is almost very good overall,' he wrote in his private journal. 'Melle Emma —— has added many things to the story that could have happened.' The scenario was largely acceptable, but the difficult weather conditions in which the film was produced affected the result. Moreover, the aesthetic qualities required some work: 'A certain necessary artistic force is not found throughout.'[80]

The film may have had its rural premiere in Verchères, but a blizzard hampered attendance. The second day was more successful, although Baillairgé complained that after giving most of the $92.80 proceeds back to the company, only 25 cents remained for himself. Baillairgé had the film come back a second time in August 1923, and this time, he attempted to enlist the support of his neighbouring colleagues in this 'beautiful Canadian history lesson.' He requested that they announce the film from the pulpit, hoping that that 'would be the sound of the whistle that would make them get in the car for Verchères.'[81] From the priest's perspective, this was not an overwhelming success either. This time, the showing netted $33, but somebody stole $15 or more from the presbytery while Baillairgé gave his out-of-town guests a tour of the church.[82]

In all, the film toured some eighty-four Catholic parishes, and the company continued to promote the film as best it could. In 1923 the company attempted to interest the National Historic Sites Branch in Ottawa in their product, offering the plan of filming other historical events.[83] For this audience, the company director announced their vocation as 'The Production of Purely Educational Pictures.'[84] But the historians in the federal department dissuaded their superiors from adopting the film. They noted matters of historical and technical inconsistency: the shape of the palisades, the modern clock in the fort, the modern apparel of the Indians, and the poor attention to continuity (for example, the sudden reappearance of Verchères's apron after being used as wadding for the cannon).[85] On behalf of the film company, S.T. Grenier acknowledged the technical problems with the film: 'We will frankly admit that the production is not up to what we planned when we first decided to make it, but the principal reasons [sic] for this is that at that time, we lacked modern instrumentation and proper technical direction.'[86] In 1924, the company planned to make a new version of the film, changing the intertitles to be more in accordance with Baillairgé's pamphlet on the heroine.[87]

Gendron and Homier stayed with the company for one more film, though tellingly, this last project moved from a historical topic to the very contemporary concerns over drug addiction. Unlike *Madeleine de Verchères, La Drogue fatale* did not pass the censors' eyes unchanged. Scenes depicting pickpocketing, assault, and shooting were considered inappropriate for the Quebec viewing public. After the scenes of crime and violence were removed, the film premiered on 20 January 1924.[88] The reaction to this second film was much more positive: 'head and

TABLE 1
Comparison of selected distributors, number of feature (sujets) and short films (parties) presented in Quebec, 1922–3, 1924–5*

	1922–3		1924–5	
	Sujets	Parties	Sujets	Parties
Le Bon Cinéma	2	7	–	–
Le Cinéma Canadien	–	–	12	44
Canadian Universal	486	1154	383	945
Famous Players	193	678	–	–
United Artists	19	152	–	–
Associated First National Pictures	–	–	209	914

*ANQ-M, E188, box 746, Opérations de chaque compagnie, 1913–1937.

shoulders above "Madeleine de Verchères,"' wrote *La Presse* the next day. For the critics, these were clearly the beginnings of a French-Canadian national cinema. There was no reason to rely on foreign countries to produce the films for French-Canadian audiences. Moreover, films could just as easily reflect French-Canadian realities as Southern Californian ones: 'The external scenes taken by Mr Homier in his film demonstrate that on celluloid the Canadian – or Québécois – sun is as beautiful as that of the tropics.'[89] This film involved much a larger investment of money and relied on a more professional cast. A special studio was constructed, and location shots took place at Montreal's Bordeaux Prison, the woman's prison, and the Recorder's court.[90] It is telling, nonetheless, that this film, unlike its predecessor, attempted to bridge French- and English-speaking audiences. An English-speaking doctor played a key role in the film, and, unlike *Madeleine de Verchères*, *La Drogue fatale* used intertitles in both English and French.[91]

In 1923, the company had changed its name to Le Cinéma Canadien Limitée in order to avoid confusion with European firms that exported films to Canada.[92] The owners made attempts to acquire the support of the Catholic clergy. They wrote to Mgr Gauthier in 1924, asking for his signed approval to acquire the exclusive rights to a film on La Petite Sainte de Lisieux and promising to follow the bishop's advice concerning the distribution of any other film they might acquire.[93] They became distributors for films from France and other countries, though their efforts paled in comparison to those of larger firms (see Table 1). They also produced tourist films for the Quebec ministry of railways.[94] Although the flyer produced to attract investors stated that *Madeleine de Verchères* had netted over $1,800, some forty years later, one of the owners of the company remembered that they had never recouped the costs of the film, even though they had sold a copy of it in France.[95]

Despite attempts by these French-Canadian entrepreneurs and others to supply appropriate films, the concerns of high-level Catholic clergymen stood in the way. In 1926, F.-A. Baillairgé asked the Archbishop of Montreal for permission to continue showing 'moral' films in his parish. These films, he stated, came from M. Paradis of Quebec and from Le Bon Cinéma, a new company owned by Amedée Rufiange for the distribution of films.[96] The parish was able to keep 35 to 40 per cent of the total ticket sales. Baillairgé argued that 'the cinema, from many perspectives, does more good than harm,' and added that the advantage of showing films in the parish was that the locals need not go into the city.[97] He was unsuccessful in his request. The tragic fire in the Laurier Cinema in east-end Montreal in January 1927, in which seventy-eight children died, put paid to his designs: 'After the terrible disaster that we have experienced,' the archbishop responded, 'I believe that it will be possible for you to make your parishioners understand the dangers that accompany the cinema.'[98]

Given the opposition of the Catholic clergy and the lack of major alternative support, the Madeleine de Verchères film did not spawn a national cinema. The Cinéma Canadien Limitée could not use its distribution links as a way of backing future endeavours of their own. The main movers behind the films, Homier and Gendron, went on to work in film journalism, establishing a twice-monthly entertainment magazine aimed at women. *La Revue de Manon* proposed to 'spread beautiful and wholesome literature, encourage French-Canadian writers, heighten interest in the beautiful ...'[99] While pruriently decrying Hollywood scandals and scenarios, the magazine primarily served the purpose of publicizing them. The magazine discussed the possibility of producing another historical film, 'an emotional love story set during the dark days of 1837–8.'[100]

The history of film in English and French Canada is almost always portrayed as the experience of noble pioneers facing daunting odds and failing to produce a distinctive national product.[101] Homier, Gendron, and their partners faced the unquestionable opposition of the Catholic Church to the art form, but they also faced the dilemma of trying to develop films that were essentially popular Hollywood pieces with a French-Canadian accent, relying on smaller budgets and less expertise.

Madeleine de Verchères, like so many others of the period, was not a great film. Nonetheless, the choice of Verchères's story for the first French-Canadian feature film reflects the apogee of her popularity as a nationalist icon. The mere commemoration of heroic figures did not serve to launch successfully the cinematographic venture in Quebec. A few other silent films were produced in the province in the 1920s,[102] but the marriage of appropriate national cultural precepts and profitability was not easy to achieve.

The use of Verchères's story ensured a degree of interest from the newspaper critics; it did not pave the way to financial success. Although the project cost a good deal of money, it was ultimately as ephemeral as the many prose and poetic attempts to guarantee the commemoration of the heroine. Yet there were still a few other attempts to inscribe the memory of the heroine in a more permanent fashion.

Other Commemorations

Quebec City's Chateau Frontenac, a late nineteenth-century version of a French Renaissance castle, built by the Canadian Pacific, includes a Salon de Verchères. This tearoom and lounge, up the staircase from the Frontenac Room, was described in 1949 as 'a rich and palatial sitting-room, not large, floored in marble, with low arches and columns, the ceiling decorated in leaves and flowers of green tones into which are introduced graceful scroll designs and cameo motifs.'[103] The Salon de Verchères provides a counterpart to the rooms named after the heroes of New France: Cartier, Frontenac, and Dollard des Ormeaux. Handbooks describing the hotel include brief retellings of Verchères's story, providing a primer on Quebec's history for tourists to the provincial capital. Before recounting the act of heroism in a 1925 tourist publication, Esther Braun described the attraction of taking tea in the Salon de Verchères: 'We are much mystified at first by the soft light (from an unknown source) which throws a tranquil yellow glow on the arches, until we discover that the urns of wrought iron on marble pedestals, though they seem to be burning incense, are really doing nothing of the sort – that they are, instead, hidden lights. The rising film of smoke is not incense, but cigarette smoke, visible only where it circles above the light.'[104] The Verchères name here conjured up images of stateliness and repose.

Verchères would also be remembered on city maps. Various municipalities, mostly in Quebec, chose to honour Verchères with a street name. The modern towns in the locations where she spent her life obviously provide this recognition. Verchères's statue is located at the end of Rue Madeleine. The small village of La Pérade, where Verchères passed her married life as wife of the seigneur, includes a Rue Madeleine de Verchères. The boundary street between Quebec City proper and the suburb of Sainte-Foy is Madeleine de Verchères. Other towns using the same street name are scattered in the region to the south and east of Montreal in relatively close proximity to the town of Verchères or in other parts of Quebec which experienced urban growth in the late nineteenth and early twentieth centuries. Appropriately enough, there is a Verchères Street in the Montreal island suburb named after Dollard des Ormeaux. Four cities in Ontario with Verchères as a street name all include a substantial French-Canadian presence (Noëlville, Sudbury, Verner, and Windsor). Calgary, Alberta, is the only other major city commemorating the heroine on its maps.[105] The signs of a number of Canadian towns, particularly ones with a strong French-Canadian presence, thus remember Verchères's exploit.

Unlike Laura Secord's case, there were few major commercial commemorations of Verchères. A line of tinned food produced in Verchères itself in the 1950s was called 'Madeleine.' A Restaurant Madeleine de Verchères (fig. 3.6) and an old age home of the same name were located in the town, as well.[106] Madeleine de Verchères was increasingly localized in her importance. In 1960, during the celebrations of the 250th anniversary of the parish of Verchères, a local beauty queen, Madeleine première, was elected. In the same year, the company Castel Madeleine de Verchères was constituted in Boucherville, not far from Verchères.[107] But there is nothing like the Laura Secord Candy Shops to secure the memory of her name among a wider public. Without this commercial recognition of Verchères, her name fails to have the resonance today that would enliven her image. Other reasons why her name has become so difficult to remember are the subject of the following chapter.

Conclusion

In their conception and their execution, both the statue and the film were 'national' projects. In the case of the statue, the issue arose over which 'nation' was commemorated in the bronze figure: the survival of French-Canadian society in the face of the foe or the transcontinental nation, which required unifying national icons. Similarly, the film could be marketed in more than one way. It was possible to attempt to sell it to

3.6 One of the few commercial uses of the Verchères image: an advertisement sign for the Restaurant Madeleine de Verchères in the village of Verchères, 1968. (Michel Saint-Jean)

the federal government as an 'educational film' at the same time that one appealed to the nationalist sentiment of dozens of parish priests. These attempts were not mutually exclusive.

They also reflected international concerns of the period about the recognition of the legitimacy of the past, and the practical desire to commemorate the past in a timely and contemporary way. What better way of retelling the story than by casting a permanent bronze monument or producing a popular film?

The erection of a statue and the production of a film in memory of Madeleine de Verchères illustrate some of the difficulties of popular historical enthusiasm. Despite the greater levels of investment, they did not necessarily stand the test of time much more successfully than did the many written accounts. The style and meaning of both are so firmly rooted in the context of the decade of their birth that it is difficult in some ways to maintain the power of the image much further. The film and its company, despite whatever limited initial success they enjoyed, would disappear into the oblivion of unfollowed pioneers. The statue exists today, of course, but the reduction in navigation of the St Lawrence River and the distance from the secondary highway that runs through Verchères force visitors to make a special effort to see the statue. Even if it had been placed more prominently, the force of the statue ultimately depended on interest in the heroic figure herself. As Madeleine de Verchères's star waned in the twentieth century, so did the impact of her more striking commemorations.

Chapter Four

Feminist and Teenager: The Decline of Madeleine de Verchères's Popularity

Although Madeleine de Verchères was one of the key historical heroic figures to be commemorated in late nineteenth- and early twentieth-century French Canada – and certainly the key lay woman – her popularity began to wane after the 1920s. There was no sudden break, but the number of poems, prose accounts, and other efforts to commemorate the heroine began to tail off noticeably. Two principal reasons explain this change: on the one hand, changing attitudes towards the role and teaching of history meant that all heroes were under threat; and, on the other, some authors were concerned about Verchères as a potential 'feminist' icon. Nonetheless, as the most famous teenager of Canadian history, her story was not forgotten, though it tended more and more to be relegated to children's school texts and to become a source of embarrassment and ironic comment for adults.

Part of the attraction of heroes and heroines of the more-or-less distant past is in fact the dearth of material relating to them. With sparse evidence of their heroic endeavours, whole tapestries of myth may be woven around them. As Graeme Morton comments on the commemoration of William Wallace (Braveheart) in nineteenth-century Scotland, 'it is the very absence of definitive source material which has made Wallace so usable and so sustaining a heritage.'[1] Thus, the conceptualization of Dollard des Ormeaux's battle against Iroquois warriors relied on a small number of contemporary and near-contemporary accounts, and the debate over his intentions always focused on the French perspectives of his endeavour. Only a significant historiographical change has permitted the view that Dollard des Ormeaux and his French colleagues were, in fact, secondary to the main conflict between the Iroquois and Dollard's Algonquin and Huron allies.[2] As we have seen, the popularity of

Verchères's story depended on the widespread circulation of her own 'authentic' narratives. But from the 1920s, attitudes towards Verchères underwent significant change. In her case, the shift primarily reflected the discovery of historical sources pertaining to Verchères's later life.

The Revenge of the Curé Lefebvre

In 1968, the researcher judge L.P. Lizotte wrote to bishop and historian Mgr Albert Tessier of Trois-Rivières about rumours concerning Madeleine de Verchères's unbridled sexuality. He wanted to present a paper on her heroism before the Société historique de Québec, and he wanted to make sure that he would not embarrass himself. Some 'storytellers' (*faiseurs d'Histoire*), he commented, had mentioned that she had had various 'romantic adventures' (*aventures amoureuses*). He wondered if Mgr Tessier attached any importance to such rumours. Lizotte acknowledged in a later letter that he could find no reference to Verchères's moral failings, apart from the court case with the parish priest of Bastican, Gervais Lefebvre. Over two centuries later, Lefebvre's gossip had returned to haunt the icon that Verchères had become.[3]

Part of the problem was that Madeleine de Verchères did not have the foresight to die at her time of bravery. While Dollard's and Joan of Arc's acts of heroism could be interpreted as the definitive moments of their lives, the same could not be said about Verchères. As Marina Warner notes, self-sacrifice represented a key element in explicating Joan of Arc's heroism: 'It is astonishing how many of Joan's apologists like her dead. Without this badge of blood, this self-obliteration in the ideal, her glory would be the less.'[4] Because Verchères continued to live beyond her act of heroism, historians beginning in the 1920s would use her later life to provide a gloss – often a negative one – on her youthful courage. Of course, Verchères could not live up to the historical virtues that she was expected to personify, if only because she outlived her exploit.

About the same time that Verchères's narratives were reprinted widely, historians were setting the groundwork for the demolition of her reputation. The rediscovery of the 1730 court case against the curé Lefebvre was particularly important in this matter. His slander accusing her of being a 'whore' provided the necessary evidence of what the woman warrior persona suggested anyway: wanton sexuality. Of course, Verchères did not remain a virgin throughout her life, bearing four children. Could she have been sexually active outside of her conjugal relationship? In 1900 the *Bulletin de recherches historiques*, one of the principal historical research publications in Quebec at the time, printed a query from a reader asking about the causes of the scandalous court case between M. and Mme de La Pérade and the curé Lefebvre.[5] Later that year, a partial account of the 1730 trial appeared in the journal. It identified Mme de La Pérade as the well-known heroine, Madeleine de Verchères.[6] The summary of the lengthy trial suppressed many of the details of the court case, particularly the raciest ones, but it revealed that the rumours were in circulation again after some 170 years.

Provincial archivist P.-G. Roy provided the first attack on Madeleine de Verchères in 1921 in a paper given to the Société Royale du Canada. Roy began his discussion by stating that 'all saints are heroes, but not all heroes are saints.' Providing a partly exaggerated list of court cases which involved Madeleine de Verchères after her marriage to Pierre-Thomas Tarieu de La Pérade, Roy called her 'an enraged plaintiff' (*une plaideuse enragée*).[7] Her husband, previously so peaceful, was led into innumerable court cases solely to please his warlike wife. Verchères was clearly an untypical woman: 'This young woman apparently so frail and delicate was endowed with so much energy that fear and temerity, despite being two sensibilities natural to women, had no place in her soul.'[8] Roy did not make an explicit link between the heroine's youthful military action and her adult litigiousness, but he hinted at such an outcome. Part of the explanation, he suggested, was genetic: their 'Norman blood' (untrue in Verchères's case) endowed them with the spirit for court cases. Women, like men, are never absolutely perfect, Roy concluded, at a time of important shifts in women's public roles; they had, after all, achieved the vote in all the provinces but Quebec and Prince Edward Island.

Roy was not alone in attempting to reveal the feet of clay of the heroes of Canadian history. From the 1920s, Canadian historians followed the lead of their colleagues in other countries in trying to debunk the heroic figures of their national past.[9] This process stemmed from changing attitudes towards history that accompanied the professionalization of the study of Canadian history, but it also had resonance among historians who were not closely connected to the academy. During the 1930s, Laura Secord and Dollard des Ormeaux were reinterpreted in new and negative ways. A clear example of this process was McGill University history professor E.R. Adair's challenge to accepted views of the primary French-Canadian hero, Dollard des Ormeaux. Dollard was little more, Adair claimed, than a fur thief, his expedition up the Ottawa River representing primarily a desire to steal furs from the Iroquois boats coming to Montreal. Adair first presented his views to the Women's Historical Society of Montreal, and the Montreal English-language press quickly reprinted his paper. He later published a version of his presentation in the *Canadian Historical Review*, the leading academic history journal of the day in English Canada. Examining the sources that recount Dollard's exploit, he concluded: 'As a saviour of his country, Adam Dollard, Sieur des Ormeaux, must be relegated to the museum of historical myths.'[10]

This was clearly a sensitive topic. Writing to the editor of the *Canadian Historical Review*, historian and librarian Aegidius Fauteux commented, 'To my mind professor Adair has at best been indiscreet and has shown a d[e]plorable lack of taste.' At a loss to explain Adair's willingness to contest the reverence of French Canadians for their national hero, Fauteux ventured that 'there is only one explanation possible of his bizarre coup d'éclat. He has come from the old country two or three years ago and, during his short stay, he has not yet learned to be modest.' Undaunted, Adair apparently wished to extend his critical eye to other elements of the received wisdom of French Canada. He had planned to launch an attack on Verchères as well, though nothing apparently came of this plan. Fauteux acknowledged that Laura Secord's story had itself been subjected to strong criticism from W.S. Wallace, 'but at least he gave some good reasons for it, and besides, he had the advantage of being of the family.'[11]

The editor of the *Canadian Historical Review* asked Abbé Lionel Groulx to provide a response to Adair's views, but the priest riposted in other publications instead.[12] Archivist Gustave Lanctot provided a measured critique in the pages of the *Canadian Historical Review*.[13] For Groulx, such attacks on his hero were as much a criticism of himself: 'If Abbé Groulx,' he bemoaned in his memoirs, 'had not become the propagandist for Dollard, would there ever have been a question about Dollard?' For Groulx, Adair's sortie was but a minor event compared to the fatal blow delivered by the use of Dollard to encourage enlistment for military service in the Second World War: 'To celebrate Dollard, now disguised as a recruiting agent for the defence of Christianity and the British Empire, would have been to acquiesce to that stupidity.'[14] The story of Dollard, Groulx implied, was part of the unique natural heritage of French Canadians, and belonged only to them.

In part, such controversies pitted those who adopted the mantle of the professional against the enthusiastic 'amateur' historian. As Peter Novick has shown for the American historical profession, the concept of 'objectivity' came to be a badge of distinction for the professionals against the romanticism of their predecessors.[15] In the context of Quebec, the professionalization of history occurred somewhat later, and the boundaries between professionals and non-professionals were less firm. Yet even before the creation of university history departments, an emphasis on the writing of 'scientific' history became possible because of the ways in which the research field was delimited: in particular, by the creation of new publication outlets and learned societies.[16] In the case of Verchères, the attacks on the heroine's stature came from writers who were not at the time of their writing part of the academy, though they were still prominent writers, even so. Yet, unlike Dollard des Ormeaux, Madeleine de Verchères did not inspire a polemical response. No historians marshalled evidence to disprove the thesis that Verchères's youthful heroism had turned her into a disagreeable adult woman. Undoubtedly because of their knowledge of the 1730 court case, historians were reluctant to develop a concerted defence. Lionel Groulx, for instance, warily maintained his distance, making it clear that whatever Verchères's qualities may have been, her heroism was secondary to that of Dollard des Ormeaux. Although he celebrated her virtues, he recognized her faults as well: 'Of Miss Madeleine, we can imagine a fair enough likeness, it seems to me, if we envisage her as beautiful, intelligent and kind, seductive and brilliant, but inside her feminine exterior she had the restless and pugnacious spirit of a muscular lad, with courage, lots of courage, her lips ready to deliver sharp rejoinders, gallant phrases and her actions closely related to her words.'[17] As had been the case during the period of her greatest popularity, the disagreements focused on her gender, not on the ideological position that she represented.

Writing in the pages of the historical journal *Les cahiers des dix*, former academic historian and senior provincial civil servant Jean Bruchési made a strong attack on Verchères in 1946. He begins his article on Verchères by declaring that 'little boys have always played at soldiers, while little girls play with dolls. When occasionally the opposite occurs, parents do not hide their discomfort.' In this context of firmly gendered spheres, Verchères was an example of the 'reversal of roles assigned to men and women, if not by divine decree, then at least by nature and indeed common sense.'[18] Bruchési acknowledged that there always have been occasional women warriors, but such instances were always rare. 'One must await our twentieth century, which has known total war, to see the acceptance of the equality of the sexes in this [military] field.'[19] Such a change clearly troubled Bruchési. His presentation occurred at a time of heightened anxiety about gender roles brought upon by the Second World War, in particular the roles women played in the military.[20] Covering the same court cases as Roy, Bruchési hesitated about using the term 'virago' for Verchères because of its negative connotations (though thereby using it nonetheless). In general, Bruchési's article has a much more negative tone than Roy's earlier piece.

Like Dollard, Verchères herself was dragged into the Second World War when her image was used in a recruiting poster for French-speaking women workers (fig. 4.1). The poster asserted that, yesterday, brave women like Madeleine de Verchères defended their country's honour against the enemy, while the modern woman joins the Canadian Women's Army Corps. Women in the CWAC provided auxiliary services to the army, freeing up men to enlist for overseas service. The parallel between the tasks of the members of the CWAC and Verchères's military feat was not exact. Madeleine had, after all, been an actual combatant. Nonetheless, the heroic image, like that of Dollard des Ormeaux, was considered useful in making the link between present and past sacrifices.

But there were other agendas also at work in such reinterpretations of heroic figures from the Canadian past. For instance, Louis Riel's significance has ranged over time from the defence of the interests of Aboriginals and Métis, to those of French Canadians, or Western Canadians, and so on.[21] With the more standard heroic figures, it is possible to measure changing attitudes to the study of history. Heroes are the province of romantic historians, and commemorations often rely on the key contributions of a small number of enthusiasts: F.-A. Baillairgé in the case of Verchères, Lionel Groulx in the case of Dollard des Ormeaux, Emma Curie in the case of Laura Secord. Although Groulx was not as distant from professional concerns as some are quick to conclude,[22] his sheer enthusiasm for Dollard des Ormeaux seems to belie the 'objectivity' of the true historian. The heroism of Laura Secord would likewise be denigrated in the name of 'objective' history. The proportion of women who celebrated Madeleine de Verchères's heroism is a case in point, in that the disciplinary structures of history in Canada were almost exclusively controlled by men, even if many Canadian women contributed serious historical research.[23] After all, professionalization was not, strictly speaking, based exclusively on intellectual merit. For instance, Lester B. Pearson merited his position as lecturer in history at the University of Toronto, not because of the depth of his historical analysis, but because of his status as an Oxford University student and his ability to coach varsity sports.[24] The study of nationalist icons such as Verchères shows

4.1 'Madeleine de Verchères, 1678–1747, Yesterday and Today.' The heroine recruits for the Canadian Women's Army Corps during the Second World War. (Copyright Canadian War Museum)

some of the difficulty of making a firm distinction between 'professional' and 'amateur' historians.

Ultimately, the perceptions of Verchères's difficult adult personality rendered the commemoration of her adolescent heroism more complicated. Henceforth, it was necessary to adopt an ironic, or sometimes a humorous, stance. Travel writers and popular historians came to echo the concerns raised by Roy and Bruchési. For Abbé Lionel Groulx, 'that she did not lack a warlike temperament in the least is evident throughout her life as much as in the exploit of 1692.'[25] Popular historian Alexander D. Angus's 1940s account of Verchères's heroism begins by commenting that the incident is one of the four best known to English Canadians (the others being Cartier's landing, Dollard's defence, and Montcalm's death). Referring to the curé Lefebvre's complaints about her, Angus adds, 'It becomes obvious that the conception of Magdelaine as simply a brave, almost legendary little girl shooting at the savages, is not quite adequate.'[26] Historian and archivist Robert de Roquebrune commented that 'it was not a good idea to attack Madeleine de Verchères, whether one were a plaintiff or an Iroquois.'[27] It became increasingly difficult to celebrate Verchères unreservedly as a heroic figure outside of school texts. Earlier images of Verchères were no longer considered adequate.

As the rumours were resurrected about Madeleine de Verchères, historians and the public have been only too willing to see her actions in the light of the accusations and interpret her experiences later in life better to understand her earlier heroism. In 1976, the magazine *L'Actualité* published an article by popular historian Jacques Lacoursière, 'The True History of Madeleine de Verchères and Her Priest ...' This article laid bare the court case between Verchères and Lefebvre in some detail, providing all the shocking quotations that previous publications had suppressed. For instance, Lefebvre's alleged litany included the sentences: 'Saint Madame with her two little pumpkins, pray for us ... Saint Boileau's hat under Madame de la Pérade's bed, pray for us ...' The piece was illustrated by a photograph of a randy priest chasing a young, nubile Verchères, much younger in appearance than the fifty-two years of age she was at the time of the court case in 1730. Barefoot and smiling, Verchères, with her scarf around her neck, runs away from the clutches of the older priest wearing sneakers (fig. 4.2). The illustrations capture the spirit of the article. Lacoursière writes that 'people whisper, in the colleges, that she was "loose."' He recounts her two acts of heroism and her lengthy court case, and implies that Lefebvre's calumnies about her

4.2 A randy Curé Lefebvre chases a much younger Madeleine de Verchères.
(Éric Daudelin)

sexuality may have been accurate. The article ends by suggesting that the
icon of Verchères had been created by English Canadians: 'At the beginning of the twentieth century, the English resurrected our heroes for us;
Marie-Madeleine de Verchères began a new life. The Order of the Daughters of the Empire (really!) sponsored a biography, and a few years later
the federal government (indeed!) provided the sum of $25,000 for the
construction of a monument.'[28] The history of Quebec was livelier and
naughtier, Lacoursière implies, than the staid emphasis on heroic exploits would suggest.

Articles like Lacoursière's and embellished retellings of the more
serious accounts contributed to making Verchères a figure of fun, sometimes gently and sometimes more cruelly.[29] In the 1980 Quebec referendum, a poster appeared which posed the question: 'Madeleine de
Verchères: would she have voted yes?' (fig. 4.3). Without providing an
exact response, the poster used the figure of Verchères to demonstrate
the central and forceful role of women: 'We can bet that she would have

4.3 Madeleine de Verchères as a contemporary nationalist icon. Referendum poster from the 1980 Quebec campaign. (Francine Serrand and Jacques Lavallée)

believed in the future! Seriously, it is not possible to study the history of Quebec without speaking of women's contributions. Since its beginnings, the colony had the privilege of counting on numerous courageous and intelligent women ... After the great heroines and female founders, our great-grandmothers contributed greatly to our survival ... Quebec was built as much in kitchens as in parliaments.' Produced by the Montreal chapter of the nationalist organization La Société St-Jean-Baptiste, the poster represented an effective political use of the heroine's persona. It also provided a reply to the controversy surrounding the 'Yvette' incident, when Parti Québécois cabinet minister Lise Payette had claimed that Québécois women who intended to vote 'no' were acting like the passive Yvette character in children's readers. Still, it showed how Verchères remained in 1980 a focus of nationalist sentiment – she could represent the nation – by this time an exclusively Québécois one.

It is difficult, of course, at any period to know how the messages concerning Madeleine de Verchères were received. In 1989, the Radio Canada program *Sameditou* ran a segment entitled, 'Who Was Madeleine de Verchères?' which can serve as an informal survey. In apparently random street interviews – mostly with men – members of the public were asked to identify the heroine. One interviewee remembered the story well, and another described her as the 'Jeanne d'Arc du Québec.' But the impact of the rumours was strikingly clear. One person commented that 'she had many more adventures than we are usually told.' Another remembered her as 'a revolutionary ... in Quebec ... for women ... for Quebec's independence ... in the nineteenth century.' One person confused her with the other standard heroines of New France and wondered if she had established a school or an institution.[30] But others could not situate her story with any accuracy. The radio presenter followed the item – without any sense of continuity – by discussing a transvestite competition in North Carolina.

Madeleine de Verchères, at perhaps the most extreme, has been cast as a 'castrating bitch.' In 1989, the Quebec humour magazine *Croc* jokingly described an exhibition of Montreal artefacts from the early years of colonization, five barrels of damp powder (the Dollard des Ormeaux collection) and a display of more than eighty-five Iroquois male genitals (the Madeleine de Verchères collection).[31] From a male perspective, it was increasingly difficult to perceive and celebrate Verchères as the virginal and brave defender of the fort. For all adults, the story required an ironic stance. Even one of the most serious contributions to the corpus of accounts, the entry on Verchères in the *Dictionary of Canadian Biography*, takes a humorous tone. Written by historian André Vachon, this account carefully examines the evidence concerning her life. Vachon examines the inconsistencies and exaggerations in her narratives and points out that the adult Verchères and her husband were certainly 'ill tempered.' He notes the large number of priests who signed the register when she was buried in 1747, 'anxious to pay her a final hommage.'[32]

Feminist

At the same time that men denigrated the traditional perspectives on Verchères, she also came under attack from some women, albeit for entirely different reasons. Just as there is no single feminist ideology, the heroic icon that Verchères represented responds better to some forms of feminism than others. In the late nineteenth and early twentieth centuries, women writers had celebrated Verchères's achievements for the mere fact that she had been there; that is, her actions allowed them to write a history of women, alongside more typical male-centred accounts. In a short speech, apparently dating from the 1930s, on 'Women's Contribution to Canadian Life,' the anonymous author used historical examples to bolster the campaign for woman's suffrage in Quebec. The text argues that 'the heroic lives of these women, Jeanne Mance, Marguerite Bourgeois and Madeleine de Verchères, form it seems, the best argument that may be brought against the claims of the opponents of the feminist movement. While filling perfectly the truly feminine vocations: Jeanne Mance that of nurse, Marguerite Bourgeois, that of teacher, and Madeleine de Verchere [*sic*] that of mother, these women did not disdain, nor were they refused the opportunity to play a large part in the social organization of their country.'[33] Thus, women's past contributions provided the precedence for the expansion of women's rights in the twentieth century.

In this way, Verchères continued to fit the needs of 'separate, but equal' feminist campaigners. In proposing an examination of what Madeleine de Verchères would be like if she were alive today, that is, in 1960, the journalist Béatrice Clément told her Radio Rurale audience that Verchères would still maintain her 'calm [*sang-froid*], courage and practical spirit,' and would be a full companion to her male partner. She would be well educated, fervently Catholic, and bilingual. She would enrol in university and join her local public library. She would raise her children in the appropriate manner to inculcate the values that she incarnated.[34] Although such statements certainly carved out a specific place for women in Quebec society, by the 1970s such statements became less acceptable for many feminists.

One clear example of the changing attitudes is the collective work *Histoire des femmes au Québec.* The first edition of this pioneering exploration of women's history, which portrays an essentialist view of women's separate and distinct qualities, includes a section entitled 'Pour en finir avec Madeleine de Verchères' – or 'Enough already of Madeleine de Verchères.' The problem with Madeleine de Verchères was that she acted more as a male than a female, and thus is an inappropriate icon for contemporary society. 'We should note,' the authors say, 'the heroine's endorsement of values based on a male, military and elitist concept of courage; she tacitly accepts the general inferiority of women and their confinement to a "naturally" female role; she justifies her heroism above all by the fact that she escaped the confines placed on women.'[35] Similarly, Verchères is mentioned only briefly in the textbook *Canadian Women: A History*, in a short discussion of women bearing arms in the early colonial period: 'Madeleine de Verchères was only one of many women who fired a gun, or took over when men were absent, in skirmishes with enemies.'[36] Where once Verchères was used as a means to introduce women's history into mainstream history, it is testimony to the development of the historiography of women in Canada that it is now possible to mention her only in passing. Such choices are also representative of a stronger essentialist view of feminist identity.

Yet not all feminists responded to the figure in the same way. The dangerous aspects of Verchères's image – her testing of boundaries and indeed her mere feistiness – are considered worth celebrating. The Acadian singer-songwriter Angèle Arsenault produced a song in 1975 which argued that the women of New France were early feminists. She lists the standard heroines, including Verchères, then laments: 'We had however begun on a good footing / The first arrivals were liberated women / They have left their name in the history of the country.'[37] Jan Noel, in a much-reprinted article on the women of New France, casts Madeleine de Verchères as an example of the range of experiences of women in the pioneering colony. 'Legend and history,' Noel writes, 'have portrayed Madeleine as a lamb who was able under siege, to summon up a lion's heart ... Perhaps the late twentieth century is ready for her as she was: a swashbuckling, musket-toting braggart who extended the magnitude of her deeds with each successive telling ... She strutted through life for all the world like the boorish male officers of the *campagnard* nobility to which her family belonged.'[38] In response to criticism that her portrayal of Verchères did not recognize how the heroine herself subscribed to a 'traditional' view of the role of women, Noel responded that 'a single, clearly defined tradition regarding womanly behaviour simply did not exist in Madeleine's time.'[39] Nonetheless, it is interesting that with the increasing interest in social history, Verchères's elite status has worked against her commemoration. Her class, as well as her actions, clearly stake her out as atypical. In a 1998 publication, Noel focuses much more on the experiences of peasant women and mentions Verchères only in passing: 'In the colony's earliest days, Madeleine de Verchères and Madame de La Tour, finding themselves the only nobles on hand during a siege, had actually commanded troops ... All in all, it seems that noble families did not conform to what are sometimes seen as "traditional" gender roles.'[40]

More recently, even Madeleine de Verchères's court case with the curé Lefebvre has been turned to her favour. Cécile Tremblay-Matte subtitled her study of women's music in Quebec *De Madeleine de Verchères à Mitsou*. Verchères, the author claims, may have written the bawdy litany that she accused the priest Lefebvre of chanting, and therefore she may be the first female songwriter in the history of French Canada. The heroine's class explains her ability to mobilize the judicial system in her favour: 'From a well-off family, with access to education – which was not the case for all women of that period – Madeleine possessed the necessary tools and courage to defend herself.'[41] Why Verchères would wish to spread a song that denigrated her is not explained in this book. But such perspectives provide a good-humoured nod to the heroic icon.

For the organizers of the 300th anniversary celebrations of Verchères's defence of her locality, what better way to recognize the heroine than to have a woman dress up as her and give an address at the base of the statue. Before a small group of listeners, which included the local political representatives and mayor, the 1992 Madeleine de Verchères read from a text commenting on the work of generations of unsung women: 'These obscure heroines worked, each day, without rest and with exemplary generosity.' The coincidence that Verchères had a woman mayor in 1992 allowed for a pleasant comparison: 'I would like to insist that many things have changed in Verchères but one thing has come back: a woman guards the fort to ensure the security and welfare of Verchères.'[42] The carefully worded text avoided any exuberant references to her heroic character.

In the twentieth century, Madeleine de Verchères has frequently been cast, both by women and by men, as a feminist, dangerous for some, fascinating for others. But her popularity is in decline. She is mentioned in popular and academic histories, but her story is much less standard fare than it was in the late nineteenth and early twentieth centuries. The spate of newspaper and magazine articles certainly tailed off after the 1920s. But she has not disappeared; she remains an appropriate figure for teaching the young about the early history of Canada.

Teenager: 'Home Alone'

Home Alone was one of the most popular Hollywood films of 1990. It is a slapstick comedy in which a young boy finds himself left alone by mistake in the large family house. By ever more improbable means, he defends the family riches from two bumbling thieves. With appropriate changes, this narrative can be seen as not much different than the story of Madeleine de Verchères. It builds on a strong sense among children of the desire to be alone within the family, and yet maintain the family's inviolability intact. Similarly, it is telling how many classic children's stories relate to orphans: *Anne of Green Gables, Heidi, Pippi Longstocking, The Secret Garden,* and so on, are all stories in which children manage to create a new family around themselves. One analysis of English-language girls' fiction examines those stories in which orphans occupy the central roles. Such stories symbolize a transition to responsibility: the ability in the appropriate circumstances to act as an adult. The authors point out how North American novels present 'impossibly well-adjusted and sunny-dispositioned children, whose own characters appeared to need very little modification.'[43] The many treatments of Madeleine de Verchères, while acknowledging and indeed revelling in her age, fail really to perceive her as a young adolescent. Verchères not only bends gender roles; in many of the accounts written to appeal to adults, she also assumes the part of the adult with ostensibly no difficulty.

In Verchères's case, she is a temporary orphan, abandoned by her mother and father, who themselves would have known how to defend the family fort. As one children's book interpreted Verchères's actions, 'even a young girl can have the bravery to defend her home if danger threatens it.'[44] For another writer, 'her story illustrates two things: first, the ever-present danger of murderous attack by the Iroquois in which the French colonists were placed in the early days; and second, the determination and heroism which this danger inspired in even the young people of that time.'[45] In many of the stories written for children, the closure of the tale is not so much Verchères's resumption of the 'normal' female place in society, but rather the return of the parents and thus the happy resolution of the temporary orphan's plight. While in Verchères's own narrative, the arrival of La Monnerie symbolizes the re-establishment of the status quo, in children's stories, the return of the parents often provides the final scene. Katherine Young's 1898 children's book ends the chapter on Madeleine with the statement: 'we may be sure that her father and mother soon came home to rejoice over the safety of their brave children.'[46] The 1913 'Story of Castle Dangerous' concludes, 'Soon the mother and father returned to their children, of whom they had good cause to be proud.'[47] Mabel Burns McKinley's account ends with the father's reaction: 'How proud her father was of her when he returned home and found out what had happened!'[48]

The resonance of Verchères's heroism is primarily as a story told to adolescents. The most famous teenager in Canadian history, Verchères's story was and is included in numerous school texts, under the premise that young readers will identify with someone who was of a similar age. This process began early on. In 1899 George Monro Grant stated confidently, 'And what school-child in Canada has not read or heard of Madeleine Verchères?'[49] Perhaps, the writers think, young girls and boys can empathize with the circumstances in which Verchères finds herself. Once she began to lose her importance as a heroic inspiration to the population as a whole after the 1920s, Madeleine de Verchères became remembered less and less for her prematurely adult courage than for her actions as a teenager. In a 1978 book produced to introduce school-children to characters from Canadian history, students are invited to discuss whether a modern fourteen-year-old could assume responsibility as Verchères did: 'Could a modern day fourteen-year-old take command of a situation and control it as effectively as Madeleine? Would a teenager today be given such an opportunity?'[50]

The stories of heroes and heroines were repeated endlessly in Canadian history schoolbooks. In the early twentieth century, provincial governments, whether through laws or the regulation of the contents of school texts, encouraged the inclusion of Canadian material.[51] As Margaret Atwood comments, until compilers wished to emphasize 'modern' literature, in school readers Canadian material was standard fare.[52] The exploits of heroic figures provided mnemonic devices, ways to render abstract principles concrete. At a time when it was the goal of educational practice in English Canada to assimilate the children of the large wave of immigrants who had arrived before the First World War,

Verchères and her Castle Dangerous provided one way among many of illustrating Canada's heroic past. Normal School examination papers provide a quick index of the importance of heroic figures to educational practice. In the published papers for Prince Edward Island, for instance, questions about Canadian heroes and heroines appeared regularly as items on the tests: Madeleine de Verchères in 1920, 1945, and 1953; Laura Secord five times between 1928 and 1936 and in 1945.[53]

Knowledge of heroes and heroines fulfilled nationalist goals. J.O. Miller, in providing a series of biographies to teachers in 1902, counselled: 'Every intelligent instructor knows the value of teaching History by examples. The interest of historical study to the young centres in persons rather than in events, in individual achievement rather than in the development of a country or the progress of a people ... Biography is History appealing to the eye of the mind.'[54] The Imperial Order Daughters of the Empire, which had earlier published Doughty's work, endorsed a book on Canadian heroines. 'We hope through these stories of Heroism, Hardship and Loyalty,' wrote the editor, 'you may more fully understand how much had to be endured by the Early Pioneers of Our Country. May it help you to give to Canada your loyal support for all things which are worthy and for the betterment and expansion of our Dominion.'[55]

Such sentiments were reflected in French Canada, even if the sense of the appropriate nation differed and much stronger emphasis was placed on her Catholic faith. For Joseph Marmette, although Verchères's bravery could no longer be imitated precisely, her story was still worth recounting. If 'our sons fall bloody on a battlefield, their sisters should not fear also confronting the bullets while they dress their noble wounds, and thus stop the draining of the purest blood of the fatherland.'[56] In a widely distributed children's book in the series Gloires nationales, Guy Laviolette invokes Verchères as a model for young women to follow. He covers her many instances of bravery and adds the important letter of 1727 concerning Verchères's appeal to the bishop to construct a new church in her seigneury of Sainte-Anne. The author adds a stirring postscript to the short book: 'give your Canadian sisters the ardour of your loving soul, the heights of your noble spirit, the force of your generous heart. Madeleine, return among us; imbue our daughters with courage, faith, and conquering values.'[57] For convent pupil Michelle Bienvenu in a publication of adolescents' work, Verchères was 'a humble girl of an intrepid race, strengthened by her patriotism and her faith.'[58]

These portrayals are often normative in narrow ways. Not only was

Verchères an epitome of selflessness, courage, and patriotism, she retained a cheery disposition throughout the Iroquois attack. For H.E. Marshall, 'hour by hour Madeleine marched round the posts, always smiling, always speaking cheering words, however heavy her heart might be.'[59] According to J.O. Miller, 'all was cheerfully done under the command of this young girl, who bravely kept a smiling face.'[60] Helen Palk suggested that 'Madeleine continued in command and cheered them all with her smiling bravery.'[61] When directed particularly at young women, some of the lessons can be especially negative about current-day practices. For Abbé J.-G. Gélinas, writing in 1915, 'fashion covers many disorders today and much craziness. And young girls who do not know how to dress and walk like marionettes, you may not know perhaps my children how nervous they are, how capricious they are, how fearful they are, how far they are, despite their frequent tantrums, from the energy of a ... Madeleine de Verchères.'[62]

Some of the accounts directly address the issue of a female being in charge. In Kay Pattinson's 1955 typescript drama, Verchères's mother informs her indignant son that Madeleine is in charge during her absence. When the attack comes, she takes command. 'I thought,' she says, 'if I wore Papa's hat, I'd feel more like your Commander.' Still, her brother tries to limit her actions, even while he accepts her authority: 'No, Madeleine. You stay here and keep guard. This [cutting down some bushes near the fort] is a man's job.'[63] For Morgan Kenney, the soldiers have difficulty with Verchères's command: 'It is evident that they don't like to accept orders from a girl, but they know that she is the one with authority.'[64]

Verchères's story also offered a pretext for providing information on the history and culture of French Canada. Sister Mary Carmel Therriault, s.m., wrote a French-language version of the story for American students studying the language: 'The need in Catholic schools for worthwhile material in French reading prompted the writing of *Madeleine de Verchères*. Madeleine's piety, courage and fortitude are splendid examples of the qualities needed today as much as in her lifetime. The dangers now are as real and as numerous as those facing the girl of early Canada.'[65] Perhaps because this book was intended for more mature students, upper high-school or college level, the author takes on some of the 'modern historians' who criticized Verchères for her litigiousness. 'It is not necessary that these few faults should make us forget the heroic acts that encircled her with a halo of bravery and pride.'[66] Grace Morrison's book for upper-level students likewise acknowledges the negative interpretations by allowing Verchères to defend herself: 'It is said in history books that I was always in a bad humour, that I mistreated my tenants, that I always wanted the last word. Well, so what! Each century has its gossips.'[67]

In recent accounts, the significance of Verchères's act of heroism is its narrative function. It serves as a scaffold upon which to hang a portrait of New France, a way of making the social history of the colony palatable to young students who may never venture near modern Quebec. Verchères's story allows teachers to discuss the various salient aspects of colonial life: the seigneurial system, the Iroquois raids, farm society, women's and children's roles.[68] Especially as women's history has become recognized as an important way of confirming the relevance of history to students of both sexes, Verchères's story (in an increasingly lay society) provides a good occasion for examining the context of women's lives at various parts of the life cycle. Thus Janet Grant's *Madeleine de Verchères* looks at her as a young woman and as an adult.[69] In particular, Verchères provides a good occasion for the thousands of French immersion students throughout Canada, and even students learning French in the United States, to practise their linguistic ability.

But the problem with using Verchères in school texts is the nature of the story. The story of defending French settlers from Iroquois attack has become less and less palatable as Aboriginal peoples become more politically active and their concerns more recognized on the national and international scene. In 1981, a fascinating attempt at rescuing the story was made for TV Ontario in both French and English versions. The theme of the story concerns the domain of what girls are allowed to do. 'I shoot as well as my brothers,' Verchères confidently announces. In this telling, Verchères is the nubile teenager who saves the fort, not from a whole host of Iroquois attackers, but from one young Iroquois man in particular, who watches her with barely subdued lust as she washes clothes by the shore. The sexual tension that Verchères herself exhibits when she chooses not to shoot him is palpable – she wonders what would be her fate if she were adopted into an Iroquois family and became the young man's wife. An old man informs her that he knew a lady captured by the Iroquois who became a princess and had four Iroquois babies. 'I let him escape,' Verchères comments to herself, wonderingly. 'Papa would have killed him.'[70] This is a sanitized version of the conflict between the Iroquois and the French, and one that gives full rein to late twentieth-century attitudes about young women's sexuality.

Other recent accounts find different ways to deal with the Aboriginal presence in the story, although the portrayals of Iroquois rely on old stereotypes. There is no questioning even in the most recent stories that European-Canadian writers are retelling the story for European-Canadian students. One 1989 children's book, aimed at grade 8 students, introduces the Hurons as potential rescuers, despite their absence from all other stories (and indeed their tiny numbers after the 1649 dispersal). Perhaps the author thought that the inclusion of friendly Natives could counterbalance the blatantly negative depiction of the Iroquois: 'The Iroquois are very evil.'[71] Jean Coté's short book on Verchères continues to convey the image of the bloodthirsty Iroquois, although their manipulation by the English may go a small way to exonerate them in the eyes of French-Canadian readers: 'They [the Iroquois] loved war more than anything, ignoring that they were merely a buffer in the age-old rivalry between England and France. Much later they would learn that they had been duped.' Madeleine de Verchères does not enjoy the central role in recent accounts that she did in earlier twentieth-century versions. Nonetheless, her actions still reveal the importance of maintaining the national community: 'The inhabitants of New France knew the meaning of the word solidarity.' This was, ultimately, the heroic lesson of the girl who was 'one of ours' (*de chez nous*).[72]

In the context of a series of biographies of Canadian celebrities, Jacques Lamarche's 1997 account downplays the Aboriginal presence and focuses instead on Verchères's court cases to recast her life story. The book begins by discussing a fight over seigneurial property lines. Verchères exclaims to her husband: 'As long as I am alive, no one will threaten our children's inheritance, Pierre-Thomas. I defended mine in the past and I have never regretted it.'[73] Lamarche discusses Verchères in the context of her genealogy and conveys the social history of early eighteenth-century New France in doing so. 'Good blood cannot lie,' the book concludes. In this recent account, the link between nation, genealogy, and history is clear.

Whether the audience of the stories is the large numbers of French immersion students in English Canada, or French-Canadian students themselves, Verchères will likely remain of interest to those who choose what stories are acceptable for teenage children. How many other significant figures of Canadian history share the same age as school children? Moreover, her chronological distance allows her story to be used as something upon which to hang a description of life in New France generally. Seigneurial tenure, the rural economy, and French-Aboriginal relations can all be summoned to round out Verchères's story. And for the inventive storyteller, perhaps, ways can be found to avoid the awkward discussion of the wars between French and Iroquois.

Conclusion

Few are the heroes who can sustain all the societal concerns that are projected onto them, especially as these concerns vary through time. It is not the icon that causes the conflicts, which are between concerns of different eras, but the icon bears the brunt of the challenges. Verchères, as an icon, has been buffeted by changing attitudes towards the role of women and of history and altered perspectives on Aboriginal peoples. Nonetheless, even such attributes as Verchères's presumed litigiousness, after being used to denigrate her character, can be used to demonstrate her unyielding personal and feminist strength. It is still possible to celebrate her heroism by focusing on her age, her sex, and her contribution to the 'nation,' but other aspects – particularly in English-speaking Canada – are more problematic. When she is remembered today, her opposition to Amerindians makes it much more difficult to celebrate her virtues.

No Canadian stamp commemorated her endeavours in 1992, despite the issue of a series of four commemorative stamps of other Canadian heroes in that very year: Laura Secord, Jos Montferrand (a lumberjack of the Ottawa Valley), Captain William Jackmann (rescuer of shipwrecked passengers off Newfoundland), and Jerry Potts (a Prairie guide and interpreter who fostered better relations between the Mounted Police and First Nations). The idea of producing a stamp for Verchères fell prey, one newspaper columnist reported, to 'other contingencies.'[74] So far, no CRB Foundation Historical Minute has recounted her heroism in the series widely shown on Canadian television in both French and English. Not entirely forgotten, Verchères has been a less compelling icon in recent decades. She is an ironic figure for adults, who know the 'truth' about her, at the same time that she remains a suitable character for school children, a means to learn about the history of New France. But she has become much less of a heroic icon to inspire the nation.

Part Two

Chapter Five

Walking to Beaver Dams:
Colonial Narratives, 1820s–1860s

25 February 1820: 'To Lieutenant-Governor Sir Peregrine Maitland. The Petition of James Secord, Senior, of the Village of Queenston, Esquire, Humbly Sheweth That your Petitioner is one of the Oldest inhabitants of this Province – has had numerous Relatives in the British army, is Brother-in-Law to the late Honorable Richard Cartwright – is a Captain in the 2nd Regiment of Lincoln Militia – was wounded in the battle of Queenston – and twice plundered of all his Moveable property. That his wife embraced an opportunity of rendering some services, at the risk of her life, in going thro the Enemies' Lines to communicate information to a Detachment of His Majesty's Troops at the Beaver Dam in the month of June 1813 ...'[1]

1840: 'To Lieutenant-Governor Sydenham. The Petition of Laura Secord, of the Village of Queenston. That your Excellency's Memorialist did in the Month of June 1813, as the following Certificate of Colonel FitzGibbon will fully coroborate, did at great Risk peril & danger travelling on foot & partly in the Night by a circuitous route, through woods mountains, the enemys lines & Indian Encampments to give important intelligence of a meditated attack of the Americans upon our troops and by which circumstance has laid the foundation of a desease from which she has never recovered & for which performance your Excellencys Memorialist has never Received the smallest compensation ... Your Excellency Memorialist would not now presume to ask any renumeration, but from the circumstances of having a large family of Daughters and Grand-Daughters to provide for for which the small means of my Husband Captain James Secord Sen'r will not meet ...'[2]

These two petitions are the earliest extant attempts to document

Laura Secord's 1813 walk from her home in the Niagara Peninsula village of Queenston to Beaver Dams (a distance of approximately nineteen miles), a journey undertaken to warn the British troops of an impending American attack. It would be, of course, anachronistic to read these texts in the same way as later narratives of Secord's journey, for they were not intended to create support for commemoration but instead for her and her family's remuneration. But they do constitute the first attempts to create a history for Secord and her family and are thus significant on a number of levels. To some degree, they can be seen as nineteenth-century histories, for the petitions attempted to create a logical and moral order out of the past to meet present needs. As such, they tell us something about the use of 'history' and its relation to the colonial state, as well as shedding light on the use to which gender and family relations were put in making such supplications. Furthermore, both the petitions and other documents produced by the Secord family that testified to her walk to Beaver Dams also hint at the discursive configuration of gender and race in this colonial context – and at later developments in the hands of the Secord commemorators. Finally, the repeated use of these documents and their embellishment make it crucial that we understand both their initial content and context.

Before discussing the writing of Laura Secord into Loyalist history, though, it is necessary to outline the gendered nature of nineteenth-century narratives of the War of 1812. Historians who have studied Upper Canadian politics have duly noted that assertions of loyalty and sacrifice during the war became the basis for many claims on the Upper Canadian state, in the competition for land and patronage appointments and for compensation for war losses.[3] Donald Akenson, for example, has pointed to the way in which claims to loyal duty during the war were used in attempts to justify the access of some residents to certain material benefits. Such claims were also made to legitimate the exclusion of others from such rewards.[4] Yet what has not been included in these historians' analysis of sacrifice in the war as a bargaining chip in the struggle for material gains in Upper Canada is the gendered nature of the narratives that were used. In Upper Canadians' commemorations of the War of 1812, the important sacrifices for country and monarch were made by Upper Canadian men, frequently in their capacity as members of the militia who risked life and limb to protect women and children, homes and hearths, from the brutal rampages of hordes of bloodthirsty Americans. During the war, and in its aftermath, women's contributions to the defence of the colony were either downplayed or ignored, in favour of the image of the helpless Upper Canadian wife and mother who entrusted her own and her children's safety to the gallant militia and British troops.[5]

In addition to the manly figures of the militia, another extremely significant masculine symbol was the British commander Isaac Brock, who made the ultimate sacrifice for the colony by dying at the Battle of Queenston Heights in 1812. Brock provided those who shaped the history of the war with a dualistic image of nationalism, one that managed to celebrate both Upper Canadian identity and colonial loyalty to Britain. He was also a Christlike figure, a man who had given both his troops and the colony beneficent paternal guidance and wisdom and, moreover, had not spared himself from the physical dangers of war: dangers that really only threatened men in the military. Those who contributed to the glorification of Brock claimed that he had provided an invaluable means whereby the colonists might resist the enemy's encroachments. Brock had inspired Upper Canadian men, who might emulate his deed of manly patriotism, and he had reassured Upper Canadian women that, come what may, they could look to their husbands, fathers, sons, and brothers for protection.[6]

This kind of narrative, which emphasized masculine suffering, sacrifice, and achievements, was not unique to the War of 1812. As Janice Potter-MacKinnon argues in her study of the experiences of Loyalist women in eastern Ontario, the history of Upper Canadian Loyalism focused on male military service and the political identification of male Loyalists with the British crown and constitution. Well into the twentieth century, loyalty was a male concept in that it was associated with political decision-making, a sphere from which women were officially excluded. The same can be said of the idea that the Loyalists bequeathed conservative values and British institutions to later generations of Canadians: women have had no role in fashioning political issues and institutions. The notion that the Loyalists were the founders of a nation had obvious and unequivocal gendered implications; the amateur historian William Caniff was right when he equated the 'founders' with the 'fathers.'[7]

There was no automatic and essential connection between military activities and masculinity, in either Canadian history or Western European culture. The woman warrior tradition, for example, was not unknown to nineteenth-century commemorators.[8] What is striking about discourses of loyalty and patriotism in Upper Canada, though, was an almost complete absence of specific female images or femininity in general as symbols of these qualities, as well as a general reluctance to admit that women could have contributed as civilians to the war effort. This silence about women and the feminine – except as helpless victims to which the masculine bravery of Upper Canadian men was inextricably linked – was unlike the discourses of the French Revolution, with their glorification of Marianne, the American Patriot's figure of the republican mother, or even the more conservative use of Britannia.[9]

Exactly how, then, did Secord's trek through the woods and fields become part of Upper Canadian history? Her symbolic journey – from obscure Queenston housewife to 'national' heroine – began with the Secord's family economy and its relation to the colonial state. As his petition mentions, James Secord was wounded at the Battle of Queenston Heights and was left a semi-invalid for the rest of his life. The family's fortunes did not, therefore, improve after the war. Unlike some of their compatriots, they did not benefit from wartime profiteering, nor, like the majority of Upper Canadians, did they see any substantial compensation for wartime losses.[10] The first petition was for a licence to the portion of Queenston's military reserve that was the site of a stone quarry. James Secord was successful in this endeavour, although he did not become wealthy from the income. In 1822 he applied for and was given a small pension by the Medical Board, which declared that he was 'incapable of earning his livelihood in consequence of wounds received in action with the Enemy.'[11] With two adults and seven children to support, though, the £18 yearly pension did not meet the family's needs; the Secords continued to press the colonial government for other sources of income, including the position of caretaker of Brock's monument. This job had been promised by Lieutenant-Governor Maitland, but with his departure from the colony, it was given by Maitland's successor, John Colborne, to Teresa Nichol, widow of militia captain Robert. In 1835 James Secord was appointed Collector of Customs at Chippewa, and the fees he collected from this position gave the family some financial security.[12]

The 'large family of Daughters and Grand-Daughters' referred to in Laura Secord's 1840 petition to Sydenham were the couple's older, widowed daughters, who had returned home (one from Ireland), and their children. The petition was aimed at obtaining the ferry concession at Queenston, and Secord's testimony to her travels was accompanied by a certificate from James FitzGibbon, the Anglo-Irish colonel to whom her message had been delivered. This request was also denied, and James's death in 1841 brought the medical pension to an end. These vicissitudes prompted more letters to Sydenham, the first one requesting that her son, Charles, be granted his father's position in customs. Upon the governor's refusal, Secord then asked for a pension for herself, the first time she had directly requested money and not a position; this request was also denied.[13] Both of her appeals cited her poverty, her lack of support since her husband's death, and her need to look after her daughters and grandchildren. After James's death, publicly distributed accounts of Secord's walk appeared, first in her son Charles's 1845 article in the Anglican paper *The Church* and, in 1853, in the *Anglo-American Magazine*; the latter was an account written by Secord herself. In 1860 Secord achieved some success in her campaign for financial recognition on the part of the state when she presented her story to the Prince of Wales during his tour of British North America. She was also the only woman whose name appeared on an address presented by the surviving veterans of the Battle of Queenston Heights to the Prince, in a ceremony attended by five hundred visitors and at which a memorial stone was laid on the site where Brock fell. Her 'patriotic services,' claimed the *Niagara Mail* in 1861, were 'handsomely rewarded' by the Prince with an award of £100.[14] When Secord died in 1868, her obituary described her as 'one of the Canadian women of the War of 1812, whose spirit and devotion to their country contributed so much to its defence.'[15]

What were the themes in these initial narratives? First, they were linked by their genre: both James and Laura used the stance of the Crown's subject offering a record of service that would justify compensation. Of course, the use of petitions as a vehicle for patronage requests was in itself not remarkable. Given the predominance of political patronage and the use of petitions in this colonial setting, it would have been surprising if the Secords had not tried to barter patriotic services for material rewards. The language of family relations also helped structure and legitimate the Secords' requests; again, given that paternalism was a defining feature of colonial politics, it was not remarkable that concepts of 'family' appear in their petitions. 'Family,' though, was deployed in slightly different, albeit related, ways. In James Secord's petition, his relations' positions in Upper Canadian society – his relatives in the army and his successful and influential brother-in-law, the Kingston merchant and politician Richard Cartwright – were offered to the colonial government as proof of James's manly probity and worthiness, the guarantors of his social and political respectability.

Laura Secord's petitions, in contrast, hinted strongly that the tribulations of war and in particular the epochal Battle of Queenston Heights had brought about a shift in gender relations in the Secord household. Although James had behaved in a manly fashion, fighting for the colonial government, this act had compromized his post-war ability to head his household and support them, an ability that, over this period, was increasingly considered the hallmark of bourgeois men's character and conduct. Colonial loyalty and subjecthood had thus devolved paternal duties onto Laura Secord's shoulders, forcing her to become a husband to James and, to some extent, both father and mother to their children. This reversal of customary gender roles within the Secord household was by no means a desirable state of affairs, particularly as it was brought about by the catastrophe of imperial conflicts. And, as such, it was only proper that the colonial government remedy matters, presumably by recognizing the Secords' contributions to the war effort and offering James support.

However, if none was forthcoming for her husband, Laura Secord was not averse to accepting some sort of employment for herself; it is quite likely she envisaged an appointment as a type of 'family enterprise.' Moreover, while the petitions display an expectation that her husband would, in the 'natural' order of things, support the family, in practice such gendered expectations might not translate into the more rigid roles of the late nineteenth century.[16] Furthermore, the ambivalence surrounding notions of appropriate masculinity and femininity, the ways that they might be transgressed (at least temporarily) in order to fulfil certain responsibilities – and thus rehabilitate the transgression – was a theme that underpinned the Secord narratives. The leitmotif of the family, as a network of connections that could legitimate individual need and as the basis of social obligations and responsibility in Upper Canadian society, was also a constant and recurring theme in later historical accounts, both of Secord and of Upper Canadian society itself.

The petitions were also marked by their reliance on the Secords' corporeal frailty, James's wounds from Queenston Heights and the 'desease' Laura contracted as a result of her walk. In light of the future development of Secord's narrative, it is worth pointing out that James himself introduced his wounds. In the more immediate aftermath of the war, such a strategy might have won Maitland's sympathetic ear in the award of the quarry licence. But the inclusion of his wounds, a theme that was repeated constantly in Secord's narrative, was more than just a demand for restitution (like the 'plundering of all his Moveable property'); they also symbolized masculine self-sacrifice and loyalty. James thus could appear, not as a questionable malingerer, but rather as one of the many men whose physical contributions were celebrated in Upper Canadian narratives of the War of 1812. No matter that these wounds were never described in detail in these narratives; their mere existence, alongside James's other proofs of manly character, was enough. And this absence of detail, this lack of any kind of visual image of James and his injuries, was one feature of the Secord narratives that did not change much over time. In contrast, Laura's physical condition, while left to the reader's imagination in the early nineteenth century, received more and more specific attention and more elaborate descriptions by the early 1900s. The details of James's body, however, remained shadowy and elusive; it thus became generalized as part of a larger massed 'body' of men who had suffered physical trauma during the war and who were not, on one level, exceptional. Laura's, on the other hand, was highly visible and to some degree very specific and extraordinary, although she too was also constructed as a 'typical' woman of her class and race.[17] In discursive manoeuvres replete with many layers of meaning and contradictions, Secord's commemorators had to make her a specific and exceptional figure in order – ironically – for her to then become domesticated and thus unexceptional. Yet the source of her physical frailty shifted, for her subsequent petitions and narratives did not mention the 'desease' she had suffered. Instead, she became a 'slender and delicate' woman prior to setting out to Beaver Dams; her ability to overcome these drawbacks pointed to the strength of her commitment to Upper Canada and to Britain.

What of the published accounts that followed the petitions? Charles Secord's narrative in *The Church* was focused on winning public recognition for FitzGibbon, whose right to £1000 for his role at Beaver Dams was being debated in the Legislative Assembly. A Lower Canadian member, Thomas Aylwin, had challenged FitzGibbon's claim, stating that a Major DeLorimer deserved recognition instead. Secord believed that 'Mr. Aylwin should be informed, and ... the country in general should know, in what way Col. FitzGibbon achieve [*sic*] so much honor for the affair at Beaver Dams. My mother living on the frontier during the whole of the late America war, a firm supporter of the British cause, frequently met with the American officers.' Exactly why and how these meetings took place is not clear in Charles Secord's narrative, nor would it be clear in that of his mother. She overheard the plan to surprise FitzGibbon and 'without waiting for further information, my mother, a lone woman, at once left her house to apprise the British troops of what she had heard.' During her journey, she passed a number of American guards and scouts but made it to FitzGibbon and told him of the American plot, whereupon he was able to prepare a successful defence and counter-attack. Laura did not, Charles informed his readers, mention a Major DeLorimer: 'Col.

FitzGibbon was the only officer who appeared to be in command to whom my mother gave the information, and who acted the part as he so nobly did in that occasion.' Thus her son's account was not about his mother and her contribution to the war; instead, her walk was told as a means of legitimating FitzGibbon's claim to patronage. The narrative also collapsed time, having Secord leave immediately upon overhearing the plot, and not dwelling upon the amount of time spent during her walk. Secord's motivations for going, and James's for staying, are not discussed; we are left to surmise that her support of the British was sufficient cause. And unlike later accounts, details of her body, clothing, and encounters along the way are absent from this narrative.

None of this may be surprising, given Charles Secord's reasons for writing this testimony. My point here is simply that the kinds of details provided by late nineteenth-century commemorators were not always obtained from earlier documentary evidence, even though they were given the aura of historical 'truth.' The 'matter-of-fact' tone of this first published account, written for both members of the Legislative Assembly and the general reading public, is also very different from the rhetorical flourishes and devices, the hyperbole and romanticism, used by Secord's commemorators. There was nothing extraordinary or transgressive about his mother's actions; in fact, they were unexceptionable, almost banal. Finally, Charles Secord's account points to a very obvious but at times overlooked aspect of historical narratives: the same story may not always be 'about' the same issues or individuals, nor is its use limited to one purpose. This narrative, while discussing Secord's walk, was not really concerned with her at all. Secord's walk was merely a way of demonstrating FitzGibbon's heroism and military leadership.[18] Yet Charles's statement would be drawn upon forty years later in order to win recognition for his mother.

Secord's account was, though, accompanied by a certificate, signed by FitzGibbon in 1837, that attested to his mother's contribution to the Beaver Dams victory. He stated that she walked from her house in 'St. Davids ... by a circuitous route of about twenty miles' to warn him of the impending attack, 'having obtained such knowledge from good authority.' Once again, the source of her information and the manner in which she obtained it was left to the reader's imagination; the 'event showed' that she was correct. FitzGibbon's comments on Secord's physical being were prescient, though, as he stated that she was 'a person of slight and delicate frame' whose walk, undertaken in very warm weather, made him 'dread at the time that she must suffer in health in consequence of fatigue and anxiety, she having been exposed to danger from the enemy.'[19] Thus, while also told for other purposes, FitzGibbon's narrative would provide an even greater basis for constructing Secord as an Anglo-Celtic heroine.

Secord's own account of 1853 is striking for a number of reasons. Its style is far removed from the poetic and dramatic strategies deployed in the narratives of the 1890s and 1900s. There are fewer discussions of her feelings, desires, and motivations – in short, her subjectivity – than would be created by Ontario women historians such as Sarah Curzon and Emma Currie. Her reason for undertaking her mission, for example, is not discussed. Like the previously published accounts, she apparently believed that her readers would see her actions arising from her natural loyalty and willingness to serve the imperial cause. And, while Secord concluded her story with the observation that she now wondered 'how I could have gone through so much fatigue, with the fortitude to accomplish it,' she did not stress her need to overcome innate physical frailty. Yet Secord's chronological organization of her narrative differed from both the petitions and her son's account. Instead of beginning with her journey or – as would become the case four decades later – her family's journey to Upper Canada, Secord starts by recounting her experience at the 'Battle of Queenston, where I was at the time the cannon balls were flying around me in every direction.' Leaving her reader wondering just how and why a female civilian was on the field, she then states that she left but upon returning to the village after the battle ended, 'there found that my husband had been wounded, my house plundered and property destroyed.' The narrative then jumps to 'while the Americans had possession of the frontier ... I learned of the plans of the American commander and determined to put the British troops under FitzGibbon in possession of them, and if possible to save the British troops from capture or perhaps total destruction.' Secord then speaks of her 'determination' to get through the American guard, and her walk of nineteen miles 'through a rough and difficult part of the country' until she reached a field in the vicinity of Beaver Dams.

It is at this point that Secord's version of the narrative differed most markedly from those previously recounted. While she had mentioned 'Indian Encampments' in her 1840 petition to Sydenham, by 1853 she chose to elaborate on her encounter with the Mohawks:

By this time daylight had left me. Here I found all the Indians; by moonlight the scene was terrifying and to those accustomed to such scenes might

be considered grand. Upon advancing to the Indians they all arose and
with some yells said 'Woman,' which made me tremble. I cannot express
the awful feeling it gave me, but I did not lose my presence of mind. I was
determined to persevere. I went up to one of the chiefs, made him understand that I had great news for Capt. FitzGibbon and that he must let me
pass to his camp or that he and his party would all be taken. The chief at
first objected to let me pass, but finally consented, after some hesitation, to
go with me and accompany me to FitzGibbon's station, which was at the
Beaver Dam, where I had an interview with him.

Secord then states that she told FitzGibbon of the Americans' plan to attack and 'benefiting by this information, Capt. FitzGibbon formed his
plans accordingly and captured about five hundred American infantry,
about fifty mounted dragoons, and a field piece or two was taken from the
enemy.' Secord, for her part, 'returned home exhausted and fatigued.'[20]

As we shall see, the Mohawk encounter, as well as the possibility of
meeting Native peoples during the walk itself, came to play a much
larger and critical role as Secord's tale was recounted; it would encapsu-
late particular configurations of gender and race in imperialist historical
writing. Secord's account, though, both differs in some crucial ways from
future narratives and simultaneously provides material for their use of
Native imagery. In the first case, there is far less sustained attention to
the threat of 'imagined Indians' throughout the journey; their absence
from the woods is in marked contrast with future narratives. However,
they do appear in the penultimate encounter in her journey, a scenario
that is full of the elements of nineteenth-century romanticism. It is
'terrifying' to Secord, who hints at her lack of contact with First Nations
(at least as a group), but, to those familiar with them, the massed bodies
of Native men, seen in the dark, presumably dressed as warriors, might
be awe-inspiring, rather than simply fearful. By the 1850s (if not much
earlier), First Nations were part of the spectrum of natural wonders that
Euro-Canadians were beginning to gaze upon as tourists.[21] It is also
possible that, for her readers, the presence of Britain's allies may have
been read as a reassurance of Britain's military presence in the area. In
the absence of any elaboration by Secord, her meaning unfortunately
remains somewhat elusive. However, the qualifying clause – 'I did not
lose my presence of my mind' – appeared only in certain future accounts. In contrast, the entire encounter with the Mohawks would take
on an ever-increasing significance, despite the reconciliation once the
chief understood Secord's purpose.

Other references to Secord began to appear in the press and in a few mid-nineteenth-century histories of the War of 1812. In 1861 the *Niagara Mail* ran an account of her walk after she had been recognized by the Prince of Wales; the author stated that Secord had overheard the Americans planning their attack during one of their 'frequent visits' to the Secord house. The paper also stated that she had walked thirteen miles, 'notwithstanding the imminent peril of falling into the hands of American scouts or hostile Indians.' It did not mention, though, her encounter with the Mohawk encampment.[22] In 1869 the American historian Benson J. Lossing, in his *The Pictorial Field Book of the War of 1812*, devoted a page to Secord and the Battle of Beaver Dams. The page's caption read, 'British Troops Saved by a Heroine,' and Secord's account of 1853 was the source that supplied Lossing with his information.[23] In 1864 the Canadian historian and government official William F. Coffin elaborated on her story by adding the cow that, he claimed, she milked in order to convince the American sentry to let her pass. While some historians regard Coffin's account as yet another example of romantically inclined nineteenth-century historians playing fast and loose with the facts of history, his placing of Secord in a context of pioneer domesticity foreshadowed the stories of the 1890s and 1900s.[24] Secord thus was not rescued from complete obscurity by her late nineteenth-century commemorators; she was, however, given a much more prominent place in their narratives of the War of 1812 and Upper Canadian loyalty. In comparison with these histories, the narratives examined here were more fragmented, particularly since they were intended to meet a more diverse set of needs. They suggest how the story itself changed depending on the narrator and his or her audience: it was not only imperialist and nationalist historians of the following decades who tailored their narratives to suit their purposes. It is to those narratives of Canadian history and of Secord's walk that we will now turn.

Chapter Six

The Lives of the Loyal Pioneers: Historical Societies and Historical Narratives

With a hurried farewell to her husband and children, Mrs. Secord took her fate in her hands, and went forth with the inspiration which comes when duty calls. It was before the early light of the summer morn, and long before the last of Boerstler's troops had halted at Queenston, when she started on her way. Her brother, Charles Ingersoll, was lying dangerously ill at St. Davids, and this excuse satisfied the sentinel for her early trip. He was at the house of her sister-in-law ... She was there but a few minutes, but in that brief time resisted all persuasion tochange her purpose, and induced her niece, Elizabeth Secord, to go with her ... This she did as far as Shipman's Corners, where her feet became so sore she was unable to proceed farther. From that point Mrs. Secord's journey was performed alone. It had been a very rainy season, the streams were swollen, and where the rude bridge had been swept away, on her hands and knees she crept over on a fallen tree. To avoid danger she had to recross the stream more than once, and to travel beyond the ordinary route. As she neared the vicinity of FitzGibbon, in coming up a steep bank, she came upon the Indians who were encamped there. They sprang to their feet upon her appearance, with piercing cries demanding to know 'What white woman wanted?' Though terrified, her presence of mind did not forsake her, but to the last years of her life she never could speak of that time without emotion. They were Caughnawagas, and did not understand English. With difficulty the Chief, who partially understood English, at last comprehended that she had a message of importance for FitzGibbon, and must see him. It was seven o'clock in the morning when she came upon the Indian encampment. After what seemed a long detention, she was at last conducted to FitzGibbon, and told him of the coming attack. There was no waste of words on either side; FitzGibbon recognized the danger, and his arrangements were promptly made.

Emma A. Currie, *The Story of Laura Secord and Canadian Reminiscences* (1900), pp. 49–50

Emma Currie, the founder in 1892 of the St Catharines Women's Literary Club (WLC), wrote her book about Laura Secord as a piece of historical commemoration in its own right and to raise funds for a Secord monument. Currie was a supporter of woman's suffrage, an enthusiastic promoter of Canadian history, and a member of groups such as the Woman's Christian Temperance Union and the Imperial Order Daughters of the Empire (IODE). Currie was joined in her efforts to memorialize Secord by women such as Sarah Curzon, the British-born suffrage activist and co-founder in 1885 of the Women's Canadian Historical Society of Toronto (WCHS), and by Mary-Agnes FitzGibbon, a descendant of James FitzGibbon. While they chose to work within all-women organizations, Currie, Curzon, and FitzGibbon were part of a much larger movement in Ontario to preserve and make known both the province's and the Dominion of Canada's history. Groups like the WLC and the WCHS worked alongside organizations such as the Niagara Historical Society (NHS), the Ontario Historical Society (OHS), the Wentworth Historical Society (WHS), and the Brant Historical Society (BHS).[1] Through the writing of Canadian history, these groups and individuals attempted to create national and imperial identities for themselves and their contemporaries, identities which in turn were shaped by their understandings of the relations of gender and race. The written narratives of Secord's walk must be read and analysed within these particular contexts of culture, nation, and history.

'History,' 'Progress,' and Modernity

During the years in which many of these groups were formed, Canadian society underwent a number of socio-economic changes, such as industrialization, urbanization, and an increase in both British and non-British immigration. It also saw the growth of social reform movements, including the women's movement, and of overtly imperialist sentiments. Late nineteenth-century imperialism has been linked by some Canadian historians to political issues, such as the Riel Rebellion, the Jesuit Estates, and the Manitoba Schools' Crisis, and imperialist desires for stronger political, social, and cultural links with Britain have been seen as being fueled by expressions of anxiety over the country's future. A cohesive national heritage was seen by such individuals as Canon George Bull of the Lundy's Lane Historical Society as the political and cultural glue that would hold a new and very fragile Dominion together, staving off threats from American expansion and dangerous foreigners.[2]

No doubt such concerns motivated many individuals to join the historical societies; prominent members often voiced their anxieties that a knowledge of Canadian history was needed to navigate fin-de-siècle changes. Yet, far from dwelling on fears of social and economic upheavals, Ontario's historical societies often went about their intellectual business with a confident desire for knowledge of the past. They were, it is true, members of the province's middle class, a group we might expect to have displayed a sense of crisis or at least profound unease with contemporary developments. Yet even to call them 'middle class' and thus expect a uniform reaction to urbanization and industrialization obscures some important distinctions between these groups. The Kingston Historical Society and the WCHS, for example, tended to draw upon intellectual, political, and social elites for their members.[3] Other societies, particularly those from outside Kingston, Ottawa, or Toronto, attracted a wider spectrum of businessmen, professionals, and politicians, many of whom came from less prosperous backgrounds.[4] Moreover, while the family backgrounds of women such as Curzon, Janet Carnochan, Augusta Gilkison, and Harriet Priddis had given them the necessary cultural capital for this work, their status as single women meant that they were denied the economic security available to many of their male counterparts.[5] Gilkison, for example, found it difficult to pay for her travel expenses to OHS meetings, while Curzon waged an ongoing struggle to make a living from her pen.[6] Yet one generalization about members' class status is possible: their ranks did not include members of Ontario's burgeoning working class, nor – as a rule – were they interested in tracing its development. Working-class intellectuals, by and large, joined groups such as mechanics' institutes.[7]

Although they may have been spurred by political and social concerns about the Dominion's future, the historical societies' members were not estranged or alienated from urban and industrial life. Many of them, men and women, equated modern developments and modernity in general with progress, improvements that would have beneficent results for Canada. Some creators of historical memory, it is true, expressed rather more yearning for the past and anxiety about the present than their counterparts, but even their faith in progress, while shaken, was not destroyed.[8] For the majority of historians, Canada's past was a linear narrative of improvement, one in which the past held the seeds of present triumphs. As James Coyne, the OHS president, told the society at its 1899 meeting,

the interest in life and the age we live in will be quickened by the perceived relation to the past ... We shall be better men and women, more patriotic citizens, and therefore ... truer cosmopolitans ... Seeing the *evolution of civilization and culture* during the hundred years of the history of settlement, we shall be inclined to face the future with a more assured faith, strengthened by knowledge of what has been done and what is being accomplished from year to year. And looking not down but up, *not backward but forward*, we may fairly hold, with the good rabbi Ben Ezra, while duly valuing the past, that the present is better, and 'the best is yet to be, The last of life for which the first was made.'[9]

Coyne's and his colleagues' interpretations of modernity as a vantage point from which to examine the past also influenced their understanding of imperialism and nationalism. In turn, these discourses also shaped their conceptions of contemporary progress. Coyne's 1901 speech claimed a *Canadian* past that made it possible to foresee a Canadian future. Of course, this strategy was by no means unique to Canada; others who have studied the writing of nineteenth-century history have demonstrated that it was integral to the formation of nation-states.[10] Being able to point to a 'history' meant that not only could nineteenth-century bourgeoisies claim a common identity based on shared collective experiences in the past, they could also assert their status as members of a modern, progressive community that, bolstered by this knowledge, would be prepared for future challenges. History, in many of the historical societies' writings, was a site of education and moral instruction for national identities and participation in the nation. With this precept in mind, the OHS and its affiliates pressured the provincial and Dominion governments for commemorations of Empire Day, more 'Canadian content' in the schools' history curriculum, and essay competitions in Canadian history for schoolchildren.[11] And the educational role of history was not confined to the classroom. Coyne's 1902 presidential address stated that history teaches both 'pride of accomplishment' but also the 'feeling of responsibility, of failure to reach the ideal aimed at, and thus comes to the incentive to more strenuous struggle and effort. Basal elements of human character, self-reliance, self-respect, patriotism, voracity, wonder, reverence, faith in an everlasting purpose and the infinite goodness are profoundly affected by the study of history. It is the searchlight we throw upon the future.'[12]

Furthermore, for many members of historical societies in southern Ontario, creating historical knowledge of an entity called 'Canada' was necessary in order to claim both national identity and imperial membership. Of course, these men and women did not completely agree whether the two were competing forms of loyalties or, at the very least, arranged in a hierarchical relationship. For Clementina Fessenden, a member of both the Wentworth Historical Society and the OHS's Flags and Monuments Committee, to lose the Canadian connection to Britain meant succumbing to the worst aspects of American society, specifically republicanism.[13] Yet positions such as Fessenden's were not unanimously held. For one, not all members of the societies equated interest in the United States with capitulation to that country's annexationist designs, a position that would have been difficult to hold given that a number of these societies frequently corresponded with like-minded American groups and exchanged historical reports and documents.[14]

And at times historians expressed admiration, bordering on a wistful yearning, for American institutions they found attractive and inspirational. In his 1914 presidential address, John Dearness told the OHS that 'the crowning achievement of the nineteenth century was the making of the nation south of us' and that Canadian and Americans shared many beliefs and institutions.[15] Yet the societies also saw Britain as contributing to modern progress through its venerable legacy of democratic institutions and respect for commercial enterprises. Moreover, such contributions had been brought to 'premodern' societies. The implementation of these imperial institutions and values was the *sine qua non* of modern, enlightened, and advanced rule over colonized peoples. 'Ontario,' pronounced OHS secretary Andrew Hunter in 1923, 'under British rule, holds a unique record in the management of its Aboriginal races, although there are a few minor similarities in the records of other countries, also under the protection of Great Britain.'[16] For these historians, the British Empire was both an inspirational and fascinating subject. The Niagara Historical Society Museum collected objects from India and South Africa, while the St Catharines Women's Literary Club frequently discussed affairs in India, Africa, Egypt, and Turkey, talks which placed these countries within the framework of imperialism and Orientalism.[17] Only by adopting values and practices that, for these writers, were coded as 'British' could the residents of such countries hope to break free of their 'medieval' chains of servitude and ignorance; they would also be spared the autocratic practices of other colonial powers.[18]

In marrying British and Canadian identity, these writers adopted a number of strategies. Their desire to depict Canada as modern and progressive *and* a country with a 'history' spurred their eagerness to trace the lineaments of imperial genealogy as a way of creating the 'imagined community' of Canada. This obsession with so-called ancestor worship or filiopietism has been seen as a fairly mundane and pragmatic way of using the past to establish claims to socio-economic superiority in the present, as when James Secord told the colonial government of his relatives in the British army or when claims to United Empire Loyalist (UEL) lineage were made in the early nineteenth century in order to qualify for land grants.[19] Late-nineteenth-century attempts to establish lines of birth and descent in historical narratives have been seen by other historians as indicative of a banal, self-interested, and narrow perspective.[20]

Yet this latter argument takes as natural the complicated processes of forging national identities and overlooks other reasons why these writers attempted to link themselves, through their ancestors, to a larger imperial community. Such endeavours might mean integrating 'family trees' into the accounts of other events or processes (for example, a detailed examination of the background of prominent historical figures such as Major-General Isaac Brock), or they could involve a presentation of genealogical research as a separate endeavour in its own right. Tracing lines of family descent, making connections between men and women from rural villages in England, from Somerset to the Scottish Highlands, and the farms they established in Peel County, was a way of creating imagined communities. This act of creation relied on images of both individuals and, in the hands of many historians, the landscapes, values, and institutions they inhabited and shaped to create discourses of shared national memories. By underpinning their work with genealogical research, men and women such as Caniff Height, William Kirby, Janet Carnochan, and Emma Currie, as well as dozens of less prominent historians, could establish that British, or even pre-republican Anglo-American values and habits, had a long and honourable past in Canada.[21]

Being 'British-Canadian' frequently meant admiration for monarchy, albeit with limited powers; parliamentary democracy, although not full adult suffrage; and the institutions of 'British' law and justice. But it also meant respect for Christianity, in particular, Protestantism. These writers' religious beliefs did not necessarily translate into explicit, detailed examinations of individual denominations; however, they pointed out that Protestant churches had played a critical role in shaping Canadian history. Hayden White has argued that historical narratives are marked by both moral meaning and their narrator's moral authority;[22] in the case of the historical societies, Christian morality underpinned the processes of imperial expansion and white settlement. It was an implicit component of narratives of progress, one that helped explain and justify the eventual success of Loyalists and other pioneers, British institutions, and the Dominion of Canada itself. No matter what the topic – from the coming of churches to pioneer communities to the spread of Christianity to Native peoples – these settlements demonstrated an innate propensity to moral conduct. Such a tendency had been passed to them from their ancestors, but it was given free rein to express itself in the Canadian context. John MacLean, whose family settled near Brockville in 1783, remembered that the community's need for a

> preached Gospel ... was met with the most earnest heed to sustain the 'church in the house.' For years no sermon was ever heard from the living preacher, and there the dead were made to speak in their real sermons; and as others settled around, a goodly band of praying men met in that house regularly, and conscientiously did they agree together to sustain the means of grace without a minister. Thus they laid the foundation of the first Presbyterian Church and Sabbath School in that vast portion of Canada.[23]

While some Protestant writers regretted that Roman Catholicism dominated Quebec's history, nevertheless the strong presence of a Christian body to some degree mitigated its lack of British institutions and values.[24] And these writers' narratives of Canadian history display a firm belief in their own moral fitness to demonstrate these triumphs; after all, were they not either literal or figurative descendants of such paragons?

Transmitting the lessons of Christian conduct in the past was not the only means of inculcating Anglo-Celtic values. An imperialist morality was also one that respected the centrality of capitalism, particularly respect for private property, in the 'building' of Canada. This position conveniently overlooked, it is true, the role mercantilism played in early British North America; those who espoused it usually pointed to the state's dominance of economic life in New France, suggesting that this state of affairs had done little to form *habitant* character.[25] These historians' understandings of community, wealth, and property were not without contradictions; it is possible that here they were expressing their own ambivalence towards late-nineteenth-century industrial capitalism. Certainly they frequently celebrated 'community' (albeit, as we shall see, in particularly gendered ways) as a beneficent force on the 'frontier.' Descriptions of bees, barn raisings, communal efforts to establish schools and churches, and of community entertainments run through their narratives of pioneer life in 'the townships.' Some of these descriptions were imbued with nostalgia for a simpler time, when people were 'contented and happy, for the rising generation are not so much as their forefathers; they have ideas that can never be realized.'[26] And the power of community loyalties as expressed through national efforts, such as fighting the War of 1812, went unquestioned. Furthermore, many of these writers were not afraid to highlight their ancestors' initial poverty on the 'frontier,' as their narratives are replete with tales of hardships and deprivation – all, of course, cheerfully born.[27] Yet the narratives celebrate those who, through thrift, sobriety, and industry, overcame the challenges of frontier life, those who managed to turn their log cabins and half-acres of crops into large, prosperous brick farmhouses with well-tended acres. Progress was to be measured by the spread of both privately owned homes and farms and private businesses; 'community' values were valued so long as they were confined to voluntary activities. It was no accident that these writers spent little time discussing the development of working-class organizations in British North America, that they did not find it appropriate to celebrate trade unions. Nor was it any accident that they found it difficult – for some, impossible – to understand Native attitudes towards private property.

Historical Narratives

The types of historical papers that were presented to the gatherings of the OHS, NHS, BHS, and the women's organizations can be categorized as belonging to three different kinds of narratives; elements of all three can be found in tales of Secord's walk. The first narrative is perhaps the best known and can be described as loyal service to the Crown and empire; into this category fell tales of Loyalist opposition to the Revolutionary government, Loyalist flight to Quebec, and the continuation of loyalty to Britain during the War of 1812. The next type of narrative was that of pioneer settlement and the development of social, economic, and political institutions. The third type of narrative, which often relied less on narrative structure and more on thematic approaches, was concerned with Native societies and Native-white contact. None of these narratives was told in isolation from the others, for they often overlapped and spilled into each other. The lessons of loyalty imbibed during the Revolution might determine the character of the communities and institutions built by Upper Canada's pioneers; they, in turn, met 'Indians' in the process of 'settling' the frontier; and the War of 1812 had been marked by the participation of Native allies such as Tecumseh.

Some societies, it is true, favoured some historical narratives more than others; the BHS was particularly fond of tales of Brant and the Mohawks' allegiance to the Crown in 1776. It also liked to discuss, however, Brantford's development as an important urban centre.[28] Other groups, such as the London and Middlesex Historical Society, were far more interested in tales of pioneer days than in commemorating the War of 1812; southwestern Ontario saw fewer battles than the Niagara Peninsula and no American occupation during the war.[29] As well, the fact that so much of the region had been settled by Anglo-American 'late loyalists' may have shaped their descendants' relative lack of interest in constructing an exclusionary loyalist mythology. And, by the 1920s, as Gerald Killan has pointed out, many historical societies were less caught up in fashioning stories of past military heroism, preferring instead to record the province's social history.[30]

Religious narratives often provided a cultural frame of reference for the coming of the Loyalists to Upper Canada. Those papers written between the 1890s and 1920 made implicit comparisons between the Loyalist experiences and those of the Israelites, with their repeated themes of persecution in the Thirteen Colonies, loss of home, flight, continuous wandering from place to place in the Canadian wilderness, and final resting place of exile in Upper Canada.[31] Another recurring theme in these papers was the stripping of personal goods, the loss of livestock, lands, agricultural equipment, and household goods, a process that extended down to the Loyalists' own bodies since some of them had their clothes taken from them. David Barker, whose genealogy was set out in the OHS papers in 1901, saw his family goods scattered on both sides of the border: his favourite arm-chair and the lady's saddle ended up in Toronto, his dishes in Napanee, and his chimney bricks in Picton.[32] This theme of loss might go further than just material goods. The Maclean family, whose tribulations were recorded in 1901, lost some of their children for a time, although they eventually rejoined their parents.[33] Yet another form of loss was that of community relations and institutions; in keeping with their desire to establish the Christian credentials of their subjects, many chroniclers of the Loyalists pointed to their most keenly felt lack of a church, both as the site of religious worship and as a central gathering place for New England communities.[34]

Since most of these narratives were told from the perspective of, or were about, male Loyalists, it was usually a *manly* dignity that survived the rapaciousness of the American government and their erstwhile neighbours. It was the losses and indignities suffered by Loyalist men, in many of these narratives, that were initially endured and eventually overcome. Unlike narratives of the War of 1812, it was not the bodies of men engaged in military victories that were celebrated; rather, it was a particular form of masculine endurance, ingenuity, and industry that rode out the sufferings of exile and rallied to build new homes and communities in the Canadian backwoods, creating a 'New Dominion' composed, as Janice MacKinnon points out, of the 'forefathers.'[35] National and imperial identities were grounded in these men, and discussions of the Canadian nation-state's formation were shaped by their authors' conceptions of late nineteenth-century gender relations.

Even though men such as David Barker occupied centre stage in these narratives, it was not possible to completely overlook Loyalist women. The Loyalist family also provided a framework for these constructions of the past. In addition to defending the Crown, Loyalist men had to defend their wives and children, if not from death, then from deprivation and poverty in the colonies and the physical hardships of exile. And it was as husbands and fathers that Loyalist men recreated communities in Upper Canada. In many of the narratives of flight and exile, women are shadowy figures and appear primarily as dependents to be protected. Given the authors' reliance on oral histories that had often been obtained second-hand, it may well be that the dominant narratives of Loyalism produced shortly after the Revolutionary War, ones in which women had been helpless dependents, influenced these reminiscences. Some historians, though, used the opportunity given to them by the centrality of family in these narratives to pay tribute to Anglo-Celtic Loyalist women's courage, strength of character, and determination. They insisted that women, too, had been inspirational historical actors in the exodus to Upper Canada, as worthy of commemoration as men. Then, as their accounts of Loyalism often segued into discussions of early pioneer life, they would expand upon this theme.[36]

Loyalism, of course, was not limited to Anglo-Celtic men and women. While today's historians of Loyalism have been quick to point out the exclusivity of the Loyalist myth and that it homogenized a fairly diverse group of refugees, at least some members of the historical societies regularly included Joseph Brant and the Six Nations in their discussions of Loyalists.[37] For the military historian Ernest Green, writing about the role played by Loyalist Indian commander Gilbert Tice, 'if the Six Nations had not taken the side of the King in the Revolutionary war there never would have been a Province of Upper Canada.' The Natives' 'fighting power' and the strategic location of their territory had proved a 'blessing' to Loyal colonists: 'so much, they, we owe to the alliance with the Six Nations.' But this was a latitude given to a particular group of First Nations and not to other, more threatening 'Indians.' Even these tributes to the Six Nations' contributions to the Loyalist cause were underpinned by racial discourses in which the figure of the savage 'Indian' always threatened to overtake the loyal, domesticated ally. Green, for example, described what violence and mayhem might have existed if the Six Nations had decided to side with the colonists; supplies would have been blocked from the upper St Lawrence 'in the teeth of hordes of hostile Indians, backed by the frontiersmen and militia of the Hudson and Ohio valleys.' And the Six Nations loyalty could be attributed, not to any innate moral propensity (as in the case of Anglo-Celtic Loyalists), but rather to the 'square deal' they received from Britain, particularly at the hands of Sir William Johnson, and because of Brant's 'controlling influence.' Brant's work 'reaffirmed the ancient alliance and kept the People-of-the-Long-House friendly to the British.' On other occasions, Tice and his fellow officers had to restrain his 'drunken and riotous' Native fighters from 'excess,' by which Green presumably meant the execution (white commentators preferred the term 'slaughter') of prisoners. During a 1781 expedition to the Mohawk Valley, the warriors (described by Green as the 'dregs of the tribe') struggled through a cold, wet October until they reached the enemy. 'Then, like a fiery blast, they swept through ... leaving a broad path of ruin in their wake.' Native warriors were thus a force of nature, elemental and volatile, lacking careful strategy but capable of fierce fighting and intimidation. On this and many other occasions, Green quoted approvingly Tice's satisfaction that the warriors abstained 'from unnecessary bloodshed,' contrary to their usual practices.[38]

The War of 1812

Narratives of the War of 1812 were similar to those of the Loyalists, particularly in their emphasis on the devotion shown to Britain by the colonists in resisting the American invasion. Again, a religious parallel was made: if the Loyalists resembled the Israelites, the colonists who fought off American invasion could be compared to Abraham, who kept the covenant made with Jehovah. They also pointed to the war as a critical moment in the development of a nascent Dominion of Canada; the process of nation-building begun by the arrival of the Loyalists was hastened by the war. The events of 1812 served as a crucible for these authors, one in which Canadian national identity was forged violently and swiftly. The war, argued Castell Hopkins, OHS president in 1910, 'brought Canadians of French and English and American extraction together in defence of their hearths and homes and laid in this way an almost invisible foundation for that seemingly vain vision – the permanent federal union of British America for purposes of common interest, defence and government.'[39] No matter that, like their treatment of the Loyalists, this analysis of the War of 1812 was teleological or that it treated events in the Canadas – particularly in the Niagara Peninsula – as being representative of the 'Canadian' experience of national identity. While historian Carl Berger has pointed to the narrowness and parochial nature of many of these narratives, for these historians local events held meanings that transcended the specificities of place.[40] As will be discussed in chapter 9, it was in the local setting, amongst significant historical landscapes, that the 'essence' of the nation could be found – just as, for their English counterparts, the 'core' of English national identity could be discovered in the English village or in the halls of Westminster.[41]

Attempts to separate the two historical phenomena – the invention of a Loyalist mythology and that of devotion to Britain – can result in overstating these distinctions, for they were closely linked in the minds of their creators and often they were narrated by the same individuals and groups. Yet it is worth considering that certain precepts of the war's mythology may have elicited even more support and had a wider appeal. One very simple and obvious reason is that the War of 1812 was less exclusive as a narrative of nation-building than the Loyalist arrival. The efforts of the UELs to trace 'Loyalist' descent meant that bloodlines might take precedence over character traits such as devotion to Britain; as we shall see, Secord's supporters had to elide this tendency in order to establish her Loyalist credentials. While, of course, it helped to have ancestors who had fought against the Americans (certainly some commemorators liked to dwell on this point), it was not as essential for those of British descent who had arrived after the war; they could claim their ancestors' imperial membership as a way of tying their heritage to that of Upper Canada. Matters were more difficult for those commemorators who had either arrived later or had ties to the United States. Even their status, though, was not an insurmountable problem. Such individuals could – and did – depict themselves as more self-consciously loyal Upper Canadians than their neighbours whose grandfathers fought at Lundy's Lane.[42]

Basing patriotism and loyalty on heroic deeds, and not primarily on descent, also helped widen their appeal in other ways. While the UELs had forged, it was said, a successful society in the wilderness, the heroism of their story was muted by their initial military defeat in the Thirteen Colonies. Ontario historians, a group who had seen an upsurge in military and 'patriotic' sentiment during the Riel Rebellion and then in recruitment for the Boer War, often found tales of armed heroism in the not-too-distant past an ongoing source of inspiration.[43] And the War of 1812 allowed for the creation of even more specific individual heroes, such as Brock, Tecumseh, and Secord, than did the Loyalists. With a few exceptions, Loyalist heroes and heroines were often, like the pioneers, composed of a mass of individuals who were not well known outside their locality. The collective efforts of the UEL Association and the historical societies turned these individuals into historical archetypes – much like the 'unknown warriors' commemorated after the First World War.[44]

To be sure, the loyal militia of 1812, the men who fought for British officers such as Brock and FitzGibbon, also served much the same function as the anonymous Loyalists. But while there were parallels between these two groups (and often one was posited as the descendant of the other), the dominant mode of narratives about the war was romanticism. As Hopkins told the OHS, 'the history of this country was, in fact, one of the most romantic and striking in the world,' a quality that historical societies should appreciate and foster. In fact, 'historical societies should be everywhere but they could only spread and succeed by making history appear interesting, vivid, life-like; the struggles of real people upon the checker-board of nations; the lives of individual heroes fighting for great objects, with real and tangible feelings, personal pluck and clear purpose.'[45] While it was this very quality that drew the scorn and amusement of twentieth-century university-based male historians, who believed that romantic desire and not 'hard facts' made these histories suspect, full of biases, and overtly sentimental, romanticism permitted these historians both to provide a founding national myth and to create heroes such as Brock. The War of 1812 had been not just a critical and cathartic moment in Canadian history, it had also been marked by the presence of extraordinary men who had displayed moral bravery, physical courage, and a Christian willingness to sacrifice themselves for a larger cause: Upper Canadian inviolability and the imperial tie.

The process of turning Brock into the personification of those who had fought and sacrificed in the war was undertaken in the decades just after 1812 and continued with even greater fervour in the 1890s and 1900s, both in the biographies but also in the lesser-known historical society reports.[46] It helped, too, that for those eager to merge British imperialism and Canadian nationalism, Brock as a symbol neatly combined the two. Originally from Jersey, Brock had served with the British army in various early outposts of empire, and ended his military career with his death on Upper Canadian soil. In a vein both similar and different to the commemorations of Brock, the Shawnee chief Tecumseh was also honoured as a stalwart and moral leader, capable of exercizing charismatic leadership over both Aboriginals and Europeans. As we shall explore in the Epilogue, the mythologizing of Tecumseh was always underpinned by colonial ambivalence; he remained a more marginal figure than Brock, particularly because he had kept his distance from white society. Yet the oft-told meeting between Brock and Tecumseh in 1812 when Tecumseh, struck by Brock's 'commanding figure and fine countenance,' is reported to have declared, 'This is a man,' was used to suggest the similarities between the two men and that, despite being an 'Indian,' Tecumseh was capable of recognizing and appreciating heroic British manliness. For his part, Brock is reported to have said of Tecumseh: '... a more sagacious or gallant warrior does not exist. He was the admiration of every one who conversed with him.'[47]

As well as the use of romantic heroism as a narrative device and its deployment around individuals, these writers also elaborated on earlier versions of the 'militia myth.' A crucial, indeed essential, aspect of this myth was that of Upper Canadian men's bodies being engaged in not just flight and stoic struggle but the same kind of physical heroism as Brock. This distinction should not, though, be seen as one that *replaced* Loyalist manliness; rather, it built upon the latter in order to deepen and enrich the virtues and moral probity of Upper Canadian manhood. But, to no small extent, the men of the War of 1812 had redeemed the military defeat of their Loyalist fathers. They had shown themselves capable of expressing physical aggression, albeit in defence of home, country, and empire.[48]

Narratives in which the central historical event was military service, written during and about a period in which armed combat was widely understood as inherently masculine, did pose certain problems, of course, for women historians. As we shall see, for women such as Curzon and Currie, celebrating Secord was a central and important response to the issue of gendered differences in both past and present contexts. Certainly some male historians, such as Ernest Cruikshank and D.B. Read, devoted vast – perhaps inordinate – amounts of time to the war to the general exclusion of all other historical events and themes.[49] Yet male historians did not completely ignore women's participation in the war (although it did not spark the same interest as details of military manoeuvres), and military narratives also received considerable attention from both men and women, *including* the women's organizations. It was no accident of historical curiosity, for example, that the first set of WCHS reports began with an account of the 'historic' banner sewed by the women of York (to be specific, women of the city's elite families).[50] This and other accounts of the War of 1812 attempted to fix clearly the link between Upper Canadian women and their descendants (literal and figurative) and loyal imperial service.[51]

The Pioneer Past

While courageous sacrifices had been made by the Anglo-Celtic 'settlers' of Upper Canada during the American Revolution and the War of 1812, the 'pioneers' of the late eighteenth and early nineteenth centuries had also performed similar feats of loyalty. As previously pointed out, narratives of Loyalist settlement, with their focus on the family, opened up the possibility that women's lives would be valued as much as men's and their contributions to nation-building prized. Such was also the case (perhaps even more so) when the subjects were not examined through the lens of Loyalist history. However, treating women as historical actors did not mean that pioneer men were forgotten. Many of these historians approached the issue of gender relations from an organic perspective, concentrating on the complementarity of and harmony between men and women in pioneer communities. In the historical accounts, pioneer masculinity was understood as being shaped by men's need to provide for their families, by their identities as husbands and fathers. Such men's experiences, it was argued, had been marked initially by hard physical labour, as they cleared bush, put up buildings, and built fences to delineate their possessions, tasks they undertook cheerfully no matter what their previous occupations had been. The men who had settled at Fergus, near Guelph, had in their homeland of Scotland been trained 'for teaching, practicing law and other vocations,' yet they set to 'hew out of the wilds of North America a home for themselves and future generations.'[52] Yet masculinity was not defined merely by physical industriousness, as these men then proceeded to take on positions of economic, political, and social leadership.[53] In addition to these accomplishments, others demonstrated a knack for carrying out the work of colonialism at local and informal levels. Catherine White's husband had been well

respected by the local 'Indians, whom he managed very well,' and Joseph
Thomas advised Brant on leasing land that belonged to the Six Nations,
with fortuitous results for Brant's people.[54] Still others, as we shall see,
came to the rescue when their families were endangered by the actions
of threatening 'Indians.'

That so many of these accounts were redolent with the Loyalist myth of
formerly prosperous ancestors who rallied speedily to the challenges of
their new environment is, of course, hardly surprising; it has been pointed
out by others.[55] Few historians, though, have demonstrated much interest in this myth's gendered and racial dynamics. These men displayed in
abundance the hallmarks of Victorian manliness: industry, self-reliance,
commitment to both family and community, and the capacity to lead and
command without becoming tyrannical. This latter quality was, of course,
extremely important, for many of these historians were interested in
constructing a history of struggle towards common ends and goals and
could not readily admit that relations of power, of inequality and oppres-
sion, had structured pioneer life. They were willing to admit that certain
hierarchies had existed, but a beneficent paternalism had prevented any
real injustices from occurring. For example, Joseph Thomas had brought
two slaves, a husband and wife, with him, who had worked for him in
return for his 'care.'[56]

Did men's and women's accounts of 'life in the bush' differ? On one
level, no. Women historians were just as interested in constructing and
celebrating manly pioneers as their male counterparts. And some male
historians were as eager to pay tribute to foremothers as to forefathers in
their constructions of the pioneer past.[57] However, while women's narratives were at times tinged with nostalgia, they were far less likely to treat
the pioneer past with the kinds of longing evident in some of their male
counterparts' writing. Unlike historian John May's desire for the more
sociable world of the bush that he contrasted to 'our more formal and
less hospitable age,'[58] women historians frequently saw the woman pioneer as having directly shaped and contributed to the progress of the
modern age: a female archetype in whom, no matter how teleologically,
was embodied the qualities that had been passed down to today's modern women. While the pioneer past was to be commemorated with great
respect, and while the pioneers' traits and habits were worthy of emulation, it was not an era to which women should hope to return, forswear-
ing their 'Ladies' Colleges' in favour of dragging pails of sap through
snowdrifts, a point which made the gendered dimensions of modernity
quite clear.

Furthermore, women historians also tended to foreground and concentrate upon the work performed by pioneer wives and mothers to a much greater extent than their male counterparts.[59] Not only had women's unpaid labour provided both health care and a degree of social welfare to their communities, matching men's official roles, the pioneer mother (usually synonymous with the pioneer woman) had shaped the nation's future by educating her children. In these accounts, women historians attempted to create pioneer women as historical subjects, with identities, goals, and motivations. As London historian Amelia Poldon wrote, 'the strong personality of the mother, her noble ambitions, her strict adherence to the principles of honour and justice, her persistent efforts for the uplift of her family and the community in which she lived were a noble heritage for her children, and in the majority of the citizens of Canada today, who are descendants of our pioneer families, we find them men and women who live to make the world better; they are loyal to God and country, and those principles of Righteousness and Freedom that uplift a nation.'[60] In many women historians' narratives, the women of the past were models for Canadian women in the present, whether in a self-conscious women's rights manner or as a reminder that such foremothers, and their descendants, were deserving of respect from these women's contemporaries and were part of the story of nation and empire.

But the representation of pioneer women as moulders of empire was not the only way in which colonial relations shaped these narratives. The pioneer past had also been marked by the presence of Native people. As has been pointed out, being able to control relations with Aboriginal people was one of the hallmarks of a pioneer man; generally this control was described as having been exercized in a benevolent and paternalistic mode (and it is worth remembering that some of these men were said to have commanded Native warriors during the Revolution). While at times men might encounter a threatening situation, or be made uncomfortable by the activities of Aboriginal peoples, their manly authority was not seriously at risk. For women, however, their relationship to colonial power was more complicated and became more of a problem. They might be entrusted with the running of the farm during a husband's absence, but they were not given any forms of official authority.

In attempting to grapple with the presence of Natives during periods of white settlement, the historical societies displayed a great degree of imperialist ambivalence.[61] Like their counterparts in military conflicts, 'Indians' could smooth the paths of those attempting to find their way in the wilderness, providing human bridges between the potential terrors of the forest and the accoutrements of civilization. Mary Warren Breckenridge's mother's flight to Canada, retold by Catherine F. Lefroy, was given added drama by the family's becoming lost in the woods. Seeing smoke and walking towards it, their arrival at an Indian campsite was heralded first by barking dogs and then by the appearance of an Indian. 'He proved to be a chief, and very politely invited them into his wigwam. They gladly accepted the invitation, and mother often speaks of that, to her, delightful night in the bark wigwam, with the blazing logs on one side and the hole at the top, where, as she lay on her bed of hemlock boughs and bear skins, she saw the stars twinkling down on them. The Indians were very hospitable, giving up with great politeness the half of their wigwam to the strangers.'[62] In such accounts, the person with whom whites have contact is often not a 'common' member of the tribe but rather a 'chief,' a figure in whom nobility of character and generosity towards whites are often vested.

Some narratives featured anecdotes, a favoured methodology of these historians, in which Natives are portrayed as potentially troublesome but, in the end, harmless nuisances, rather than actual threats.[63] In such passages, Natives were constructed as effeminate and childlike, infantilized for their fascination with women's clothes and their inability to understand the rules of private property and the sanctity of domestic space (private property, as I have argued, was an important signifier of successful colonial expansion). Yet 'Indians' could not only impinge upon whites' hospitality, they could also transmogrify from bothersome juveniles to more threatening figures with the potential for physical violence. One Sunday, while Breckenridge's mother and aunt were alone, a group of 'Indians' arrived at their farmhouse bearing furs and demanding whiskey. The women refused to supply them with alcohol, whereupon they 'became so urgent and insolent and so constantly increasing in number that they became terrified and sent the French girl to beg my grandfather to return' (he had gone to visit a neighbour). When their servant came back, she was even more frightened, telling her employers that she had seen 'squaws' hiding knives in their camp, supposedly a common practice when their men were drunk. As well, the Native women had chased her back to the house. From that point on, the story became even more heavily laden with images of threatened and besieged white Christian womanhood:

> Some of the Indians were intoxicated before they came to the house, and their threats were awful. They had collected to the number of forty, and

those poor girls still held out stoutly in refusing the whiskey, which was kept beneath a trapdoor in the kitchen, in a sort of little cellar. At length my aunt thought of the large, handsome family Bible, in two volumes, in which they had been reading, and opened them and pointed out the pictures to try and attract their attention, while my mother knelt down at the other end of the table and prayed to God loudly and earnestly. In this position my grandfather found them, and fearful was the shock to him.

But even white masculine intervention (neither the grandfather's nor God's) was not enough to quell the 'Indians,' who became increasingly primordial and collectivized in this narrative. After one of the group threatened to kill the neighbour who had arrived with the grandfather, on the grounds that he had killed his brother, the latter acquiesced to their demand for whiskey. 'Nothing else probably saved their lives.' Other white male settlers were called in, and the two women slipped into a small room 'inside my grandfather's [a striking piece of spatial symbolism], while he and his friends kept watch, and those horrid creatures set to for a regular orgy. There was a great kettle of food for hounds on the fire, made of bran and potato peelings and all sorts of refuse. This they ate up clean and clever; then they drank, danced and sang all night long, and in the morning off they went, to the relief and joy of the family.'[64] Although Breckenridge's story reversed the setting of nineteenth-century captivity narratives, with the Euro-Canadian home and not the Native encampment becoming the scene of white women's entrapment, it clearly made use of those tales' central symbol: besieged and pure white womanhood threatened by Aboriginal men's bestial savagery.[65]

At the hands of these historians, Native peoples in the past could 'become' any number of entities: romantic and charismatic heroes dedicated to racial and imperial uplift; individuals who welcomed whites into their midst, providing spaces that not only approximated but in some ways superseded white domesticity; mischievous tricksters who might annoy but not seriously disrupt whites' lives; and, finally, a bestial, subhuman mass whose presence became more threatening as it multiplied. In these narratives, 'Indians' were unstable figures whose identities might shift and who lacked solid and fixed values, the essence of colonial identity. Thus the work of colonialism could be justified by its attempts to secure, not just socio-economic and political institutions, but also the subjectivities and identities of Aboriginal peoples – although this project never completely achieved its aims. And by including Native peoples in their accounts of Canadian history, these historians were able to stake out an identity both Canadian and imperial, one linked to, but also distinguished from, that of Britain's. Moreover, for Anglo-Celtic middle-class women, who were themselves in many ways defined as others in Canadian society (through medical, legal, and, in some contexts, religious discourses), claiming the historian's authority that allowed them to pronounce upon Native peoples was also a means of asserting their own historical subjectivity and their contemporary status as imperial subjects. Their work on Natives, particularly Native men, who had been historical actors and subjects but who had become subjected (a reversal of what these women believed to have been their own sex's fate), affirmed their capacity to speak and write as 'civilized' individuals, akin to Anglo-Celtic men. Through history, these women could participate in the larger projects of modern nation-building and imperialism.[66]

Laura Secord

What, then, did all of this mean for the narratives of Secord's walk? First, the campaign to memorialize her cannot be said to have been strictly 'women's work,' since male historians supported and, at times, participated in it. Nevertheless, it was women such as Curzon and Currie who wrote the most extensive histories of Secord. Furthermore, narratives of Secord's contribution to the British cause were, no less than other creations of the historical societies, marked by the interplay of locality, nationality, gender, and imperialism. They usually opened by exploring Laura and James Secord's backgrounds and tracing their genealogies, thus placing them within the Loyalist tradition of suffering and sacrifice. For those writers who were concerned with strict historical accuracy, such a task was considerably easier for the Secords than for Laura's family, the Ingersolls. James's male ancestors had fought in the Revolutionary War for the British, and the many military ranks held by the Secord men were duly listed and acclaimed. Moreover, the Secords could claim as part of their history both allegiance to the British Crown and a desire for the protection of the British Constitution; they were descended from Huguenots who arrived in New York from La Rochelle in the late seventeenth century.[67]

But it was not only the Secord men who had served their country and suffered hardships. The Loyalist legacy inherited by both Laura and James had, it was pointed out, been marked by gender differences. As Curzon told her audiences, James Secord's arrival in Canada had been as a three-year-old refugee; he had been part of his mother's 'flight through the wilderness,' with four other homeless women and many children, to escape the fury of a band of ruffians who called themselves the 'Sons of Liberty.' After enduring frightful hardships for nearly a month, they finally arrived at 'Fort Niagara almost naked and starving.' Curzon went on to comment that these were by no means 'uncommon experiences,' for Loyalist men frequently had to flee 'for their lives' and leave their women and children behind (as well as their 'goods, chattels, estates, and money'). Their loved ones were then left to endure the terrors of the wilderness

> unprotected and unsupported, save by that deep faith in God and love of King and country which, with their personal devotion to their husbands, made of them heroines whose story of unparalleled devotion, hardships patiently born, motherhood honourably sustained, industry and thrift perseveringly followed, enterprise successfully prosecuted, principle unwaveringly upheld, and tenderness never surpassed, has yet to be written, and whose share in the making of this nation remains to be equally honored with that of the men who bled and fought for its liberties.[68]

Unfortunately for Laura's popularizers, the Ingersoll family did not fit as neatly into the Loyalist tradition. Her father, Thomas, had fought against the British in 1776 and had seen his 1793 land grant cancelled as the result of British officials' efforts to curb large-scale immigration of American settlers.[69] As J.H. Ingersoll noted in his 1926 OHS paper, 'The Ancestry of Laura Ingersoll Secord,' Laura's inability to claim the United Empire Loyalist pedigree 'has been commented upon.'[70] However, some historians argued that Thomas Ingersoll came to Upper Canada at Simcoe's request.[71] For those poets and novelists, such as John Price-Brown, who felt free to create Laura's loyalism in a more imaginative manner, her patriotism was traced to a long-standing childhood attachment to Britain. They insisted that she chose Canada freely and was not forced to come to the country (many of these writers felt free to also claim that 'Canada,' often construed as Ontario, Quebec, and the Maritimes, existed as a national entity in the late eighteenth century) as a refugee.[72] Moreover, despite these historians' fascination with lines of blood and birth, they were as equally determined to demonstrate that these could be transcended by environment and force of personality. Laura's commitment to Britain was yet another reminder to the Canadian public that a sense of imperial duty could overcome other relationships and flourish in the colonial context.

Therefore, these historians argued, it should come as no surprise that both Laura and her husband felt obliged to perform their patriotic duty when American officers were overheard planning an attack on the British forces of Lieutenant FitzGibbon. This act of patriotic eavesdropping was explained by the presence of billeted American officers in the Secord home; some historians claimed that they had been rude to the Secords' black servants and thus Secord, who was protecting the servants from their abuse, had taken over their duties and was nearby. (Secord's own account, we should remember, had been silent on this issue.) In some histories, it was James who heard them, and, in others, Laura. James was still suffering from wounds sustained at the Battle of Queenston Heights, and it therefore fell to Laura – over her husband's objections and concerns for her safety – to walk the twenty miles from Queenston to warn the British troops at Beaver Dams. Here the linear chronology of the narratives was frequently interrupted to explain that Laura had come to his aid after the battle when, finding him badly wounded and in danger of being beaten to death by 'common' American soldiers, she had attempted to shield him with her own body from their rifle butts. In some narratives, the Secords were finally saved by the intervention of American officers, proof that not all members of the enemy were brutes, although in Price-Brown's account American personal grudges overrode even an officer's duty, when an officer whom Laura had rejected in favour of James refused to intervene. But whatever role the Americans played, this incident was further evidence that Laura was no stranger to wifely and patriotic duty.[73]

Her journey took on wider dimensions and greater significance in the hands of Secord's commemorators. It was no longer just a walk to warn the British; instead, with its elements of venturing into the unknown, physical sacrifice, and devotion to the British values of order and democracy, Secord's walk symbolized the entire pioneer woman's experience in Canadian history. Leaving the cozy domesticity and safety of her home, the company of her wounded husband, children, and loyal servants, Secord ventured out into the Upper Canadian wilderness. Some of these historians contrasted the settled nature of the Niagara Peninsula of the late nineteenth and early twentieth centuries – the beauty of fertile agricultural land, the spires and tall chimneys of manufacturing villages, and those stupendous pieces of modern engineering, the locks of the Welland Canal – with the wilderness of 1813, with its swamps and underbrush, in which threatening creatures, such as rattlesnakes, bears, and wolves, might lurk. A few historians chose to comment on the beauty of the landscape. Curzon's 1887 play, for example, which was one of the better-known celebrations of Secord, includes several monologues delivered by Secord that were meditations on the loveliness of the June woodland. However, even the tranquillity of Curzon's forest was disrupted by the howling of wolves.[74]

But most serious of all, in the majority of the accounts, was the threat of the 'Indians' whom she might meet on the way. If Secord's commitment to Canada and Britain had previously been presented in cultural terms, ones that could be encouraged by the colonial tie and that might transcend race, it was at this point that her significance as a symbol of white Canadian womanhood was clearest. While her feminine fragility had been the subject of comment throughout the stories, and while her racial background might have been the underlying subtext for this fragility, it was in the discussions of the threat of Native warriors that her gender became most clearly racialized. Like the women in the narrative of pioneer society, her fears were not as much of sexual violence by Native men (at least not explicitly) as they were of the tactics supposedly used by Native men in warfare (scalping being the most obvious one).

Some stories mentioned that Secord had had to stay clear of open roads and paths 'for fear of Indians *and* white marauders' (emphasis added).[75] But even those that downplayed her fear of a chance encounter with an 'Indian' during her journey were scrupulous in their descriptions of her fright upon encountering Mohawks outside the British camp. As described in chapter 5, Secord herself had stated that she had stumbled across the Mohawks' camp and that they had shouted 'woman' at her, making her 'tremble' and giving her an 'awful feeling.' It was only with difficulty, she said, that she convinced them to take her to FitzGibbon. As this meeting with the Natives was retold, they became more menacing and inspired even greater fear in Secord. In these accounts, at this penultimate stage in her journey she steps on a twig that snaps and startles the Indian encampment. Quite suddenly Secord is surrounded by Indians, and 'the chief throws up his tomahawk to strike, regarding the intruder as a spy.'[76] In some narratives, he shouts at her, '"Woman! what does woman want!" Only by her courage in springing to his arm is the woman saved, and an opportunity snatched to assure him of her loyalty.'[77]

Moved by pity and admiration, the chief gives her a guide, and at length she reaches FitzGibbon, delivers and verifies her message – 'and faints.'[78] FitzGibbon then goes off to fight the Battle of Beaver Dams, armed with the knowledge that Secord has brought him and manages to successfully rout the American forces. In a number of narratives, this victory is achieved by using the threat of unleashed Indian savagery when the Americans are reluctant to surrender.[79] While the battle is being fought, Secord is moved to a nearby house, where she sleeps off her walk, and then returns to the safety of her home and family. She tells her family about her achievement but, motivated by fear for their security (as American troops continue to occupy the Niagara area), as well as by her own modesty and self-denial, she does not look for any recognition or reward. Such honours come first to FitzGibbon.[80]

Like other historical narratives, these tales of Secord were imbued with their authors' concerns with the relations of gender, class, and race and the way in which they perceived these identities to structure both Canadian society and history. For one, Secord's 'natural' feminine fragility was a major theme of their writings. As a white woman of good birth and descent, she was not physically suited to undertake the hardships involved in her walk (although, paradoxically, as a typical 'pioneer woman' she was able to undertake the hardships of raising a family and looking after a household in a recently settled area). Her delicacy and slight build, first mentioned by FitzGibbon in his own testimony of her walk,[81] were frequently stressed by those who commemorated her, thus contrasting her physical frailty with the manly size and strength of British soldiers such as FitzGibbon and Brock. Nevertheless, the seeming physical immutability of gender was not an insurmountable barrier to her patriotic duty to country and empire. The claims of the latter transcended corporeal limitations. Even her maternal duties, understood by both conservatives and many feminists in late nineteenth-century Canada to be the core of womanly identity, could be put aside or even reformulated in order to answer her country's needs. In Curzon's play, Secord is asked by her sister-in-law, the Widow Secord, if her children will not 'blame' her should she come to harm. She replies that 'children can see the right at one quick glance,' suggesting that their mother's maternal care and authority are bound to her patriotism and loyalty.[82]

Furthermore, in making Secord appealing and as a reflection of their own conceptions of 'Canadian womanhood,' there were other ways in which historians constructed her image. Many of them created Secord as an icon of respectable white heterosexual femininity. Anecdotes that were supposedly told by her family were often added to the end of the narratives of her walk, especially those written by women. These tales stressed her love of children, her kindness and charity towards the elderly, her solicitude for her black servants, and also her very feminine love of finery and gaiety (making her daughters' satin slippers, for example, and her participation as a young woman in balls given by the Simcoes at Newark). The clothing that she wore upon her walk was discussed. Her daughter Harriet told Currie that she and her sisters saw her leave that morning, wearing 'a flowered print gown, I think it was brown with orange flowers.'[83] Elizabeth Thompson, who was active within both the Ontario Historical Society and the Niagara Historical Society and was also a member of the IODE, wrote that Secord wore a print dress; she added a 'cottage bonnet tied under her chin ... balbriggan stockings, with red silk clocks on the sides, and low shoes with buckles' (both shoes were lost during the walk).[84]

As we shall see, much of this material was used by authors of Canadian history textbooks and children's readers; it was also used and elaborated upon by other writers. John Price-Brown's *Laura the Undaunted: A Canadian Historical Romance*, published by Ryerson Press in 1930, offered readers an even more independent-minded Secord whose loyalties to 'Canada' were formed at a very early age upon meeting General Burgoyne and Joseph Brant in her family's Barrington home. Her memory of these encounters is evoked while she is gazing on miniatures of her dead mother and George III, thus compelling Secord to insist that her father take the family to Upper Canada.[85] As well, Secord's fitness for her later exploits is foretold during her family's voyage to Upper Canada. She answers a reproach from a male friend who is saddened that she is not spending more time with him, with 'I don't see why, for on this trip I'm not a girl any longer, but only a boy, like the rest of you.' Secord tells her friend that they are similar to 'soldiers on the march.' Although she becomes tired and footsore during their tramp through the woods, she enjoys herself, and the young men draw lots to follow her, admiring her 'steady, regular step ... her trim figure ... [and] the ease with which she carried her burden, despite the warm weather.'[86] At dinner, while all prepare the food, it is Secord who sets out the damask tablecloth and then sings 'a dainty woodland ditty' from *As You Like It*.[87]

Later in the book, she refuses a proposal of marriage from her cousin, David Ingersoll, because he will not move to the Upper Canadian woods, in which she is very happy, despite being the 'solitary white woman' in a thousand-mile radius (Ingersoll insists instead on returning to Massachusetts).[88] Ingersoll later appears in the novel at the Battle of Queenston Heights, where he fails to protect James Secord from being battered by two American soldiers. Laura, who had already expressed anxiety about the fate of women and children at the hands of the invading force ('what of the women and children? ... We cannot have them shot down like rats.

The women could fight if they have guns; but not the children'), rushes in to shield her husband, calling the soldiers 'Brutes! Cowards!'[89] Secord's reunion with her 'American cousin' ends on a defiantly patriotic (if not terribly familial) note. He asks her why the Canadians are bothering to 'hold out,' since they 'can't win,' a prediction that Secord denies vehemently. Faced with her defiance, David Ingersoll leaves his cousin and Canada – for good.[90] Price-Brown had a distinct taste for thwarted romance, as he then proceeds to describe a doomed love affair between Tecumseh and one of the Secords' older daughters (a match that did not meet with Laura's approval). Their engagement was ended, of course, by Tecumseh's death at the Battle of Moraviantown.[91]

Price-Brown's heroine thus emerges as a paragon of Canadian pioneer womanhood: physically fearless and hardy, loyal to her country and family, sensible of the benefits of her 'British' heritage, and equally 'at home' in the elite society of Newark as she was in the Upper Canadian bush with her Huron companions. In Merrill Denison's 1931 radio play 'Laura Secord,' a similar picture emerges. Denison characterizes his protagonist as 'a cultivated woman of much charm and beauty ... sought by American officers when in Queenston to act as their informal hostess, although both she and her husband are known as rabid loyalists.'[92] This Secord is a decidedly firm, albeit caring and fair, white mistress to her two black servants, Pete and Floss; she also tends faithfully to her bed-ridden husband. But it is her demeanour towards the American officers that allows Denison to add an extra dimension to the Secord legend: that of the diplomat and would-be spy. These roles are quite explicitly gendered not only female but also middle-class and white. As a paragon of genteel white womanhood (fig. 6.1) (remember her skilful management of black servants), the 'hostess' Secord is able to disarm the officers. She serves them a delicious meal and deflects their observations that Canada should join the United States by offering the household's prized thirty-year-old cherry brandy (telling them that 'my husband would be furious if he knew').[93] In other ways, too, she exercises great tact and diplomacy, keeping Pete away from them, for example, after an officer – originally from Maryland – verbally abuses him; she also counsels James to be patient and quiet as she suspects the officers are planning something.[94] Yet it is Pete who awakes the Secords two nights later, telling them that Queenston is 'full of Yankees,' and it is James who grasps the significance of certain clues, all pointing to an attack on Beaver Dams. Pete begs to be sent to FitzGibbon but is instead sent to bed while Laura, telling James 'what is a fifteen-mile walk?' insists on going.[95]

6.1 Illustration by Lawrence Smith from Merrill Denison's radio-play script, 'Laura Secord.'

Although she keeps off the trails 'for fear of Indians and American scouts,' Secord is only 'fatigued,' not terrified, upon meeting the Mohawks, who have already deduced by the noise of her skirts that it is a woman coming up to their camp.[96] FitzGibbon and Dominique Ducharme, the captain of the Kahnawake Mohawks, are amazed by Secord's bravery.[97] Upon leaving the officers, Secord asks them if they had already heard her news, to which they reply that 'we might have had an inkling of something in the wind, but that in no way detracts from your courageous deed ... nor our opinion of it.'[98] In all probability, Denison was responding to contemporary attacks on Secord's legend which, as we shall see, were being mounted at the time. His introductory notes state that 'the plays [are] reasonably accurate from the standpoint of historical veracity, but I confess to having been more interested in dramatic development than with historical minutiae, although, in certain instances, dramatic possibilities have had to be scarified in the interests of historical fact.'[99]

Historical Revisionism: W.S. Wallace

To present-day readers, all these narratives might seem to be so much invented tradition, their telling subject to revision and embellishment. Yet it is probably fair to point out that, for their narrators, they represented the 'truth.' Many writers recognized that both historical fact and legend were being created in this process, that Secord was, like many other historical figures, 'larger than life,' the repository of a number of fantasies, fears, and desires. For Price-Brown and Denison, then, marrying historical to fictional or dramatic narrative was a logical use of a story that had already reached mythic proportions. Yet her supporters could also remind their readers that Secord had been an 'actual' figure, a flesh-and-blood woman, one whose former home could be seen and whose descendants could be consulted in order to achieve the degree of authenticity needed for her commemoration. Thus it was not her authenticity as a historical figure that was attacked in 1932 by the University of Toronto librarian and historian W.S. Wallace; instead, it was the meaning and significance of the walk itself.

Wallace began his 'dethroning' of Secord with an acknowledgment that he was tampering with a national symbol:

> Few episodes in Canadian history have gained a wider fame, or touched more deeply the popular imagination, than the story of Laura Secord's journey ... Nor is this surprising. The story has a romantic quality such as

endears it even to the hard heart of the professional historian; it illustrates
in a dramatic way the patriotism of the Canadian loyalists during the War of
1812; and it is typical of the heroism of the mothers and daughters of the
Upper Canadian pioneers.[100]

Wallace thus recognized the strength of the historical societies' narrative
typologies and the ways in which Secord encapsulated their elements. Yet
no less than Secord's commemorators, professional historians had their
own moral responsibilities and obligations. Wallace was not alone in his
doubts: 'within recent years, however, there has been evident among
historical scholars a tendency to regard the story of Laura Secord with
some skepticism.' He went on to cite three other writers, Colonel William
Wood, L.L. Babcock, and Dr Milo M. Quaife, who believed that Secord's
contribution had been negligible, indeed non-existent.[101] He set out the
documents in which FitzGibbon and Secord made their claims (his 1837
deposition, the 1839 and 1841 ferry and pension petitions, and her 1853
account from the *Anglo-American Magazine*) and then moved to Lossing's
and Coffin's histories.[102] Wallace now contrasted the narratives of these
accounts with his own, based on Cruikshank's 'invaluable' collection of
documents; he argued that, based on military sources, 'Caughnawaga'
(Kahnawake) scouts had already informed FitzGibbon of the impending
attack and that, while FitzGibbon negotiated the American surrender,
Kahnawake warriors should receive credit for the victory, for it was they
who had done all the fighting.[103] Certainly Wallace was not trying to
completely deny that Secord had made her journey. He concluded that
Secord's 'picture of her encounter with the Indians has about it a strong
air of verisimilitude,' and that 'of her courage and patriotism there is not
question.' 'But truth compels one to say,' he continued, 'that the story
she told from memory in later years (and no doubt sincerely believed)
was seriously at variance with the facts, and that she played no part in
determining the issue of the battle at the Beaver Dams.'[104]

Wallace's argument was, on one level, based on the nature of historical
sources, the veracity and 'truth' of some records and the uncertain and
shifting nature of others. For Wallace, factual evidence resided in military archives: Colonel Boerstler's narrative, an American major's journal, and an 1815 Baltimore court of inquiry's findings.[105] In these writings
was to be found reality, not evidence that was less than, in Wallace's
words, 'first-class.' His main objection to Secord's and FitzGibbon's stories was that they were based on memory: a 'notoriously treacherous and
fallacious medium for the transmission of historical truth'; so that 'a

story told twenty-five years after the event is not likely to be as reliable as a story told at the time, especially when it lacks contemporary corroboration.' Wallace admitted that if 'such a story is not inconsistent with the known facts, as established by contemporary evidence, then it may be regarded as admissible. It is only when such a story is irreconcilable with the known facts that one is justified in questioning it.'[106]

But there was more to Wallace's objections than a simple preference for 'just the facts' in writing Canadian history, for his discussions of Secord's narratives, particularly her petitions, sought to discredit them by pointing out their venal nature. 'Mrs. Secord's statement of her services had a financial object – first, the lease of a ferry, and secondly, a pension. Consequently it is not likely that her story lost anything in the telling.' That the American military accounts may also have been shaped by various motives did not, it seems, occur to Wallace; productions of the official, legitimate – and, not coincidentally, masculine – discourse, they were not subjected to a similar critical scrutiny. Instead, the narratives of these men were accepted as the raw material of real historical truth. Wallace also told his audience that the Upper Canadian government 'was not impressed' and instead chose to either ignore Secord and her husband or reject her petition – yet another 'fact' that, it seemed, should persuade them of Secord's negligible role in the war.[107] Wallace also – possibly conveniently – chose to ignore the fact that the compiler of these military documents, Cruikshank himself, had claimed that Beaver Dams 'is indissolubly linked with the memory of one of the most patriotic and courageous women of any age and country.'[108] Cruikshank's *Fight in the Beechwoods* had recounted the Battle of Beaver Dams with Secord's walk as pivotal to the British success and described her as a 'principal actor' and 'one of the bravest and most loyal of Canadian women.'[109] (Cruikshank, it must be remembered, was treated by self-fashioned 'professionals' as a 'expert' and an 'authority' on the War.)

Wallace's immediate target may have been Secord, but his larger offensive was waged, as his pamphlet demonstrates, on the issues of historical methodology and epistemology. His inveighing against unreliable memory highlights an important means by which professional historians attempted to distinguish themselves from the amateurish 'others': their preference for the solid, weighty document found in the archives, as opposed to the supposedly ephemeral, insubstantial, and unverifiable reminiscences that many societies used (what present-day historians might call oral histories). This is not to argue that the latter may not have been filtered through layers of memory; altered by successive historical contexts that suppressed some accounts and encouraged the telling of others; and told with the help of particular tropes (such as 'welcoming Natives' or 'hardy struggle'). Indeed, my analysis of the Secord narratives has attempted to demonstrate these processes at work. But the production, collection, and retention of documentary sources did not take place at a level of scholarship so rarefied as to be unsoiled by these same processes – quite the contrary, as a number of scholars have shown.[110] Moreover, there was a central contradiction in Wallace's contention that those who had commemorated Secord were more interested in romantic myth-making than hard historical 'verisimilitude,' for at least until the late 1920s university libraries continued to request the historical societies' publications for their Canadian history collections.[111]

But Wallace's notions – however contradictory – of historical methodology and epistemology were no less shaped by gender than were those of the historical societies. It was not just that Secord's claims were based on her own and FitzGibbon's narratives. It was of Secord's own memory that Wallace was most sceptical, for in his writing a narrative shaped by 'memory' takes on a profoundly gendered meaning: it is fleeting, fickle, capricious, and self-interested, all qualities that had been assigned feminine meanings in Western philosophy.[112] Memory could only be trusted when found in the solid currency of a military document written by and presented to a particular group of men. And it was no coincidence that Wallace was not just the first self-styled 'professional' historian to seriously challenge the Secord story – he was also a male historian. And while there were other accounts of the War of 1812 and other historical figures no less suspect than Secord that Wallace could have scrutinized, he made a self-conscious choice to attack a female figure whose place in Canadian history had been secured primarily because of the work of women historians. As Donald Wright's work on the professionalization of Canadian history in the first half of the twentieth century shows, it was certainly no coincidence that the historical profession identified itself, and its work, as masculine and masculinist.[113] For most of the twentieth century, the playing field of Canadian academic history would be defined by its denial of romantic desire for the past (although archival research and documentary evidence also came to hold their own romantic allure) in favour of cool-headed, rational, scientific, and objective inquiry, qualities with a long-standing association with bourgeois manhood.[114] The realms of the fantastic, the anecdotal, and the downright quirky would be left to the so-called amateur historians, the antiquarians, genealogists, and the dabblers, many of whom were women –

6.2 Charles Comfort's vision of Secord: 'Laura Secord, the woman who made Confederation possible.'

6.3 Laura Second tells her story to Lieutenant James FitzGibbon, 1813. From
C.W. Jefferys, *Picture-Gallery of Canadian History* (1945).

although this division of intellectual labour was never as complete as
some historians (on either side of the divide) might have wished.

Wallace's attack on Secord did not go unnoticed, for her supporters
were quick to rebut his account – and not just as indignant supporters of
romantic nationalism. A lengthy article in *Saturday Night* cited an 1820
certificate of FitzGibbon's that was published in the NHS *Transactions* of
1924, a document that was more precise than the 1837 deposition. The
author (who was also responsible for the Peel Historical Series) claimed
that, furthermore, her detractors did not understand the 'nature of
secret information in warfare' and its transmission. But the desire to
'own' Secord also motivated this counter-attack, as the writer concluded
that 'justice should be done to this early Canadian heroine, for the
reason, among others, that through her father's settlement in 1805 on
the banks of the Credit as lessee of the Government House tavern, she

may fairly be regarded as a daughter of Peel.'[115] Other defences of Secord appeared, particularly in the Niagara area.[116] Yet, as we shall see in the next chapter, Wallace's denigration of Secord's contribution may have achieved at least some of his desired effect.

Conclusion

Narrative forms of historical memory imbued the past with certain kinds of meanings, ones dependent not merely on the subject matter chosen and the facts that were presented but also on the kinds of narratives that were written: romantic tales of flight and survival, military triumphs, and the hard work of creating prosperous communities. These narratives overlapped, and their key elements and characters spilled into one another, to no small extent because they were overdetermined by the relations of gender, imperialism, and national identities. Yet even these structural frameworks allowed for degrees of flexibility and mutability: women could be threatened and feeble creatures, on the one hand, brave and unyielding wives and mothers, on the other; First Nations could be heroic allies with whom racial reconciliation and harmony was a distinct possibility, as well as menacing and sinister adversaries. The centre of many of these narratives, however, that of bourgeois manliness, was for the most part fixed and constant. These contradictions and ambivalences were not just the result of individual historians' own outlooks on gender and race: they were part of Canadian society's discourses on the position and character of women and Natives, gender and colonialism. And the work of the historical societies, as we shall see, also helped shape the lessons of history taught to Ontario's schoolchildren.

Chapter Seven

Lessons in Loyalty:
Children's Texts and Readers

While the historical societies were crucial in shaping narratives of Ontario's past and lobbying various levels of government for historical preservation and commemoration, school texts and readers in Canadian history were also influential sites in the creation of historical memory. From at least the 1880s, history texts used in the elementary and secondary schools have attempted to fulfil a number of functions; in particular, they have been vehicles used to inculcate and develop national identity. The 'story' of Canada's past was often the imagined and desired narrative of her future. Of course, school texts and readers were not the only source of historical knowledge developed for students. As chapter 8 will show, historical plays and pageants written and staged for Ontario children, both within and outside the school, drew heavily on historical narratives to frame their displays of loyalty. As well, over the course of the twentieth century, historical museums, exhibits, and tourist sites became important places in which both adults and children were educated about the past.

Nevertheless, school texts and readers remain an important source in attempting to understand just what versions of the 'story of Canada' were presented to children. For many students, textbooks were an important, perhaps the first, genre that shaped their understanding of the past. Unlike the reports presented by the historical societies, which generally examined the specific and particular, the texts were intended to present the 'whole story' of Canada, to create entire narratives that culminated in the nation of 'today.'[1] Therefore these narratives allow us not only to track continuities and changes in Secord's story and image, they also lend themselves to an examination of their wider context, to see what relationship Secord's tale bore to other narratives and to representations of other historical actors.

Furthermore, the historical societies' relation to various levels of the Canadian state might be described as multi-layered and ambiguous, given the lack of continuity of state funding and the societies' consequent need to pressure the state to carry out preservation and historical conservation.[2] At the same time, however, the societies did the work of the nation-state through their creation of national narratives. By contrast, the relation of history texts to the state was far less ambiguous, for in Ontario their production and use were mediated by the provincial department (later ministry) of education, which worked to regulate the form and content of materials used by teachers. Texts purchased by school boards and used in classrooms had to win the state's stamp of approval. But texts, of course, were not produced in a vacuum. They were shaped, first, by the historical narratives that were available to their authors; and, second, by decision-making processes within the Ontario publishing industry. The stories that were told in school histories were a product of the debates among the various individuals and institutions involved. While in the Ontario context this is a narrative that generally has yet to be written, nevertheless it is possible to glimpse how the provincial state, the publishers, and, by the mid-twentieth century, various community groups debated the forms of representation that were deployed in textbooks. However, all of these parties simultaneously agreed that 'the nation' provided the major narrative framework in which these representations were embedded. To the 'textbook' we must add the 'reader,' a related but not identical vehicle for conveying historical information to younger children, a medium that has survived – albeit in a somewhat different format – in children's stories of today that tell the thrilling tale of Laura Secord and other heroes of the Canadian past.

The Texts and Their Authors

Ontario's historical textbooks, along with their counterparts in other humanities and social science disciplines, have attracted the attention of historians of education interested in such issues as Egerton Ryerson's promotion of the 'Irish readers,' the use of nineteenth-century American texts and their promotion of republicanism, and changes in pedagogical methods in Canada West.[3] Contemporary studies tend to focus on issues of 'bias' and 'prejudice' towards women, Aboriginal peoples, and racial and ethnic minorities, examining the inclusion and exclusion of particular groups and the types of language and visual imagery used to describe them.[4] Yet, apart from Viola Parvin's study of textbooks' authorization in nineteenth- and twentieth-century Ontario, which ends in 1950, there are no comprehensive studies of the production and regulation of textbooks in nineteenth- and twentieth-century Ontario, nor do we know much about the content of these works.[5]

Parvin's work provides a useful overview of the varied policies that governed textbook use. According to Parvin, the various approaches of the Ontario Department of Education towards texts can be roughly divided into three stages: the nationalistic and more centralized control of Conservative George W. Ross's tenure as minister during 1883–99; the delegation of educational services to specialists by Liberal minister R.A. Pyne and his successor, Henry Cody, during 1906–36; and a shift from the 1930s into the 1950s as John Dewey's child- and activity-centred pedagogy became increasingly popular, with the result that textbooks became not the sole source of authority but instead resources for students' research. And if we compare a text of the 1900s to one of the 1950s, there are direct contrasts in both subject matter and its presentation. Turn-of-the-century textbooks were more overtly committed to the work of creating national identity, especially by their adoption of an authoritative voice; they also relied on political and military events as central structural features of their narratives. In contrast, books of the post-war decades included far more social history, and, when they did include discussions of the War of 1812, they invited their readers to imagine themselves as part of the narrative, to merge their own subjectivity with that of historical actors.

The authors of history texts and readers were frequently teachers or professors of history, many of them graduates of, or associated with, southern and central Ontario schools or universities. Out of the seventy-five texts and readers examined, fifteen were written by women, and most of the women historians, such as Luella Creighton or Edith Dyell, were published during the post-war decades. Authors such as Blanche Hume or Emily Weaver, who wrote in the first half of the century, tended to produce readers and historical sketches that were used either in the elementary grades or as supplements to the central texts. It is tempting to see this phenomenon as yet another example of women authors lacking or being denied the supposedly more authoritative voice of the senior instructor. However, we should not forget that the readers were the initial (and possibly more lasting) influence on children's conceptions of Canadian history. They are particularly significant from the 1880s to the 1920s, decades when many Ontario children left formal instruction at the age of fourteen.[6] Works such as Blanche Hume's *Laura*

Secord, published by Ryerson Press in 1928 as part of its Canadian History Readers Series and authorized by both the Imperial Order Daughters of the Empire (IODE) and the Department of Education, may well have performed a greater role in forming historical consciousness than W.L. Grant's *Ontario High School History of Canada* (1914).[7]

What, then, did the textbooks tell their readers about Canadian pasts? While Parvin's chronological distinctions are useful in understanding particular dimensions of state policy, the texts explored here should, I think, be divided somewhat differently: from the 1880s to the First World War; the inter-war decades to the Second World War; and the post-war decades to the 1970s. These divisions, of course, are far from discrete; the authors' preferences for particular narrative contents and styles, their choices of material deemed historically significant, and their rationales for teaching history in the first place overlapped from period to period in these books. Nor can we isolate nationalism, imperialism, and colonialism as being relevant only in the late nineteenth century; these relationships and discourses appear and reappear in these books (and, indeed, it would be naïve and condescending towards the past to assume they do not appear in today's 'multicultural' textbooks). Yet the form and shape they took varied significantly throughout the twentieth century. And the 'lessons' in gender relations offered by the texts' authors were linked to, and were shaped by, those in national and imperial identities; in turn, learning about the 'Canadian' past for the good of the country's future was frequently a profoundly gendered exercise. Moreover, the textbooks were not just indicative of past departmental or pedagogical practices: they are also artefacts of historical commemoration.

Textbooks from the 1870s to 1920

What was the significance of the War of 1812 in the first group of texts? Their authors usually paid respect to the bravery and heroism of the founders of New France. Yet it was the spread of British institutions and values that marked the true beginning of 'Canada': New France and Acadia were dress rehearsals for an authentic performance of nationhood that really only began after 1763. And, even within that particular production, it was the act of war and military defence that contained the denouement to this drama. The arrival of the Loyalists was seen, of course, as the significant, penultimate step in constructing Canada, but it was the War of 1812 that brought matters to a climax. From the war on, 'Canada' could be imagined as a national community.

Yet some authors suggested that such a 'Canada' was present even before the arrival of the Loyalists. J.N. McIlwraith's *The Children's Study* (1899) suggested that Canada had offered the refugees, including a 'greater part of the Mohawk nation,' a wide welcome, as well as being a land of freedom for fugitive slaves.[8] And a few of these writers saw great significance in the life and works of Sir William Johnson, the British Indian agent who, from his residence on the shores of the Mohawk River, managed to gain the trust and respect of the Six Nations (a very tiny minority of writers conceded that Molly Brant, his Mohawk wife and sister of Joseph, had acted as her people's ambassador and representative). Few writers provided many details as to just how Johnson had gained such acceptance among the Mohawks, although David M. Duncan's *The Story of the Canadian People* argued that he had joined in their games and dances and adopted their dress and manners, thereby prompting the Mohawks to adopt him and make him a warrior.[9] Most of the narratives that mentioned Johnson, however, simply stated that his character and the British government's equitable treatment of Natives – as opposed to the nascent United States' government's policies of land-grab and removal of Aboriginal peoples – accounted for the transformation of the Mohawks from Britain's feared adversaries to her loyal allies.[10]

Many of these themes continued on into expositions of the War of 1812, itself a defensive action triggered by international and imperial forces over which the colonists had little control and in which, some writers suggested, they were initially reluctant to become involved. Still, once war had been declared, the white settlers of Upper Canada invoked the legacy of their United Empire ancestors; farmers and their sons were transformed into a brave and martial force who left wives and younger children behind to tend the family farm or business and, for their dependents' own protection, defended their country. Then these writers mentioned, either in great detail or in some cases merely as a list, the many battles fought by the men of Upper Canada and their outcomes. Thus the narrative of the war as it was taught to children – and, by extension, the meta-narrative of the Canadian nation – became one of male heroism, patriotism, resistance, and defensive action.

Not surprisingly, Isaac Brock figured prominently as a central character in these tales. His death at Queenston Heights was often portrayed as pivotal in inspiring Canadian identity and patriotic duty. Brock, as in other accounts, provided Canadians with an almost superhuman figure, whose sacrifice and devotion to both Canada and empire should be emulated. Brock's humanity was also recognized, in his ability to manage his troops with paternal firmness, his acknowledgment of their own family responsibilities that might conflict with their military duty, and his last words of love to his sister in Guernsey.[11] All these qualities helped shape Brock as a character both heroic and human, a man whose place in Canadian history was assured by both his physical sacrifice and his character, and whose great service to Canada, the writers often reassured children, had already been commemorated by the Queenston Heights memorial.

If Brock became a stock character for those wishing to create an individual example of Anglo-Celtic male heroism, then Tecumseh was in many ways his Native counterpart. Given the work of the historical societies, the textbook writers' choice of Tecumseh as a model of Native heroism is, of course, not overly surprising. By virtue of his role in the war, itself a nation-founding narrative, Tecumseh was placed within the 'mainstream' of Canadian history. Like Brock, Tecumseh was made to conform to the archetype of the sacrificial hero and warrior. Furthermore, in many of these narratives, Tecumseh appears as the first Native whose character, motives, and actions are comprehensible and reasonable, who can be deemed 'knowable' by a non-Native audience; however, as the Epilogue explores, such an appearance was not without its contradictions and ambiguities.[12]

Central characters such as Tecumseh and Brock, and the texts' general focus on military and political affairs, could not help but impart lessons in gender relations, most specifically concerning masculinity. The books' approaches did not lend themselves to discussions of women as historical actors (which was, as we shall see, a critical difference between the texts and the readers), nor of men who did not fit that particular ideal of masculine loyalty manifested in physical, military bravery. A few texts in this period widened their narrative scope to include social history and discuss 'pioneer life' in Upper Canada, and, in some of these passages, women's work in manufacturing clothing and the skills they learned from 'friendly Indians' were acknowledged. Even in these discussions, though, the 'work' of pioneer communities was just as likely to be cast as masculine endeavours, which might range from land-clearing, home-building, and crop-planting, to the work of itinerant preachers who represented an important link to morality and civilization.[13] These passages, though, were always brief digressions from the central narratives of nation-building, a process understood as unfolding in the imperial theatre of war and diplomacy. The texts' authors, it is true, did link the two processes, thereby suggesting to readers the morality of the white settlers, men and women. Such a morality, along with the willingness to defend the colony, was immanent in the collective *and* individual consciousness of pioneer society, an inheritance of the UELs that – in an almost biological manner – simply needed to be triggered by the threat of American invasion. Yet the figure which embodied that response was almost always masculine, a member of the militia who, in turn, was defending a Crown and colony that were often – if not always explicitly – embodied as vulnerable, feminine figures.[14]

But there was an exception to this narrative of masculine nation-building. The textbook writers' were consistent in their choice of an exemplary figure of Anglo-Celtic womanhood: the figure of Laura Secord. Other women, it is true, made brief appearances in some books: Madame de La Tour, Madame de la Peltrie, Jeanne Mance, Madeleine de Verchères, Anna Jameson (an honorary Canadian), Susanna Moodie, and Catharine Parr Traill, as well as a number of well-known contemporary Canadian women: Agnes Machar, Marjorie Pickthall, Isabella Valancy Crawford, and Pauline Johnson.[15] Yet it was Secord's name that appeared in both these texts and those that mentioned no other woman; she was a recurring figure and symbol in children's classroom readings from the 1870s to the 1920s. In some books, her walk was mentioned as a twenty-mile journey to warn the British of the impending American attack at Beaver Dams; while it was certainly an act of patriotism, few details were given.[16] Other accounts, however, were slightly more elaborate and added details regarding Secord's family and person; Nellie Spence, for example, described her as a 'brave young woman.'[17] Some narratives, while seeking to elevate Secord to the pantheon of Canadian heroism, appeared to have difficulty reconciling femininity with national service. William H. Withrow praised her as a heroine who had undertaken her mission because of her wounded husband and pillaged house, thus suggesting that domestic, personal reasons guided her actions.[18] Other writers, though they might mention James's inability to go and depicted Secord as feminine, insisted that there was nothing untoward about her actions.

W.L. Grant told his readers that 'FitzGibbon had known nothing of the coming of the Americans, and would undoubtedly have been surprised had it not been for the valour of a woman. At Queenston, Sergeant James Secord was lying helpless from his wounds. Both he and his wife, Laura, were children of Loyalists, and hated the Americans for the wrong done to their parents. When the American troops reached Queenston, Secord and his wife at once suspected they were on their way to startle FitzGibbon.' Borrowing liberally from Cruikshank (and footnoting the latter's work), Grant stated that Secord 'was already in her thirty-eighth year, and the mother of five children. The roads in many places were ankle deep in mud, the country was sparsely settled, and the woods were known to be haunted by bands of Indians and white marauders, who hung upon the skirts of the armies, yet she never faltered in her resolution.' Grant debunked the story of the cow, preferring instead to believe that Secord probably used the excuse of visiting her sick brother, 'who lay dangerously ill some miles away.' After a journey that included the threat of wolves, rattlesnakes, swollen streams, and becoming lost in the woods, Secord crawled along a downed trunk and up a

> steep bank [where] she stumbled into the midst of a group of sleeping Indians who sprung to their feet with piercing yells. It was with great difficulty she made her object understood by their chief, who understood but a few words of English, and some delay ensued before she was entrusted to FitzGibbon ... The modesty of this heroine of Upper Canada led her to make no record of her adventures, and the story only came out more than forty years later. Uncertain and contradictory accounts of some of the details have therefore grown up, but the main facts are undoubted. It is pleasant to think that Laura Secord lived to a vigorous old age, dying in 1868 at the age of ninety-three.[19]

Grant's account acknowledged, at least, that Secord's story had been subject to partiality and subjectivity. Emily Weaver's narrative told her readers that, when a 'wounded militiaman named James Secord' overheard the Americans' plot and was unable to go, his wife decided to warn FitzGibbon. 'For a whole day she toiled through the woods, afraid of being stopped or questioned, but reached her journey's end in time to put FitzGibbon on his guard.' Beaver Dams was 'one of the most brilliant exploits of the war.' In contrast to Grant, Weaver felt that FitzGibbon had received much of the credit for the victory and thus Secord's name appeared in bold type alongside the story in order to help rectify 'Canadians'' memory lapse.[20]

Why, though, is Secord's presence in these texts of any significance? To many of today's historians, it is important to know if women were included in narratives of the nation that were presented to Ontario's schoolchildren; moreover, it is also important to know *which* women made appearances in the pages of these books.[21] However, Secord's incorporation is significant not just because of the frequency and consistency of her appearances and the tributes paid to her as a brave Canadian woman (although those were certainly important): for these Ontario writers, the War of 1812 itself was deemed as a watershed, the formative moment in the development of Canadian national identity. While the books' authors did not agree about the material gains of the war for Canada, judging them either quite considerable or completely unremarkable (and a few claimed that Canada's economy had been damaged by the war), almost all writers summed up the war as having developed Canadians' 'patriotism and loyalty,' muting party feeling and thus inter-party strife, and uniting all 'in a firm determination to uphold the honour of the country's flag.'[22] Canadians, wrote McIlwraith, gained a great moral victory, as they discovered they could defend themselves and their country. Duncan believed that in 1812 men and women of UEL descent sacrificed comforts for loyalty and thus proved themselves the stuff of nation-builders. And, wrote Grant,

> to Canada the war gave an heroic tradition. Men of French, Scotch, Irish, English descent had stood side by side the regulars of Great Britain and had fought as gallantly as they. It was our baptism of blood, and so far in this world that has been the only real baptism of a nation.
>
> It is less pleasing to think of the long years of hatred of the United States which date from the war; but to many men patriotism is impossible without a little hatred, and memories of the war did much to steady Canadians in the years of trial which were to come.[23]

Thus Canada was said to have achieved young adulthood in the crucible of the War of 1812, a state attained not just in Ontario but throughout the entire spectrum of British North America. Charles G.D. Roberts told the readers of his *History of Canada for High Schools and Academies* that, while Canada had been left with the destruction of her homes and blood of her sons, 'these were not too great a price to pay for the bond of brotherhood between the scattered provinces. The bond of brotherhood that then first made itself felt, from Cape Breton to the Straits of Mackinaw, grew secretly but surely in power till it proclaimed itself to the world in Confederation, and reached out to islands of the Pacific.'[24] In this passage, the war took on a mysterious yet undeniable life of its own, transmogrifying into a being – that of national identity – which, like a child growing up, matured quietly yet surely until it was confident of announcing its majority.

It is, then, the identification of Secord, the sole *individual* woman discussed in narratives of the War of 1812, with this process of nation-forging that makes her story more than a mere anecdote of historical interest. She was held up as an example of individual heroism: a woman who stepped out of her ordinary prescribed roles and relations and who should be admired for this; yet, paradoxically, she was also meant to symbolize the qualities of loyalty, self-sacrifice, and devotion to country that all of Ontario's children might emulate on a less dramatic scale. And, in particular, Secord could serve as an inspirational model for girls. While the heroism of Brock, Tecumseh, and the gallant militia may have cut across gender (their strength of characters, moral virtues, and so on), it was also dependent upon, and was exercised within, a military framework in which physical courage and corporeal self-sacrifice were integral to the definition of a 'hero.' I do not wish to imply that Secord's narrative took on equal weight – she was, after all, the *only* woman commemorated – merely that, as in the historical societies' accounts, her contribution to the war must also be understood within the context of 'nation-building.' In the textbooks, Secord became even more unequivocally the central symbol of Anglo-Canadian female loyalty than in the historical societies' accounts. Furthermore, given the insistence by many authors that the War of 1812 had united French and English Canada, it is possible that her English-Canadian commemorators saw her as a female symbol for both groups.

When we place Secord's story and her image within the context of a critical moment of nation-building, how does that affect their relationship to the narratives and images of Native men? While the authors did not explicitly address this issue, Natives disappeared from historical narratives once the War of 1812 was over (except for brief appearances as deluded and/or 'bloodthirsty savages' in 1885); in their discussions of Loyalists, a few texts mentioned that Brant's descendants lived at the Bay of Quinte and on the Grand River, although 'it is doubtful if there is a full-blooded Iroquois among them.'[25] Native peoples, in general, and Native men, in particular, then vanished from the texts. Even their descendants' claims to a legacy of loyalism might be suspect, unlike the assertions made by their non-Native contemporaries. In contrast, the rest of the country – by virtue of the war – progressed into Canadian adulthood. Native peoples' actions in the war were always understood as emanating from motives that placed them outside the main narrative of nation-building. It was never easy or really possible to place them at the centre of a drama that, from its inception, had been seen as having been shaped by non-Native needs and desires. Yet, while Secord's gender might make her participation exceptional and noteworthy, deserving special titles and typefaces, her racial and ethnic background made it harder to turn her into a commodity as Native men were thus transformed, useful for their military contributions. It was possible for these writers to imagine and map Secord onto the grid of the Canadian imagined community and to attribute to her specific desires and motivations that could simply not be ascribed to Native peoples.

Textbooks in the Inter-war Decades

The texts of the 1870s to the end of the First World War were shaped by discussions of the need to promote national identity, discussions that were themselves influenced by debates over imperial unity, the threat of American annexation (geographical and cultural), increased immigration, and urbanization. Those texts published between the 1920s and '40s were written, it is true, within different contexts – both of political, socio-economic, and cultural developments within Ontario, and of changes within educational policy and pedagogy. It would be tempting, therefore, to see these texts as part of a national 'identity' that had been tempered by the war, by the influence of commercial and consumer modernity, and by changes in gender relations; an identity that represented a break from the imperial-national hybrid of the pre-war years. It would be tempting, then, to see these texts as changed with the times.

Tempting it might be, but it is another question as to whether this scenario accords with the content and discourses of these books. For one, efforts to locate national identity within an imperial orbit continued. To be sure, a number of writers, both pre- and post-war and in venues such as Ontario Historical Society meetings, insisted that Canadian children must learn Canadian history and not just memorize lists of queens and kings. Even those earlier histories that had linked Canada to Britain argued that 'there is no lack of Canadian historians – their name is legion – yet there is a painful lack of historic knowledge among Canadian youth.'[26] Nevertheless, Canadian identity was still presented as being moulded by 'British' values and 'tradition.' W.S. Wallace's *A History of the Canadian People*, published in 1930, divided Canadian history into three periods: the 'pre-British,' British North American, and Canadian. Thus 'Canada,' Wallace's taxonomy suggests, either was simply waiting for the British to arrive, was under British rule, or, in its final phase, was the beneficiary of the British legacy: that first half-century 'determined the form and character of Canada today.'[27] Using what he called a combination of topical and chronological approaches to organize his material, Wallace did not approach the War of 1812 as a series of important battles that might tell the reader something valuable. For Wallace, 'the actual details of the war, comprising as it did what were merely, according to present-day standards, a series of skirmishes, are of little importance even to the military historian.' (The reaction of military historian Ernest Cruikshank, who had devoted much of his career to documenting those 'skirmishes,' can only be imagined.) What the war could tell Canadians, though, was 'its many episodes of gallantry and heroism illustrating the determination of Canadians to be free.' It had also 'exerted a powerful influence on feeling and opinion in Canada since that time; and for this reason, some at least of the details of the war deserve to be described.'[28] Furthermore, while the war could not be described as a source of pride for either the British or the Americans, Canadians 'showed on many stricken fields of battle their ability to defend their own country against overwhelming odds.' The War of 1812 was the Canadian equivalent of the Italian War of Liberation, as such conflicts 'have frequently given birth to a strong national feeling; and this War of 1812 – which might not improperly be called the Canadian War of Independence – did in Canada. It bound together, as nothing else could have done, the scattered and diverse elements in the country; and it gave Canadians memories which are invoked to this day.'[29]

In other contexts, particularly in his attacks on the Secord story, Wallace had expressed a great deal of scepticism about the use of the War of 1812 as a romantic tale of Canada's national formative moment. As we have seen, it was precisely those details of 'skirmishes' that Wallace found important. Here, though, he had no such intellectual scruples. And in his estimation of the war's legacy, Wallace was joined by other textbook authors. James Bingay's *A History of Canada for High Schools* assessed the war's impact in a number of ways: it had brought trade to Canada and had given British North America (especially Upper Canada) a reputation in England as a desirable destination for emigrants. Most importantly, it had instilled a 'spirit of self-reliance' in Canadians, with the 'tendency to unite the two races who had shared in its perils but had hitherto looked upon each other with mutual distaste and suspicion.'[30] Writing in 1942, George W. Brown found that in the war's aftermath the Canadas united, 'which was not forgotten even though later years brought quarrels and misunderstandings.' The conflict also strengthened Canada's tie to Britain through the 'cherished memory' of the fight against

American invasion; simultaneously, 'there was planted in the soil of British North America a new patriotism which was to become in later years a part of Canada's heroic tradition.'[31]

Not all of the texts produced within these decades were, it is true, dedicated to teaching national loyalty through the commemoration of this military endeavour. Edwin C. Guillet's and Jessie E. McEwen's *Finding New Homes in Upper Canada* (1938) was framed by political and military events, but the central focus of their narrative was the effects of such episodes on Canadians' (both ordinary and extraordinary) lives. The women of Acadia and New France – Madame de La Tour, Marguerite Bourgeoys, Jeanne Mance, and Madame de la Peltrie – were given a nod of respect as being either 'heroic' in a military context or providing their communities with much-needed services. When the authors turned to Upper Canada, though, the War of 1812 was not mentioned; instead, they chose to focus on the process of pioneer settlement.[32] Yet, as we shall see, the children's readers, which also chose to examine individuals' place in history, were not slow to create heroes and – in the case of Secord – a heroine out of those military and civilian figures affected by the War of 1812.

While Wallace may have deliberately chosen to omit Secord, other authors professed to believe in the story's historical veracity. J.E. Wetherell's *Handbook to Nelson's Pictures of Canadian History* (1927) narrated the story in great detail. Although James had overheard the American plot, his wounds made it impossible for him to go, and so he 'consented to allow his wife, Laura, to make her way through the forest ... a daring project for a woman of thirty-eight years of age, the mother of five young children.' Acting with her husband's permission and not as an independent agent, the wife and mother used her cow as a decoy to fool the American sentries and 'struggled on through the thick wilderness, by unfrequented paths, for nearly twenty miles.' After losing her way and crawling on her hands and knees, Secord 'pressed on,' even though night was falling and wolves and 'deadly rattlesnakes' posed a threat. 'Suddenly, at dusk, she found herself near an Indian camp. She knew these Indians were friendly, and she did not fear their savage yells when they first saw her. With much difficulty she made them understand the purpose of her mission and they conducted her to FitzGibbon. She gave her message and sunk utterly exhausted.' FitzGibbon went on to win a bloodless victory, as the 'whoops' of his 'dusky allies' so 'terrified' the Americans that they surrendered. Secord, for her part, 'enjoyed the honours poured on her by grateful Canadians for more than fifty years, for she lived till 1868, fifty-five years after her heroic adventure.'[33]

In this version, then, Secord's actions are shaped by pioneer domestic life – the cow, her relation to her children – and, what is more, a particular kind of domesticity in which even a heroine must obtain her husband's consent before serving her country. Yet, once she began her journey, this middle-aged wife and mother displayed neither feminine weaknesses nor feminine fears of either the Niagara landscape or its inhabitants. Not even the 'Indians,' who were very close to being part of the topography, could frighten her, armed as she was with 'knowledge' of their alliance with the British. Yet a very different image of Secord's relation to the Mohawks was depicted in Henry Sandham's illustration (fig. 7.1). This sketch accompanied the written narrative and in it Secord, a blonde woman with her hair hanging loose, emerges from the forest into a clearing, where she is accosted by two 'Indian' men. Secord and one of the men are placed at the centre of the picture; he stands at her right hand, holding up a gun and wearing a feathered headdress. Her face is turned towards him. The other crouches in the bottom right-hand corner of the drawing with his left hand raised, his body muscular, wearing feathers on his head, an earring, and no shirt. The linking of Secord's 'whiteness' and femininity is highlighted even further by the contrast of her blonde hair and fair skin and the complete clothing of her body with the Native men's dark, muscular physiques, their lack of upper-body covering, and the ornamentation of their hair and bodies.[34]

Wetherell added yet another dimension to this narrative in his conclusion, which followed the picture. Not only did Secord's story give his young readers a chance to be educated about Canadian heroism, it also served to contrast 'Canada then' with 'Canada now.' The illustration of Secord's encounter with the Mohawks, Wetherell told his readers, was not just about Native-white relations or the War of 1812; rather, 'the predominant feature of this picture is the impression which it conveys of the wild and uncultivated character of the region through which the heroine had to travel on her famous journey.' By using the Niagara region as a model for 'untamed Canada' of the early nineteenth century, Wetherell was able to point to the great national progress that had occurred over the following centuries:

> Today this district is a rich farming and industrial country, populous and busy with fruit growing, manufacturing and the business of transportation; traversed by steam and electric railways, motor roads, power transmission lines, and the great waterway of the Welland Canal. In 1813, doubtless, it looked very much as it appears in the picture. Large tracts were still

7.1 Illustration by Henry Sandham, from J.E. Wetherell, *Handbook to Nelson's Pictures of Canadian History* (1927).

covered with the original forest, swamps and muskegs spread for miles, and the only paths were narrow trails through the thick underbrush and among the tangle of fallen trees. It was the home of wild beasts and the hunting ground of the Indians. It circled the more settled country along the shores of the Niagara River and Lakes Erie and Ontario, and as yet was penetrated only by an occasional clearing around a homestead, or a few sawmills on some of the small streams. From the security of this position the British patrols and outposts and their Indian scouts were able to watch the movements of the American invaders, to ambush marching forces, as at Beaver Dams, and to make raids upon the enemy's encampments, as at Stoney Creek. The picture, with its tangle of brilliant colour, its suggestions of intricate foliage, and the vigorous movement of the figures, expresses the feelings of perilous action in this wilderness country.[35]

Although Wetherell did not state this explicitly, the picture also managed to equate Native peoples with 'time past,' residing in an era of warfare and 'primitive savagery,' not as participants in 'settlement,' a meta-narrative represented through the symbols of industrialization, agricultural prosperity, and 'modern' transportation. 'Time past' also might have been stirring and romantic, a temporality that encouraged action even on the part of Euro-Canadian women – but it was also an epoch potentially threatening for such women.

But where would Canadian women – or, at any rate, Ontario's – be found outside of these stirring tales of heroic deeds? After all, Wetherell's scenario of modern progress could make little, if any, room for Anglo-Celtic women as historical actors, as they were not recognized as creators of factories, canals, and railroads. It was entirely possible for these women, like Natives, to be atavistic, to stand outside of modern time if the latter was designated solely as public temporality, removed from home and family. Yet at least one other writer was eager to identify Canadian women with modernity and the 'public sphere.' In a chapter entitled. 'The March of Progress,' Wallace's *A History of the Canadian People* told students of the striking changes in women's status that had occurred over the last sixty years. In 1867 most women 'were almost wholly excluded from business life. Domestic life was considered to be their sphere.' However, the invention of the typewriter meant that women were drawn into the business world as stenographers and secretaries; recently 'they have come to fill highly-paid and responsible positions in business.' Other changes had also come about in this period: women had won the 'right of admission' to universities and the professions. And in all of the provinces – except Quebec – they had the right to vote, to be elected to Parliament, and to sit in Cabinet and the Senate.[36]

Other texts written in the 1930s told Secord's story and repeated the themes of earlier narratives: her domestic context, which, however, did not stop her from displaying bravery and determination; the perils of her journey; and her meeting with the Mohawks. Some books, it is true, either omitted Secord entirely or at least disciplined their narratives in accordance with 'professional' standards, possibly because their authors agreed with Wallace, or because they had little space for the War of 1812.[37] Bingay's work represented a desire to find a place for Secord's heroism while at the same time distancing his history from the supposedly naïve and romantic versions attacked by Wallace. He included Secord's walk but undercut its dramatic impact by stating that although she 'told her story to a chief,' the 'Indians had already warned FitzGibbon' and the American surrender was achieved through fear of the Aboriginals. 'The battle of Beaverdam was a purely Indian victory. Here, as frequently throughout the war, they proved themselves valuable allies to the Canadians.'[38] Another means of telling Secord's story was to simply sidestep the issue of her 'contribution.' George Brown's *Building the Canadian Nation* told readers that 'it was at Beaverdam that Laura Secord risked her life in carrying a message through the American line to the British commander. Her name, like that of Madeleine de Verchères in Lower Canada, became in later years a symbol of the spirit with which the people of Upper Canada stood firm in defence of their homes.'[39]

Was the omission or refashioning of Secord's 'contribution' (at least in the historical texts) accompanied by a rethinking of Native peoples' role in Canadian history? As we have seen, some accounts pointed out that Beaver Dams must be told as a narrative of Native 'victory.' Such a triumph, however, was not to be understood in the same terms as the Battle of Detroit or the Battle of Queenston Heights. While Native knowledge reached FitzGibbon first, it was British willingness to trade in Anglo-American fears of Native warfare and of the 'other,' not the 'heroic' deeds of Native warriors themselves, that won the battle. Earlier narratives had focused on Tecumseh's individual heroism as a quality and stated that it helped to mitigate the 'primitive savagery' of his supporters. Thus, the historical agency of Native peoples could only be recognized intermittently: their construction as non-European allies was always laced with imperial ambivalence and apprehension.

Moreover, downplaying or ignoring Secord's contribution to the imperial tie did not necessarily lead to a greater 'appreciation' of Aboriginal peoples. Wallace, for his part, while designating Tecumseh as 'the greatest soldier the Indian ever produced' (and we should note that it was Aboriginals, not Europeans, who served as his reference point), did not mention the Six Nations in his discussion of Loyalism.[40] His *A First Book of Canadian History* told Ontario's schoolchildren that the early 'Indians' were 'savages of a very low order,' an illiterate group that had left no written records. What information historians had about these people came from the (more reliable) narratives of the early explorers, who described a society in which men hunted, fished, and fought, while 'the women performed the drudgery of life, and even took the place of beasts of burden.'[41] Life for these people was lived not just crudely and brutally, but it was also unchanging, outside the realm of historical time, until Europeans such as William Johnson, the great 'Indian tamer,' arrived, bringing both civilization and history.[42] Wallace's determination to narrate the nation as a triumph of modern British democracy and socio-economic 'progress' had much to do with his denigration of Native society, for as we have seen he was not averse to chronicling the 'rise' of women's status as part of the panorama of 'the' Canadian nation bound up with empire and imperial developments (although, with the exception of Madeleine de Verchères, his list of individual women who were important figures includes only writers).

Much of this treatment of Native peoples in the texts was not drastically different from their representation prior to the First World War. Yet the absence of Aboriginal peoples from narratives of 'the' nation after the Loyalists and the War of 1812, and the denial or suppression of their political subjectivity during the mid-nineteenth century, a period that was designated one of first incipient and then flourishing Canadian nationalism, must also be examined in light of the intensification of Native peoples' own activism in the decades after the First World War. The experience – let alone the 'contribution' – of Native soldiers in the war, one which helped precipitate the formation of the League of Indians of Canada, was simply not reflected in these texts, even as the 'experience' of forging the Canadian nation was written into the historical narratives.[43] The textbooks of the inter-war decades generally worked diligently to consign First Nations to the borders of Canadian history, designating them at certain critical moments as the 'saviours' of British military supremacy but then rendering them absent once such supremacy was guaranteed.

Children's Readers and Biographies

The textbooks were not, of course, the only sources for Ontario children to learn about the past. School readers and biographies of 'famous Canadians' that were written for children from the early 1900s to the early '30s were also intended to teach children about the past by using individual examples of heroism. Such literature was not unique to either the early twentieth century or Ontario. As recently published popular historical literature demonstrates, these books continue to be produced.[44] While the readers and biographies share many things with the textbooks used in classrooms and school libraries, particularly in their general choice of subject matter, they were not identical. Certainly both textbooks and readers shared a desire to celebrate individuals, and considered the impact of individual personalities and actions a major force in historical change. Textbooks often interrupted their linear narratives of cause and effect with biographical sketches of the central characters or by providing such sketches in a side panel. However, while the readers did not take their subjects out of context (there was usually some discussion of the historical period under consideration), they instead shifted the narrative's focus and made the individual historical actor's life, whether that of a famous individual or a historical archetype, occupy centre stage. In the eyes of their authors, such choices were not made merely to introduce a 'human interest' to the study of history that would be more engaging to younger children and capture their attention. As more than one author wrote, the 'inherent' interest in biography made it 'the best medium through which to approach the study of history. The dry, dull facts of social and political changes are coloured, illuminated, and given an interest through their intimate association with the great men and women of the past.'[45] By examining the many 'picturesque and striking' figures who populated the pages of Canadian history and 'about whom cluster the great events in the evolution of our national institutions ... one may obtain ... a clear and comprehensive grasp of the history of their times.'[46]

However, history also was a roll-call of national characteristics in the pages of these books, whereby 'the self-sacrifice of a Brébeuf, the determination of a La Salle, the heroism of a Brock, the persistence of a Baldwin, the enthusiasm of a Ryerson, the vision of a Macdonald, the moral earnestness of a Brown, the integrity of a Mackenzie, the fervour of a McGee, the fearlessness of a Tupper, the inspiration of a Laurier, the straightforwardness of a Whitney'[47] could be seen as not just individual traits, important though they might be. Like the landmarks and sites that, as chapter 9 will argue, were perceived as the repository of historical and national meanings, or the local and regional events documented by the historical societies, individuals were seen as both representatives of a larger process, the formation of the nation-state, and as component parts of the 'national character,' whose relationship to the state was, of course, symbiotic.

While the preceding quotation suggests that the authors of readers and biographies envisioned Canadian heroism as masculine, many of the books studied here included women. Individual books and series that took as their main focus explorers, soldiers, and politicians conceived of heroism and nation-building as the province of Euro-Canadian men – Macmillan's Canadian Men of Action being an example. The Ryerson Canadian History Readers Series, while it included a few studies of Canadian women, published far more books about men.[48] Yet readers and biographies generally produced more portraits of Euro-Canadian women than did the textbooks; some were about both men and women, and others focused only on women. These studies were not governed as tightly by linear narratives of political and military events (although they did organize their portraits in chronological order) in which women's activities were rarely deemed relevant, nor were they governed as strictly by the need to examine only 'great deeds.' Thus the books covered the lives of women who were mentioned only briefly in the texts, such as Madame de La Tour or Madame Hébert. As well, their authors granted themselves a degree of historical licence. They created composite, fictional characters such as 'great-grandmother' and provided their readers with portraits that dealt with the social history of particular periods. The early to mid-nineteenth-century period of pioneer 'settlement' was a favourite topic, one in which women's contributions to colonial society were discussed. However, the ubiquitous image of the pioneer home often lacked specificities of time and place, and thus Euro-Canadian women might appear outside of history – or at least have a much fuzzier relationship to historical time than their male counterparts.[49]

Secord, like Madeleine de Verchères, made frequent appearances in the books of the late 1920s and early '30s. In these narratives, both her and James's devotion to the British Crown was foregrounded, but the expression of Secord's loyalty was invariably placed firmly within the context of unusual circumstances, a breakdown in the ability of the husband and father to perform his duty. In some accounts, James initially was the central character, as he overheard the American officers and was tormented by his inability to pass on the news, a responsibility that his wife offered to shoulder.[50] In other readers, though, Laura Secord heard the plot and determined to go, overriding her husband's fears for her safety.[51] Some authors gave her company on her journey, either in the form of the cow (fig. 7.2) or her niece, while others believed that she used the excuse of her critically ill brother as a means of passing the American sentry.[52] As well as her husband and children, these figures helped link Secord to domesticity and familial relations, thereby grounding her in the expected and conventional.

Yet no matter what variations in the narrative concerning the impetus to go or the structure of her journey, Secord's encounter with the Mohawks is surprisingly similar in these texts: it is one of great fear. In Mabel Burns McKinley's *Canadian Heroines of Pioneer Days*, Secord finds herself

suddenly ... in the midst of a band of Indians. When they saw her the braves started up and rushed toward her, yelling their ear-splitting war-whoops. Many were the tales Laura had heard of the cruelty of the Indians. The settlers knew to what dreadful torture the savages put those who fell into their hands. During the war the Indians had been even more cruel than before. It was indeed a terrible situation for the footsore and weary woman. But Laura did not lose her presence of mind. She must have courage if she were to deal with the Indians. She looked quickly at the band of yelling savages and saw one whom she thought would be their leader or chief. At once Laura beckoned to him. She got his attention, and by signs indicated that she must see FitzGibbon, without delay. She made him understand that she had an important message for the leader of the British forces. Even the safety of the Indians themselves might depend upon it! It was fortunate that the band of Indians were allies of FitzGibbon's, and that Laura had been able to explain her errand before the savages had harmed her. They led her at once to Beaver Dams.[53]

McKinley's account was one of the most explicit and detailed discussions of Secord and the Mohawks. It repeats and re-emphasizes that not only were 'Indians' primordial, ambiguous beings to be feared, but that they could also be tamed by the presence of mind and superior judgment (Secord's 'knowing' who was the chief) of a white woman who was armed with knowledge of their viciousness. Even their position as allies of the British did not render them harmless; this passage suggests that their violence was not cultural, but rather an innate, biologically driven trait that the war had unleashed.

7.2 'Driving a cow before her, Laura Secord passed the American sentries.' Illustration by J.R. Skelton, from H.E. Marshall, *Canada's Story, Told to Boys and Girls* (1919).

Not all accounts of her meeting with the Mohawks used the same kind of language and imagery. W.J. Karr suggested that, while Secord had good reason to be afraid, it was because of her gender and the historically specific beliefs and practices of Aboriginal peoples. 'As she approached FitzGibbon's position she came unexpectedly upon some Indian scouts. She was much frightened, for the Indians *at that time* showed scant respect to women. Though they could not speak English, she made them understand that she had a message for FitzGibbon and at length she was conducted to him' (emphasis added).[54] But no matter what motives were given to the 'Indians,' almost all the readers collapsed the Mohawks into one homogeneous group of savage and brutal creatures, forces of nature far more deadly than rattlesnakes and wolves. Secord's dealings with them were strictly because of their alliance with the British, a temporally bound and contingent state of affairs, in contrast with the qualities that formed the essential and transcendental core of their being.[55] And while, as in the texts, the readers could honour 'good Indians' such as Tecumseh and Brant, these men were either exceptions or products of colonial hybridity.[56] Furthermore, as in the historical societies' narratives, the readers also included tales of pioneer settlement in Upper Canada that featured homes and Anglo-Celtic women threatened and besieged by drunken and vicious Native men.[57]

Textbooks in the Post-war Years

The subject matter of textbooks published in the decades after the Second World War did not depart dramatically from those of the previous decades. Many authors, for example, continued to celebrate the War of 1812 as the 'dawning' of Canadian nationalism. As in the earlier texts, certain key figures continued to appear, personifying individual traits either as ones that defined the individual as having risen above his social and racial context (such as Tecumseh) or, in Brock's case, as ones found in the population represented by him (or, in a few cases, her). Secord's story, while told less and less often, still appeared in a number of these books, albeit with the explanation that her courage, and not her news, was the more valued commodity (fig. 7.3). Arthur Dorland's *Our Canada* (1949) made much of her courageous determination 'to run the gauntlet of American patrols' and her struggle 'through dense underbrush' to reach FitzGibbon. Dorland told his audience that 'it does not detract from the bravery of the exploit' to know that FitzGibbon's 'Indian scouts' were already aware of the Americans' plans. While the victory of

7.3 'She walked bravely up to them.' Illustration from Donald French, ed., *Famous Canadian Stories* (1945).

Beaver Dams must be attributed to the Mohawks, Dorland pointed out that 'Laura Secord has become a legendary figure, who typifies the brave qualities of the pioneer women of English-speaking Canada, just as Madeleine de Verchères typifies the same qualities for French-speaking Canada.'[58] In Aileen Garland's *Canada Our Country* (1961), Secord was a determined figure who walked twenty miles on a 'steaming hot day through thick forest and dense underbrush.' Upon giving her news to FitzGibbon, he 'recognized what a heroic effort she had made and thanked her warmly. He had already learned from his Indian scouts about the proposed attack, but that does not alter the fact that Laura Secord is entitled to honour as a brave patriot.'[59]

The post-war texts tended, however, to personalize historical narratives to a much greater extent than did their predecessors. The romanticism of earlier texts had always included a degree of appeal to emotion and sentiment, but the texts' narrators generally adopted a tone of omniscience and objectivity. While such approaches were not completely abandoned, more and more authors attempted to appeal to students, not by simply telling the meta-narrative of Canada's history (for that was included as the overarching story), but also by including narratives of the 'micro level' through tales of individuals, both famous and humble, and their roles in historical events. Of course, the readers had always adopted this approach, yet their subjects generally were well-known individuals whose places in the historical narrative were invariably guaranteed. In contrast, the post-war texts often created quasi-fictional, almost generic characters, such as the immigrant family who came to Upper Canada in 1832 and whose journey was narrated in the pages of a daughter's diary.[60] The authors also appealed to the historical consciousness and location of 'individual' readers, by reminding them of past events that had taken place in their hometown or county. Garland's text included a chapter, 'Our Own Province in 1800,' that ran through various regions of Ontario and told students what their hometowns would have looked like 161 years ago.[61]

These post-war accounts of 'Canada's story' also included greater amounts of what academic historians might call 'social history': narratives of immigration, settlement, and the daily chores of pioneer life. Many of these books presented these studies in a vignette form; their authors inserted them at an appropriate chronological point but did not attempt to link them to other historical developments. Not all authors, though, agreed that this was the most appropriate approach to take. Donalda Dickie, author of *The Great Adventure: An Illustrated History of Canada for Young Canadians* (1950), called for a more connected teaching of history, rather than the 'bits and patches' of the social studies approach. 'The history of Canada is a thoroughly good story; a "movie" in Technicolor, enacted on a vast stage, by characters lively, intriguing, romantic, wise and foolish, good and bad, but hardly ever dull. It is full of excursions and alarms; hair-breadth escapes with life and fortune perched upon a paddle blade; great attempts made boldly, lost or won gaily; important events with at least one development that has played, and is playing, an important part in the evolution of the free world of today.'[62]

Yet Dickie's book also included a chapter entitled 'The Pioneers,' which consisted mostly of details of daily life and was illustrated with pictures of 'pioneer clothing' for men and women, girls and boys. These garments, though, were those of the Victorian urban middle class: top hats, frock, and cut-away coats for the men; fitted jackets and hoop skirts for the women; and a dress with three tiers of trim, ruffled pantalets, and a long cape for the girls (the boys were given a similar version of the men's attire).[63] While sketches of such clothing were accompanied by text that discussed the intense physical labour of those who produced the 'pioneer' farm and home – its crops, food, home-clothing, and household goods – the collapsing of these two different groups for a young audience suggests how social history might be flattened and homogenized, so that two ostensibly different socio-economic – and political groups – were represented through the medium of fashion as being indistinguishable. Moreover, what was presented to such texts' readers was social history without political history's traditional reliance on the themes of conflict and struggle. While 'progress' occurred, it was understood to have occurred through the media of individual achievement, self-discipline, and hard work. No clear analytical framework for this material existed; in content, it resembled some of the 'new' social history of the 1960s and 1970s, but it lacked an intellectual reason for its inclusion in these texts – other than the desire to make history 'relevant' and 'alive' to children and not merely a handmaiden to nationalism.[64]

One of the effects of including narratives of pioneer settlement was a greater inclusion of women, even if Secord's story was told in a revised version or was completely omitted. Of course, there was no automatic or essential reason for including women pioneers; earlier works had demonstrated just how easy it was to construct masculinist narratives that focused on male land-clearing and farming. Yet the post-war texts tended to discuss the hardships of these women's lives, the loneliness from which many had suffered, and their need to organize community-based institutions, such as the bees (themselves supposed to reflect women's work in textile production), to combat their isolation.[65] Edith Dyell's work took this theme of women's involvement in 'community building' even further, pointing out to her readers the links between reform work, especially temperance, and campaigns for women's suffrage.[66] But 'women' as historical agents and actors were, generally, to be understood as either French- or English-speaking and middle-class, although discussions of men tended to pick subjects from a greater variety of backgrounds. The hardships (followed by successes) of an 'East European' immigrant family on the Canadian prairies were chronicled by their twelve-year-old great-grandson.[67] Workers, male or female, who had gone on strike and formed unions were, however, not part of these studies.

The increased appearance of 'women' in the 'pioneer period' may have been underpinned by assumptions about their improved position under conditions of modernity; the same could not be said, however, for

Native peoples. Certainly turn-of-the-century histories generally saw Aboriginal peoples only in terms of their intrinsic value and worth to Anglo-Celtic military and political expansion. Such a construct did little to explore Aboriginal motives and subjectivity, nor did it allow readers to see Native people as historical actors, with the exception of well-known figures such as Tecumseh and Brant. These trends continued in the post-war period, with many stories, for example, of Tecumseh's bravery, physical attributes, and moral superiority.[68] Yet, no matter how much individual Natives were celebrated, other shifts in the textbooks' narratives made it increasingly difficult to see them as anything but a vanished race relegated to anachronistic time. The expansion of the chronological parameters of 'Canadian history' made Native peoples even more marginal to these tales of progress and advancement. Their disappearance after either the War of 1812 or the Northwest Rebellion made their absence from the time of modernity even more pronounced. Occasionally, Aboriginal peoples would be mentioned in tales of Western settlement and the formation of reserves.[69] But as Canada's 'story' expanded into the twentieth century, it did not include figures such as the Native leader Fred Loft or the League of Indians of Canada. To discuss such First Nations movements would have meant disturbing the triumphal nature of these historical narratives, which were often represented on the books' covers by a parade of masculine historical figures, usually starting with blanket- and feather-clad 'Indians' and ending with railroads, schoolhouses, farmers, and – not coincidentally – Royal Northwestern Mounted Police officers.[70]

Whose Story? Whose Nation?

Although these post-war narratives seem to indicate that modernity was the antithesis of Native culture, it would be misleading to suggest that their authors or publishers were unaware of competing claims over 'accuracy,' 'authenticity,' and 'positive depictions.' As has been mentioned, the texts were always subject to the regulation of the provincial state and its consultants; however, it is possible to glimpse the concerns and frustrations of those who felt excluded from the textbooks' presentation of the 'Canadian' past. One such individual was Milton Martin, a Mohawk from the Six Nations reserve who had fought for Canada during the First World War. After the war, Martin became a public school-teacher, principal, and secretary of the Ontario Public School Men Teacher's Federation.[71] During the 1930s and 1940s, Martin charged the

Ontario school system with perpetrating stereotypes of Mohawk and, in general, 'Indian' savagery, dishonesty, and barbarism in its textbooks; he also called for the extension of the franchise.[72]

Further research would be needed in order to determine if others echoed Martin's concerns. In the 1950s, though, a variety of communities called upon the state for a more inclusive curriculum. Part of their interest stemmed from the Ministry of Education's efforts to involve various organizations and individuals in the process of 'vetting' textbooks prior to their inclusion in Circular Fourteen, the Ministry's list of approved texts and readers. Yet the Ministry's own correspondence also reveals that various organizations were concerned over the place of women, First Nations, ethnic and racial minorities, and, occasionally, working-class people and unions in historical texts and readers.

Some of these concerns were expressed by Ministry officials. Writing to S.A. Watson of W.J. Gage Publishing in 1952, J.R. McCarthy, the Ministry's Superintendent of Curriculum, offered an assessment of one of Gage's publications, Margaret Avison's *History of Ontario*. While McCarthy enjoyed Avison's 'interesting introduction' (the 'story of the Indian boy'), was enthusiastic about the book as a work of Canadian history written by a Canadian 'authoress,' and liked its maps, drawings, and interesting anecdotes, he felt that 'there seems to be an unnecessary elaboration for young children of cruelties of the Iroquois.' Whether or not McCarthy's concern stemmed from the impropriety of young children hearing about such practices and being unable to contextualize them, the suitability of discussions of violence for that age group, or the teaching of anti-Aboriginal attitudes through the book (or a mixture of all three), is unclear; however, the book was recommended for inclusion in Circular Fourteen's Schedule A (a category that permitted boards to buy and use approved texts for classrooms and libraries).[73]

By the late 1960s, though, concerns such as McCarthy's had intensified. For one, the Ministry increasingly insisted on the use of Canadian-authored and -produced books.[74] Such attitudes were, of course, not new; as we have seen, nationalism had been a close companion to the writing and teaching of Canadian history in Ontario. But during this period, the provincial government displayed a greater desire to produce more inclusive and less 'biased' versions of the country's past. By 1970, a Ministry review of books listed in Circular Fourteen began with the goal of inclusivity, buttressed by the beliefs that ethnic and racial minorities should have the same kinds of 'positive' representation as the Anglo-Celtic majority, and that 'sex-role' stereotyping must be excised. Using the 1948 United Nations' human rights declaration as their inspiration, the report's authors called for the greater 'balance' in history and other textbooks that Canada's new immigrant population demanded. Much of the report focused on the representation of Native peoples, identifying problems of language, perspectives, and structures. Too many books – the Macmillan series was targeted as a special offender – continued to use derogatory nouns, adjectives, and adverbs ('squaw,' 'half-breed,' 'massacring,' and 'bloodthirsty') to describe Native peoples and Native activities. Quotations were being lifted from earlier texts or from documents written by Europeans; in the case of the latter, textbook authors were not being sufficiently careful to indicate that these passages emanated from European perspectives, left by those who had observed scenes they could not fully comprehend. In addition to these issues, the structure of history texts was in itself a problem. By attempting to cover an overly large sweep of time, their authors were forced to make generalizations. In doing so, they fell back on European perspectives, explored European motives, and discussed only Euro-Canadians as historical actors.[75] The report's authors recommended that 'correct' knowledge be produced and disseminated about Natives, for the benefit of both Native and non-Native children.

Individual school texts were also sent to a number of groups in order to be evaluated for 'bias.' More research would be needed to determine the degree to which parents, teachers, and organizations concerned themselves over specific texts, and the curriculum in general, in order to understand how textbooks were, in Michael Apple and Linda Christian-Smith's words, 'sites of cultural struggle' among teachers, parents, boards of education, and ministries.[76] However, the Ministry's files present glimpses of such struggles as representatives of certain organizations, parents, and, on one occasion, a grandparent wrote with complaints of racial and sex-role stereotyping.[77] In October 1972, William Mahoney, the National Director of the United Steelworkers of America, wrote to Minister of Education Thomas Wells that, while he welcomed the Ministry's report on eliminating bias in school texts, labour had been excluded. Mahoney pointed out that the Ontario Institute for Studies in Education's report 'Teaching Prejudice' stated that twentieth-century labour history in the schools emphasized violence (by dwelling on events such as the Winnipeg General Strike) and that students were taught very little about labour's present significance. Mahoney asked Wells point-blank what he planned to do in order to include 'working people and their movement' for, as matters stood, the Ministry was simply perpetuating class-based bias.[78] Wells replied that he was aware of these concerns and had just had a 'most worthwhile and pleasant meeting with the Ontario Federation of Labour.' Although the research and action on this matter was 'quite complex,' the Ministry was studying the problem and looking for anti-labour bias.[79] And, in August 1974, N. Keith Lickers, Director of the Woodland Indian Cultural and Educational Centre on the Six Nations reserve, offered the Centre's services to Eileen McAlear, a member of the Canadian Book Publishers Council. Lickers asked her to let the publishers know that the Centre could investigate printed material on 'Indian affairs,' so that 'misinformation or errors be corrected *before* publication.' The Centre could contact 'qualified' Indian people, and, Lickers pointed out, the best way to have 'Indian' input would be to have an Indian person as an editor: 'who better to know the subject matter well enough to criticize than the Indian himself?'[80]

Such concerns suggest that Canadian history and its representations, far from being unimportant or irrelevant in a period of mass, American-influenced popular culture, may well have been an important arena in which contests over national and cultural identities took place. During the 1960s and early 1970s, Canadian nationalists saw history as part of an important wider cultural program that included literature, film, and music. However, far from being the concern of an elite group of academics, politicians, and writers, the writing and teaching of Canadian history (as well as other subjects) was, these letters suggest, a real concern for 'ordinary' members of the public. What that history should be – whether it would reflect the dynamics of power relations and struggles in the past, whether it was simply a liberal inclusiveness of various groups' contributions and their recognition – is a question that textbooks alone cannot answer, given the dynamics of classroom practice and students' own interpretations. Finally, whether this history simply reclothed the body of the imperial nation in a suit of liberal multiculturalism is an issue that has yet to be resolved.

Conclusion

As this conclusion is being written, passionate debates over the nature and place of Canadian history are being conducted in the newspapers, in academic journals, on television, and in classrooms. The rhetorical devices often used to frame these arguments are no stranger to any student of commemoration and memory: most common is the tragic narrative of a Golden Age, a period when all Canadian schoolchildren 'knew their history' (one might hope that Laura Secord's walk formed part of this sacred corpus of knowledge!) and thus assured the security of Canadian national identity. Of course, being a tragic narrative, the inevitable Decline and Fall of this Age, with the consequent damage to 'Canadian history,' follows. Knowledge of the nation's past has been undermined and dealt an almost fatal blow by (pick any or all): the rise of social studies in the schools; multiculturalism and its evil twin, 'politically correct' pedagogy; globalization and its undermining of national sovereignty. Some participants blame a generation of academic historians who (the argument runs) care little for history's place in Canadian schools; who no longer produce national narratives, focusing only on the local, the fragmented, and the trivial; and who, moreover, write these works in language that is 'inaccessible' and replete with 'jargon,' thus making their work incomprehensible to the 'general public.'[81] Another truism often made in some of these exchanges is that Canadian 'history' (rather than historians) has not produced heroes and heroines, a statement which is often linked to the supposedly benign and placid – or just downright dull – nature of 'our' national narratives. Others, though, believe that stirring and heroic symbols of national identity have existed but, like the fairy-tale character Sleeping Beauty, have been condemned to eternal slumber in the nation's collective consciousness unless and until they are kissed back to life by a patriotically minded historian.[82]

But, as this chapter has shown, myth-making and the creation of heroes (and some heroines), as well as narrating the 'nation's' progress, have been essential to the writing of Canadian history for the schools. Nor have these narratives remained static or, as some proponents of 'the national story' would have it, focused solely on political and military history. Examining the place of Secord's narrative, along with those of the War of 1812 and the role of Aboriginal peoples, allows us to see that teaching children about 'the past' was not a simple matter of reciting 'the facts' of Canadian history. No matter where they were presented or the age of the audience, the telling of historical narratives was – and continues to be – a performance that mingles description *and* interpretation, one that cannot be seen in isolation from the context in which it is staged.

Chapter Eight

'Seeing' the Past: The Monuments and the Candy Company

Writing to a colleague in the Ontario Historical Society in 1901, OHS secretary David Boyle argued that 'there is nothing better calculated to promote patriotism than the honor paid by posterity to those who in the past have served the public. Monuments are not less honorable to those who erect them than to those whom they seek to honor. They are at once an index to the character of a people and constant object lessons of the civic virtues, of heroism, and public and private gratitude. Their educational influence can hardly be overestimated.'[1] Boyle's observations were nothing if not timely, being made in the same year that the province's first monument to Laura Secord at Lundy's Lane was erected. It was not the first such structure for, as Norman Knowles has pointed out, a number of Loyalist monuments were erected between 1884 and 1914. Yet it would not be the last, as it was followed ten years later with a second monument at Queenston Heights.

Although the historical commemorators tended to privilege written narratives as the foundation of the nation's history, they also appreciated the significance of visual representations of the past. As a number of scholars have pointed out, the nineteenth century was a highly visual era, one that saw the proliferation of popular theatre, advertising, exhibitions, and museums.[2] And much time, effort, and fund-raising went into ensuring that Secord's memory would receive a suitable tribute in granite. Others, less convinced that monuments were the appropriate form of commemoration, named Queenston's elementary school after their heroine. Visual representations of the Dominion's history, such as the Canadian Historical Exhibition in 1899 and the collection of the Niagara Historical Museum, also included artefacts – most notably a tea kettle – that had belonged to Secord.[3] Her story was also dramatized for audiences in historical pageants and plays.

But the most obvious and effective example of the use of Secord's image as a metonymic medium for the past was the advertising of the Laura Secord Candy Company. The company's use of the past for the purposes of commercial capitalism, coupled with its attitude towards modernity, meant that Secord's history was reinterpreted and represented in somewhat different forms than in monuments or pageants. Yet the company was not alone in seeing the financial potential in her story; even Boyle believed that monuments offered more than just lessons in civic consciousness. 'There is also a material benefit ... in the added interest that historical sites thus marked acquire in the stimulation of travellers. Hundreds of thousands every year visit the monuments of Europe, and countries possessing such memorials are benefitted pecuniarily to a large extent from these pilgrimages. As an investment, apart altogether from the patriotic side of the questions, the money spent on monuments is a good investment.'[4] 'History' thus had the potential to be an economically productive enterprise.

Memories in Stone: The Monuments

The story of the campaign to build a monument to Laura Secord at the Drummond Hill cemetery on Lundy's Lane in 1901 has been narrated by a number of historians, popular and academic. They have located the monument's construction within the context of late nineteenth-century Loyalist commemoration and have also pointed to the pivotal role played by women commemorators, particularly Sarah Curzon and Emma Currie.[5] It is possible, though, to add some nuances to the history of the Secord monument at Lundy's Lane, to delve further into the symbolism and meaning of the monument itself, and to explore the relatively neglected, yet equally (if not more) important, 1910 Queenston Heights monument to Secord.

What were the objectives of those involved in the campaign for the Lundy's Lane monument? As we have seen, other forms of commemoration took shape during this period; the monument was by no means the sole form of tribute to individuals. Why, then, was a piece of granite or marble, as well as prose, poetry, and drama, a particularly appropriate medium for historical memory's conveyance? Certainly historical monuments were a form favoured by nineteenth-century historical commemorators in Ontario and Quebec. The supposed permanency of such a medium – one literally 'etched in stone' – would triumph over public capriciousness and reach a larger audience than that of the historical societies. Yet, as Marina Warner's work has shown, for the most part monument committees tended to choose the female form to convey allegories. Rarely was the figure of a historical woman memorialized in market squares or on public buildings.[6] In Secord's case, the monuments continued the process of singling her out as an individual while simultaneously attempting to inform the viewer that here were qualities found in all loyal and virtuous Canadian women.

Moreover, like those put up to Verchères, these commemorations were intended to demarcate the Niagara area as a region rich in 'history' and fix locality to her story. And, in her case, they were more successful. The Niagara Peninsula, particularly Niagara-on-the-Lake and Queenston, became a place where, as we shall see in chapter 9, groups such as the St Catharines Women's Literary Club could make self-styled 'pilgrimages' to visit historical shrines such as the monument and the Secords' Queenston homestead.

As well as promoting an Ontario locality, the commemorators also drew attention to the work of Mildred Peel, sister of the London, Ontario, painter Paul Peel. They thus continued both the process of celebrating Canadian women's achievements and ensuring that Anglo-Celtic women were integral to Secord's recognition. After viewing the sculpture (a bust of Secord placed on a granite pedestal) before it was installed at Lundy's Lane, the OHS Monuments and Tablets Committee was happy to report that 'Miss Peel has been very successful with the likeness with the assistance of a granddaughter of one of Laura Secord's sisters who bears a striking likeness to the Ingersolls and particularly to Laura Secord. She has been able to give us a beautiful [representation] of the brave and noble woman who did so much for King and country in 1813 ... It is worthy of note that the Laura Secord monument will be the first public memorial to a woman, erected in Canada and will be the work of a Canadian woman.'[7]

Although it is true that Secord's femininity was a essential component in the process of her commemoration, the monument's inscription (arrived at after various consultations) celebrated not only Secord but the other Beaver Dams participants (fig. 8.1):

To perpetuate the name and fame of Laura Secord who walked alone nearly 20 miles by a circuitous, difficult and perilous route through woods and swamps and over many roads to warn a British outpost at De Cew's Falls

8.1 Laura Secord monument, Lundy's Lane. This photograph was taken 22 October 2000; note the carnations left at the foot of the monument.

of an intended attack and thereby enabled Lieut. FitzGibbon on the 24th June, 1813, with less than 50 men of H.M. 49th Regiment, about 15 militiamen and a small force of Six Nation and other Indians under Captains William Johnson Kerr and Dominique Ducharme, to surprise and attack the enemy at Beechwoods (or Beaver Dams), and after a short engagement to capture Col. Boerstler of the U.S. Army and his entire force of 542 men with two field pieces.

Moreover, the monument itself (which replaced the marble slab grave-stones that marked James and Laura Secord's graves, which were trans-ferred to Holy Trinity Church, Chippewa) did not stand alone in the cemetery. As Ruth McKenzie has pointed out, the eight-foot Secord monument was placed near the Battle of Lundy's Lane soldiers' memo-rial, a forty-foot granite shaft.[8] The narratives of Secord's walk had always included male actors and depicted masculine heroism; women authors, though, made it clear that Secord was their protagonist and women's heroism their major theme. However, the placement of the Lundy's Lane monument could (according to the viewer's predilections) allow the viewer to see it as either an interesting historical curiosity, a possible diversion from the central narratives of male heroism during 1812, or as an irrefutable reminder of Canadian women's importance and their support for their country. The latter position, of course, was taken by those responsible for the monument. It was reiterated at the unveiling ceremony, held 22 June 1901, by a number of the speakers who stressed Secord's loyalty and devotion to her country during the war. The presi-dent of the Manitoba Historical Society, George Bryce, did mingle, however, the themes of women's service to the country with their domes-tic role, as he spoke of 'the debt we owed to the memory of those early settlers, particularly the women who had been the home makers.'[9]

However, not all felt the event had been an unqualified success. Four days after the ceremony, Mamie Strobel, of the Women's Wentworth Historical Society, wrote to Boyle and asked why 'were we not notified of the unveiling ... A dozen or more of our members, including myself would have gone down had we known of it in time, and we feel rather sad at being overlooked ... We are greatly disappointed at not being invited to go to Lundy's Lane – How came you to forget us?'[10] The problem, it appeared, was that an invitation had been sent to the president, Mrs Calder, who, Strobel stated, was 'too full of trouble to take any interest in the society.'[11] Nevertheless, Strobel was troubled herself, since 'you could not make some of our members believe that the notice was not sent to

Mrs. Calder purposely to keep our society away as in her trouble she could not think of anything.' Strobel could not believe that the women in her organization would 'do a mean thing [but] after the way Mrs. Fessenden cheated Mrs. Holden out of the curatorship of Dundurn I can't say the same for her.'[12] Apparently Laura Secord's commemoration had opened up old wounds among the Hamilton historians.

Nine years later, this form of memorializing Secord did not go uncontested. Upon hearing that the Dominion government had granted two thousand dollars for a Queenston Heights monument, Edna Lowrey, Secretary of the Women's Institute of Queenston and St David's, wrote to John Jackson, Manager of the Niagara Parks Commission (NPC), protesting the proposed expenditure. Lowrey suggested that instead of a monument, a memorial hall should be built and named after Secord. The building *must* be put up, she informed Jackson, on government-owned land and controlled by the park commissioners. The Women's Institute (WI) had received contributions from their sister institutes across the province, from the public schools, and from private donations; moreover, the residents of Queenston and St David's had raised four hundred dollars. 'The citizens of the vicinity,' wrote Lowrey, 'feel that they should have some voice in the expenditure of money in their own community and *do not* want another monument erected. Anything that could be erected would be far surpassed by Brock's Monument.' She also believed that more buildings were needed at Queenston Heights: '... and in the vicinity are more relics which should be preserved for the country but cannot now because there is not [a] suitable building.' The hall, Jackson was told, should be of brick or stone, thus making it a suitably permanent structure. 'We think it absurd to have a monument and a Hall erected at the same place to the memory of the same person and a Hall of such description would be ... of great benefit to the community and to the travelling public.' Lowrey had heard that the work on the monument was to start immediately: '... and we are very anxious not to have it proceeded with until we have heard from Mr. Borden to whom we have applied to have the grant used if possible in connection with our building.' She closed by hoping that Jackson approved of these plans and that he would use his influence in her group's favour.[13]

The Women's Institute's request was duly passed on to NPC chairman John Langmuir, but on 1 February Jackson wrote back to Lowrey to tell her that those who had obtained the Dominion government's grant 'do not see fit to consent to a change in the purpose of the Grant.' As well, a contract had been signed and thus 'the Commissioners have no power to

divert the monies appropriated for the purpose you have in mind,'
although if another grant turned up the NPC would consider putting it
towards park lands.[14] However, the Commission did not brush the Institute off completely. Three months later, Langmuir met personally with
Lowrey and her colleague Mrs Hudson Usher to discuss a site for the
Hall.[15]

Even after the Queenston Heights monument to Secord had been
built and unveiled, the Women's Institute refused to let the matter of the
hall drop. In May 1911, Mrs H.C. Bradley, the WI president, and Lowrey
wrote once again to the NPC, advising them that suitable land might be
available for the Secord hall. Negotiations among the WI, the NPC, and
the Dominion government (who would be the purchaser) carried on
throughout the rest of the year and into the following, but stalled over
the purchase price. The WI did not take the delay kindly; in early 1913,
Lowrey implored the Commission to 'take the land as I believe [the
Commission] has the power to do so?' And, if not, then could they not
consider other property, as the WI was anxious to go ahead with the hall
and 'things are dragging altogether too long.'[16] The WI continued to
raise funds and reported in April that they had $2,500 in an account and
wanted to have the hall built for the upcoming peace celebration. Thus
they needed to start immediately and asked Langmuir what support they
might expect, telling him to 'instruct Jackson to draw up a plan with
working specifications and send some to us immediately – must we pay
an architect four to five thousand to do this for us? You seemed so
interested in our Hall when we interviewed you on the subject that we
hope you will see it is consistent to put this through promptly.'[17] Their
faith in Langmuir, though, was badly shaken, as by September Lowrey
had called Jackson and written Langmuir, demanding, 'Can you not
give me an answer? When talking to you you said you would in two or
three days. I think it is two or three weeks since then and still no answer.
Please give me an answer this week so I may have something to report to
the committee. They are becoming impatient. It would be very much
appreciated if I might have an answer very shortly.'[18]

But when the answer came, it was not quite what the WI had in mind.
On 27 November, they were told that the board had considered their
request the previous week, 'when it was decided that in as much as
permission has been given to erect the proposed Laura Secord Memorial Hall upon commissioners' property, the Board could not see its way
clear to make any further contribution or undertake further responsibility.'[19] Far from being deterred, however, the Institute continued with

its plans and in 1914 opened Memorial Hall as part of Laura Secord School in Queenston. A plaque was put up near the entrance with the inscription

Laura Secord Memorial
In Loving and Honored Memory of
Laura Ingersoll Secord
A Resident of Queenston and
A Heroine of Upper Canada
Who Saved Her Country
From the Enemy in 1813.

The WI's vigorous campaign in opposition to the monument was matched by Emma Currie's support of it and her determination that she have a say in its direction. Although Ontario premier George Ross believed that 'Mrs. Currie will agree to anything we [he and Langmuir] decide,' his belief in her malleability was somewhat misplaced.[20] Currie pressed Langmuir and Ross on the media of the prototypes used to guide the stonemasons and on the amount of money available.[21] She was also particularly concerned about the procedures of the unveiling ceremony and requested that Jackson visit her at home (one of many requests that he, Langmuir, or Ross come to her house, as she was finding it increasingly difficult to travel) to discuss these '*soon* for there are certain things that need to be prepared for the day ... it is my desire and has been from the first to do nothing without consultation with those who are responsible that everything should be done satisfactorily.'[22] Jackson and Langmuir themselves believed that the initial sketch submitted for the monument was 'very ordinary and it seems a pity to slight the memory of one of our greatest Canadian heroines by a tribute that is unworthy, when by the addition of a few dollars we might have a suitable monument.'[23] Currie, for her part, was ready to admit her gratitude and approval of the proceedings to Jackson and Langmuir, telling the former that 'I assure you and Mr. Langmuir (who has met my wishes so kindly in every way) that you can make any arrangements – feeling that they will be in every way satisfactory ... Please express to him that the site selected by him is most gratifying and will be appreciated by every woman ... My *aim* from the commencement has been to erect a suitable monument for a brave woman – *without any extravagance*, and yet fulfilling a brave woman's deed.'[24]

She was unwilling, however, to simply turn over all responsibility for

8.2 Laura Secord monument, Queenston Heights.

the unveiling ceremony to the commissioners and reminded them a number of times that Laura Secord's grandchildren must be invited. Her granddaughters, who were in their seventies and eighties, 'are all that are left of the second generation from Laura. There are others of a later generation but not of Laura.'[25] These spectators, unlike any others, would thus combine both genealogy and authenticity, reminding the audience that Secord was no mere mythical heroine, confined to an abstract and hazy 'times past,' but instead had flesh-and-blood ties to the present. Currie was temporarily diverted from her concern that the unveiling be comfortable for the 'grandchildren' when she heard of Queenston residents' plans for the hall. She expressed her disgust with the idea to Jackson. 'Did you hear that the opposition of Queenston to Queenston Heights *being made a cemetery*, is that the two largest fruit growers want money to build a fruit growers hall on *the grounds – if this can be done* they will *desecrate* the name of Laura Secord by *giving* it her name.'[26] Once the monument was in place, Currie paid a visit of inspection and was quite pleased. 'It is fine in every way,' she told Jackson, 'without being pretentious: material, design, and execution, excellent.'[27]

The unveiling ceremony had been postponed until the following summer in order to ensure fine weather; except for a few minor obstacles, it went off smoothly. However, two months later Currie told Ross that the inscription on the monument was incorrect, as the date of the Battle of Beaver Dams had been given as 23 July 1813, not 23 June 1813.[28] Langmuir commented wryly to Ross that 'I thought that inasmuch as the designer was in touch with Mrs. Emma Currie that the inscription would be absolutely perfect,' but promised to have the offending date altered.[29]

Yet even with the monument in place and open to the many tourists who visited Queenston Heights, Currie was not done with memorials to Secord. Langmuir received another letter from her the following March, in which she asked him if Mr Munro, the designer and sculptor of the monument, could also execute another statue of Secord 'in the costume in which she performed her historic deed.' This figure would be placed at the base of the Queenston Heights monument. Such an object, she reassured Langmuir, would not cost the NPC a penny, as there were funds in Toronto and St Catharines banks that had been raised for the addition. The accounts had been collecting interest for ten years and now totalled four hundred dollars; they could also, she pointed out, be used to pay for a shelter for the monument.[30] Langmuir replied that this request would have to be submitted to the board and enclosed a newspaper article about a sketch for a bronze statue of Secord.[31] Currie's response was swift and emphatic. 'Yours of March 29 1912,' she wrote, 'helps to correct a difficulty arising from an unauthorized press statement.' Everything pertaining to Secord's memorial must be vetted by the NPC. 'I wish Mr. Langmuir to believe that his sanction is the first thing to be submitted for additions or changes. A bronze statue was never thought of. The memorial is Vermont Granite. Canada does not furnish any thing suitable for such purposes. Have notified the parties who published that announcement that their services are dispensed with.'[32]

Whoever the hapless and indiscreet 'parties' were, they were soon forgotten as Currie pursued the issue of an addition to the monument. She wanted to draw attention to an aspect of the Secord story that appeared in the second (although not the first) edition of her book. In this incident, Secord took off her shoes and stockings so that she might bathe her sore feet, but 'to her dismay' was unable to get them back on. She tied them together, hung them around her arm, and in that state met FitzGibbon. Currie had been given a sketch of her heroine, drawn up by David Secord's great-granddaughter, which she proposed using for the granite-stone addition. She reminded Langmuir that, although she was not in a hurry, he should not 'forget that I am a very old woman. If I live until the latter part of November will be eighty-three years old. My *broken hip* makes me very lame. Cannot move without a crutch. My sight has failed me very much within the last few months – my general health is good. Rarely out of my home.'[33] Langmuir passed on the matter to Ross, telling him that the NPC felt such an addition 'will be a great disfigurement of the Statue ... As Mrs. Currie is getting very old I should like the refusal to accede to her request couched in the most courteous terms possible, and I know of no one who can advise her not to press this matter better than yourself. You have taken such an interest in the Laura Secord Memorial Monument that I know she will act on your advice.'[34] Ross acquiesced, telling Currie that the Commission did not wish to proceed with the addition:

> ... and in this view I fully concur. I do not think it possible as the monument was not designed to bear a statue or even a bust, or that any figure large or small would harmonize with the monument. And unless it did it would very much destroy the effect and beauty of the work already accomplished. Had it been part of the original design, even if both were not completed at the same time, there would be no danger of destroying the artistic effect of either. I know your zeal for the memory of Laura Secord and the extraordinary energy you have exhibited in recording her life and doing honour to her memory, and I fear that my letter will make a painful impression upon a mind so sensitive to all that pertains to Laura Secord's history, but I hope that on reflection you will see that the conclusion arrived at by the Parks Commission is correct.

Ross concluded with a further attempt to assuage her feelings by congratulating her on her new edition and hoping she was happy with her publisher.[35] There is no record of Currie's reaction to Ross's letter or the NPC's rejection of her proposal. Ross, though, forwarded a copy of his letter to Langmuir and enclosed a note telling Langmuir that coping with the matter was no easy task. 'I know,' he confessed to Langmuir, 'it will hurt the old lady's feelings,' but the proposal would turn a 'respectable ... monument into a grotesque deformity.'[36] Langmuir concurred, telling Ross he was grateful 'for the kind and tactful manner' in which he had avoided embroiling Langmuir himself; all members of the NPC had agreed that the figure would have 'destroyed all its [the monument's] beauty and artistic effect.'[37]

While Currie's campaign to have a statue of Secord added to the monument smacked of an obsession with her heroine, there may well have been good reasons for her strategy. Although the Lundy's Lane monument had a bust of Secord, the Queenston Heights one (taller than the former by four feet) depicted only her bonneted face – and that in the form of a bronze medallion. In contrast, Currie's suggested addition would have represented Secord in her entirety, as a flesh-and-blood woman whose body bore the marks of her struggle to serve her country, just as statues of wounded soldiers bore signs of their sacrifice. And, like the Lundy's Lane monument, the Queenston Heights edifice was placed metaphorically – and almost literally – at the feet of Brock's. His was a much larger and more prominent monument that – as the WI of Queenston was well aware – could easily overshadow that of Secord. Moreover, the inscription on the Queenston monument read:

> To Laura Ingersoll Secord
> Who saved her husband's life
> In the battle of these heights
> October 13th, 1812
> And who risked her own
> In conveying to Capt. FitzGibbon
> Information by which he won
> The victory of Beaver Dams.

Like the first monument, this tribute could be read in a number of ways. Both of Secord's brave acts were hereby commemorated and the rationale for placing the monument on Queenston Heights made clear. Those students of Canadian history who might have been familiar only with her walk would thus be told that, far from being exceptional or even aberrant, it was part of a continuum of bravery and patriotic service. Like her counterpart Brock, Secord would be exceptional, but not so exceptional that 'ordinary' Canadian girls and women would feel daunted when they tried to emulate her loyalty. Yet the monument also continued to domesticate Secord, since the first act of heroism was directed towards her husband. As well, the omission of details in the second half of the inscription meant that a spectator – such as an American tourist – unfamiliar with Canadian history would not have known that her walk took place one year later and was more than a trip across the street.

The depiction of Secord on the medallion as an elderly 'lady' was more ambiguous. On the one hand, it could be read as an attempt to downplay her status as a heroine. Instead of depicting her as a larger-than-life, mythic figure – a Canadian Boudicca, for example, the saviour of her people – it emphasized her ordinariness and normality and thus prevented Secord from attaining true mythic status. But an alternative reading – and probably one closer to the heart of Emma Currie, who had no compunctions about domesticating Secord – was that the medallion suggested that in their lifetimes such 'ordinary' women were capable of acting to protect their country. Thus they should not be underestimated and thought to be feeble creatures, themselves in need of protection. Furthermore, the fact that she was commemorated as an individual woman was, as I have noted, an anomaly in the tradition of monument building. Despite the fact that Currie's hope for additional embellishments was thwarted, the monument's depiction of Secord did transgress some of the more dominant conventions of Victorian and Edwardian commemorative edifices. In these memorials, the genre of allegorical representations of women as outside and transcendent of history took precedence over attempts to place women firmly within historical time and as historical actors.[38]

Historical Pageantry

Monuments, of course, were stationary, recognitions of the past fixed in one spot. While pictures of them might travel, by and large their creators expected future generations to come to the monument to venerate their ancestors and their deeds. But as has been argued in chapter 3, often such edifices end up being taken for granted, becoming invisible yet, paradoxically, permanent features of the landscape. Other, more mobile ways of remembering the past through visual media have also been found necessary. One such means was the historical pageant. By the early twentieth century, historical pageants had become increasingly popular in Britain and the United States, serving a number of purposes: civic pride, patriotism, and popular entertainment.[39] Such spectacles also demonstrated the belief that 'history could be made into a dramatic public ritual' in which the participants 'could bring about some kind of future social and political transformation.'[40] And, as historians have argued, pageants provided a way of creating historical memories through performance and the use of music, song, dance, and costumes, as well as sometimes (for the more lavish and sophisticated) make-up, scenery, props, and lighting.

Much of the literature on pageantry examines those enacted on a fairly grand and very public scale, such as the Quebec tercentenary or pageants organized by an entire town to commemorate its history. However, the pageants in which Secord was featured – or at least those that have come to light in the historical record – were far less grand, performed by both adults and children at the local level or in schools. Such events did not leave extensive records of their planning or staging (unlike the Quebec pageant), but there are hints of their popularity and their subject matter. Pageants might be given some coverage by the local newspaper, particularly if the participants were prominent citizens. In June 1927, for example, the IODE staged such an event at Massey Hall 'as its contribution to the celebration of the Diamond Jubilee of Confederation.' Nine scenes were presented, each one with 'an accompanying tableaux, and effectively suggested the major episodes which developed the history of Canada.' The episodes, linked by prologues, covered events such as Cartier's landing, Henry Hudson 'discovering Hudson's Bay' (*sic*), the expulsion of the Acadians (adapted from Longfellow's *Evangeline*), the Battle of the Plains of Abraham, 'Alexander Mackenzie discovering the Pacific Ocean,' the arrival of the Loyalists ('Canada's First Parliament'), the War of 1812, and the meeting of the Fathers of Confederation. Social history was also presented in 'The French Court in Canada (amidst the alarms of warfare with the British and the Indians),' the country's first school, the coming of the Ursulines, and Western homesteading. The pageant's conclusion, 'Sixty Years of Confederation,' 'revealed in a highly attractive ballet the social and industrial progress of Canada.' Both Madeleine de Verchères and Secord had their turn in the spotlight, although the latter shared the stage with Brock and Tecumseh. *Saturday Night* was pleased to report that 'the pageant was entirely satisfactory from the point of view of patriotic sentiment and many of the scenes had artistic appeal.' A 'powerful' episode was that of the 'French Court,' and the eviction of the Acadians was 'dramatically moving.' 'Particularly attractive,' the magazine noted, 'was the episode, "1812," in which the jolly dances of the farmer folk were immensely pleasing to the audience.'[41]

Although she did not warrant special mention in the review's text, Mrs. C.J. Campbell, who played Secord, did manage to get her picture in the magazine, wearing a bonnet, long-sleeved, full-skirted dress, and (unlike Currie's imagined statue) leather shoes or boots.[42] The other characters who appeared in the pages of *Saturday Night* were a Mr R. Edmunds, who posed as Frontenac in full wig, moustache, sword and sash, and lace-cuffed embroidered jacket, and Mrs Colin Sabiston, who dressed as Champlain, clutching a sword and sporting bobbed hair, a false moustache, and seventeenth-century tunic, short pantaloons, and tights.[43] Such a costume hinted at a transgressive element to these events, with 'respectable,' middle-class women cross-dressing and performing as masculine historical figures who might also be from a different ethnic background. Whether any of them were conscious of prodding at the limits of propriety, or whether dressing as men was seen as just a harmless lark – tamed because the subject matter was the entirely respectable past – is difficult to determine.

For adults, another form of 'performing the past' was the fancy-dress party structured around historical figures. The St Catharines Women's Literary Club (WLC) held such an event in 1935 as a celebration of their thirty-fifth anniversary. Held in the home of club member Mrs J.B. McIntyre, with its 'spacious rooms, old wall tapestries, and handsome crystal chandeliers,' the 'old-fashioned party' featured a musical program of vocal solos with piano accompaniment, followed 'by tea, served on a lace cloth, with single and double mums, antique silver candlesticks with crystal prisms [that held] three-branch ivory candles.' The guests represented a number of historical figures, almost all of them female. English personages, such as Boudicca or the Duchess of Richmond (Mrs James Brighty), wearing a lavender satin frock with 'over drapery of exquisitely embroidered net of pink and blue rosebuds on an ivory background, topped by pearl strands and a pink feather in her hair.' Scotland was also depicted in the Highland dress worn by Mrs McIntyre and by the anonymous woman who came as Flora Macdonald. And Canadian figures, such as Susanna Moodie (grey taffeta with brown velvet bands and a taffeta bonnet), Pauline Johnson, and, of course, Laura Secord, also came to tea.[44]

Records of children's pageants have also survived in the form of their scripts.[45] Isobel McComb Brighty's 'Blazing of the Trail' was written for and performed by the St Catharines Girl Guides in the inter-war decades. Brighty, a long-standing member of the WLC, wrote the pageant 'with the hope that it would inspire the youth of our nation to follow in the footsteps of those whose love and devotion to country led them to the Blazing of the Trail.' As set out by Brighty, the pageant made use of a very large cast of characters, well over one hundred (although double-casting would have been possible). The Guides and their leader acted as a chorus; the pageant opened with a prologue in which the leader told them:

Ye have heard around your campfire
Tales of love and valour too,
Listen now, and I will tell you
Tales as strange but also true.
Ye are told in your Guide duty
'Be prepared and your best,
Lend a hand to help each other
Trust to God to do the rest'
So these Guides who came before you
And as heroes now we name
Only tried to do their duty
Not to win undying fame.[46]

Brighty chose fairly familiar characters and scenes for her youthful performers. The pageant began with Native peoples and then moved to depict their contact with Cartier and Champlain. This encounter was followed by the story of New France, in which fur traders and *coureurs de bois*, nuns and priests, French ladies and seigneurs, soldiers, and Madeleine de Verchères were brought on stage. All of these characters were followed by the arrival of the British and the UELs, the War of 1812 (with Brock, the Secords, an American sentry, Indians, and FitzGibbon), and Upper Canadian pioneers; in turn, these scenes and characters made way for the nine provinces and 'Maple Leaf Maidens' of 1867. Once nationhood had been firmly established, representatives of the armed forces and a Red Cross nurse arrived to demonstrate Canada's service to the Empire in 1914. They shared the stage with farmerettes and knitters who, the audience was told, had served on the home front. The pageant's penultimate scene was the 'youth of the nation' singing 'O Canada'; it concluded with a Girl Guide finale.[47]

Such scenes and personages were fairly predictable and corresponded to the lessons of the textbooks. Quite likely this was Brighty's intent, as such pageants were intended to reinforce and enliven material already taught in the classroom, not to introduce children to new historical knowledge. Like the Quebec tercentenary, the past was presented as a romantic epic, full of 'heroism, nobility, grandeur, paternalism, community harmony, Christian sacrifice, mission, [and] loyalty.'[48] Furthermore, Brighty's script followed a well-established tradition of pageantry, in that the exhibited past was 'a highly selective and idiosyncratic representation' of Canadian history.[49] But the pageant also imitated its predecessors in its ambivalent treatment of colonialism and its power struggles, both those that involved Native peoples and the colonization of French Canadians. Brighty acknowledged the presence of Native peoples and the existence of Native societies prior to European contact (although the scene jumbled various First Nations together for a homogeneous 'Indian life': they were shown living in wigwams, drumming on tom-toms, and with Native women performing the Sun Dance); but the arrival of the French was a peaceful, even joyous event. Aboriginals pressed gifts on Cartier and eagerly embraced the message of Christianity offered by Champlain's Recollets and Jesuits, who 'taught those poor benighted Indians, that their life was more than chance.'[50] However, in the following scene of Madeleine de Verchères, the 'poor benighted Indians' quickly – and somewhat confusingly – turned into 'sneaking forms' who 'spied' and were known for their 'cruel cunning' (and were held off by Verchères until she was rescued by La Monnerie, to whom she offered her father's sword). The French regime's end was signalled, not by a battle and the 'conquest' of New France, but simply by the entrance of General Wolfe, who came with 'glowing banner' (the Union Jack) and some British soldiers to the accompaniment of 'Rule Britannia.'[51] Wolfe was quickly followed by the Loyalists, and they, in turn, were succeeded by the War of 1812.

The text then deals quickly with Brock's sacrifice at Queenston Heights, although the cast was not instructed to enact it. The Secords, he leaning on her for support, then entered. Laura's overhearing the American plan was performed and, with James's reluctant consent, she left, passing an American sentry and exiting the stage.[52] As she reappeared, 'stumbling and weary, showing fatigue and terror,' a group of 'Indians' entered, whereupon they 'immediately seized' her and dragged her to the chief. Secord was directed to plead for her life and tell her errand; having done so, she was given an escort to FitzGibbon. Secord and the 'Indians' having left the stage, FitzGibbon then entered, deep in meditation, but 'hear[ing] alarming sounds at right,' called a soldier, who brought in Secord and her new companions. She told FitzGibbon her news and was 'helped – fainting' – off stage to left followed by all. To the music of 'The British Grenadiers,' FitzGibbon, leading a company of soldiers and band of Indians 'advanced and won the day.'[53] This scene was the end of Natives' appearance in the pageant.

It was not new, as we have seen, to write out First Nations after 1812 – Brighty was merely participating in a well-established historical trope. Yet because of the form of the pageant itself, the stage directions, and the content of the verse, the disappearing act of Aboriginal peoples was unmistakable: they literally exited off stage – both for the audience and for Canadian history.[54] Secord, after all, was followed by a group of pioneer folk, boys and girls, women and men, so that her presence as a historical actor and signifier of women's role in history was clearly marked.[55] As well, the lack of stage directions for wars between Aboriginals and Europeans, and the British and French, may have been motivated by Brighty's desire that children not perform violent acts. But events such as war and military conquest would not, after all, have been news to the participants or the audience, as school textbooks made it clear that these events had been part of Canada's past. And there was no compunction about having children in other scenes portray Aboriginals as violent, bloodthirsty characters and forces of nature.

However, such considerations were not uppermost in the mind of the local paper's reviewer. 'Historic Pageant Scored an Extraordinary Success,' read the headline. The Brownies and Girl Guides, performing under Brighty's direction, had appeared before a standing-room-only audience in the local Collegiate Institute's auditorium. There, 'encouraged by the vast crowd which had gathered to witness their historical and educational pageant of Canada, the Guides excelled in their efforts, winning the merited applause of the audience.' The highlights of the evening were the dancing of the Brownies, the Indian love song ('a beautiful haunting melody of real artistic merit'), the 'most excellent Sun Dance,' and the costumes which 'throughout were realistic and lent the required backing to the production.' Laura Secord's shawl, along with the actress who played her, merited special attention, as did a two-hundred-year-old Indian buckskin coat, originally from the Northwest. The pageant was a decided triumph, and much of the credit for that went to Brighty.[56]

As this review suggests, pageants might be an impressive – or, at least, entertaining – presentation of the past for their audiences' consumption. They also offered imaginative opportunities for the participants to perform the past and create historical characters' subjectivities and identities for themselves, something that was not so easy to accomplish with monuments. It is difficult to be more than speculative on this score, as there are no extant records that could tell us how the pageant participants – who were, after all, children – felt as they 'became' Native warriors, French soldiers, or loyal pioneers. Also, we can only speculate how certain children felt about re-enacting a 'history' far removed from their own. The pageant's performative aspect was underscored by having Euro-Canadian schoolchildren playing Native peoples, a mimicry reminiscent of black-face minstrel shows. Any attempts to understand their characters as historical actors, with their own motivations and desires, may have been subsumed by stereotypical costumes, gestures, and vocal expressions. For many children, the entire experience might have been less educational than simply entertaining – a chance to dress up and dance, sing, and 'run wild.' Certainly the format of the pageant, which presented a succession of tableaux that were held together by a highly selective and, at times, disjointed narrative, did not – in fact, could not – even hint that certain historical events had been more complicated, let alone engage with such complexities.

The Secord story caught the attention of other children's dramatists, ranging from Alexander Maitland Stephens, whose 'Laura Secord' was published in his 1929 *Classroom Plays from Canadian History*, to playwright Norman Symonds and the students of Guelph's King George Senior Public School, who penned the collaborative effort *Laura and the Lieutenant: A Musical Play* in 1974. And, as the Epilogue will discuss, Secord's story is still being used for its dramatic potential in the CRB Foundation's *Heritage Minutes* (albeit with a very different racial subtext than Sarah Curzon's play). Canadian nationalism of the 1970s also helped shape the 1974 CTV production of *The Cow That Never Was*, a half-hour play written by Lister Sinclair and narrated by Pierre Berton that was part of the company's Heritage Theatre Series.[57] As its title suggests, *The Cow* was intent on debunking the myth of Secord's bovine companion, which, according to Berton, first turned up in a 'shoddy biography.' But the dramatization of Secord's story was not intended to rescue her contribution to the nation from Wallace's denunciation. Although her encounter with FitzGibbon was duly depicted, Berton expressed scepticism about the timing of her hearing the news. Moreover, the viewer saw only her interview with FitzGibbon and not the walk itself.

Rather than foregrounding Secord and brave Canadian femininity, the real subjects of *The Cow* were different kinds of military masculinity. The bravado exhibited by the American and English soldiers, one that dissolves at the threat (usually imagined) of 'Indians,' is contrasted with the forceful, effective, and somewhat raffish manliness of the Anglo-Irish FitzGibbon (played by R.H. Thompson). FitzGibbon, who commands a regiment he dubs the 'Bloody Boys,' has not only proved himself physically adept in Canadian terrain (having waded through the 'Black Swamp' that Secord crossed), but he is also a clever strategist, one who keeps a vigilant eye out for American spies (donning farmer's clothes over his uniform in order to trick them and remaining sceptical of Secord until she, in turn, convinces him of her loyalty). He also tricks the Americans

into surrendering by his use of the menace of 'Indians.' In this presentation of the Secord narrative, it is FitzGibbon who is the true 'Canadian'
patriot; martial masculinity, not civilian femininity, provides the bedrock
for this national narrative.

Consuming the Past: The Laura Secord Candy Company

Pageants, monuments, and other visual and material presentations of
the past have often tended to reach limited – and already converted –
audiences. Ironically, the survival of Secord in popular consciousness is
primarily owing to the use of her name to head a major candy company.
Its advertising has probably been the most influential visual deployment
of Secord's image. As Ruth McKenzie puts it, 'mention Laura Secord to
the man in the street and the chances are his thoughts will turn to
chocolates' (and the cover of McKenzie's 1971 book used the Secord
company's trademark signature, itself an adaptation of Secord's own).[58]

Unlike the historical societies, there is little in the way of corporate
records that would permit a full exploration of the Secord company
history. A skeletal history exists, which starts with Frank O'Connor's
1913 founding of the company in Toronto. O'Connor, a future member
of the Senate, began his confectionery career as a Chiclets manufacturer
in Peterborough. According to the company's narratives (themselves an
example of the formation of corporate historical memory), O'Connor
chose the name Secord out of a desire to identify his products with
wholesomeness, purity, domesticity, and cleanliness. He opened his first
set of stores in Toronto and Montreal; their success prompted the company's expansion across Ontario and Quebec and then to Winnipeg in
the 1930s. It also used drugstores as retail outlets for the candies. In 1964
the corporation bought the Smiles n' Chuckles company, thus acquiring
its own source of chocolate and expanding into the mass confectionery
market; it followed this move by placing its products in Canadian department stores, having already set up shops in shopping centres. From the
1960s on, the corporation also changed hands a number of times. In
1969 John Labatt Ltd bought Secord (and, as will be discussed in the
next chapter, bought and renovated the Secord homestead in Queenston),
then sold it to Rowntree in 1974. After a number of changes in focus and
production in the 1970s, in 1989 Rowntree, in turn, sold its interest to
Nestlé. In an ironic turn of corporate fate, in June 1999 the company
announced it had been sold to Fanny Farmer, an American chain established by O'Connor shortly after forming Secord.[59]

Whether or not the company's founder would appreciate the irony of his first business venture being bought out by his second is, unfortunately, unknowable. What is clear from the company's early advertising of the 1910s and 1920s is that it did not choose to make Secord's historical significance the centrepiece of its advertising (although, as we shall see, it was an important undercurrent). Very few – if any – advertisements from these decades refer to her walk or to her status as a heroine; none featured Secord walking to the nearest candy outlet as an act of patriotic consumerism. They did use a picture that was purported to be of her, a beribboned cameo of an elderly woman wearing a white bonnet tied with a large white bow. Moreover, the advertisements were framed with rows of maple leaves suggestive, of course, of devotion to and pride in Canada (see figs. 8.3 to 8.5). And, particularly in the context of the inter-war years, there probably would have been no need to remind customers of the Secord story and its significance.

Instead, the company chose to create its own history, that of its dedication to purity of materials and care in preparation, to the importance of the candy-maker's craft, and to a determination to give the Canadian (or, at least, the Ontario and Quebec) customer the very best quality possible. An advertisement from May 1920 was typical of the company's approach. With the heading 'For Old Time Sake,' it appealed to the candy-buying public as 'Dear Friends,' a phrase commonly used in its advertisements of these decades, and asked them to let the company 'take you back – not so many years ago – to a small shop in a very inconspicuous place where Laura Secord candies were originated. Commencing with this modest little shop and using methods that have never changed, Laura Secord Candies have won for themselves world-wide distinction and fame.' However, this was not because of 'the usual business method of advertising'; rather, it 'was the inevitable result of the consistent goodness of the candies.' The overture to the company's 'friends' went on to insist that 'this remarkable growth, which now includes the larger cities of Canada, is a wonderful tribute to quality and goes to show how goodness will survive. By means of quality, dignity and simplicity, so many friends have been made by Laura Secord Candies, that today our dainty little candy shops are sought and frequented by folks of every walk of life.'[60]

The company's determination to distinguish itself from the techniques of modern advertising and mass production, to address its customers as 'friends,' not consumers, and to rely on a reputation for quality products painstakingly built up over a number of years, suggests its attempted

QUALITY

Dear Friends :

The question of quality is never debated in

Laura Secord

STUDIOS. That important question was settled when these dainty little white shops first made their debut to a critical public. They were then and are now

THE ACCOMPLISHMENT OF ARTISTS

and the result of using materials that are only

THE PUREST, BEST

and most WHOLESOME that are obtainable

FOR OLD TIME SAKE.

Dear Friends :

Let us take you back—not so many years ago — to a small shop in a very inconspicuous place where

Laura Secord

CANDIES were originated.

Commencing with this modest little shop and using methods that have never changed, Laura Secord Candies have won for themselves world-wide distinction and fame. This was accomplished without using the usual business method of advertising, and was the inevitable result of the consistent goodness of the candies.

This remarkable growth, which now includes the larger cities of Canada, is a wonderful tribute to quality and goes to show how goodness will survive.

By means of quality, dignity and simplicity, so many friends have been made by Laura Secord Candies, that to-day our dainty little candy shops are sought and frequented by folks of every walk of life.

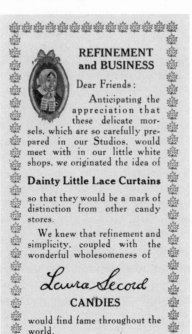

REFINEMENT and BUSINESS

Dear Friends :

Anticipating the appreciation that these delicate morsels, which are so carefully prepared in our Studios, would meet with in our little white shops, we originated the idea of

Dainty Little Lace Curtains

so that they would be a mark of distinction from other candy stores.

We knew that refinement and simplicity, coupled with the wonderful wholesomeness of

Laura Secord

CANDIES

would find fame throughout the world.

8.3–8.5 Advertisements for Laura Secord Candy Company, circa 1920s.

disassociation from the world of post-war commerce and manufacturing – in short, from the milieu of post-war modernity. Certainly many of the company's strategies – not least, its use of a historical figure who was herself a figure of loyalty – evoked continuity, stability, and tradition in the face of a changing and possibly confusing (not to mention deceptive) world. The woman or man who bought Secord products would thus be assured of the very best of Canadian goods and craftsmanship. Of course, there were a number of ironies and contradictions involved in these strategies. As Keith Walden has pointed out, in the latter decades of the nineteenth century, companies had to work hard to inculcate brand loyalties in Canadian consumers.[61] Thus, the company strategy – suggesting that a customer would buy its product based on a long-standing loyalty – was itself a product of 'modern' advertising and retailing techniques. But the Secord company, while invoking brand loyalty and using Laura Secord's image, was also helping to inculcate that image, as it intertwined the two kinds of loyalty for Canadian consumers: dedication to the product and dedication to the nation.

Other themes that connected the company implicitly to Secord's image ran through its advertising. The company also loved to point to the plainness and simplicity – both of which were tied to purity and, it is likely, to pioneer women's domesticity – with which their goods were purveyed. As Walden has also argued, the issue of how goods were marketed, whether, for example, they were left to 'speak' for themselves or whether they needed to be surrounded by a host of other signifiers to intensify their appeal, was a serious problem for turn-of-the-century retailers.[62] In this case, the company hoped that its customers might not need the flashy trappings of consumerism. 'Heart to Heart talk with Our Friends' was another advertisement that ran in the early 1920s: 'dainty, simplicity, small shops, inexpensive fixtures, no ribbon or fancy fixings on the boxes, no commercial advertising and the enormous increasing popularity with those folks who have ever tasted Laura Secord Candies – are some of the reasons why we have maintained a comparative low price for these wonderful good candies.'[63] In this case, the goods would be backed, not by advertising spectacles, but by the company's history.

The Secord company did not market its products on the basis of their cheapness alone. It emphasized that while its candy was not merely for the rich, its quality was guarenteed; at the same time, neither was it a decadent luxury. Secord candy could be bought by the working woman or the Rosedale matron, since it was sold in a number of weights and as little – or as much – as was affordable could be purchased at a time. But those 'working girls' who stopped at the local shop on their way home from the office or department store could be assured that they were participating in a ritual of refinement and gentility, one structured by the relations of gender, class, and race. 'Refinement and Business,' yet another advertisement from this period, told the 'Dear Friends' that, 'anticipating the appreciation that these delicate morsels, which are so carefully prepared in our Studios, would meet within our little white shops, we originated the idea of Dainty Little Lace Curtains so that they would be a mark of distinction from other candy stores. We know that refinement and simplicity, coupled with the wonderful wholesomeness of Laura Secord Candies would find fame throughout the world.'[64] Just as the narratives of Secord had worked hard to create her as an icon of respectable bourgeois white femininity, so too did the candy company use the latter's signifiers – respectability, wholesome attractiveness, modesty, and cleanliness (the 'dainty little lace curtains' hung at the 'little white' windows) – in order to appeal to those paragons of womanhood who might buy the truffles and peanut clusters.[65]

In many other advertisements created during this period, the company continued to play upon these gendered themes of whiteness and respectability. Not only were the shops' interiors and exteriors white (see figs. 8.6 and 8.7), so too were the candy boxes, with gold trim around the Secord cameo and black lettering (see fig. 8.8), and the company's delivery trucks, which had the trademark Laura Secord black signature painted on their sides (see fig. 8.9). Of course, assuring their 'friends' that they were buying a pure and fresh product was a very practical strategy when marketing foodstuffs. The company often encouraged people to place their orders ahead of time, particularly during the busy holiday seasons of Christmas and Easter.[66] It announced in the 1920s that, while the Secord company had received 'a tremendous collection of applications for agencies ... including at least one from practically all cities and towns of importance between Halifax and Vancouver, as well as several from England,' a collection which was 'being added to at the rate of several per day,' nevertheless 'in order to assure the careful handling that the delicate freshness of Laura Secord old time homemade candies demands, and that they be presented to our friends in only the delicious condition in which they leave our studios, we desire to point out to all that we do not establish agencies.'[67] Yet, while the tropes of purity and freshness were being put to practical use, they also worked to create a corporate image that linked femininity and whiteness to Canadian identity.

8.6 One of the 'dainty' Laura Secord candy shops.

8.7 One of the white, respectable looking exteriors of a Laura Secord candy shop.

8.8 Panels from Laura Secord candy box, circa 1930.

8.9 The Laura Secord Candy Company 'Studio,' Toronto, circa 1920s.

Of course, these advertisements were also helping to create consumer demand; their somewhat coy statements about not accepting external agents, or being unable to meet their 'dear friends' needs, reinforced the message of the candies' desirability and exclusivity. The advertisements also made use of another theme, as they emphasized that those responsible for Laura Secord candies were 'artisans' who deployed their carefully executed and perfectly timed craft in 'studios'; that is, they were not 'workers' who laboured on assembly lines in 'factories' and who could be pressed to produce vast quantities upon demand.[68] 'The accomplishment of artists' could be read as yet another reassurance that by buying a one-pound box of candy, a Canadian customer was helping to resist the forces (possibly construed as American) that were transforming her or his society: efficiency experts and time-management strategies that resulted in both the speed-up of work and the degradation of artisanal skills. For his part, O'Connor decided to introduce a profit-sharing plan, as he announced in 1923 that 'the success we have enjoyed would not have been possible had it not been for the steadfast loyalty of my employees, many of whom have been with me for the full ten years. They have made not only our Kingston friends welcome in our shop, but they have made people from other places and other countries go home and tell about Kingston's Laura Secord shop' (the announcement was made in that city).[69]

Not all of the advertisements of the inter-war decades used only pictures of Secord. Notices of new shops in Montreal, Toronto, and London ran text above pictures of figures from the sixteenth or early seventeenth and the mid-nineteenth centuries (see figs. 8.10 and 8.11). In one, a pleasantly surprised gentlewoman and her (presumed) daughter accepted a box of Secord candy proffered by a dashing gentleman who, with his short cape, manicured beard, high-heeled and ribboned shoes, and large, plumed hat, resembled a French gentleman of Louis xiv's court. In another, a 'lady' wielding a fan and wearing a huge hoop skirt looked on at the same gift offered to her by a dapper gentleman dressed in a frock coat, his top hat resting at his feet. All of these figures, the advertisements hinted, would have been happy to have had Secord candies in their respective periods. The visual images also suggested, with their use of clothing to evoke particularly 'romantic' periods (the age of gallant gentlemen and the charm of the antebellum era), that buying Secord candy for a 'lady friend' was itself a romantic – yet still highly respectable – gesture.

After the Second World War, the company decided to make some changes to its image, starting with the design of the candy box. It hired Canadian graphic designers W.R. Cockburn and Clair Stewart and an advertising agency, Cockfield Brown, to come up with new packaging and a promotion campaign, asking them to 'retain something of the character of the well established old design and yet bring it up to date.' As well, the box had to be 'characteristic of Laura Secord Shops and would at no time look like a drug store or grocery store product' and would not cost more to produce than the old box.[70] The firms went to work, producing a box with a 'young and beautiful Laura Secord in a miniature style painting in full colour rather than the old portrait with an embossed gold frame which had a slightly funereal appearance' (see fig. 8.12). White was still the predominant colour of the box, although a 'grey-blue colour has been added on the side and brought over a quarter of an inch to the top,' a change made to emphasize the whiteness of the box's top.[71] At the corporate luncheon held to launch the new packaging, 'everyone present felt that Laura Secord had gone a long way to modernise their package and bring it in tune with the times. Each

8.10 Advertisement for Laura Secord Candy Company, circa 1920s.

8.11 Advertisement for Laura Secord Candy Company, circa 1920s.

luncheon guest was presented with a three-pound box of Laura Secord candies, when leaving.'[72]

Yet despite this vaunted leap forward into 'modern times,' the company did not completely jettison its link to historical time. As we have seen in the inter-war decades, during the post-war years the company generally preferred to make implicit use of Canadian history. For one, the cameo was not of a 1950s woman, but rather an early nineteenth-century maiden, albeit one presented in ways that might appeal to a 1950s sensibility. Her white dress was much more revealing than the bonnet, large bow, and black frock of the older Secord, and her head was bare, with centre-parted hair in a wavy, yet demure arrangement, her gaze directed at the spectator (see figs. 8.12 and 8.13). And as Secord's image became more 'modern,' that of an attractive youthful woman and not a rough-hewn 'pioneer foremother,' it also became more 'ladylike,' her skin tone whiter and more delicate. This Secord would definitely have employed servants, either black or white; her unseen hands would not have been calloused or darkened by manual labour.[73] The 1950s Secord (and her 1980s successor) would have been far more at home attending balls at Newark than working alongside Native people in the Upper Canadian bush.

A 'traditional quality' advertisement from the 1950s, produced after the new box, told the 'Laura Secord story.' Its author, Bernard K. Sandwell (himself a 'distinguished author, lecturer, and editor ... an ardent advocate of the best in Canadian life'), narrated her walk to Beaver Dams, describing its great significance in keeping Canadian British as well as the monuments that a grateful country had erected to her memory. He concluded that 'her name has become for Canadians a symbol for courage, devotion, and loyalty,' which the company repeated in a sidebar under its new cameo of Secord. And, underneath the narrative of Secord's walk, with the heading 'Traditional Quality,' was a presentation of the company's own history, that of 'quality,' 'old-time treasured recipes,' and the use of 'the finest foods obtainable, carefully prepared and blended by experts in the art of home cooking.' A new line of baked goods also contained 'this same recognised quality,' one that has made the candies 'famous for flavour and freshness everywhere.'[74]

The use of 'experts' to dish up 'home-cooked' goodies combined modern scientific appeal with reassuring tropes of domesticity and femininity. Such a combination may have seemed quite appropriate in a post-war world that was seeing the increased promotion of convenience foods

Today is Laura Secord's 200th birthday. The lady is a legend, a Canadian heroine.

But to us, the legend isn't nearly as important as the lady behind it – a strong, compassionate, and very real woman.

A woman with enough love to seek out her wounded husband on the field of battle, and take him home to care for him.

A woman calm enough to feed American soldiers who came to her home demanding a meal; and alert enough to catch their plans for a surprise attack on a Canadian detachment at Beaver Dams.

A woman with enough courage, strength and conviction to leave her home at dawn and walk 20 miles to warn the endangered detachment. And a woman with enough self-esteem to seek recognition for what she did. Because what she did changed the course of the Battle of Beaver Dams in 1813. The Canadians were prepared, and won. It was one of the turning points of the War of 1812.

The recognition Laura Secord sought, she's received – from the Crown, the country, from Canadians everywhere.

And each year at this time, we commemorate her birthday and feel doubly proud of our association with the Canadian heroine who played such an important part in the history of our country.

Two hundred years ago today, a great lady was born. Come celebrate with all of us at Laura Secord.

Laura Secord
CANDY SHOPS

The Laura Secord Homestead in Queenston, Ontario.

1775 1975

8.12 The pioneer foremother: Laura Secord as an elderly woman, with white bonnet and large white bow.

and a steady stream of women into the paid labour force. At the 1954 Canadian National Exhibition, the company's booth again mingled these themes, with its signs advertising 'home baking' hung on the walls of a streamlined, modular-shaped, white-and-chrome booth, lit by stark white globes. And, as a playful take on the story of the cow, the company helped promote 'Elsie the Cow' at the CNE, with a 1950s 'milkmaid' (possibly a dairy princess) who posed with 'Laura Secord's milking stool.' The company also experimented with other forms of promotion, such as sponsoring a Highlanders Band in a 1950s Grey Cup parade. Young women were part of this spectacle of sport and advertising, marching as the Laura Secord majorettes and presenting a wholesome (albeit potentially disruptive – note the short skirt and show of leg in figure 8.14) display of Canadian femininity.

8.13 The post-war Laura Secord: young, beautiful, and more modern.

8.14 Laura Secord Candy Company junior majorette, Grey Cup parade, 1954.

Wholesome femininity, the nuclear family, and the company's self-created past also dominated the company's stock of images into the 1960s and 1970s. A May 1965 advertisement for Mother's Day gifts juxtaposed portraits of three generations of blond and fair-skinned 'mothers' (representing the turn of the century, the 1940s, and the present) who smiled on the reader from their respective frames. 'There's a sentimental reason to give Laura Secord Candies to your Mother,' read the caption, '(She probably gave them to hers).' Below the portraits was a picture of an open box of candy (displaying the product in the advertisement became more popular in the post-war years), and under it the text stated that 'for over 50 years, mothers have received Laura Secord Candies for Mother's Day.' The reader was reminded of the 'wide assortment' at local Secord stores, assortments 'all made from time-treasured recipes.'[75] Twelve years later, a Toronto Eaton's Centre store advertisement featured a (once again) smiling brunette woman who held up a box of candy with the cameo prominently displayed (fig. 8.15). The text urged customers to drop in soon, for 'Canada's best loved gifts with that old-fashioned goodness will put smiles on the faces of your family, friends and business associates.'[76] But the company also began to target male customers. Its Father's Day advertisements, for example, urged families to 'give him Laura Secord candies.' In one such advertisement, the open box of confectionery, with a very brief description of some of its contents next to the cameo, was the main attraction for customers.[77]

While generally shying away from a direct use of Secord's history, at certain strategic times the company chose to use it. Although it appears to have been silent on the controversy surrounding Secord's walk, the Laura Secord Candy Company refused to drop its association of her image with Canadian loyalty and heroism. In the 1960s, the opening of a new Secord outlet in Niagara Falls prompted the company to contact a St Catharines resident, Laura (Secord) McKinnon, a descendant of the 'colorful and controversial Laura Ingersoll Secord.'[78] The Niagara Falls *Evening Review* told its readers that 'it's hard to imagine that this pert, charming, attractive wife and mother could have anything in common with her austere looking forebear.' Laura McKinnon, though, kept a scrapbook on Laura Secord and admitted to being 'fascinated by the adventurous tale.'[79] The store itself was unique, as it marked a 'departure from the traditional Laura Secord decor' and featured 'prints of the Niagara area and of the central figures of the War of 1812.'[80] Even in the 1960s, it seems, lineages and genealogies still carried some weight and sparked some interest.

The Laura Secord Candy Shop in the Eaton Centre is brimming with fine candies, cookies and our own irresistible ice cream.

Canada's best loved gifts with that old-fashioned goodness will put smiles on the faces of your family, friends and business associates . . . especially at Christmas. Drop in soon.

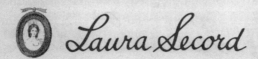

8.15 Advertisement for Laura Secord candies, circa 1970s.

As well, on the two-hundredth anniversary of Secord's birth, September 1975, the company ran an advertisement that featured the first Secord cameo, a sketch of the Queenston homestead, and a commemorative medal (on one side was written the dates 1775–1975, and on the other, the current Secord portrait). The text told readers that she was a

legend, a Canadian heroine. But for us the legend isn't nearly as important as the lady behind it – a strong, compassionate, and very real woman. A woman with enough love to seek out her wounded husband on the field of battle, and take him home to care for him. A woman calm enough to feed American soldiers who came to her home demanding a meal; and alert enough to catch their plans for a surprise attack on a Canadian detachment at Beaver Dams. A woman with enough courage, strength, and conviction to leave her home at dawn and walk 20 miles to warn the endangered detachment. And a woman with enough self-esteem to seek recognition for what she did. Because what she did changed the course of the Battle of Beaver Dams in 1813. The Canadians were prepared, and won. It was one of the turning points of the War of 1812. The recognition Laura Secord sought, she's received – from the Crown, the country, from Canadians everywhere. And each year at this time we commemorate her birthday and feel doubly proud of our association with the Canadian heroine who played such an important part in the history of our country. Two hundred years ago today, a great lady was born. Come celebrate with all of us at Laura Secord.[81]

By the 1970s, the company thus felt it necessary to remind Canadians precisely who Secord was and what she had done. However, the company thus also presented itself as an upholder of Canadian national identity and aligned itself with those who were calling for greater recognition of Canadian cultural and historical figures. This advertisement also argued quite clearly that women's image did not have to transcend or reside outside historical time; in fact, it was important to recognize women such as Secord as historical actors, creators of history.

Yet other displays of Secord's image, as we have seen, while using it to evoke 'history,' 'loyalty,' and 'Canada,' subordinated her historical role to that of the company's own narrative. And in this process, the role of Aboriginal peoples was generally completely omitted from the Secord story. From being either threatening warriors or loyal allies, the Mohawks simply vanished from the narratives that were told through the advertisements. Apparently they had no role to play as purveyors of candies to the Canadian nation.

The company's advertising demonstrated just how mutable history could be, particularly when presented in this particular genre. By changing Secord's image to 'move with the times,' for the purposes of commercial modernity, the advertising showed that, far from crystallizing history and fixing it for the viewer, 'history' could be rearranged and represented to accord with contemporary fantasies, desires, and needs. In this particular context, the desire was to sell candy – but as respectably, and in as nationalistic a manner, as possible.

Conclusion

As work on historical memory has demonstrated, the past crops up in a number of places, being created and used (some might say abused) by a variety of actors, some of whom are linked by common interests in the past (as in the case of the museum founders and monument builders). Others have little or no connection, other than being the recipients of certain historical codes and symbols.[82] What is interesting is the varied and multiple uses to which the same historical narrative may be put, as it shifts locations and contexts.

Visual representations of the past did allow a quick assimilation of 'history.' They might stir the interest of those who had not considered history interesting, or who did not have the patience, time, or inclination to wade through historical societies' reports and records. Yet objects and images also ran the risk of freezing the past, of reifying it and not illustrating the processes that they might represent. And, no less than the written records, objects and images could be manipulated and made to 'tell a story.' Paradoxically, though, they might be thought to represent the 'reality' of history, to be more trustworthy than the slippery device of the written narrative (even though such narratives were needed to decipher and decode their significance).

But material traces of the past did not exist in a physical, let alone metaphorical, vacuum. The Secord monuments, for example, were set in a geographic region, the landscape of Niagara and Queenston. Through the efforts of various historical actors, these areas became sites of loyalty, history, and – David Boyle would have approved – tourism.

Chapter Nine

Laura Secord, the Niagara Region, and Historical Tourism

'An Historical Outing: The Women's Literary Club Spends a Delightful Day Revisiting the Scenes Made Famous by Sir Isaac Brock, Laura Secord, and Other Heroes of Long Ago,' read the headline in the *St Catharines Standard.* The group had spent a July day in 1904 visiting the village of St David's, Brock's monument, the site of his death, and, in the village of Queenston, William Lyon Mackenzie's home (now in ruins) and the Secord house. Fortunately for her commemorators, the latter building was still habitable and occupied by the Sheppard family, who gave the club a cordial welcome and a tour of the house. Their 'pilgrimage' ended with a tour of the Alexander Hamilton house on the road between Niagara-on-the-Lake and Queenston, where their guest speaker, Janet Carnochan, delivered a paper on the Battle of Queenston Heights. Emma Currie closed the meeting by reading a letter from William Kirby, who expressed his regrets at not being able to join them but reminded them of the importance of their work. 'But for the women of the Dominion, we should be too much engrossed in considerations of business and money; and material advancement to remember those higher duties of patriotism and literature, on which after all the true prosperity of a country is founded. It is the women who, like the vestal virgins of Rome, keep the perpetual fire of love and devotion to our country.' After reminding them of the significance of their work to the Empire, Kirby closed by discussing the holiness of Queenston Heights, suggesting that visitors to the spot should remove their shoes and thank God for Isaac Brock.[1]

Although Kirby's omission of Laura Secord may have secretly irritated some club members devoted to their heroine, his point about the sacred nature of the landscape was probably well taken by many commemorators.

Those who saw Secord and Brock as the redeemers and saviours of the imperiled Canadian nation also believed that the geographic sites where their stories had been enacted held special meanings. Queenston Heights was, in historian John Sears's words, a 'sacred place,' a site where spiritual renewal could take place and a connection with the imagined community of the nation was made.[2] In addition to the paintings, written narratives, monuments, and advertisements, for her commemorators Secord's narrative was both represented by and embedded in the landscape of Queenston and Niagara-on-the-Lake.[3] For the members of the WLC, and many others, visits to the places where she had performed her heroic deeds were yet another way of seeing the past and imagining the nation: past, present, and future. While the club had always thought of Queenston Heights and its monuments as a sacred place, a site of devotion to the nation, they never forgot to visit Laura Secord's home. For these women, 'history' and 'memory,' the 'public' and 'private,' were firmly intertwined.

Sacred places, though – Kirby's somewhat hyperbolic tributes notwithstanding – were not immune from the worlds of commerce and money. Over the course of the twentieth century, the historical societies, the Niagara Parks Commission (NPC), the Ministry of Tourism, and, finally, the Laura Secord Candy Company worked to create the areas of Queenston and Niagara-on-the-Lake as sites, not just of 'history,' but of historical tourism. However, the priorities of these organizations, particularly those of the state, meant that in this enterprise Secord's presence was often subsumed by masculinist narratives of the War of 1812.

The Delights of Historic Niagara

From the 1890s, the area north and west of Niagara Falls had attracted a number of tourists.[4] Brock's monument at Queenston Heights had brought in sightseers, particularly after the creation of Queenston Heights Park by the NPC. Here opportunities were offered for both serious historical reflection and entertainment, as a trip to the top of the monument (which itself gave a fine view of the landscape north of the Heights) could be combined with dancing in the pavilion, dining in the restaurant, or picnicking on the grounds. After World War I, parents could pursue all these activities and leave their offspring in the park's crèche.[5] Lake-going steamers docked at Queenston, where their passengers could make rail connections to the Falls. Such 'visitors' also landed at the Niagara-on-the-Lake dock and might spend some time in the town before proceeding to the Falls. The predominant form of tourism, however, was practised by the 'summer folk,' the well-to-do Americans and Canadians who built large homes in the village and along the River Road between Niagara and Queenston, as well as their less wealthy counterparts who rented summer cottages in Niagara Township's Chautauqua area.[6]

These visitors came for a variety of reasons, for to be a tourist to this area (then and now) meant that one's experiences were not organized around one particular site but instead were shaped by multiple sensations and activities. Different, yet overlapping, forms of tourism existed: landscape viewing, whether of the Niagara River, Lake Ontario, the Escarpment, or of the surrounding fruit orchards; the tourism of rest and relaxation from urban life that sojourns in the spacious houses, the large hotels, or the cottages of Chautauqua might bring; and historical and educational tourism, in which knowledge of the past could be attained by visits to the Niagara Historical Museum, historical landmarks such as Brock's monument or Butler's Burying Ground, and leisurely walks around Niagara-on-the-Lake itself to view examples of 'historic' architecture, much of which had not been disturbed since the 1820s and 1830s.[7] An annual summer army camp in Niagara-on-the-Lake, while not officially designated a 'tourist site,' also brought in hundreds – sometimes thousands – of army officials and soldiers, all of whom had to be provisioned by local businesses. In turn, the soldiers provided entertainment for both residents and tourists.[8]

These activities, of course, were not discrete entities. Those who wrote to the local paper about their experiences spoke not just of the range of pleasures offered by Niagara-on-the-Lake and Queenston, but also penned paeans to the area's harmonious 'nature' that united all these delights.[9] Moreover, for middle- and upper-class tourists, the primary consumers of Niagara's and Queenston's tourism, spending leisure time in this area was not a frivolous enterprise. Instead, it was self-improvement, an opportunity to become immersed in Canadian history by simply moving through the local landscape. The anonymous author of 'Chautauqua Breezes,' for example, was eager to quash any suspicion of hedonism that might be attached to a Niagara vacation. Although something was 'in the air of this delightful place that produces such a feeling of calmness and contentment,' the town and surrounding area were immersed in reminders of Canadian history:

There is floating in the air of Niagara and its environs memories of bygone days. Memories that will never fade away from Canada's patriotic sons, for the noble exploits and hardy endurance of the defenders of the Empire, who in 1812, counted not their lives dear that they might hand down to their descendants the country that was their heritage, and to this day this Canada, 'the brightest gem in the British crown,' is ours to hold intact to hand down to our descendants ... Then what more fitting place for Canadians than Niagara and its district (with its magnificent orchards and fruit farms) to spend their vacation, where love of nature and love of country is in the very air we breathe, and among whose dwellers you imbibe the very spirit of contentment.[10]

Janet Carnochan's work, though, went even further to create the area as a site of history that would attract visitors. Many of the writings of the Niagara Historical Society's co-founder focused on Niagara as both the cradle of Canadian history (as an important theatre in 1812) and a place shaped by great national experiences. Her 'Old Niagara' recounted the area's history from 1678, starting with La Salle and then pointing out that he was followed by many officials, 'civil, military, commercial, ecclesiastic, scholastic.' A number of historical narratives touched one another in Niagara: it was the first capital of Upper Canada, the chief naval and military station, and a distribution centre for the Hudson's Bay Company and Indian Department. It had also been a refugee landing, had seen the passage of the Loyalists' Hungry Year, had been burned by the United States' army, and had grown after that with an assembly for the county, military regiments, a courthouse, and shipbuilding. Niagara had been the home of the province's first newspapers, churches, and agricultural society; it had housed the first public library and one of the earliest grammar schools; and, most notably, had hosted the trial of Robert Gourlay.[11] In her 'Early History of Canada as Exemplified by Visitors at Niagara,' she amplified these points and added that the first capital saw refugees from the underground railroad, two of whom were killed in a riot when slave-catchers attempted to drag their contemporary, Walter Moseby, back across the river. It also saw, however, the much happier arrival (told by a museum visitor who had lived as a small boy at Fort George) of a small boat, filled with black people, 'evidently a family, as there seemed to be husband, wife, children. When the boat touched the shore, they sprang out and knelt, kissing the earth, and I shall never forget the thanksgiving to God in the prayer that they were now in Canada, in a land where slavery did not exist.' Carnochan's liberalism also prompted her to tell the tale of Maria Waite, wife of the exiled rebel

Benjamin, who had passed through the town on her way to interview Lord Durham and then plead with Queen Victoria for her husband's life ('Was she not a heroine?'). The town had also seen other interesting women, such as the 'brilliant' Mrs Jameson and Sally Carter, who had led the town's 'coloured women' in helping Moseby escape. As well, Niagara had been the seat of mid-nineteenth-century commercial enterprises (Augusta Gilkison's family's shipbuilding firm) and had been visited (more than once) by the Prince of Wales, Joseph Brant, and the Seneca chief Red Jacket.[12]

And because Canadian history had been an ever-present force in Niagara, Carnochan believed the town's residents should work hard to preserve the places where 'history' manifested itself. Nowhere was this issue more pressing than at the military reserve, an area adjoining the town's southeast border. Carnochan was an indefatigable campaigner to ensure that the Dominion government did not sell the land to private developers. Her 1905 appeal, 'Military Reserve at Niagara,' also used a similar panoramic view of history to make a case for the area's value. After all, the reserve included in its history the passage of laws, the colonial government's dispensation of hospitality to Americans, French, and Indians, the presence of Brock, and the burial of English regular troops and the militia. And, for the last thirty years, 'these plains have been the camping ground for the youths of our country, where they have learned what has enabled not a few of them to fight even unto the death on African veldts for the honor of their country. And to how many generations have these plains been endeared by early associations when earthen ramparts, rifle pits, and powder magazines have been explored and patriotic feelings roused?' (Carnochan combined a liberal political outlook with a commitment to imperialism.) All of this history was to be sacrificed for a few dollars, which the country could well do without. 'But it does need that these historical sites should be preserved, so that the youths of our country may proudly point to the spots where daring deeds were done in days of yore, and thus encourage all that constitutes true patriotism.'[13]

Of course, Carnochan was not the only person who was busy creating Niagara and Queenston as landscapes replete with history and sacred meanings for the Dominion. The WLC made yearly ritualistic 'pilgrimages,' as they were dubbed, to Niagara and Queenston, starting in the 1890s and continuing into the 1970s.[14] In 1905 the group laid a stone tablet in front of the Secord house, marking the spot from which the historic journey had begun (in 1972, John Burke-Gaffney of Labatt's would congratulate them on the marker, calling it 'the only reassuring, tangible fact of my life when we [the company] were trying to document the fact that James and Laura Secord actually lived in the house that we eventually restored').[15] As well, Frank Yeigh's 'A Pilgrimage along the Historic Niagara,' run in *The Globe*'s Dominion Day edition, 1899, made observations similar to Carnochan's (and with the benefit of photographs). Yeigh adopted the voice of the omniscient historian to narrate the tale of 'a little band of historical pilgrims [who] landed on a recent Queen's birthday at Old Niagara': '... the town was captured without a struggle and a triumphal entry was made in one of the archaic buses for which the town is noted. Here, indeed, is an inviting field for the lover of history, though the multitude pass by the ruined forts and mossy parapets lamentably ignorant of the stirring tales they tell.'[16] Yeigh then guided the reader through a number of buildings in Niagara, such as Forts George and Mississauga, the Anglican church of St Marks, and the courthouse, before moving on to Queenston. While one 'would scarcely think that Queenston is, like Niagara, haunted with the memories of three centuries of history,' Yeigh pointed out that it had been visited by La Salle and Father Hennepin. 'And, between the visits of the men of France and the settlement of the men of English speech, the Indian still looked upon the land as his own by right of possession.'

However, 'the pilgrims of the nineteenth century were in search of more tangible shrines than the Frenchmen left; and these they found': Queenston Heights, Brock's monument, and William Lyon Mackenzie's former home and printery.

> The home of Laura Secord may also be visited, although it has been somewhat modernized since the day, eight-six years ago, when the courageous woman made her all-day journey of warning to FitzGibbon and his company, fifteen miles away. Many hold to the opinion that Brock's body was hidden in this house on the day of his death; others think it was laid in the old stone house across the street from the Secord residence. One of the old-time cavernous receptacles beneath a fireplace is a feature of the local hotel – the Monument House.

Yeigh's suggestion that Brock and Secord shared an intimate connection was a fancy typical of many late-Victorian and Edwardian commemorators. Famous individuals were often linked through such anecdotes, thus demonstrating a greater plan in history than mere happenstance or arbitrary trajectories (as we have seen, a similar fictive tale was that of Tecumseh's wooing of Secord's daughter and her family's friendship with Joseph Brant).

From Queenston the pilgrims progressed to Chippawa, formerly a 'busy centre of trade' but now a 'dozing' village, whose name

> recalls the Chippawa tribe, who made the locality a camping centre when they came to worship the spirit of the cataract that demanded its human tolls each year. It recalls the legend that on one occasion the choice of a propitiatory victim fell on the only daughter of an aged chief, the maiden being cast adrift on her canoe, which was soon caught in the fatal current. Before the first line of rapids had been reached, another canoe shot out suddenly from the banks, and lo! the chief followed his child to the abode of the hungry god of the Horseshoe!

Navy Island was the next stop for the pilgrims, where they reflected on the misfortunes of Mackenzie in 1837 and the burning of the *Caroline*. On their return, they stopped at the house where Laura Secord died, then proceeded to Lundy's Lane, a site of many military graves, a monument to the soldiers, and her grave, enclosed by a 'rude wooden paling.' Yeigh's account of the pilgrimage ended with an homage to the Niagara River and a meditation on military deaths and Christian salvation.[17]

The Niagara landscape, then, was not just composed of forest, riverbank, and water; it was also made up of memories. At Queenston Heights, Yeigh even reversed the usual device of seeing the historical landscape as populated by ghostly figures. With the help of J.G. Currie (the husband of Emma), who related the story of the battle, 'we saw the succession of scenes: the battlefield, the first advance of American troops, their repulse, "the tremor of excitement, as the sound of musketry and cannon filled the air," Brock's "stalwart form" galloping up the battle, his leading "a little band of soldiers, in that splendid fearless, reckless dash up the hillside" ... we seemed to catch sight of the tall figure as it reeled and fell; we saw Brock die!' In this passage, the dead were raised for the imaginations of the living, yet Yeigh wrote as though time had been reversed: he and his pilgrims had simply stumbled upon the battle, which they then watched. While this literary device was not sustained throughout the rest of the piece – certainly there was no doubt that, for the most part, the group was gazing upon time past – it did suggest just how 'real' and 'true' Yeigh wanted to make the past. Its narration was not an arbitrary act but rather a tale of truth, especially because the past could be seen in bricks and mortar, hillside and rock.

Yet, like boxes of candy, landscapes could not 'speak' for themselves. Historical interpreters, like Carnochan and Yeigh, had to translate their messages for the public. Without their expertise, the ordinary tourist would never know the 'real' significance of the military lands or that Niagara had been a way station on the underground railroad. The founders of the Niagara-on-the-Lake museum, along with the creators of Queenston Heights and Lundy's Lane monuments emphasized that the area held a number of shrines to Upper Canadian loyalty, ones that should be visited by outsiders and appreciated for their historical significance. Tourism, therefore, was to no small extent implicit in and integral to historical preservation. For one, without the support of a wider public – whether town residents, summer visitors, or groups from other parts of the province – it was much harder for even elites to garner legislative and financial support from governments for historical commemoration and preservation. As well, the historical societies saw their work as the education of the Dominion's people. What point, after all, was there in displaying Secord's tea caddy or honouring her with a monument if only a small group of men and women came to gaze upon them?

But it was a fine line between wanting a public for museums and monuments and working to create a tourist industry based on the region's history. Carnochan and other commemorators did not urge the town to develop tourism for its own sake or as a substitute for commercial ventures and small-scale industrial production (saw and grist mills, basket and canning factories, and boat building) that had helped support Niagara and Queenston from the early to mid-nineteenth century. Others in the town, though, argued much more vehemently that encouraging tourism was its only hope of prosperity. Writers to the local paper called for improvements to the town, such as ending the practice of letting cattle and horses graze in certain spots and making sure people maintained their property in an attractive manner.[18] They also argued that the town's lack of adequate rail service was hampering tourist traffic.[19] 'Thoughts by the Wayside' wondered why the electric rail line stopped at Queenston, since an extension to Niagara would bring in thousands of people each year, who would fill up the town's hotels and boarding houses and buy summer homes. Niagara, the anonymous writer reminded the readers, had many interesting historical landmarks, such as Butler's Barracks, the Military Commons, and Fort George.[20] Other voices, though, counselled caution in trying these ventures.[21]

However, unlike their counterparts in other areas (notably Nova Scotia), boosters of tourism did not actively attempt to suppress the area's collective memory of commerce and industrial production (although it was not this period that was created for tourists' edification).[22] They often invoked those days in arguing that the towns' economies would benefit from more tourists. The past had shown exactly what, given the right circumstances, Niagara, Queenston, and their residents were capable of achieving. There was no doubt, though, that the conditions of the 1820s and '30s were gone and would not return. The notion of the towns, especially Niagara, as a feminine 'sleeping beauty' to be awakened by the masculine force of modern improvements and modern visitors is a recurring image in these writings.[23] Modern times demanded modern solutions and what could be more modern and forward-thinking than exposing the area's 'resources' – its scenery, architecture, and history – to a greater number of tourists, a fast-growing sector within early twenti-eth-century Canada? Tourism, they argued, had already brought some measure of prosperity to Niagara and Queenston; certainly it had worked wonders for the economy of Niagara Falls. Given care – plus the fact that Niagara and Queenston already attracted the 'right kind' of tourists and had many historical attractions – the two villages could avoid the traps of mass tourism and 'tawdry amusements' found to the south.[24] With assist-ance from various forms of government, tourism would ensure the area's future progress and prosperity.

During the early 1900s, rail companies and steamship lines occasion-ally attempted to improve their service to the area.[25] But it was the NPC's work on the River Road during the late 1920s and early '30s that im-proved transportation into Niagara-on-the-Lake and Queenston and dem-onstrated a new degree of state interest in the area as a site of history that could bring in tourist dollars. However, unlike historical commemora-tion from the 1880s to the 1920s, in which women such as Currie, FitzGibbon, and Carnochan had played a prominent role, state-funded historical tourism in Niagara during the twentieth century generally was the province of men, such as NPC officials John Langmuir and John Jackson, Minister of Tourism James Auld, and local MPP Robert Welch. And the narratives they constructed around various sites generally fo-cused on the activities of Euro-Canadian men.

The Niagara Parks Commission and Fort George

The NPC's extension of the Parkway was by no means the first sign of its presence in Queenston. The Commission owned the park at the Heights in which both Brock's and Laura Secord's monuments stood (although not the Secord 'homestead,' which remained in private hands). Prior to the 1920s, it had worked to ensure that Queenston Heights' Park maintain a respectable, wholesome image through the regulation of concession booths, amusements, placement of cab stands, and the behaviour of both tourists and the Commission's staff.[26] All these endeavours, of course, were not unique to Queenston Heights for, as Karen Dubinsky has argued, the NPC also ran Queen Victoria Park in a similar manner.[27] But the Commission's work on the roadway to Niagara-on-the-Lake increased its ability to manage and shape the tourist landscape, for in the course of this work it expropriated various properties along the road and river. By doing so, the NPC was not only able to turn the road into a spacious boulevard, one with large, grassy verges and plenty of trees, it was also able to control the appearances of many riverside properties and establish a number of historical landmarks.[28] The overall effect was that of a gateway into Niagara-on-the-Lake that mingled the pastoral with the historic, themes the NPC had worked to create in Queenston. Running alongside the parkway was the Niagara River. With the American villages of Lewiston and Youngstown and the restored Fort Niagara clearly visible on the opposite bank, the river view was more than just a continuation of the scenic backdrop; it also might remind the visitor (who may very well have been from the U.S.) not only of the two countries' shared history but also of Canada's determination to maintain a separate historical – and thus national – identity. And, on a practical level, the Niagara Parkway was also designed to draw more tourists from Niagara Falls northward, so that they might discover the refined delights of Queenston and especially those of Niagara-on-the-Lake.[29]

Once the road extensions were complete, the Commission undertook a number of projects in Niagara-on-the-Lake, such as supervizing the construction of a sea wall along Lake Ontario.[30] The NPC had already assumed some responsibility for Butler's Burying Ground, a two-acre plot on the outskirts of Niagara-on-the-Lake that it bought in 1909.[31] As the Historic Sites and Monuments Board placed a number of markers in Niagara-on-the-Lake and along the parkway (and in other spots), the NPC was asked to take responsibility for their maintenance.[32] But the most highly visible manifestation of the NPC's presence in the town, and probably the Commission's major contribution to historical tourism in it, was the restoration of Fort George.

The commissioners were not the first to notice the presence of historic sites in the town, undertake their preservation, and designate the area as 'historical.' As Patricia Jasen has shown, during the early nineteenth century tourists had been drawn to Niagara's ruined battlefields and forts. By the late nineteenth century, however, such ruins were no longer entrancing, but were instead a cause of civic shame and concern over the loss of the past.[33] Since the 1890s, the Niagara Historical Society (NHS) had lobbied various levels of government for the preservation of Forts George and Mississauga, Navy Hall, and the 'ordnance lands,' a large open expanse on the edge of town owned by the Department of National Defence (DND).[34] Yet, so far as the NHS was concerned, little had been done to prevent these buildings from rapid deterioration. Indeed, the NPC's correspondence files contain numerous requests from local historians and politicians that the Commission take over the forts and Navy Hall; Fort Mississauga, in particular, was the object of much concern. Located on the town's golf course, open to curious tourists and their children, and said to be literally falling apart, for many concerned citizens it was the site of numerous imagined accidents and maimings; its sorry physical state also represented a distressing lack of concern for Canadian history.[35]

Fort George, however, was a different bundle of mortar and bricks. The NPC understood it to be a historical landmark, a symbol of loyalty to Britain, and a potential tourist attraction. Not only did the restoration promise to realize all three possibilities, it also began in 1937, when the town was searching for work for those residents on relief and was more than happy to draw upon the Commission's funds. Relief workers had been used to build the sea wall and, judging by correspondence among the NPC, the Department of Labour, and municipal officials, few had any qualms about using forced labour in the service of patriotic pride.[36] By 1940 the work was completed, and the fort was unofficially opened to visitors.[37] After the war, Fort George began to attract a growing number of schoolchildren, as principals and teachers targeted it as a suitable site for field trips.[38]

Thus, by the end of the Second World War, various levels of government were involved in shaping both the historical and the tourist landscapes of Niagara-on-the-Lake and Queenston. The monuments at Queenston Heights, the markers along the parkway (such as the stone laid at Brown's Point, the spot where Brock supposedly rallied the York Volunteers to fight at Queenston Heights), Butler's Burying Ground, and Fort George were all reminders to both residents and visitors of Canadian loyalty to Britain: the arrival of the Loyalists and the War of 1812. While such a theme would seem obvious, almost 'natural,' given the NPC's choice of sites to protect and restore, it is worth pointing out that the Commission carried out this work in ways that reinforced certain aspects of the landmarks' history and downplayed others. The period chosen for Fort George's reconstruction, for example, was that of its original state as built by Lieutenant-Governor John Graves Simcoe in the 1790s, not the structure put up by American troops in 1813 after they had destroyed much of the original building. This latter incarnation of the fort was, according to the NPC's historian Ronald Way, 'never actually attacked and had few historical attractions for Canadians.'[39] The NPC's decision not to restore Fort Mississauga was partly based on its lack of any stirring military history during the war (Fort Mississauga was built during 1814–15 on a site that offered a greater command of the river's mouth).[40] And, once Fort George was opened as a tourist site, it was (and continues to be) marketed primarily as a material reminder of the war, despite the fact that those events occupied a very brief part of the building's history.[41]

Forts, monuments to wartime heroes, and military graveyards were not only about loyalty to the nation and empire; such sites also commemorated national identity and the past in a militaristic and masculinist fashion. Certainly the Queenston Heights memorial to Laura Secord demonstrated that female patriotism had existed and was remembered. Yet, as we have seen, the NPC refused to become involved in the building of a hall dedicated to her memory. Even more significantly, it also refused to purchase the Secord home in Queenston. Such a purchase was considered, though; in 1908, NPC superintendent James Wilson corresponded with R.E.A. Land (the author of the original pamphlet that called for a Secord monument) about the home's purchase. Land had raised thirteen thousand dollars for the house and hoped that the Commission would contribute an additional five hundred; once the house had been bought, Land's plan was to turn it over the NPC.[42] However, Wilson argued that legislative permission would have to be granted for this and that Land should approach the Dominion government, which had just given $300,000 to the Plains of Abraham fund. Why should it not, Wilson suggested, give a 'small moiety' to Secord?[43] At some point during these discussions, the house's owner, F. Sheppard, wrote to the Commission to describe it: two and one-half lots, a frontage of forty by twenty-two feet, with a kitchen, coal and wood house, and closet at the back, an upstairs bathroom, and verandahs up and down. The house, Sheppard wrote, had a small mortgage, which he 'could take up at any time do not care to sell but will take three thousand for it no less.'[44] In 1931 the Commission looked into the purchase of Secord's home in Chippawa, as it has 'a great historical value and requests have been received that it be preserved.' J.R. Bond, the NPC's engineer, reported that the brick home, owned by Mrs. W.E.B. McKenzie of the village, had had its interior and roof gutted by fire. Mrs. McKenzie had not made up her mind about selling, and her husband, who opposed the idea, was considering repairing the house and turning it into a museum. Bond told the Commission that 'I really do not think he has any serious intentions of doing this as his ideas were vague, and in my opinion were expressed to influence any sale that might be in the offing.' In any case, the list of things the house needed was extensive: a completely new roof, rafters, window frames, sashes, doors and frames, and floors and stairs. The cellar floor and walls had to be repaired, the exterior walls needed to be painted and fixed, and the south wall needed a new foundation. All told, the repairs would cost $2,800; the land was valued at $1,200–$1,500; and the house's current assessment was $200.[45] The matter was dropped.

After the war, with the acquisition and restoration of the MacFarland house on the Parkway (chosen because it had been a British battery and a hospital for both sides during 1812), scenes of recreated colonial domesticity would be added to the historical landscape; its parlour, kitchen, and bed chambers reminded tourists of women's historical presence.[46] The one anomaly in the NPC's collection of battlefields and barracks was the Mackenzie house in Queenston, which the NPC purchased and renovated during the 1930s in order to commemorate the struggle for British democracy in Upper Canada.[47] But in the 1920s and '30s, the NPC generally chose to focus on military deeds and structures that were, for the most part, the province of men.[48]

And not just any men for, while the 'gallant militia' and British soldiers were not forgotten, it was the officers whose way of life, by and large, was recreated in Fort George's furnished quarters and whose presence in the area was celebrated. This formation of the past also had a racial component; the NPC records do not suggest that the area's Colored Corps was the subject of commemoration (if, indeed, the commemorators were aware of its existence). While it is less clear just how – or if – Natives, as Loyalists, members of Butler's Rangers, and Britain's allies in the War of 1812, were depicted for the tourist audience, at least one observer of ceremonies in 1950 to honour Brock and the soldiers of 1812 was less than pleased. Writing to the *Globe*, C.N.A. Ireson of Toronto claimed that there had been no mention of 'Brigadier Tecumseh or Captain Brant ...

Indian allies were most completely ignored and their descendants could take such an omission as an affront to the red race of Canada.' Pointing to the textbooks' history of Native support for the British, Ireson argued that

> the white man's gratitude must be short-lived, when a government-sponsored ceremony cuts the Indians dead at an international ceremony of an event in which they were so conspicuous. Any one who saw the Six Nations Indian pageant and the costumes in use on their reserve near Brantford last year could not help but wonder who neglected to take advantage of such a wealth of readily available pageant material to add more colour to the Fort George ceremony, and to honor the Indian people who have spilled so much of their blood in the defense of Canada in all wars, including the last one. Let us hope such a glaring omission of our red UELs will not occur again at similar historic ceremonies.[49]

This is not to suggest that the inclusion of Aboriginal peoples in historic re-enactments and ceremonies would have automatically resulted in a re-visioning of Canadian history. As other scholars have pointed out – and as Ireson's letter suggested – by the mid-twentieth century there were well-established tropes of 'Indianness' that could be performed for non-Native audiences, who might have no notion of the complexities and heterogeneity of Aboriginal cultures.[50] It is merely to point out that even up to the post–Second World War period, the narratives of Canadian history presented by the state in this location were shaped by a vision of national identity that did not draw upon Native definitions of nationhood or even acknowledge that such concepts might have existed. Nor is it the point to engage in contemporary finger-wagging at the NPC, for the Commission was involved in 'selling' the area's history to an audience that would be drawn to Niagara by recognizable names and events. What is important to realize, though, is that this process was neither 'natural' or 'inevitable.' It was not dictated by the simple 'facts' of the area's history, for the NPC designated certain events and processes 'historical' and deployed the state's cultural and financial capital accordingly. Other aspects of Niagara's and Queenston's past, such as the pre-contact presence of Natives, the formation of a small yet visible African-Canadian community, or industrial and commercial expansion after the War of 1812, were ignored or downplayed in favour of a historical landscape marked by military structures and artefacts.[51]

Preserving Niagara: The 1950s and 1960s

In the immediate aftermath of the Second World War, the future of Niagara-on-the-Lake came under increased scrutiny. Various levels of government put forth a number of suggestions concerning the preservation of the town's nineteenth-century buildings: turn the town into another Williamsburg; preserve the central core through a mixture of zoning, public acquisition of 'historic' buildings, and the establishment of special arrangements with private owners; and develop a 'comprehensive, historically authentic, effective and exciting restoration and interpretation program to cover the early history of Niagara-on-the-Lake and Niagara Falls area with special emphasis on the War of 1812.'[52] And the town's residents also became involved in the preservation of historic buildings, often out of frustration with the slow pace of the state's conservationist efforts. The Niagara Foundation (NF), a voluntary group made up of a number of prominent residents, organized to protect the town's 'unique historic architectural character.' The Foundation asked that, as local government was being reviewed, Niagara-on-the-Lake be treated as a separate entity, much like Ottawa's National Capital Commission. Local-level 'modifications' had to be made in order to accommodate growth while simultaneously protecting 'certain valuable qualities' presently offered by the town. They did not provide a detailed outline as to how these goals should be achieved but argued that there was more to 'the development of regional government of this area than the purely physical problems of providing and administering such necessities as water, roads, schools, sewers, housing, and buildings.'[53]

Although the members of the NF achieved some of their goals, their perceptions of the state's role in historical preservation was not always shared by their provincial representatives. In 1952, James Auld, the minister of tourism, told James Allan, the provincial treasurer, that while 'there can be no doubt that the preservation of the original area of Niagara-on-the-Lake and the restoration of some of the early buildings within this area would be a major historical attraction ... I don't think the province should become involved in any undertakings of Niagara-on-the-Lake, but I do think that some financial encouragement should be given. As you know, a number of the citizens there are presently restoring, correctly, their own homes, and the congregation of the Anglican Church have [sic] done a magnificent job in its restoration.'[54] Auld's attitude resembled the NPC's measured approach to preservation. However, like the Parks Commission, the Ministry was confronted with local residents and others concerned with Niagara's fate. Correspondence to the minister, newspaper editorials, and letters to the various editors spoke of the potential of Niagara-on-the-Lake, the need to act swiftly before its 'history' was desecrated and destroyed by development, and the hope held out by sites such as Quebec City.[55] Auld was also confronted with the indefatigable lobbying of Robert Welch, the MPP for Niagara, who wrote innumerable memos and letters on behalf of the town's preservation. Welch urged Auld to take action so that both the area and the province might reap the benefits of the increased tourist trade that would result from 'Niagara conserved.'[56]

Not all agreed that the town would automatically gain from such provincial undertakings as the purchase by the Ontario Historical Foundation (OHF) of private property. Municipal politicians, for example, objected to the Foundation's non-profit and therefore tax-exempt status. George Voth, the town's treasurer, pointed out to Auld that, while the entire province benefited from restoration, the community was left to absorb the loss of revenue. 'As our area, one of the oldest in Ontario could, in the future, be adversely affected by numerous acquisitions by the foundation we must express concern.' Voth was advised by Auld not to worry unduly, since it was unlikely that the OHF would be acquiring the private homes that comprised the bulk of Niagara-on-the-Lake's historic properties. He was also reminded that in 1968 the council had passed a resolution agreeing that the tax loss would be outweighed by the advantages: 'the restoration of this beautiful and unique historic site will be a source of pride and educational benefit to residents of the Niagara area. Undoubtedly it will greatly enhance the town's attraction to tourists and visitors and the support and stimulus to business and industry thereby provided.'[57]

Restoring the Secord Homestead

While so much attention was being paid to buildings in Niagara-on-the-Lake, what of Queenston? In 1964 the province had decided that the Secord homestead was not in any danger: D.F. McOuat (who was also the provincial archivist) had placed the building on a list of the area's landmarks deemed to be 'safe.'[58] However, others were not so sanguine about its future. As we have seen, the NPC had been asked earlier to buy the building from its owners, the Sheppard family, but it consistently refused these requests. In January 1968, E.W. Bertinger, a contractor from Elmira and a history enthusiast, wrote to James Allan to express his concerns about the Queenston house. The owners had allowed him to tour it, and he noted 'with alarm that this old shrine is rapidly deteriorating.' Bertinger attempted to negotiate with the owners for its restoration in order that the house might be open to the public. Unfortunately 'it seems there is a tangle in the estate of the owners, meanwhile a Canadian landmark is rapidly disappearing through sheer neglect.' Having heard that the Laura Secord Candy Company had been bought by Fanny Farmer, he wondered if the NPC could encourage the company to buy the house and open it to the public, 'especially our school children.' Allan's reply to Bertinger – that the NPC 'has not been actively engaged in the restoration of historic landmarks' – was curious, given the Commission's activities in just that field. Auld's response, however, was far more commonplace: the Ministry and the OHF were very concerned about the Queenston house (and Secord's former home in Chippawa, also privately owned), but while 'great things' were expected from the Foundation, it was just getting organized and he hoped that private funds would also come to the government's rescue.[59]

On this occasion, Auld was right. The Sheppards sold the house to the Laura Secord Candy Company (by this date owned by John Labatt), and the company proceeded to renovate the house and also set up a nearby candy store. The company's publicity during the course of renovations stressed the care that was being taken to respect 'historical authenticity'; a number of additions had been made to the house, and the architect, Peter Stokes, had to take it apart section by section to determine the original size and shape (Stokes specialized in historical renovations and reconstruction). All the woodwork had been done by hand, using methods and materials 'similar' to those of Secord's day, and the house was furnished with 'authentic' furniture from 1800–35. The company also staffed the house with costumed guides, all of whom were from Queenston or nearby.[60]

The story of her walk was not told in the interior of the house, which focused on genteel domesticity, but instead on a series of placards erected outside, which featured an attractive, youthful Secord, with a 1970s hairdo and make-up. Those who stopped to read the placards were told that Laura Secord, wife of James, overheard American officers plotting an attack on FitzGibbon's troops. Acting out of patriotic duty, Secord walked to Beaver Dams to deliver the news, undetered by the presence of wild animals and unfriendly Indians. Her message delivered, FitzGibbon went on to win the battle and ensure Canada's safety. Newspaper articles about the home's opening focused on Secord as a historic and heroic figure; many writers mentioned that the WLC had played an important role in preserving her memory.[61]

One month prior to the homestead's opening, the WLC held a 'pilgrimage' that was sponsored by the candy company, wishing to honour the charter members who had placed the plaque.[62] As we have seen, Burke-Gaffney was grateful to the club for their 1905 marker, and wishing to reciprocate, took advantage of 'the opportunity to meet the present membership whose antecedents had the conviction to place a stone marker on a piece of property in Queenston long before most of our compatriots had come to understand the special nature of Laura Secord's contributions to our country ... Please accept my congratulations on the celebration of your eightieth year and, above all, the thanks of everyone associated with the Laura Secord Candy Shops Ltd. for your guidance, for the confidence you gave us, and for permitting us to share in your eightieth pilgrimage.'[63] The Club met Burke-Gaffney at the Laura Secord School in Queenston for a presentation and then walked to the house for a preview of it and a re-dedication of the marker. The pilgrimage honoured not just Secord's memory but that of her commemorator and WLC founder, Emma Currie. After leaving the homestead, the group visited Secord's Queenston Heights monument, where a tribute to Currie was read that stressed her knowledge of, and dedication to, Canadian history and, too, her altruism in dedicating her royalties to the monument. After this ceremony was complete, the group concluded their trip with a bus ride to the Lundy's Lane monument.[64]

No representatives of the provincial or municipal governments were reported as participating in this event. However, when the house opened on 2 June 1972, it was not the members of the Women's Literary Club but rather Ontario premier William Davis, who, flanked by company executives, urged the public to save their cultural heritage.[65] To be sure, the state *had* taken responsibility for the preservation of Brock's and Mackenzie's and, to some extent, Secord's (with her Queenston Heights monument) historical memories. Yet it had repeatedly refused to save the Queenston house, leaving the most direct and visible reminder of a woman as a historical actor in the Niagara area to be shaped by private enterprise: a 'sacred site' where tourists were induced to remember the past and celebrate Canadian identity by buying chocolate.

Conclusion

Historical tourism was only part of the area's tourist landscape.[66] But the

9.1 Sacred site and tourist destination, the Women's Literary Club's marker at the Laura Secord homestead, Queenston.

LAURA INGERSOLL SECORD 1775-1868

Born in Great Barrington, Massachusetts, Laura Ingersoll came to Upper Canada with her father in 1795 and settled in this area. About two years later she married James Secord, a United Empire Loyalist, and within seven years they had moved to this site from nearby St Davids. From here, during the War of 1812, Laura Secord set out on an arduous 19-mile journey to warn the local British commander, Lieutenant James FitzGibbon, of an impending American attack. The courage and tenacity displayed on this occasion in June 1813 places her in the forefront of the province's heroines. Mrs. Secord's house, a simple frame building, was restored (1971-72), and remains as a memorial to this exceptional act of patriotism.

Erected by the Archaeological and Historic Sites Board, Archives of Ontario

9.2 Tourist plaque at the Laura Secord homestead, Queenston.

lure of gazing upon the past helped imbue the two towns with respectability; a vacation spent touring Fort George was meant to educate and inculcate national pride. Furthermore, designating Niagara and Queenston as sites of history was a strategy that gave residents a weapon to wield against certain types of development – a strategy that is still being used today. But such weapons came with their own price tags; nor were they entirely effective, since private capital was given considerable latitude by the Canadian and Ontario governments. 'History' was nobody's preserve; rather, it could be and was harnessed, appropriated, and marketed by the tourist industry.

Furthermore, the past was (and still is) no less amenable to particular forms of reification and particular kinds of commodification when the state was involved. Whether or not increased government intervention would have provided a 'solution' suggests that, first, the state would have offered a different kind of vision and, second, that the only question worth asking centres on the merits of public versus private tourist devel-

9.3 The Laura Secord homestead, Queenston, 22 October 2000.

9.4 The Laura Secord Candy Company candy store, Laura Secord homestead, Queenston, 22 October 2000.

opment. There is no indication that more substantive intervention by either the NPC or the Ministry of Tourism would have offered anything more than historical tourism grounded in the meta-narratives of imperial expansion and national identity. Was it possible, anyway, to create alternative narratives of the past when 'history' was understood as being captured by artefacts and buildings, not processes and struggle? Did not the very methodology of presentation tend to freeze the past, making it seem static and homogeneous and flattening out its complexities and ambiguities? And given the kinds of historical narratives drawn upon by the NPC, the Ministry, and residents' groups, narratives that shaped their understanding of historical tourism in Niagara and Queenston, it would be difficult for the latter to be anything but fundamentally conservative.

A shift in gender relations, and the meanings of gender in historical commemorations, also occurred with the involvement of the state (even at such a grudging and sometimes recalcitrant level). The fact that masculinist narratives were being presented by state bodies run by middle-class men is not, on the whole, surprising. Nor did women historical commemorators present completely radical or alternative visions of the past and the nation; as we have seen, some middle-class women could be as conservative as their male counterparts. Yet the inclusion of Anglo-Celtic women in history was at least understood as a process of struggle, a fight for recognition and valuation of women's work and deeds; it was also done in the face of other narratives that saw women as existing outside of history. And as the work of historical commemoration became part of the state's purview, those who made significant legal and financial decisions about which narratives were to be preserved in the landscape (and which were not) were male bureaucrats, not the women's organizations. At the Secord homestead opening, it was the candy company and the architects who were recognized by the state, not the women historians, even though they bore much of the responsibility for Secord's initial and ongoing commemoration.[67]

What of historical tourism and Secord's narrative in the twenty-first century? The tours of the Secord home have varied considerably in their content and emphasis. Some guides stress Secord's act of heroism and tell, quite quickly, the 'story' of her walk. Laura Secord is a Canadian heroine, audiences hear, since during the War of 1812 she walked twenty miles to deliver news of an American attack to the British troops. Other guides make no mention of her as a historical figure and instead describe the contents of the house. And the tours either downplay Aboriginal peoples' presence in the Secord story, or completely omit them from their accounts. They have also started and ended in the attached candy shop, thus making a not-so-subtle link between Canadian history, female heroism, and consumption.

To further update the story of the tourism industry's presentation of Laura Secord, in 1998 the Laura Secord Candy Company donated the Secord house to the NPC. In the words of the Commission's website, the Company 'enabl[ed] The Niagara Parks Commission to ensure the Homestead's preservation and safekeeping for future generations.' The website tells viewers that Laura Secord, 'heroine of the War of 1812,' overheard an American plot to attack British troops. Her husband's wounds from the Battle of Queenston Heights made it impossible for him to deliver the warning; thus 'despite the danger and harsh unsettled country,' Laura set out on a thirty-two kilometre (twenty-mile) 'treacherous route' which 'took her more than 18 hours to complete.' Despite the threat of 'American patrols, wolves, wildcats ... rattlesnakes [and] unfriendly Native forces,' the discomfort of 'exceedingly hot temperatures and wild, unsettled land,' and 'blistered and bleeding' feet, she reached Beaver Dams. There Laura encountered Native forces allied with the British who, upon hearing her news, accompanied her to FitzGibbon. Her message delivered, 'the Native forces, under the command of John Norton and Dominique Ducharme, ambushed the invading Americans and defeated them at the Battle of Beaverdams, June 24, 1813.' The website also mentions that Secord's heroism was 'soon forgotten,' even though she deserves much of the credit for the British victory. Not until 1860, during the visit of the Prince of Wales, was Laura Secord given her due.[68] Although Aboriginal people now play a greater role in the Secord story, other aspects of its presentation by the tourist industry have not changed much.

The website also informs the public that 'the Secord Homestead in Queenston was reconstructed in 1971 by Laura Secord Inc. Open for tours during the summer months, the Homestead feature[s] authentic furnishings of the 1812 period.' The potential visitor to the Secord home is promised that 'costumed interpreters [will] thrill you with tales of her adventure as they guide you through this lovingly restored homestead ... This tranquil location also offers ice cream, Laura Secord fine chocolates, and refreshments for your enjoyment.'[69] Consuming history is, it seems, still an important way of remembering Laura Secord.

Epilogue: The Iroquois Presence

The power of the nationalist narratives that developed around Madeleine de Verchères and Laura Secord stems from the danger the women faced and their acts of heroism in overcoming it. Central to the two stories are the actions of Aboriginal peoples, in both cases Iroquois. For Verchères, the Aboriginal attack was the *sine qua non* of her heroism as it precipitated the historic event. For Secord, the pleasant reversal of the Paul Revere story acquires additional force from her encounter with the Iroquois in the forest on the way to Beaver Dams. Whereas the Iroquois were the enemy in Verchères's defence (though the English sometimes lurk in the background), in Secord's heroic action, the Iroquois turn out to be friends. They accompany Secord to the British encampment, and the intelligence she provides allows the British to defeat the American invaders, the real enemy. Her encounter with the Iroquois – and the readers' encounter with them – represents a temporary, gothic threat to the woman's progress. Yet even though they are the silent reasons for much of the tension in the stories, the Iroquois fulfil little active role themselves.

It is true that the Iroquois have often performed a merely narrative function to stand for all the threats, past and present, to French Canadians (or all Canadians). Historian Patrice Groulx sums up the significance of the Iroquois presence in the Dollard stories recounted in French Canada: 'The speeches on Dollard Day repeated endlessly that the enemy today is not the Iroquois, but Anglo-Saxon dominance and its effects, uncontrollable economic and social modernization, the penetration of foreign capital and workers, the degradation of national culture, the increasing marginalization of French Canada and the incessant attacks on its institutions.'[1] In a similar way in the women's heroic narratives, the Iroquois represent not so much themselves as all other potential enemies. They are absent, yet present, in the narratives – necessary but excluded. Despite the implicit discursive assumption that Iroquois people would never read the stories, they remain potential readers of the narratives of heroism, with the potential of reformulating them according to their own perspectives.

Iroquois Motivations

In Verchères's two accounts of the defence of the fort, there is but a brief mention of Iroquois motivations. In her second version, dating from the 1720s, Verchères recounted what the Iroquois later told the governor of Montreal, M. de Callière: 'And in truth the Iroquois, with all their astuteness and skill in warfare were completely deceived, as they afterwards avowed to M. de Callière. They told him they had held a council with a view to assaulting the fort during the night, but that the increased vigilance of the guard had prevented them from accomplishing their design, especially in view of their losses of the previous day (under the fire maintained by myself and my two brothers).'[2] Represented in this fashion as little more than dupes, the Iroquois display little agency. Suffering casualties at the hands of the small troop inside the Verchères fort, the Iroquois decide that it is better to withdraw. No account of their motivations in the attack is given, which is assumed to be unremitting blood thirst.

It is difficult in the absence of supporting documentation to determine the specific goals of the Iroquois attack. But a model of revisionist analysis is John Dickinson's treatment of the Dollard des Ormeaux story. According to Dickinson, the 'traditional' historical narratives that place Dollard at the centre of the story are incorrect. French traders were not the goal of the Iroquois attack. Rather, the Huron allies of the French were the goal, and some of them quickly decamped to the Iroquois. In this fashion, Dollard and his unfortunate colleagues were little more than 'collateral damage' in the on-going struggle between Iroquois and Huron. Depleted by warfare and disease, the Iroquois attempted to boost their own numbers by assimilating the few Huron who remained after the 1649 dispersal. The encounter with Dollard des Ormeaux merely continued this strategy.

Much of the history of seventeenth-century New France is imbued with a perspective based on the French colonists' heroic and successful struggle to survive in the challenging circumstances they faced. It is sometimes difficult to acknowledge the marginality of the French presence in the seventeenth century. Even Louise Dechêne's magisterial *Habitants and Merchants in Seventeenth-Century Montreal* quickly passes over the 721 Amerindians in the Montreal area in 1691 – more than one-third of the total population – to concentrate on the population of French origin, who were of course much better represented in the archival source material.[3] Historical accounts of the early French colony tend to place at the centre of the narratives those groups and those individuals who left the most archival material.

In relying on Madeleine de Verchères's own accounts of the 1692 episode, historians have almost always tended to ignore the rationality of the Iroquois attackers. Current evaluations of the nature of Iroquois warfare in the seventeenth century allow us to pursue this issue further. In a tightly argued analysis of Iroquois-French relations in the seventeenth century, José Brandão argues that the Iroquois pursued their military strategies with different purposes than those of the Europeans: the capture of hostages was one of the most important aims of their incursions. Over time, their purposes seem to have changed, focusing primarily on attacks on the Indian allies of the French, to begin with, with a view to incorporating captives into their villages, replacements for previous casualties of war or the victims of epidemics. By the late seventeenth century, French policy had come to threaten the very existence of the Iroquois Confederacy, as the French built military posts, armed their Indian allies, and encouraged Christian Iroquois to settle near the French towns. Governor Denonville's attack on the Seneca in 1687 was the final provocation for the Iroquois, who henceforth overcame their divergent political structures to pose a distinct threat to the French colony. It is worth bearing in mind the size of the respective populations. Brandão posits an Iroquois population of some 23,000 in 1681, with 2,430 Mohawks in 1689 (1,170 in 1691). The French population of the St Lawrence Valley in the late seventeenth century numbered around 15,000. By the time of the 1692 attack, the Iroquois goal was apparent: the destruction of the French colony. But the Iroquois recognized the necessity of English help to achieve that aim, and they unsuccessfully requested that aid again and again. Even acting primarily alone, they achieved a great deal of military success. Between 1680 and 1698, the Iroquois captured some 2,500 French men, women and children.[4]

While it is impossible to discover the specific goal of the attack on the fort of Verchères in 1692, it is easy to situate the particular raid in the larger context of Iroquois hostility to the French. The attack on the fort of Verchères was probably of little importance to the larger Iroquois strategies, given the minor strategic importance of the settlement. It is highly unlikely, as Madeleine de Verchères implies, that the Iroquois launched an eight-day siege of the fort. Such tactics were not typically part of Iroquois military strategy. But a clear military strategy attempting to displace the French from the St Lawrence Valley existed that would last until the Great Peace of 1701, when the Iroquois and French achieved a long-lasting treaty.

Despite the establishment of peace between the French and the Iroquois, many authors who cover Verchères's later act of heroism in saving her husband in the 1720s carelessly impute the attack again to the Iroquois. Verchères's second narrative is clear on this matter: it was a group of Abenaki who tried to kill the de La Pérade family. Yet for some writers it was too complicated to introduce another potential enemy when the Iroquois represented such a convenient scapegoat. As Eugène Achard writes, 'the Iroquois, who forgive nothing, had sworn a great hatred toward Madeleine ... Therefore, they did not hesitate, each time they passed by Sainte-Anne de la Pérade, to give her some indication of their resentment.'[5]

'Iroquois' Voices

For all the importance of the Iroquois to the narratives, it is difficult to discern many specific elements to their actions. In the many retellings of Madeleine de Verchères's heroism from the 1740s to the present, the Iroquois are usually voiceless – essential participants in the event, but without individuality or agency. Indeed, many of the visual depictions of the event do not include Aboriginal people at all – they are faceless attackers beyond the gaze of the viewer. When they are included, they are often depicted with the feather headdress accoutrements of Plains Indians, the archetypical 'visual' Indian for non-Aboriginal North Americans and Europeans (fig. E.1). Moreover, they are often drawn from behind, as if the artist were surreptitiously keeping guard over them as they, in turn, were watching over the fort (fig. E.2).

The logic of the Iroquois' actions is denied by invoking stereotypes of Aboriginals. In one children's book, *Famous Canadian Studies Re-told for Boys and Girls*, the readers are addressed: 'You remember that the Iroquois Indians were very cruel and wicked. Everyone was afraid of them.'[6] Many versions of Verchères's heroism say little more about the Iroquois context for such raids. Rather, writers draw on figures of the 'barbarian' again and again. One children's book of the 1950s stated that the

E.1 An Iroquois warrior grabs Verchères's scarf. (Louis Brouilly)

consequences of capture by the Iroquois would have been horrid for Verchères: 'They would have treated her like a beast of burden. They would especially have destroyed her innocence. Later she would have become the third or fourth wife of an Iroquois brave: which means an ignoble barbarian without laws and without conscience. Far from all religious instruction and living in the middle of the worst decadences, one becomes practically a beast.'[7]

Such blatant racism silenced the Amerindian characters in these stories. The imputed silence of the Iroquois could exacerbate instances of technical problems. In one performance of Rodolphe Girard's romanti-

E.2 Hidden in the forest, Iroquois warriors watch the fort of Verchères. The artist's perspective is from behind the Iroquois. (Joseph Forte)

cized stage drama, Madeleine de Verchères prepares to fire the cannon, calling to the Chevalier de Briac to throw himself on the ground. After the cannon shot, de Briac kills the Iroquois characters. But when the cannon momentarily did not fire, the Iroquois characters could do little but stand and await their deaths, their role being to 'be cut down by the sword without saying a word.'[8] Without words in the play, there was little scope for improvization to rescue the scene.

In a minority of cases, Iroquois are given voices in the narratives, even voices that are not entirely unsympathetic. In Pierre Mariel's *Une héroïne canadienne* (1967), published in France, the Indian chief La Grangula laments, 'But are riches and fire-water worth so much that we give up inch by inch the territory of our ancestors, that we let our ancestral traditions disappear and mock the Great Spirit?' It is true that the rest of Mariel's book portrays the Iroquois in a savage if enticing fashion, reflective of French concerns for the exotic. Indeed, it is telling that the book makes the stunning remark that the Iroquois no longer exist.[9] A more recent book aimed at schoolchildren includes a short section on the Aboriginal way of life, foreshadowing the fate of dispossession that awaited them: 'The Indians showed the explorers the routes to follow, without guessing that they were preparing themselves for a tragic destiny.'[10]

Elsewhere, the Iroquois voices serve to accentuate the danger Verchères faced. Thus, in a book for adolescents, Richard A. Boning has the Indian chief state: 'Men of the Iroquois, six suns have passed, still you have not crushed this tiny fort. If you cannot crush this fort, how can you take Montreal? Up and down the river your brothers await news of our victory. As soon as they hear, they will join us.' Madeleine de Verchères in the story hears the speech, understands it, and therefore understands what is at stake in the whole episode.[11] Likewise, in Launcelot Cressy Servos's operatic drama, the Iroquois sing their war song:

When joyous vision from a rocky brow
We spie [*sic*] our enemies in the vale below
Our strength revives our hearts rise at the sight
And every heart glows with a fierce delight
While silently our guns we charge with care
Make loose the hatchet and for fight prepare
Around the woods a circle wide we drew
and get before them where the bushes grew.[12]

A few versions of the story give a more prominent role to the Iroquois characters. In Ida Davidson's 'Madeleine de Verchères' (1929), a short three-act play for the classroom, the second act is devoted entirely to the Iroquois warriors. 'Have you forgotten,' the character Eagle Feather intones, 'that the last Onontio [Governor] of the French seized a number of our warriors and sent them across the big sea water in chains? ... We must wipe out the insult to our race.' But his rival Lone Wolf convinces the assembled warriors that 'to attack the fort now would be folly.'[13]

One of the ironies of the Verchères narratives relates to those accounts which do ascribe feelings and words to the Aboriginals. For instance, in the children's plays which give clear roles to the Natives, such roles must have been as compelling, if not more so, than the actions of the heroine and her colleagues within the fort. What Euro-Canadian children would not prefer the role of the Indian attacker in the staid classrooms of the early twentieth century?

This is not to say that the roles in any way approximated what Aboriginal people of the seventeenth century would have been like, or what contemporary Aboriginal people might prefer, but it does demonstrate the intense and ongoing desire on the part of non-Aboriginals to experience the apparent freedom of Aboriginal society. Baron de La Hontan played on this sense in the seventeenth century, and his fictitious philosophical exchange with the Indian Adario provided a key influence on the French Enlightenment's concept of the 'noble savage.' In the twentieth century, the great fraudster Grey Owl, born in Hastings, England, but probably the best-known Canadian 'Indian' of the century, also fitted this mould – as did Ernest Thompson Seton, who launched the League of the Woodcraft Indians, an early version of the Boy Scouts. Margaret Atwood points out that such depictions, however romantic, were not necessarily negative: 'at least Seton created a generation of quasi-Native children, some of whom would grow up to be ardent conservationists and sympathetic to Indian claims once they had made their way onto the agenda again. It's harder to collude in the destruction of a people and a way of thinking if you feel that this people and this way of thinking are partly your own.'[14] Portrayals of First Nations people can have complicated consequences, both for the Aboriginal peoples themselves and for those who project their anxieties onto them.

Aboriginal Reactions

No Aboriginal versions of the Madeleine de Verchères story have been located. Nonetheless, it is possible in a couple of cases to gauge Aborigi-

E.3 The Iroquois attack on the Verchères fort. Still from the film *Madeleine de Verchères*, 1922.

nal reaction to the use of the story. One intriguing piece of information comes from the recollections of one of the producers of the 1922 film *Madeleine de Verchères*. Mohawks from Kahnawake participated in that film, although they resented the role assigned to them by the story and the directors. Arthur Larente recollected, some sixty years after producing the film, that they had difficulties with the Mohawk actors: 'We used to kick them to make them do what we wanted. They didn't want to do what we wanted to do. We had to kick them to make them move.'[15] We can only speculate which specific parts of the filming caused difficulties. Reviewers at the Board of Historic Sites and Monuments also noted difficulties with the Mohawk actors. Not only was the dress of the Indians wrong, as they were wearing 'modern' trousers and shirts, but also their attacks were poor, presumably not blood-curdling enough (fig. E.3).[16] Nonetheless, as one viewer of the film recognized, in this film of the early days of the colony, even with the poor filming conditions and less than sumptuous costumes, the role of the Mohawks could not be underestimated. 'Colour is provided by the Indians,' he wrote, 'and as they are real Indians, there is a feeling of truth in it.'[17] Likewise, in the 1908 Champlain Tercentenary Celebrations, the Aboriginal actors were by far the most popular participants in the pageant.[18]

Undoubtedly, Aboriginal readers could not escape the racist connotations of the story. Aboriginals were invariably cast as the unrelenting enemies of French or Western civilization. In 1992, Jim Commandant, an Iroquois parent in Barrie, Ontario, complained to his local school board about the depiction of the Iroquois in a French-language school text, *Madeleine de Verchères: Héroïne canadienne.*[19] He brought the issue to the attention of the press, and threatened to remove his son from school unless the book was withdrawn. Commandant acknowledged that the English version of the textbook was much better than the French.[20] After a meeting between the parent, the local band council, the publisher, and the school board, it was agreed that the text would be dropped from the curriculum. This had been a popular book up to that point, as the French-as-a-second-language consultant confirmed: 'I still have teachers who ask me when they can start teaching this book again.'[21] Commandant's success in this incident says much about the changing political status of Aboriginal people in Canada, as well as the attitude of the press concerning what constitutes a noteworthy story.

The construction of the 'heroic woman' imagery in the accounts of Verchères's bravery depends on the assumption of unthinking Aboriginal cruelty. If an Aboriginal perspective were possible on this nationalist narrative, it could begin with the words of a Mohawk orator after the destruction of Iroquois villages by Governor Denonville in the late 1680s: 'The Governor of Canada ... has started an unjust war against all the [Iroquois] nations.'[22] The heroism of a fourteen-year-old girl could still form part of the story, but the moral weight of the narratives would not remain in the same place.

Secord and the Mohawks

In 1999 an Internet poll devoted to the naming of Canadian heroes named Laura Secord as one of Canada's top ten, ranked with Terry Fox, Sir Frederick Banting, Tommy Douglas, Sir Isaac Brock, Lester B. Pearson, John A. Macdonald, Louis Riel, Billy Bishop, and Nellie McClung. The poll was compiled by the Dominion Institute and the Council for Canadian Unity; at least one media report pointed out the omission of sports figures such as Lionel Conacher, artists (the Group of Seven was conspicuously absent), or the silent screen star Mary Pickford. Rudyard Griffiths, the Institute's director, conceded that the results 'were coloured by how the Web is still dominated by wealthier, highly educated Canadians.'[23]

To what extent such domination accounts for Secord's presence on this list is difficult to know. But as the poll confirms, Laura Secord's story continues to be told and her image deployed in Canadian culture in a number of ways and in various genres. Canadian cartoonists have relied on the associations linked to Secord's name to poke fun at the vagaries of the country's politicians (fig. E.4). And the recent sale of the Secord company to the American Fanny Farmer chain has inspired at least one political cartoon, based on the theme of her capture through the medium of international commerce. In Canadian novelist Jane Urquhart's *The Whirlpool*, set in late nineteenth-century Niagara Falls, one of the novel's central characters is so obsessed with Secord that he has his bride dress up as her to act out his sexual fantasies.[24] Hardly a figure of which Emma Currie would have approved!

Other Canadian artists have also used Secord's figure to ground their work in Canadian history and nationalism; however, they do so in ways that reflect 1980s and 1990s sensibilities. Canadian artist Barbara Klunder's engaging chair, 'Laura Secord: Our Patron Saint of Guerrilla Warfare,' sold at the Eighth Annual PEN Canada benefit, is one such representation. A sturdy arrowback, the kitchen chair is painted a deep blue with Secord's bonneted face painted on the top rail and three eagle feathers on the back rails. In this representation, Secord, domesticity, and patriotic duty are once again combined, but without the suggestion that Secord must be defined primarily as a wife and mother (fig. E.5).[25] As in the folk group Tanglefoot's song 'Secord's Warning,' bravery does not necessarily have to be explained and understood in gendered terms; instead, conceptions of gender equality underpin these uses of the past.[26] And, as discussed in chapter 7, children's books – particularly those aimed at girls – continue to be written about Secord. Like their early twentieth-century predecessors, these works offer her as an example of heroic conduct and of women's agency in history. Their authors also depict a 'human' – and very modern – Secord, embedded in family relationships and as concerned with the details of daily life on the Niagara frontier as she is with military and political matters.[27]

While it would be impossible to strip away the colonial and imperial contexts of Laura Secord's walk, in the 1990s her encounter with the Kahnawake Mohawks has been retold in ways that do not depend on the trope of endangered white femininity. In the CRB Foundation's Heritage Minute on Laura Secord, the dramatic impact of this historical narrative does not come from her meeting with the Mohawks. Instead, as she runs through the bush, she hears animal noises and glimpses blurred figures of American soldiers. The rough terrain is itself a danger to Secord – she faints as she scrambles up a crumbling hillside. Upon

E.4 'The ride of Sinclair Stevens?' (Ed Franklin, *Globe and Mail*, 23 July 1979)

*

from
Barbara Klunder, visual artist:
Laura Secord (1775-1868) is one of the genuine
heroes of Canadian history. During the War of
1812, she walked 30 kilometres (from
Queenston to Beaver Dams) to warn the British
garrison of an impending surprise attack by
American forces. In 1991, Klunder made the
Secord story the focus of an important one-person
exhibition involving period-style craft pieces as
well as paintings. Now she returns to the
theme with this arrowback kitchen
chair entitled "Laura Secord, Our
Patron Saint of Guerrilla Warfare".
The artist points out that she is
connected to the historical Laura
Secord "through her husband's
brother and my father's family."

*Silent auction item 11   Minimum bid: $350

E.5 Laura Secord period–style chair, entitled 'Laura Secord, Our Patron Saint of Guerrilla Warfare,' designed by Barbara Klunder for the Eighth Annual PEN Benefit, Toronto, 1998.

opening her eyes, the first sight visible to her is that of the bodies of Mohawk men. Wearing feathers and paint, but only partially clothed, these warriors are not, however, threatening. Without missing a beat, she immediately requests that they take her to FitzGibbon. The men help her to her feet, and together, arm in arm, they walk off-camera, with a voice-over telling the viewer that Laura Secord and the Kahnawake Mohawks alerted the British and helped save Canada.

Thus the Heritage Minute reconciles the Native man and the Euro-Canadian woman; it also manages to give both credit for the British victory at Beaver Dams. Racial harmony in the creation of the nation and the historical contributions of these two groups are wrapped up neatly in one narrative. Moreover, it is possible to simply omit Secord's story completely from contemporary presentations of the War of 1812. In 1999, Terence and Brian McKenna's television series on the war chose to exclude the Battle of Beaver Dams. Instead, much of its narrative focused on the position of Aboriginal peoples in the conflict, and their contributions to it.

Despite such contemporary desires to make Native-white relations more palatable, the position of Aboriginal peoples in Secord's narrative and that of the War of 1812 in general has been an ambivalent one. It has been fraught with Euro-Canadians' fears, desires, and fantasies, and their need to create 'imaginary Indians.' Such representations were deployed to help create notions of a concordant and intact national community, instead of the fragmented and often conflict-ridden reality of the British North American colonies. The two most obvious examples of such a process can be found in the narratives of Joseph Brant and, in particular, Tecumseh. In many ways, they were Secord's Aboriginal male counterparts, 'heroes' who were both outside of, and yet an integral part of, the commemorative processes of Euro-Canadians: outsiders because of their race, yet also integral because their presence in the narrative was proof that the 'story' of Canadian history was that of, in Mary Louise Pratt's words, the 'anti-conquest.' Canadians had not only chosen a different path than their southern counterparts when it came to Aboriginal peoples, having extended beneficence towards them, they had also incorporated these two leaders into their narratives of the 'nation,' claiming them as their own.[28] Both Brant and Tecumseh can be categorized as Homi Bhabha's 'mimic men,' members of a subaltern group that embodies colonial authority's 'desire for a reformed and recognizable Other ... [the] *subject of a difference that is almost the same, but not quite.*'[29]

Time and again, Ontario historians told their audiences that a great deal of credit for the integrity of British North America's border must go to her Native allies, partially because of their 'natural' affinity with the colony's landscape, their ability to move through forests undetected, and their knowledge of terrain, all these attributes so deeply a part of them they were almost inherent.[30] No matter that First Nations might not live in the areas where they fought, as in the case of the Kahnawake Mohawks in the Niagara Peninsula. This identification of Native peoples as being at 'one' with their environment was, of course, by no means new. Such a strategy had been an important part of the 'noble savage' archetype, and it continued (and continues) to be used by whites in multiple, often overlapping ways of either admiration or denigration, depending on the context and aims of those fashioning the discourse.

Furthermore, these narratives did much to make 'Native' synonymous with 'masculine.' As was mentioned in chapter 7, a few textbooks dealt with the 'sorry plight' of Aboriginal women, and occasionally commemorators of the Loyalists mentioned the work of Molly Brant. Yet in both the aggregate and as individual leaders, Native 'people' were understood as Native men – and 'heroines' as Euro-Canadian women. To be sure, perhaps such an absence was more blessing than blight, given the racist treatment of Aboriginals. However, the representation of Native peoples as 'male' worked to marginalize Aboriginal women on a number of levels. At a most obvious one, it ignored Native women as historical actors, omitting their contributions to Native society and to Native-European relations. To an even greater extent than Native men, they were thus consigned to anachronistic time, without agency or subjectivity. If they were discussed at all in these narratives of Canadian history, it was only as figures of pathos and tragedy, remnants of a 'dying race.' As such, Aboriginal women were subjected to the brutality of Native men and therefore were in desperate need of rescue and redemption at the hands of Euro-Canadian missionaries and the Canadian state. In these histories, Native women were not even the dangerous, contaminating influence that they became in Western Canadian discourses around Aboriginal peoples.[31] It should be remembered, though, that these narratives were produced just as various levels of the Canadian state formally stripped (or were about to strip) Native women of their political power in their own communities, while simultaneously refusing to include them as members of the Canadian body politic, a decision made on the grounds of both their gender and their race. Thus, while Euro-Canadians – and Euro-Canadian women, in particular – used the medium of 'history' to posit white women's agency and subjectivity as members of the nation, both the state and historians attempted to confine Native women to political subjection and historical irrelevancy.

Like that of Verchères, though, irrelevancy appears to be the appropriate term with respect to the interest of the Mohawks in the Secord story. There is no evidence to suggest any interest on their part in her narrative. So far as the meaning of War of 1812 to Aboriginal peoples is concerned, historian Carl Benn has shown that the Six Nations had their own goals and objectives which influenced their decisions governing when to participate in – as well as to refrain from – the conflict. Moreover, far from being a definitive moment in a narrative of triumph and progress, perhaps for the Six Nations the War of 1812 should be understood as the apogee, the last peak in an account that then became one of decline and marginalization. The War of 1812, after all, would be the last time Aboriginal peoples in Canada fought as allies, not subjects, of the imperial power.[32] Historical 'time,' then, did not always have the same meaning for Native peoples as it did for Euro-Canadians.

Although Aboriginal peoples may have been indifferent to Laura Secord, they were certainly concerned about the writing of Canadian history. While the subject deserves its own separate treatment, members of the Six Nations sat on the Ontario Historical Society's executive from 1897 until 1911. According to Gerald Killan, they did so out of a desire to win sympathetic whites' support for Aboriginal opposition to increased state control over the reserve, and abandoned these efforts once such support was either not forthcoming or was clearly only lukewarm.[33] However, while they were involved with the OHS, Native historians such as Asa Hill, Evelyn Johnson, and John Brant-Sero frequently refused to become convenient symbols of antimodernism. Instead, they reminded non-Native audiences of their former importance to national 'progress' in order to justify demands for 'progressive' solutions to present problems.[34]

And, while their formal association with the OHS ended in disappointment, at the local level members of the Six Nations continued to pursue affiliation with the Brant Historical Society (BHS). For well over two decades, Evelyn Johnson (Pauline Johnson's sister) pressured the Society to badger the Dominion government for the restoration of Chiefswood, the home built by her father, Mohawk chief George Johnson, and for better care of both the Mohawk cemetery and Joseph Brant's monument.[35] By the 1930s, members of the Six Nations were attending BHS meetings, reading papers, performing musical solos, and staging historical pageants.[36] In 1937, Six Nations' members also sat on the Society's executive, and by 1941 Elliott Moses, a member of the Delaware, was the Society's vice-president.[37] From the late 1940s into the 1960s, the BHS records testify to the ongoing and increasing presence of Six Nations members in the society. Their participation appears to have been fuelled by their desire to have some control and power over the displays and discussions of Native history that were so dear to the BHS. Such displays were, after all, a prominent part of the Society's work, as Brantford residents, schoolchildren, and visitors from outside the area were encouraged to come to the museum and gaze upon its exhibits in order to become 'educated' in Six Nations' history.[38]

Furthermore, some individuals from the Six Nations reserve were able to take their narratives to an audience beyond Brantford. In addition to his work with the BHS, Moses spoke to groups around the province about

Six Nations history, served on a number of provincial committees, and in the early 1970s corresponded with the anthropologist Sally Weaver about her work on Six Nations history.[39] The Mohawk writer Ethel Brant Monture spent much of her life lecturing and teaching about Aboriginal history in southern Ontario. Out of a desire 'to see a history of the Indian people that had been written by an Indian person,' she published work on leaders such as Brant, Crowfoot, and Oronhyatekah, and worked with American author Harvey Chalmers on popular histories of Native peoples, particularly that of Brant.[40] Chalmers credited her with leading him 'to the realization that Indians actually are generous, good-tempered and blessed with an excellent sense of humour,' thus changing his notions of them as 'sadistic, vindictive, treacherous people with a racial obsession for murder and torture.'[41] To be sure, it might be argued that Chalmers simply replaced one set of stereotypes with another, for his discussion of 'Indians' has overtones of the 'noble savage'; 'their simplicity and honesty,' for example, are lauded.[42] Monture's own work, though, written quite explicitly from the vantage point of an 'Indian' writer and historian, attempted to move beyond such stereotypes. Her portraits of Brant, Crowfoot, and Oronhyatekah depicted these leaders as having developed more complex and nuanced masculine identities than other writers had attributed to Aboriginal men.[43] Readers of Canadian history were thus offered more than the unidimensional heroism of a Tecumseh, a heroism always overdetermined by colonial ambivalence.

Conclusion

By focusing on First Nations within the narratives of Madeleine de Verchères and Laura Secord, it is possible to provide yet another 'de-centring' of their stories. Since the late nineteenth century, the stories of these women's heroism have proved vital to the creation of a broader sense of national identity, whether pan-Canadian or French-Canadian. The presence of First Nations actors in the stories reminds us of the difficulties of portraying Canadian (or French-Canadian) national development as an unproblematic victory over the anonymous 'enemies' of the past. Their presence also provides evidence of the importance of the gendered nature of Canadian nation-building. The compelling feature of both of these narratives rests on the women's encounter with First Nations men. The sexual tension and danger provides the subtle subtext for the successful establishment and defence of European settlements in the colonies.

As contemporary focus shifts to the Aboriginal presence in these narratives, the retellings of Madeleine de Verchères's and Laura Secord's heroism reveal the anxiety of commemoration in the Canadian context. As the two key heroines of the country's past, both women participated in paramilitary actions to defend their home and family from attack. They came to personify the survival of the Canadian peoples against the odds, providing reassurance that Canada (or French Canada) was, too, destined to assume its proper place among the nations of the world. Yet their messages were never univocal. As women acting outside the usual fields of women's actions, they also came to represent claims that European women could make on Canadian history and politics. Yet as women they also were subject to denigrations of their actions based on their sex. Ultimately, heroines face the trials of history – and of historians' judgments – in ways that heroes do not.

Notes

Introduction: Why Heroines, Why History?

1 Benedict Anderson, *Imagined Communities: Reflections on the Origin and Spread of Nationalism.* For a critique of Anderson's inattention to gender, see Catherine Hall, Jane Lewis, Keith McClelland, and Jane Rendall, 'Introduction,' *Gender and History* 5, no. 2 (Summer 1993): 159–64.

2 Pierre Nora, 'Between Memory and History,' in *Realms of Memory: Rethinking the French Past*, vol. 1, *Conflicts and Divisions*, 2.

3 Ibid., 6.

4 Raphael Samuel, *Theatres of Memory*, vol. 1, *Past and Present in Contemporary Culture*, x.

5 See Nora, 'From Lieux de mémoire to Realms of Memory,' and 'General Introduction: Between Memory and History,' in *Realms of Memory*, vol. 1.

6 J.A. Dickinson, 'La conception populaire de la tenure,' in Joseph Goy and Jean-Pierre Wallot, eds, *Évolution et éclatement du monde rural.*

7 Nicole Guilbault, *Il était cent fois La Corriveau: Anthologie.*

8 See Carl Berger, *The Writing of Canadian History: Aspects of English-Canadian Historical Writing, 1900–1970.*

9 For work on the Canadian context, see C.J. Taylor, *Negotiating the Past: The Making of Canada's National Historic Parks and Sites*; Ian McKay, *The Quest of the Folk: Antimodernism and Cultural Selection in Twentieth-Century Nova Scotia*; *Histoire sociale/Social History* (hereafter *Hs-SH*) 29, no. 58: *Spectacle, Monument, Memory* (November 1996); Jonathan F. Vance, *Death So Noble: Memory, Meaning, and the First World War*; Norman Knowles, *Inventing the Loyalists: The Ontario Loyalist Tradition and the Creation of Usable Pasts*; Beverly Boutilier and Alison Prentice, eds, *Creating Historical Memory: English-Canadian Women and the Work of History*; Alan Gordon, 'Contested Terrain: The Politics of

Public Memory in Montreal, 1891–1930' (Ph.D. thesis, Queen's University, 1997); Ronald Rudin, 'Contested Terrain: Commemorative Celebrations and National Identity in Ireland and Quebec,' in Gérard Bouchard and Yvan Lamonde, eds, *La nation dans tous ses états: Le Québec en comparaison*, 183–204; Robert Cupido, '"Sixty Years of Canadian Progress": The Diamond Jubilee and the Politics of Commemoration,' *Canadian Issues* 20 (1998): 19–33; Patrice Groulx, *Pièges de la mémoire: Dollard des Ormeaux, les Amérindiens et nous*; H.V. Nelles, *The Art of Nation-Building: Pageantry and Spectacle at Quebec's Tercentenary.*

10 Alon Confino, 'Collective Memory and Cultural History: Problems of Method,' *American Historical Review* 102, no. 5 (Dec. 1997): 1386–403, especially 1400; John Bodnar, *Remaking America: Public Memory, Commemoration, and Patriotism in the Twentieth Century.*

11 The extent of the literature on commemoration, memory, and history is already large and is rapidly growing. See Nora, *Realms of Memory*, vols. 1–3; Bodnar, *Remaking America*; Samuel, *Theatres of Memory*; Michael Kammen, *Mystic Chords of Memory: The Transformation of Tradition in American Culture*; John R. Gillis, ed., *Commemorations: The Politics of National Identity*; George Lipsitz, *Time Passages: Collective Memory and American Popular Culture*; David Lowenthal, *The Past Is a Foreign Country*; Eric Hobsbawm and Terence Ranger, eds, *The Invention of Tradition.*

12 Gillis, ed., *Commemorations*, 3.

13 Vance, *Death So Noble*, 9, 166–7.

14 It is possible to elide the power relations that are part of commemoration. On this point, see Donald Wright, 'Myth, Memory, Meaning,' *Literary Review of Canada* (Dec. 1998): 25–7.

15 See, for example, Inderpal Grewal, *Home and Harem: Nation, Gender, Empire, and the Cultures of Travel*; Anne McClintock, 'Family Feuds: Gender, Nationalism, and the Family,' *Feminist Review: Nationalisms and National Identities* 44 (Summer 1993): 61–80.

16 These scholars have argued this most successfully, although the processes that have been studied are not quite the same as those examined here. See T.J. Jackson Lears, *No Place of Grace: Antimodernism and the Transformation of American Culture, 1880–1920*; McKay, *Quest of the Folk*; Donald Wright, 'W.D. Lighthall and David Ross McCord: Antimodernism and English-Canadian Imperialism, 1880s–1918,' *Journal of Canadian Studies* (hereafter *JoCS*) 32, no. 2 (Summer 1997): 134–53.

17 Kammen, *Mystic Chords of Memory*, 9.

18 As Kammen points out for the U.S. South in the 1870s and '80s, a society may have many 'memories' and much 'history' but have few resources to

devote to their public inscription and preservation (*Mystic Chords of Memory*, 113).

1: Like Mother, like Daughter: The Woman Warrior Tradition

1 Anthony Smith, 'The "Golden Age" and National Renewal,' in Geoffrey Hosking and George Schöpflin, eds, *Myths and Nationhood*, 57.
2 Philippe Aubert de Gaspé, *Mémoires* [1866], 402–4.
3 Allan Greer, *The Patriots and the People: The Rebellion of 1837 in Rural Lower Canada*, 216–18.
4 National Archives of Canada [hereafter NA], Archives des Colonies, Collection Moreau de St-Méry, MG1, vol. 6 (reel F-382), 341–2.
5 Ibid., (reel F-383), 434–7.
6 C.-C. Le Roy de La Potherie, *Histoire de l'Amérique septentrionale* (1722), vol. I: 324–8; vol. III: 152–4.
7 For example, similar sentences appear in the two. Verchères: 'je conservé, dans ce fatail moment, le peut d'asseurance dont une fille est capable et peut estre armée'; La Potherie: 'elle conserva dans ce moment plus d'assurance que n'en pouvoit avoir une Fille de quatorze ans.' André Vachon discusses the strong resemblance between La Potherie's second narrative and Verchères's petition in 'Jarret de Verchères, Marie-Madeleine,' in *Dictionary of Canadian Biography* [hereafter *DCB*], vol. III, 308–13.
8 La Potherie, *Histoire de l'Amérique septentrionale*, vol. I: 367.
9 'ce fust dans cet endroit que la fille du dit seigneur repoussa les ennemis qui estoient prests d'entrer dans ce fort et mesme tira du canon sur eux. Son action a esté gratifiée de Sa Majesté' (Gédéon de Catalogne, 'Report on the Seigniories and Settlements ...' in William Bennett Munro, ed., *Documents relating to the Seigniorial Tenure in Canada, 1598–1854*, 114). Unless otherwise noted, all translations are by the author.
10 P.-F.-X. de Charlevoix, *Histoire et description générale de la Nouvelle France* (1744), vol. III: 124.
11 Ibid., vol. II: lviii.
12 Frontenac and Bochart de Champigny to the Minister, 11 November 1692: '... il y a eu seulement pendant deux jours diverses escarmouches et quelques gens de tués de part et d'autre après quoi ils se sont retirés voyant que nous étions sur nos gardes et en résolution de les recevoir bien' (*Rapport de l'archiviste de la Province de Québec* [1927–8], 123).
13 'Les ennemis avoient tué et pris prisonniers quelques personnes à Vercheres, emmené les bestiaux dans le bois et levé la chevelure a un soldat a

St Ours ...' (NA, Archives des Colonies, MG1 series C11A, General correspondence, Canada, Transcriptions, vol. 12, 'Relation de ce qui s'est passé
en Canada depuis le mois de septembre 1692 jusques au depart des
Vaisseaux en 1693,' 358–420).

14 'Ce que la fille du Sr de Verchere expose dans la lettre qu'elle s'est donnée
l'honneur d'ecrire a Madame la Comtesse de Pontchartrain, est veritable'
(ibid., vol. 18, Champigny to the Minister, 15 October 1700, 69).

15 For a fascinating evaluation of some other themes in Verchères's narratives
and a comparison to the stories of Joan of Arc and Jeanne Hachette, see
Diane Gervais and Serge Lusignan, 'De Jeanne d'Arc à Madeleine de
Verchères: La femme guerrière dans la société d'Ancien Régime,' *Revue
d'histoire de l'Amérique française* [hereafter *RHAF*] 53, no. 2 (Fall 1999):
171–205.

16 James Douglas, 'The Status of Women in New England and New France,'
Queen's Quarterly 19, no. 4 (April-May-June 1912): 359–74; Natalie Zemon
Davis, *Women on the Margins*; Jan Noel, *Women in New France.*

17 Olwen Hufton, *The Prospect before Her: A History of Women in Western Europe,*
vol. I: *1500–1800*; Allan Greer, *The People of New France*, chap. 4.

18 'Quoyque mon sexe ne me permette pas d'avoir d'autre inclinations que
celles qu'il exige de moy, cependant permettez moy, madame, de vous dire
que j'ay des santiman qui me portent à la gloire comme a bien des
hommes.'

19 Louise Anne May, 'Worthy Warriors and Unruly Amazons: Sino-Western
Historical Accounts and Imaginative Images of Women in Battle' (Ph.D.
thesis, University of British Columbia, 1985), 56.

20 'Philis de Lacharce,' in *Biographie universelle ancienne et moderne*, vol. 23
(1819), 51; John A. Lynn, *Giant of the Grand Siècle: The French Army, 1610–
1715*, 343.

21 'Je scay, Madame, qu'il y a eu en France des personnes de mon sexe dans
cette derniere guerre, qui se sont mises a la teste de leurs paisant pour
s'opposer à l'invasion des ennemis qui entroient dans leur province.'

22 La Potherie, *Histoire de l'Amérique septentrionale*, vol. III: 151; Charlevoix,
Histoire et description générale, vol. III: 124–5.

23 May, 'Worthy Warriors and Unruly Amazons,' 19.

24 Ibid., 21.

25 Céline Dupré, 'Jarret de Verchères, Pierre,' in *DCB*, vol. II: 295–6.

26 'Souvenez-vous des leçons que mon pére vous a si souvent donné, que des
gentils hommes ne sont nés que pour verser leur sang pour le service de
Dieu et du Roy.'

27 Megan McLaughlin, 'The Woman Warrior: Gender, Warfare and Society in

Medieval Europe,' *Women's Studies* 17, nos. 3–4 (Jan. 1990): 196–7; Rudolf M. Dekker and Lotte C. van de Pol, 'Republican Heroines: Cross-Dressing Women in the French Revolutionary Armies,' *History of European Ideas* 10, no. 3 (1989): 360–1.

28 Natalie Zemon Davis, 'Women on Top,' in *Society and Culture in Early Modern France*, 124–51; Marina Warner, *Joan of Arc: The Image of Female Heroism*, chap. 7; Dianne Dugaw, 'Balladry's Female Warriors: Women, Warfare, and Disguise in the Eighteenth Century,' *Eighteenth-Century Life* 9, no. 2 (Jan. 1985): 1; Julie Wheelwright, *Amazons and Military Maids: Women Who Dressed as Men in the Pursuit of Life, Liberty and Happiness*.

29 'je crus qu'il estoit de la prudence pendant que l'on faisoit feu sur l'Ennemy de Représenter a ces femmes désolées et a ces enfans le danger d'etre entendus de l'Ennemy malgré le Bruit des fusils et du canon je leur ordonnay de se taire afin de ne pas donner lieu de croire que nous estions sans Ressource et sans esperance.'

30 'extrémement peureuse, comme il est naturel a toutes les femmes parisiennes de nation.'

31 'je me métamorphosay pour lors en mettant le chapeau du soldat sur ma teste.'

32 'je jettay ma coëffe, j'arboray un chapeau.'

33 Charlevoix, *Histoire et description générale*, vol. III: 123–5.

34 Louise Dechêne, *Habitants and Merchants in Seventeenth-Century Montréal*, 9.

35 Pierre-Georges Roy, ed., *Un procès criminel à Québec au dix-septième siècle: Anne Edmond accusée de s'être travestie en homme et d'avoir répandu de fausses nouvelles.*

36 Leslie Choquette, *Frenchmen into Peasants: Modernity and Tradition in the Peopling of French Canada*, 137–40.

37 Dugaw, 'Balladry's Female Warriors.'

38 Wheelwright, *Amazons and Military Maids*, 15.

39 Davis, 'Women on Top.'

40 Marjorie Garber, *Vested Interests: Cross-Dressing and Cultural Anxiety*.

41 '– Monsieur, vous soyez le bien venu, je vous rends les armes.
    – Mademoiselle ... elles sont en bonnes mains.
    – Meilleures que vous ne croyez.'

42 Ulinka Rublack, 'Wench and Maiden: Women, War and the Pictorial Function of the Feminine in German Cities in the Early Modern Period,' *History Workshop Journal* 44 (Autumn 1997): 18.

43 Gervais and Lusignan interpret this incident in a different fashion. For them, by leaving the scarf in the Iroquois warrior's hand, Verchères enters a liminal phase during which she abandons for a time her femininity ('De Jeanne d'Arc à Madeleine de Verchères,' 187).

44 On Zenobia, see Antonia Fraser, *The Warrior Queens*, 107–28.

45 Jean Blain, 'La moralité en Nouvelle-France: Les phases de la thèse et de l'antithèse,' *RHAF* 27, no. 3 (Dec. 1973): 408–16.

46 'Elle se battit avec toute l'intrepidité que le plus aguerri soldat auroit pû faire' (La Potherie, *Histoire de l'Amérique septentrionale*, vol. I: 327).

47 'Elle se battit de la sorte pendant deux jours, avec une bravoure & une présence d'esprit, qui auroit fait honneur à un vieux guerrier ... Bien honteux d'être obligé de fuir devant une Femme ... que pour faire éclater la valeur et l'intrépidité de deux Amazones' (Charlevoix, *Histoire et description générale*, vol. III: 124).

48 NA, MG1 series C11A, vol. 27, fol. 144, 1707.

49 Lord Kames (Henry Home), *Sketches of the History of Man* (1788), vol. I: 44–6.

50 Thomas Anburey, *Travels through the Interior Parts of America in a Series of Letters by an Officer* (1789), vol. I: 172–5.

51 D. Dainville [Gustave Bossange], *Beautés de l'histoire du Canada* (1821), 180–1.

52 'nos deux grand'tantes de Verchères, qui défendirent à la tête d'autres femmes en l'année 1690, et en l'année 1692, un fort attaqué par les sauvages, et les repoussèrent' (*Mémoires*, 402–4).

53 For instance, the discussion in F.-X. Garneau, *Histoire du Canada depuis sa découverte jusqu'à nos jours*, 2nd ed. (1852), 313, is very short compared to that in the 8th edition (1944), 194–6.

54 David Gosselin, *Tablettes chronologiques et alphabétiques des principaux événements de l'histoire du Canada* (1887), 16; Frédéric Gerbié, *Le Canada et l'immigration française* (1884), 46.

55 Régis Roy, 'Une vaillante canadienne,' *Le monde illustré* (21 Oct. 1893), 296–7.

56 'Je ne sçaurois passer sous silence l'action heroïque de Mademoiselle de Vercheres'; 'L'action de Mademoiselle de Vercheres (Fille d'un Officier qui a cinquante ans de service) me paroît trop héroïque pour la passer sous silence' (La Potherie, *Histoire de l'Amérique septentrionale*, vol. I: 324; vol. III: 152).

57 'entrer dans un détail de toutes les circonstances qu'il fallut encore donner à la Cour pour confirmer une chose que l'on avoit cachée jusques alors' (ibid., vol. I: 328).

58 Guy Frégault, 'Politique et politiciens,' in *Le XVIIIe siècle canadien: Études*, 176–8.

59 'Je mandai il y a deux ans l'action de Mademoiselle sa Fille à Monsieur le Comte de Pontchartrain, qui est le Protecteur des Canadiens' (La Potherie, *Histoire de l'Amérique septentrionale*, vol. I: 327).

60 'Ce que la fille du Sr de Verchere expose dans la lettre qu'elle s'est donnée l'honneur d'ecrire a Madame la Comtesse de Pontchartrain, est veritable ... son père qui étoit gentilhomme et la disgrace que sa famille vient d'eprouver par sa mort ... une pension pour ayder a tirer cette pauvre famille de la plus profonde misere' (NA, MG1 series C11A, vol. 18, Champigny to the Minister, 15 October 1700, 69).

61 Ibid., vol. 19, Callière and Champigny to the Minister, 5 October 1701, 30–1.

62 See, for instance, ibid., vol. 113, 'Gratiffications ordinaires,' 1707, fol. 213v., and 30 September 1726, fol. 374v.

63 I analyse this case in 'Authority and Illegitimacy in New France: The Burial of Bishop Saint-Vallier and Madeleine de Verchères vs. the Priest of Batiscan,' *Hs-SH* 22, no. 43 (May 1989): 65–90.

64 NA, MG1 series C11A, vol. 106, pp. 232–6, letter of M. le Coadjuteur, 29 September 1731.

65 'Dieu ne craint ni héros ni héroine' (Archives nationales du Québec à Québec [hereafter ANQ-Q], 'Verchères-Naudière – Procès avec le curé de Batiscan,' ZQ27, 183).

66 Fraser, *The Warrior Queens*, 11–12.

67 ANQ-Q, Collection des pièces judiciaires et notariales, M67, no. 550½, Jean Ricard vs. Pierre Thomas de la Perrade, 1715.

68 NA, Nouvelle-France, Archives judiciaires, MG8 B4, vol. 1, 664, 691.

69 'À ce moment, un peintre me voyant auroit bien pu tirer le portrait d'une Magdelaine décoéffée, mes cheveux epars et mal arrangés, mes habits tout déchirés, n'ayant rien sur moy qui ne fut par morceaux. Je ne ressamblois pas mal à cette sainte, aux larmes près qui ne coulèrent jamais de mes yeux.'

70 NA, Nouvelle-France, Official correspondence, MG8 A1, 3rd series, vol. 12, pp. 2657–8, 15 October 1730; MG1, series B, vol. 58, pp. 132–3, 6 May 1733.

71 On Moreau de St-Méry's collection, see Édouard Richard, ed., *Supplement to Dr. Brymner's Report on Canadian Archives by Mr. Édouard Richard (1899)*, 4–5.

72 'Voylà la narration simple et juste de mon aventure.'

73 'il estoit d'une consequence infinie qu'ils n'entrassent dans aucun fort françois, qu'ils jugeroit des autres par celuy-cy, s'ils s'en emparoient, et qu'une pareille connoissance ne pourroit servir qu'à augmenter leur fierté et leur courage.'

2: Images of Heroism and Nationalism: The Canadian Joan of Arc

1 'on croirait entendre un chant de l'Iliade! ... J'ignorais que ce pays nouveau eût des annales déjà si glorieuses ... Je plaidais une cause en effet,

Excellence, celle des miens, celle de l'héroïsme français et de son droit au
respect, à l'espace, à la survivance, à la liberté ... Je vois en effet que le fort
de Verchères est encore français, et que, malgré le siècle écoulé, l'ombre
de la petite Madeleine revient parfois, la nuit, dans le Château, monter la
garde!' (Frère Marie-Victorin, *Peuple sans histoire: Fantaisie dramatique en un
acte et trois tableaux* [1937], 21–2).

2 Denis Martin, *Portraits des héros de la Nouvelle-France: Images d'un culte
historique*, xiii; Norman Knowles, *Inventing the Loyalists*, 119.

3 'Donnez une idée du courage militaire de la femme dans la Nouvelle
France' (F.-X. Garneau, *Additions à l'histoire du Canada de F.X. Garneau*
[1864], 54–5).

4 Archives du Séminaire de Québec, Fonds Verreau, Faucher de Saint-
Maurice to Rev. M. Verreault, 15 December 1869, 30, no. 15.

5 R. Brunet, 'Chronique européenne,' in *Le monde illustré* 14 (1897–8): 68–
70. In 1888, J. Frémont had published Verchères's first narrative: 'Notice
sur Mademoiselle de Verchères,' *Annuaire de l'Institut canadien de Québec* 12
(1888), 69–72.

6 É. Richard, ed., *Supplement to Dr. Brymner's Report*, 5–6.

7 See Serge Gagnon, *Le Québec et ses historiens de 1840 à 1920*, chap. 1–2;
Fernande Roy, 'Une mise en scène de l'histoire: La fondation de Montréal
à travers les siècles,' *RHAF* 46, no. 1 (Summer 1992): 22–30; Jacques
Mathieu and Jacques Lacoursière, *Les mémoires québécoises*, 319–23.

8 Pierre-Georges Roy, *Les monuments commémoratifs de la Province de Québec*,
vol. 2: 65–6.

9 Patrice Groulx, *Pièges de la mémoire*, 206–10; Susan Mann Trofimenkoff,
L'Action française: French Canadian nationalism in the twenties, 43–4.

10 Jacques Chevalier, 'Myth and Ideology in "Traditional" French Canada:
Dollard, the Martyred Warrior,' *Anthropologica* n.s. 21, no. 2 (1979): 144;
Ramsay Cook, *The Maple Leaf Forever: Essays on Nationalism and Politics in
Canada*, chap. 8–9.

11 See Gagnon, *Le Québec et ses historiens*, chap. 1.

12 Maurice Agulhon, *Marianne into Battle: Republican Imagery and Symbolism in
France, 1789–1880*, 3, 183.

13 'Souvenons-nous toujours, Français, que la patrie chez nous est née du
coeur d'une femme, de sa tendresse, de ses larmes, du sang qu'elle a
donné pour nous' (Michelet, quoted in Michel Winock, 'Jeanne d'Arc,' in
Pierre Nora, ed., *Les lieux de la mémoire*, vol. 3, *Les France 3: De l'archive à
l'emblème*, 701).

14 Eugene Weber, *Peasants into Frenchmen: The Modernization of Rural France,
1870–1914*, 111–12; Marina Warner, *Joan of Arc*, chap. 13; Martha Hanna,

'Iconology and Ideology: Images of Joan of Arc in the Idiom of the *Action française*, 1908–1931,' *French Historical Studies* 14, no. 2 (Fall 1985): 215–39.

15 Poincaré quoted in Gerd Krumeich, 'Joan of Arc: Between Right and Left,' in Robert Tombs, ed., *Nationhood and Nationalism in France: From Boulangism to the Great War, 1889–1918*, 71.

16 Winock, 'Jeanne d'Arc,' 710–14; Robert Gildea, *The Past in French History*, 164–5.

17 Martha Vicinus, *Independent Women: Work and Community for Single Women, 1850–1920*, 266; Elaine Showalter, *Sexual Anarchy: Gender and Culture at the fin de siècle*, 29; Judith Walkowitz, *City of Dreadful Delight: Narratives of Sexual Danger in Late-Victorian London*, 62.

18 On Joan of Arc's cult in Quebec, see *Nova Francia* 3 (1927–8): 381; and 4 (1929): 318.

19 'Pleine à déborder du souvenir de Jeanne d'Arc ...' (Groulx, *Mes Mémoires*, vol. I: 128).

20 'J'ai prié ce matin Jeanne, la bienheureuse et la vaillante, pour ceux qui, au Canada, luttent comme elle au service des traditions françaises et catholiques' (Centre de recherche Lionel Groulx, Fonds Joseph Gauvreau, P39, Joseph-P. Archambault to Dr Gauvreau, 19 August 1913).

21 Sharon Macdonald, 'Boadicea: Warrior, Mother and Myth,' in Sharon Macdonald, Pat Holden, and Shirley Ardener, eds, *Images of Women in Peace and War: Cross-Cultural and Historical Perspectives*, 57; see also Antonia Fraser, *The Warrior Queens*, 299.

22 Maximilien Bibaud, *Les Machabées canadiens* (1859), 17.

23 L'Annaliste, 'M. Rodolphe Girard: L'Homme du jour dans le domaine des lettres,' *Le monde illustré* (7 March 1903): 1061. Frédéric de Kastner makes the same comparison in *Héros de la Nouvelle France* (1902), and Charles Colby pursues the allusion in a negative fashion by saying that 'New France had no Maid of Orleans' (*Canadian Types of the Old Régime, 1608–1698* [1908], 338).

24 Marie-Louise d'Auteuil, 'Vos Doctrines?' *L'Action française* 16, no. 6 (Dec. 1926): 381.

25 Louis Fréchette, *La légende d'un peuple* (1887); Jacques Cézembre, 'Les romans de la vie: Madeleine de Verchères, la Jeanne Hachette canadienne,' *Dimanche-illustré* (14 Sept. 1930): 5.

26 'C'en était fait: le Canada avait droit de se comparer à la France en ceci: il avait eu son héroïne' (P. de la Chatre, 'L'Héroïne de Verchères,' *Le Nouvelliste des Trois-Rivières* [8 Aug. 1929]).

27 Martin, quoted in Naomi Griffiths, 'Longfellow's *Evangeline*: The Birth and Acceptance of a Legend,' *Acadiensis* 11, no. 2 (Spring 1982): 36.

28 Ginette Pellerin, dir., *Evangeline's Quest* (National Film Board of Canada, 1996).

29 Cf. Roy, 'Une mise en scène de l'histoire.'

30 Bibliothèque municipale de Montréal, Salle Gagnon, Lot 10, C1, Concours littéraire Société St-Jean-Baptiste de Montréal, Valmoral, 7 November 1918, 'Petite héroïne de quatorze ans'; F. Sophronius, 29 November 1918, 'Une Héroïne de quatorze ans (Nouvelle historique).'

31 Francis Parkman, *Count Frontenac and New France under Louis XIV*, vol. II [1877]: 224.

32 'Vierge sainte, mere de mon Dieu, vous scavez que je vous ay toujours honorée et aimée comme ma chere mere, ne m'abbandonnez pas dans le danger ou je me trouve; j'aime mille fois mieux perir que de tomber entre les mains d'une nation qui ne vous connoit pas.'

33 'forte de l'Évangile' (Baillairgé, *Marie-Madeleine de Verchères et les siens* [1913], 22).

34 John Reade, *Madeleine de Verchères* (1890).

35 Alan Sullivan, 'Madeleine Verchères,' in Ontario Women's Liberal Association, *Hearts of Gold: Being Chronicles of Heroism in Canadian History* (1915), 26.

36 'Battons-nous jusqu'à la mort. Nous combattons pour notre patrie et pour la religion.'

37 Diane Gervais and Serge Lusignan, 'De Jeanne d'Arc à Madeleine de Verchères,' 178–9.

38 Arthur Doughty, *A Daughter of New France: Being a Story of the Life and Times of Magdeleine de Verchères, 1665–1692* (1916), 4.

39 'C'est leur seule réponse mais combien juste écho de la voix de l'enfant du fort de Verchères' (Pierre Homier, 'À travers la vie courante,' *L'Action française* 3, no. 6 [June 1919]: 266).

40 Albert Larrieu, *Madeleine de Verchères*.

41 On Drummond's appeal, see Roy Daniells, 'Minor Poets, 1880–1920,' in Carl F. Klinck et al., eds, *Literary History of Canada: Canadian Literature in English*, 2nd ed., vol. 1: 438; Mary Jane Edwards, 'Drummond, William Henry,' in *DCB*, vol. XIII: 284–6.

42 William Henry Drummond, *Phil-o-rum's Canoe and Madeleine Vercheres* (1898), 6–12.

43 McGill University, Osler Library of the History of Medicine, William Henry Drummond Fonds, P103, Box 2, 5.7, draft of 'Madeleine Vercheres,' no date.

44 Carl Berger, 'The True North Strong and Free,' in J.M. Bumsted, ed., *Interpreting Canada's Past*, vol. 2, *After Confederation*, 164–5.

45 Daniel Francis, *The Imaginary Indian: The Image of the Indian in Canadian Culture*, chap. 4.

46 McGill University, Osler Library, Drummond Fonds, P103, Box 11, 32.3/6/3, clipping from the *Chicago Chronicle*, 30 Jan. 1899.

47 Ibid., Box 9, 17.2/35, Major L. G. Drummond, Governor General's Secretary to Drummond, 28 December 1898.

48 Ibid., Box 8, 17.3/77, Louis Fréchette to Drummond, 22 June 1898.

49 Showalter, *Sexual Anarchy*; Walkowitz, *City of Dreadful Delight*.

50 Ramon Hathorn, *Sarah Bernhardt's Canadian Visits*.

51 Susan Mann Trofimenkoff, 'Henri Bourassa and "the Woman Question"' in Trofimenkoff and Alison Prentice, eds, *The Neglected Majority: Essays in Canadian Women's History*, vol. II: 104–15; Trofimenkoff, *The Dream of Nation: A Social and Intellectual History of Quebec*, chap. 12; Andrée Lévesque, *La norme et les déviantes: Des femmes au Québec pendant l'entre-deux-guerres*.

52 'La femme-homme, le monstre hybride et répugnant qui tuera la femme-mère et la femme-*femme*' (Henri Bourassa, *Femmes-hommes ou hommes et femmes? Études à bâtons rompus sur le féminisme* [1925], 41 [article dated 28 March 1918]).

53 *House of Commons Debates*, Session 1918, vol. I: 655.

54 'L'idée, pour une femme, de se faire homme est contre nature ... Pourquoi ne faire qu'un, là où Dieu veut qu'il y ait deux?' (F.-A. Baillairgé, *Jeunesse et folies* [1925], 40).

55 Marc de Germiny, 'Une héroïne de quatorze ans: Marie-Magdeleine de Verchères,' *Le Devoir* (31 Aug. 1912): 4.

56 Frédéric de Kastner, *Héros de la Nouvelle France* (1902), 82–91. Another aristocratic author emphasizing Verchères's social class was Thérèse de Ferron; see 'Une héroïne de la Nouvelle-France: Marie-Madeleine de Verchères,' *Revue hebdomadaire* (4 Oct. 1924): 89–102.

57 M. Hodent, 'Philippe Hébert: Le maître de la sculpture canadienne,' *La Canadienne* [Paris] 11, no. 9 (Sept. 1913): 164.

58 Martin, *Portraits des héros*.

59 Rev. Aen. McD. Dawson, 'The Heroine of Vercheres,' *Canadian Antiquarian and Numismatic Journal* 6 (1878): 142–5. Poems by William Chapman ('L'Héroïne de Verchères,' in *Les Quebecquoises* [1876], 150–6); Drummond (*Phil-o-rum's Canoe and Madeleine Vercheres*, 6); and Sullivan ('Madeleine Verchères,' 25) employ the same trope.

60 'Oui, Madeleine, qui était forte, n'en était pas moins douce et sensible' (Baillairgé, *Marie-Madeleine de Verchères et les siens*, 30).

61 Agnes Maule Machar and Thomas G. Marquis, *Stories of New France: Being Tales of Adventure and Heroism from the Early History of Canada* (1890), 216.

62 'Madeleine était une petite fille et ... une petite fille n'est pas un petit garçon ... On doit suppléer quelquefois les hommes, mais leur rendre les armes pour les batailles qui leur reviennent' (Lionel Groulx, *Notre maître, le passé*, 1st series [1924], 61–9).

63 Chapman, 'L'Héroïne de Verchères'; J.M. LeMoine, *Les héroïnes de la Nouvelle-France* (1888), 16.

64 'elle devint à son tour, la conquête de celui dont elle avait sauvé les jours' (François Daniel, *Histoire des grandes familles françaises* [1867], 519).

65 'Magdelon fut une femme parfaite, aussi habile ménagère que bonne mère de famille' (T.G., 'Magdelon la Canadienne,' *Le Temps* [14 Aug. 1912]).

66 Raoult Renault, 'Une héroïne canadienne,' *La Revue canadienne* 31 (1895): 347.

67 'comme autant d'étoiles, de flambeaux conducteurs destinés à nous piloter à travers les sinueux sentiers de notre existence, comme autant de patrones [sic] pour nos jeunes canadiennes, comme autant de modèles de fidélité conjugale' (LeMoine, *Les héroïnes de la Nouvelle-France*, 23).

68 de Briac: 'Je meurs pour avoir trop aimé Madeleine de Verchères, qui m'a aimé, elle aussi.'
Madeleine de Verchères: 'Et si vous faites feu, eh bien! nos deux corps tomberont en même temps, notre sang se mêlera, nous serons unis dans la mort et dans l'éternité, puisque nous n'aurons pu l'être dans la vie ...' ('Fleur de lys: Page littéraire empruntée au drame de M. Rodolphe Girard,' *Le monde illustré* [7 March 1903]: 1067). The play was published in thirteen parts in Ottawa's *Le Droit* newspaper from 19 February to 4 March 1936. The wording of the above extract was slightly different in the 1936 version.

69 'Madeleine de Verchères' (no. 9), *Le Droit*, 28 February 1936.

70 'Pardonnez-moi, chevalier de Briac. Moi aussi, j'ai une réparation à vous faire. Prenez ma fille, capitaine, prenez-la, et puissiez-vous avoir des fils dignes de vous et des filles dignes d'elle' (ibid., [no. 13], 4 March 1936).

71 'M. Girard a adopté le grand genre romantique, c'est-à-dire le genre le plus en vogue de nos jours' (L'Annaliste, 'M. Rodolphe Girard,' *Le monde illustré* [7 March 1903]: 1061; Madeleine Charlebois-Dirschauer, *Rodolphe Girard (1879–1956): Sa vie, son œuvre*, 131, 29).

72 Carolyn Heilbrun, *Writing a Woman's Life*.

73 For similar projects by other English-Canadian women during this period, see the articles on Agnes Maule Machar (by Dianne M. Hallman), Sarah Anne Curzon (by Beverly Boutilier), and Isabel Skelton (by Terry Crowley) in Boutilier and Prentice, eds, *Creating Historical Memory*.

74 Mary Sifton Pepper, *Maids and Matrons of New France* (1902), 4.

75 Teresa Costigan Armstrong, 'The Heroine of Vercheres,' *Women's Historical Society of Ottawa: Transactions* 5 (1912): 71.

76 'L'histoire, c'est fait surtout pour les garçons ... à cause des batailles et des soldats ... Et Madeleine de Verchères? Ce n'était pas un garçon ... Et l'on en parle dans l'histoire' (Marie-Claire Daveluy, 'Le cours improvisé' [1920], in *Aux feux de la rampe* [1927], 11–12).

77 'On dit que les peuples heureux n'ont pas d'histoire. Si cet épigramme s'applique aux individus, il faut croire que les premières Françaises établies en Amérique furent des femmes heureuses, car on n'en parle pas ... ou si peu que c'est tout comme!' (Corinne Rocheleau, *Françaises d'Amérique: Esquisse historique* [1915], 3).

78 'Puisque je suis femme, ma sympathie doit d'abord se porter vers des femmes' (Madame Donat Brodeur, 'Deux héroïnes de la Nouvelle-France,' *Canadian Antiquarian* 3rd series, 5 [1908]: 65).

79 Emma A. Currie, *The Story of Laura Secord and Canadian Reminiscences* (1900), 83.

80 Pepper, *Maids and Matrons*, 228–9.

81 E[thel] T. Raymond, *Madeleine de Verchères* (1929), 8–9.

82 Mary Constance Du Bois, 'Captain Madeleine (Wild Flower of Chivalry),' *St. Nicholas Magazine* (June 1928): 610.

83 Glasgow, quoted in Crowley, 'Isabel Skelton: Precursor to Canadian Cultural History,' in Boutilier and Prentice, eds, *Creating Historical Memory*, 173.

84 Isabel Skelton, *The Backwoodswoman* (1924), 77.

85 John Reade, *Madeleine de Verchères* (1890).

86 Mme Boissonault, 'Magdelaine de Verchères,' in *L'Huis du passé* (1924), 80.

87 Colby, *Canadian Types*, 343.

88 Yves Roby, *Les franco-américains de la Nouvelle-Angleterre, 1776–1930*, 290–300.

89 'L'émule canadienne de Philis méritait d'être signalée à nos compatriotes, étant fille d'un Dauphinois. Bon sang ne sait mentir' (Marie-X. Drevet, 'Une héroïne de la Nouvelle-France: Marie-Madeleine de Verchères,' *Le Dauphiné* [Grenoble] 3520 [19 Oct. 1924], 143–4). Likewise, Mlle Françoise Mournaud, *Les Allobroges au Canada (suivi de relation des faits historiques de Mlle Marie-Magdeleine de Verchère)* (1935).

90 Archives nationales du Québec à Trois-Rivières [hereafter ANQ-TR], Fonds de la famille Baillargé, P29, Marie Antoinette Young to Abbé Baillairgé, n.d.

91 'Nous conservons, dans nos vieilles familles françaises, un sentiment très tendre et plein d'admiration envers nos frères du Canada qui n[ou]s sont demeurés si fidèles ...' (ibid., de Ferron to Abbé Baillairgé, 30 Jan. 1923).

92 Léon Ville, *Madeleine de Verchères: Une héroïne canadienne* (1928), 70.

93 Ibid., 53; Georges Cerbelaud-Salagnac, *Mademoiselle de Verchères* (1958), 95; Nicole Vidal, *La nuit des Iroquois* (1983), 157.

94 *Riddarna och de röda. Madelon I* (1981); *I de rödas krig. Madelon II* (1982); *Fredens hemliga Stig. Madelon III* (1983). Lars Furuland et al., *Ungdomslitteraturen: Historik, kommentarer, texturval* (1994), 109–10.

95 Arthur Doughty and William Wood, *The King's Book of Quebec* (1911), 251.

96 Fréchette, *La légende d'un peuple*, 77.

97 Lester B. Pearson, *Mike: The Memoirs of the Right Honourable Lester B. Pearson, vol. 1, 1897–1948*, 15. My thanks to Donald Wright for this reference.

98 Arthur R.M. Lower, *Colony to Nation: A History of Canada* (1946).

3: Representing History: The Statue and Film of Madeleine de Verchères

1 'Et les siècles jamais ne pourront, sous leur lime, / De l'histoire effacer son nom' (Chapman, *Les Quebecquoises* [1876], 155).

2 'Madeleine de Verchères,' arrangement and words by I.S. Henri (to ancient Irish air) (1929).

3 Armstrong, 'The Heroine of Vercheres,' 79.

4 'Les Romains n'auraient pas oublier [sic] d'élever un monument ou une statue à la mémoire d'une si jeune et si brave héroïne' (N.E. Dionne, 'Une héroïne canadienne,' *La Kermesse: Revue hebdomadaire* 6 [28 Oct. 1892]: 96).

5 Henry James Morgan, ed., *Types of Canadian Women and of Women Who Are or Have Been Connected with Canada* (1903), vol. I: 80; See also Frédéric de Kastner, *Héros de la Nouvelle France*, 91.

6 Doughty, *A Daughter of New France*, 2, 4.

7 H.V. Nelles, *The Art of Nation-Building*.

8 Doughty, *A Daughter of New France*, 129.

9 Richard Jebb, *Studies in Colonial Nationalism* (1905).

10 ANQ-TR, P29, Fonds de la famille Baillargé (sic), Thérèse de Ferron to Abbé Baillairgé, 30 Jan. 1923.

11 Ottawa City Archives, Ottawa Municipal Chapter IODE, MG43, vol. 1–3/4, Magdelaine de Vercheres Chapter, Treasurer's Report, 10 February 1917 to 14 February 1918. The first annual report (vol. 1–3/1) does not provide a breakdown of any receipts from the book, and the expenditures for printing, binding, and commission are detailed in the 1917–18 report.

12 NA, Picture Archives, Acc. 1984–4–13654.

13 'Les hommes ont la faculté de se taire, et jouissent même souvent du triste privilège d'oublier; les pierres, au contraire, ne sauraient garder le silence,

et les monuments rendent les souvenirs impérissables ...' (quoted in Pierre-Georges Roy, *Les monuments commémoratifs de la Province de Québec*, vol. 2: 41–2).

14 Eric Hobsbawm and Terence Ranger, eds, *The Invention of Tradition*.

15 'C'est activer le patriotisme que deposer une plaque commémorative, une colonne, une marque quelconque, dans un lieu où le passant ne voit rien aujourd'hui qui frappe son imagination' (Benjamin Sulte, 'Report of the French Secretary,' *The Historical Landmarks Association of Canada, Annual Report* [1915]: 17).

16 C.J. Taylor, *Negotiating the Past*.

17 Richard Handler, 'On Having a Culture: Nationalism and the Preservation of Quebec's *Patrimoine*,' in George W. Stocking, Jr, ed., *Objects and Others: Essays on Museums and Material Culture*, 213.

18 'Un acte d'héroïsme dont la gloire, appartient à la race Canadienne Française, mais dont tout Canadien a le droit de s'enorgueillir' (Archives nationales du Québec à Montréal [ANQ-M], Comité du monument Dollard, P3/1/1, Livre des minutes, Charles A. Doherty to Emile Vaillancourt, 23 May 1910).

19 'Comme glorification première de ces héros par leurs coréligionnaires et conationaux' (ibid., J.A. Lemire to Emile Vaillancourt, 11 June 1910).

20 Ibid., undated and unsigned letter on *Montreal Herald* stationery.

21 Roy, *Les monuments commémoratifs*, vol. 1: 245–6, vol. 2: 249–50 (Louis Marcoux); on the 1895 monument to the Patriote Dr L.-O. Chénier in Montreal, see Alan Gordon, 'Contested Terrain,' 174, 182–3.

22 Roy, *Les monuments commémoratifs*, vol. 2: 261.

23 William Cohen, 'Symbols of Power: Statues in Nineteenth-Century Provincial France,' *Comparative Studies in Society and History* 31 (1989): 499.

24 Compare Daniel J. Sherman, 'Monuments, Mourning and Masculinity in France after World War i' *Gender and History* 8, no. 1 (April 1996): 82–107.

25 ANQ-M, Fonds Marie-Claire Daveluy, P1000/1/115, Daveluy to Abbé Azarie Couillard-Després, 21 October 1916.

26 Alain Gelly, Louise Brunelle-Lavoie, and Corneliu Kirjan, *La passion du patrimoine: La Commission des Biens Culturels du Québec, 1922–1994*, 26.

27 ANQ-TR, P29, Livre de compte personnel, 96–9.

28 Musée des beaux-arts de Montréal, État de la recherche, Louis-Philippe Hébert, 'Madeleine de Verchères,' 1988.3.

29 NA, Parks Canada, RG84, vol. 1255, File HS-7–25 vol. 1, Philippe Hébert to William Pugsley, Minister of Public Works, 8 June 1911.

30 'Tantôt je sentais que pour vouloir traduire toute sa belle énergie, j'allais

faire de ma jeune héroïne une virago ... transfigurée par l'idée de sauver les siens et de défendre la maison natale' (quoted in M. Hodent, 'Philippe Hébert,' 164).

31 'Ce n'est ni une virago, ni une amazone, encore moins un mousquetaire en jupon, c'est une personnalité bien féminine, toute vibrante, frappée d'une marque spéciale, que l'artiste offre au ravissement de nos yeux' (J.-Edmond Roy, 'Madeleine de Verchères,' in P.-G. Roy, *La Famille Tarieu de Lanaudière* [1922], 176).

32 NA, Grey of Howick Papers, MG27 II B2, Grey to Lord Strathcona, 11 March 1909, vol. 28, 7411.

33 NA, Fonds Rodolphe Lemieux, MG27 II D10, vol. 10, Lord Grey to Lemieux, 16 May 1910, 11878.

34 NA, MG27 II B2, vol. 5, file 50, pencil note of 24 May on letter of Grey to Lemieux, 16 May 1910.

35 Barbara Messamore, 'The Social and Cultural Role of the Governors-General in Canada,' in C.M. Coates, ed., *Imperial Canada*, 78–108.

36 Nelles, *The Art of Nation-Building.*

37 NA, MG27 II B2, vol. 28, drawer 4, file 2, Lord Grey to Mr MacBride, Premier of British Columbia, 9 November 1907.

38 NA, RG84, vol. 1255, File HS-7-25, vol. 1, Lord Grey to Mr Pugsley, 2 November 1910.

39 'Je suis bien aise de voir que ce digne curé aura pour contempler dans sa propre paroisse une superbe statue de Madeleine de Verchères ... Voilà la réponse du gouvernement Laurier à l'agitation créée par l'abbé Baillairgé' (*Débats de la Chambre des Communes*, vol. civ, Session 1911–12, vol. ii: 2889).

40 NA, RG84, vol. 1255, File HS-7-25, vol. 1, Arthur Boyer to J.B. Hunter, 7 September 1911.

41 Women were thanked for organizing the brunch as well. The information on the unveiling comes from *Le Devoir* (22 Sept. 1913): 4–6; and *La Presse* (22 Sept. 1913): 8.

42 'Elle a vécu notre vie ... Il y en a eu d'autres Madeleine de Verchères dernièrement, alors que des institutrices canadiennes-françaises préférèrent perdre leur salaire plutôt que de ne pas enseigner le français à leurs élèves ... Si le royaume de France fut délivré et réhabilité par Jeanne d'Arc, cette colonie, alors française à son berceau, fut illustrée par Madeleine de Verchères ... Elle jouissait de l'admiration de l'élite, mais son image n'était pas gravée dans l'imagination des foules' (*Le Devoir* [22 Sept. 1913]: 4–6).

43 Jonathan F. Vance, *Death So Noble*, 156.

44 'Plus d'un canadien qui l'apercevra en remontant le fleuve dira qu'il n'est pas de plus jolie fille sous le ciel bleu' (Hodent, 'Philippe Hébert,' 164).

45 NA, RG84, vol. 1255, HS-7–25, vol. 2, part 1, A. Pinard to J.B. Harkin, 10 December 1923.

46 Ibid., part 1, Baillairgé to ?, n.d.

47 Quoted in Daniel J. Sherman, 'Art, Commerce, and the Production of Memory in France after World War I,' in John R. Gillis, ed., *Commemorations*, 206.

48 NA, RG84, vol. 1255, File HS-7–25, vol. 2, part 2 (1924–5), F.W. Howay to J.B. Harkin, 23 September 1924.

49 Ibid., Harkin to Cruikshank, 6 Oct. 1924.

50 Ibid., Fauteux to Harkin, 14 September 1925.

51 ANQ-TR, P29, J.B. Harkin to F.A. Baillairgé, 28 July 1924.

52 'Peu de monuments ont été érigés avec autant d'amour, autant de conviction, autant de foi en l'avenir de notre race. M. Baillairgé avait, pour ainsi dire, la dévotion de Mademoiselle de Verchères qu'il appelait la Jeanne d'Arc de la Nouvelle-France' (Bibliothèque nationale du Québec, Fonds Réjean Olivier, MSS-48, carton 2, chemise 2, 'Allocution du Révérend Père L.J. Morin, c.s.v.,' 4).

53 NA, RG84, vol. 1255, File HS-7–25, vol. 3, pt 1 to vol. 4, pt 3, reports by the caretaker.

54 Roy Rosenzweig, *Eight Hours for What We Will: Workers and Leisure in an Industrial City, 1870–1920*, 198–204; Lary May, *Screening Out the Past: The Birth of Mass Culture and the Motion Picture Industry*, 151–3.

55 Rachael Low, *The History of the British Film, 1918–1929*, 91–8; Susan Hayward, *French National Cinema*, 23.

56 Quoted in Yves Lever, *Histoire générale du cinéma au Québec*, 75.

57 Ibid., 65–6.

58 Peter Morris, *Embattled Shadows: A History of Canadian Cinema, 1895–1939*, 47–8.

59 Bibliothèque municipale de Montréal, Salle Gagnon, Documents divers, Lot 2, C-50, 'Madeleine de Verchères sur l'écran' [undated, unidentified press clipping, possibly from Sherbrooke].

60 'Le cinéma tel qu'il existe actuellement au Canada, exportation de l'industrie américaine, est fatal à notre langue, à nos moeurs, à nos traditions' (Pierre Homier [Joseph-Papin Archambault, SJ], 'À travers la vie courante,' *L'Action française* 6, no. 3 [Sept. 1921]: 572).

61 'une oeuvre essentiellement moralisatrice et féconde au sens national du mot' (advertisement in *L'Action française* 11, no. 1 [Jan. 1924]: 2 [the same advertisement had appeared since June 1923).

62 'il est urgent d'entrer en lutte avec le cinéma américain inepte trop souvent, à tendances généralement corruptrices, fatalement anglifiantes,

par un cinéma catholique de mentalité, donc honnête et propre, et essentiellement canadien-français de direction et de ton ... c'est du moins ce que touchent 95% des fabricants de films qui sont des Juifs. Une compagnie canadienne qui n'a rien à craindre de par la nature de ses "vues" de la redoutable concurrence juivo-américaine, ne peut-elle pas obtenir aisément des résultats aussi marqués' (Archives de la Chancellerie de Montréal, dossier Cinéma [campagnes de censure], 773–80, 924–1b, 'Des noms qui sont une solide garantie d'habile et honnête administration,' investment flyer for Le Cinéma Canadien).

63 On this early film, see Germain Lacasse, *Histoires des scopes (Le cinéma muet au Québec)*, 65–7.

64 *La Patrie* (12 Dec. 1922): 8.

65 NA, National Film Archives, Hye Bossin Collection, reel 2, file 27, no. 27, Arthur Larente to Hye Bossin, 31 May 1964.

66 ANQ-M, Régie du cinéma, E188, Direction du classement des films, box 62, November–December 1922.

67 *La Presse* (11 Dec. 1922): 15.

68 D. John Turner, 'J.-A. Homier photographe: Le pionnier oublié du cinéma québécois,' *24 images* 11 (Dec. 1981): 54.

69 'La petite intrigue sentimentale, très naive qu'on a greffée, ne nuit pas du tout à la trame' (*La Patrie* [12 Dec. 1922]: 8).

70 'anticipant de deux siècles le geste héroïque [de] Verdun: "Ils ne passeront pas"' (Film poster reproduced in Pierre Véronneau, *Montréal: ville de cinéma*, 17).

71 'Vous avez sauvé le pays ... Je n'ai fait que mon devoir.'

72 'C'est bien une page de la vie de nos pères' (ANQ-TR, P29, Journal of F.-A. Baillairgé, 22 Dec. 1922).

73 Hughes-Hallett, *Cleopatra: Histories, Dreams and Distortions*, 3.

74 'Madeleine de Verchères,' *L'Action catholique* (8 Feb. 1923): 10.

75 Tim Edensor, 'Reading Braveheart: Representing and Contesting Scottish Identity,' *Scottish Affairs* 21 (Autumn 1997): 153.

76 'C'est une belle vue, qu'il faut faire voir le plus possible à cause de la bonne leçon d'histoire qu'elle donne' (*La Presse* [16 Dec. 1922], 43).

77 'Ce sont de pauvres gens, dans de pauvres habitations dans un pauvre pays. Pas d'uniformes somptueux, nulle caresse pour le regard ... On dirait un homme qui admire le portrait de ses ancêtres – brossé par un artiste d'occasion. C'est une émotion plus patriotique qu'esthéstique' (*Le Devoir* [11 Dec. 1922], 2).

78 Gustave Comte, 'Produits indigènes et produits importés,' *La Patrie* (12 Dec. 1922): 8.

79 *La Presse* (19 Dec. 1922): 15; *Quartier Latin* (14 Dec. 1922): 2.

80 'Le film de Madeleine est Presque Tres Bien dans son ensemble. Melle Emma ____ a ajouté plusieurs choses très vraisemblables ... Il faut aussi une certaine force artistique qu'on ne trouve pas partout' (ANQ-TR, P29, Journal of F.-A. Baillairgé, 22 Dec. 1922).

81 'belle leçon d'histoire du Canada'; 'le coup de sifflet qui ferait prendre l'auto pour Verchères' (ANQ-Q, Fonds Georges F. Baillairgé, P715/1–6.2, letter of 17 August 1923).

82 Ibid., P715/1–6.1, journal entry, 21 August 1923.

83 NA, RG84, vol. 1255, File HS-7–25, vol. 2, part 1, S.T. Grenier to J.B. Harkin, 11 June 1923.

84 Ibid., S.T. Grenier to J. B. Harkin, 5 Oct. 1923.

85 Ibid., memorandum on Madeleine de Verchères film, J. Pinard, 12 Oct. 1923.

86 Ibid., S.T. Grenier to J. B. Harkin, 11 June 1923.

87 Ibid., vol. 2, part 1, S.T. Grenier to J.B. Harkin, 7 January 1924; ANQ-TR, P29, S.T. Grenier to Rev. Fred A. Baillargé (sic), 7 February 1924.

88 ANQ-M, E188, Direction du classement des films, box 69, January–February 1924, 14 January 1924.

89 'Mille coudées au-dessous de Madeleine de Verchères ... Les scènes extérieures prises par M. Homier dans son film, montrent que le soleil canadien, québécois, est aussi beau que celui des tropiques sur les pellicules' (*La Presse* [21 Jan. 1924]).

90 'La Drogue Fatale,' *La Presse* (19 Jan. 1924): 55.

91 Turner, 'J.-A. Homier photographe,' 53.

92 Advertisement, *L'Action française*, 9, no. 4 (April 1923): 2.

93 Archives de la Chancellerie de Montréal, dossier Cinéma (campagnes de censure), 773.80, 924-1a, E. Gariépy and S.T. Grenier to Sa Grandeur Monseigneur George Gauthier, 7 January 1924.

94 Lacasse, *Histoire des scopes*, 63.

95 Archives de la Chancellerie de Montréal, dossier Cinéma (campagnes de censure), 773.080, 924–1b, 'Des noms qui sont une solide garantie d'habile et honnête administration,' investment flyer for Le Cinéma Canadien, Limitée; NA, National Film Archives, Hye Bossin Collection, reel 2, file 27, no. 27, Arthur Larente to Hye Bossin, 31 May 1964.

96 ANQ-M, Raisons sociales, TP11, S2, SS20, SSS48, no. 1108, vol. 2, C.F.S., 'La compagnie Le Bon Cinéma National Limitée' was founded 8 May 1925. Declaration, 3 March 1926.

97 'Le cinéma, à beaucoup de points de vue, fait plus de bien que de mal' (Archives du diocèse de St-Jean-de-Québec, Ref. St.Frs.Xavier, no. 55,

Fred-A. Baillairgé to Mgr Gauthier, Archbishop of Montreal, 28 Dec. 1926).

98 'Après le désastre terrible que nous venons de subir, je crois que vous auriez l'occasion de faire comprendre à vos paroissiens les dangers qui accompagnent le cinéma' (ibid., Georges arch. coad. de Montréal to M. l'abbé Baillargé [*sic*], 16 January 1927).

99 *La Revue de Manon*, 1, no. 1 (15 Feb. 1925).

100 Quoted in Turner, 'J.-A. Homier photographe,' 54.

101 Morris, *Embattled Shadows: A History of Canadian Cinema, 1895–1939*; Marcel Jean, *Le cinéma québécois*; Lever, *Histoire générale du cinéma au Québec*.

102 Lacasse, *Histoire des scopes*, 69–74.

103 Joan Elson Morgan, *Castle of Quebec* (1949), 169. Thanks to Judith Nefsky of the Canadian Pacific Archives for this information.

104 Esther Braun, *A Quebec Sketch Book* (1925), 22.

105 Data compiled from the CD-Rom, Select Phone. Thanks to Eileen Lim of the National Library of Canada for her assistance in acquiring these data. The list of street names is not exhaustive.

106 Advertisements for 'Conserves alimentaires "Madeleine"' and for the 'Foyer Madeleine de Verchères' in *Programme souvenir 1710–1960. 250e anniversaire, Paroisse Saint-François-Xavier, Verchères, Québec* (1960).

107 ANQ-M, TP11, S2, SS20, SSS48, no. 1402, vol. 24, C.F.S., 7 Dec. 1960.

4: Feminist and Teenager: The Decline of Madeleine de Verchères's Popularity

1 Graeme Morton, 'The Most Efficacious Patriot: The Heritage of William Wallace in Nineteenth-Century Scotland,' *Scottish Historical Review* 77, no. 2 (Oct. 1998): 224.

2 John Dickinson, 'Annaotaha et Dollard vus de l'autre côté de la palissade,' *RHAF* 35, no. 2 (Sept. 1981): 163–78.

3 Archives du Séminaire de Trois-Rivières, Fonds Tessier, 0014-Q1–80, L.P. Lizotte to Monseigneur Albert Tessier, 18 Dec. 1968; 4 Jan. 1969.

4 Warner, *Joan of Arc*, 263.

5 'Questions,' *Bulletin de recherches historiques* 6 (1900): 160.

6 Philéas Gagnon, 'Le curé Lefebvre et l'héroïne de Verchères,' *Bulletin de recherches historique* 6 (1900): 340–5.

7 'Tous les saints sont des héros, mais tous les héros ne sont pas des saints' (Pierre-Georges Roy, 'Madeleine de Verchères, plaideuse,' *Transactions de la Société Royale du Canada*, 3rd series, 15 [1921]: 63–72).

8 'Cette jeune femme à l'apparence si frêle et si délicate était douée de tant

d'énergie que la crainte et la peur, deux sentiments pourtant bien naturels à son sexe, n'eurent jamais de place dans son âme' (ibid., 66).

9 Patrice Groulx, *Pièges de la mémoire*, 249.

10 E.R. Adair, 'Dollard des Ormeaux and the Fight at the Long Sault,' *Canadian Historical Review* (hereafter *CHR*) 13, no. 2 (June 1932): 121–38, quotation from 138.

11 University of Toronto Archives, George Brown Collection, A86–044/005, Aegidius Fauteux to George W. Brown, 10 May 1932. Thanks to Donald Wright for this reference.

12 Ibid., George Brown to Aegidius Fauteux, 13 May 1932. See Lionel Groulx, *Le dossier de Dollard: La valeur des sources, la grandeur du dessein, la grandeur des résultats* (1932).

13 Gustave Lanctot, 'Was Dollard the Saviour of New France?' *CHR* 13, no. 2 (June 1932): 138–46.

14 'Si l'abbé Groulx ne se fût constitué le propagandiste de Dollard, y aurait-il eu jamais une question Dollard? ... Fêter Dollard, maquillé en agent recruteur pour la défense de la chrétienté et de l'Empire britannique, c'eût été se faire complice de la bêtise' (Lionel Groulx, *Mes Mémoires* vol. ii: 57–8).

15 Novick, *That Noble Dream: The 'Objectivity Question' and the American Historical Profession*.

16 Ronald Rudin, *Making History in Twentieth-Century Quebec*; Patrice Régimbald, 'La disciplinarisation de l'histoire au Canada français, 1920–1950,' *RHAF* 51, no. 2 (Autumn 1997): 163–200.

17 'De Mademoiselle Madeleine, on se fera une image assez juste, ce nous semble, si on se la figure belle, intelligente et fine, séduisante et brillante, mais portant, dans son enveloppe féminine, l'âme d'un gars remuant et batailleur, fortement musclé, avec du cran, beaucoup de cran, ayant facilement aux lèvres le mot à résonance de métal, la phrase à panache et le geste proche parent de la parole' (Lionel Groulx, *Notre maître, le passé*, 3rd series [1944], 99).

18 'Depuis toujours les petits garçons jouent au soldat et les petites filles, à la poupée. Le contraire arrive parfois, mais, alors, les parents ne cachent pas leur inquiétude ... le renversement des rôles assignés à l'homme et à la femme, sinon par décret divin, du moins par la nature, voire par le bon sens' (Jean Bruchési, 'Madeleine de Verchères et Chicaneau,' *Les cahiers des dix* 11 [1946]: 25).

19 'Il faut attendre notre vingtième siècle, qui a connu la guerre totale, pour que l'égalité des sexes, dans ce domaine, soit une chose admise' (ibid., 26).

20 Ruth Roach Pierson, *'They're Still Women after All': The Second World War and Canadian Womanhood*.

21 Douglas Owram, 'The Myth of Louis Riel,' *CHR* 63, no. 3 (Sept. 1982): 315–36.

22 As Ronald Rudin argues in *Making History*, chap. 2.

23 See the essays in Beverly Boutilier and Alison Prentice, eds, *Creating Historical Memory*; and Donald A. Wright, 'Gender and the Professionalization of History in English Canada before 1960,' *CHR* 81, no. 1 (March 2000): 29–66.

24 John English, *Shadow of Heaven: The Life of Lester Pearson, Volume One: 1897–1948*, 97–101.

25 'Que l'humeur belliqueuse fût peut-être ce qui lui manquait le moins, le reste de sa vie l'allait démontrer autant que son exploit de 1692' (Groulx, *Notre maître, le passé*, 3rd series [1944], 98).

26 Alexander D. Angus, *Old Quebec: In the Days before Our Day*, 140.

27 'Il ne faisait pas bon de s'attaquer à Madeleine de Verchères, qu'on fût plaideur ou Iroquois' (Robert de Roquebrune, *Les canadiens d'autrefois: Essais*, 118).

28 'Sancte Madame avec ses deux petites citrouilles, ora ... Sancte le bonnet à Boileau sous le chevet de Madame la Pératte, ora pro nobis ... On chuchote, dans les cegeps, qu'elle avait la cuisse légère ... Au début du vingtième siècle, des Anglais nous ressuscitent des héros; Marie-Madeleine de Verchères commence une nouvelle vie. L'Ordre des Filles de l'Empire (really!) commande une biographie, et quelques années plus tard le gouvernement fédéral (eh oui!) fournit la somme de 25 000 dollars pour la construction d'un monument' (Jacques Lacoursière, 'La véridique histoire de Madeleine de Verchères et son curé ...' *L'Actualité* 1, no. 3 [Nov. 1976]: 36). Lacoursière's chronology is incorrect.

29 See for instance, the treatment of Verchères in Claude Falardeau's comic history of Quebec, *Des Zéroquois aux Québécois* (1969), 36–7.

30 NA, Sound and Visual Archives, Société Radio-Canada, CAVA 1989–0542, 'Sameditou,' 1989–09–25, Mouffe, animateur, 'Qui était Madeleine de Verchères?'

31 Michel Lessard, 'Déficit 1642–1992 ou le programme des festivités du 350e de Montréal,' *Croc* 118 (May 1989): 29.

32 André Vachon, 'Jarret de Verchères, Marie-Madeleine,' in *DCB*, vol. III: 308–13. One of the few other critical analyses of Verchères's story is J.-Edmond Roy, 'Madeleine de Verchères' (1922), reprinted from *Le Soleil*, 20 March 1909.

33 Bibliothèque municipale de Montréal, Salle Gagnon, Fonds de la ligue des droits de la femme, Lot 4, 0/8, 19, 'Women's Contribution to Canadian Life,' n.d.

34 ANQ-M, Fonds Béatrice Clément, P43, vol. 3, 32.5: transcript.

35 Clio Collective, *Quebec Women: A History*, 27.

36 Alison Prentice et al., *Canadian Women: A History*, 50.

37 'Nous avions pourtant commencé sur un bon pied / Les premières arrivées c'taient des femmes libérées / Elles ont laissé leur nom à l'histoire du pays' (quoted in Marie-Thérèse Lefebvre, *La création musicale des femmes au Québec*, 23; Arsenault, 'Les Héroïnes,' on *Première* [SPSS, PS-19901, 1974; éditions de l'Échelle]).

38 Jan Noel, 'New France: Les femmes favorisées,' in Alison Prentice and Susan Mann Trofimenkoff, eds, *The Neglected Majority: Essays in Canadian Women's History*, vol. 2: 34 (first published in *Atlantis: A Women's Studies Journal* 6, no. 2 [Spring 1981]: 80–98).

39 Jan Noel, 'Women in New France: Further Reflections,' *Atlantis* 8, no. 1 (Fall 1982): 126 (in response to a critique by Micheline Dumont).

40 Jan Noel, *Women in New France*, 10–11. Likewise, in Allan Greer's social history survey of the history of New France, the chapter entitled 'Women of New France' makes no mention of Verchères (*The People of New France*, 60–75).

41 'Issue d'une famille aisée, ayant eu accès à l'instruction – ce qui n'est pas le cas de toutes les femmes de son temps – Madeleine possédait les outils et le courage nécessaires pour se défendre' (Cécile Tremblay-Matte, *La chanson écrite au féminin, 1730–1990: De Madeleine de Verchères à Mitsou*, 18–19).

42 'Ces héroïnes obscures ont oeuvré, chaque jour, sans répit et avec une générosité exemplaire ... je tiens à souligner que bien des choses ont changé à Verchères depuis 300 ans mais une chose est revenue: une femme veille au fort à la sécurité et au bien-être de Verchères' (Verchères, Hôtel de ville, Dossier Madeleine de Verchères, 300e anniversaire).

43 Mary Cadogan and Patricia Craig, *You're a Brick, Angela! A New Look at Girls' Fiction from 1839 to 1975*, 89.

44 Mabel Burns McKinley, *Canadian Heroines of Pioneer Days* (1929), 13.

45 W.J. Karr, *Explorers, Soldiers and Statesmen* (1929), 77.

46 Katherine A. Young, *Stories of the Maple Land: Tales of the Early Days of Canada for Children* (1898), 79.

47 E.L. Marsh, *The Story of Canada* (1913), 65

48 McKinley, *Canadian Heroines of Pioneer Days*, 13.

49 George M. Grant, *French Canadian Life and Character* (1899), 129.

50 Robert Livesey, *Footprints in the Snow: The Heroes and Heroines of Canada* (1978), 16.

51 For instance, Quebec passed the Choquette Law in 1925 encouraging the purchase of Canadian publications (Elvine Gignac-Pharand, 'L'Évolution

de la littérature de jeunesse au Canada français,' *Cultures du Canada français* 3 [1986]: 7).

52 Margaret Atwood, *Strange Things: The Malevolent North in Canadian Literature*, 10.

53 Prince Edward Island, Department of Education, Annual Report, examination papers, 1917–1957.

54 J.O. Miller, *Brief Biographies Supplementing Canadian History* (1902).

55 McKinley, *Canadian Heroines of Pioneer Days*, 1.

56 'si par malheur un jour, nos fils tombaient sanglants sur un champ de bataille, leurs soeurs ne craignissent point d'affronter aussi les balles pour panser de nobles blessures, et arrêter l'effusion du plus pur sang de la patrie!' (Joseph Marmette, *Héroïsme et trahison: Récits canadiens* [1930], 26).

57 Guy Laviolette, *Marie-Madeleine de Verchères: Châtelaine de la Pérade, 1678–1747* (1944), 31.

58 'une humble fille de race intrépide, forte de son patriotisme et de sa foi' (Michelle Bienvenu, 'Madeleine de Verchères,' in *Fidélité à Ville-Marie: Récits et légendes* [1942], 102).

59 H.E. Marshall, *Canada's Story Told to Boys and Girls* (1920?), 83.

60 Miller, *Brief Biographies*, 93.

61 D.J. Dickie and Helen Palk, *Pages from Canada's Story: Selections from the Canadian History Readers* (1932), 134.

62 'La mode couvre bien des désordres aujourd'hui et bien des folies. Et puis ces jeunes filles qui ne savent plus s'habiller et marchent comme des marionnettes, vous ne savez peut-être pas vous autres, comme elles sont nerveuses, comme elles sont capricieuses, comme elles sont peureuses, comme elles sont loin, malgré leurs colères fréquentes, de l'énergie ... d'une Madeleine de Verchères' (Abbé J.-G. Gélinas, *En veillant avec les petits de chez nous au foyer: Causeries historiques*, vol. 1 [1915]).

63 National Library of Canada, Kay Pattinson, 'Commander at Fourteen' (typescript drama, copyright August 1955), 17, 20.

64 'Il est évident qu'ils n'aiment pas accepter des ordres d'une fille, mais ils savent que c'est elle qui a l'autorité' (Morgan Kenney, *Madeleine de Verchères: Héroïne canadienne* [1989], 11).

65 Sister Mary Carmel Therriault, s.m., Foreword, *Madeleine de Verchères* (1951).

66 'il ne faut pas que ces quelques fautes nous fassent oublier les actes héroïques qui ont entouré sa tête d'une auréole de bravoure et de fierté' (ibid., 28).

67 'On raconte, dans les livres d'histoire, que j'étais continuellement de mauvaise humeur, que je maltraitais mes censitaires, que je devais toujours avoir le dernier mot. Eh bien, tant pis! Les mauvaises langues sont de toute

époque' (Grace Morrison, *Vignettes d'histoire du Canada, les premières années: Magdelaine de Verchères* [1989], 7).

68 Ibid.

69 Janet Grant, *Madeleine de Verchères* (1989).

70 NA, Sound and Visual Archives, TV Ontario and Rosebud Films, *Madeleine de Verchères* (screenplay by Barry Pearson; French version by Marie-Hélène Fontaine), 1981, 24 minutes.

71 'Les Iroquois sont très malins' (Kenney, *Madeleine de Verchères*, 26).

72 'Ils aimaient la guerre par-dessus tout, ignorant qu'ils servaient de tampon dans une vielle rivalité opposant l'Angleterre à la France. Beaucoup plus tard, ils découvrirent qu'ils avaient été dupés ... Les habitants de la Nouvelle-France connaissaient le sens du mot solidarité' (Jean Coté, *Madeleine de Verchères: l'Intrépide 'Magdelon'* [1995], 37, 69, 74).

73 'de mon vivant, personne ne contestera l'héritage de nos enfants, Pierre-Thomas. J'ai défendu le mien avant le leur, je ne l'ai jamais regretté ... Bon sang ne peut mentir' (Jacques Lamarche, *Madeleine, héroïne de Verchères, seigneuresse de La Pérade* [1997], 3, 59).

74 Denis Masse, 'Quatre héros légendaires,' *La Presse* (5 Sept. 1992): G15.

5: Walking to Beaver Dams: Colonial Narratives, 1820s–1860s

1 James Secord's petition, from Ruth McKenzie, *Laura Secord: The Legend and the Lady* (1971), 74–5.

2 Ibid., 84–5. The document's spelling mistakes are uncorrected.

3 See, for example, David Mills, *The Idea of Loyalty in Upper Canada, 1784–1850.*

4 Donald H. Akenson, *The Irish in Ontario: A Study in Rural History*, 134.

5 See Cecilia Morgan, *Public Men and Virtuous Women: The Gendered Languages of Upper Canadian Religion and Politics, 1791–1850*, chap. 1.

6 Ibid.; see also Keith Walden, 'Isaac Brock: Man and Myth: A Study of the Militia Myth of the War of 1812 in Upper Canada 1812–1912' (M.A. thesis, Queen's University, 1971).

7 Janice Potter-MacKinnon, *While the Women Only Wept: Loyalist Refugee Women in Eastern Ontario*, 158.

8 The first section of this book deals with precisely this tradition; see also Marina Warner, *Joan of Arc.*

9 See Morgan, *Public Men and Virtuous Women*, 24, for a lengthier discussion of these issues.

10 See George Shepherd, *Plunder, Profit, and Paroles: A Social History of the War of 1812 in Upper Canada*, 136–7, 139–47.

11 McKenzie, *Laura Secord*, 73.

12 Ibid., 73–7.

13 Ibid., 84–5.

14 *Niagara Mail*, 27 March 1861; 3 April 1861.

15 Ibid., 17 Oct. 1868.

16 For a discussion of Upper Canadian married women's work in family businesses, see Elizabeth Jane Errington, *Wives and Mothers, School Mistresses and Scullery Maids: Working Women in Upper Canada 1790–1840*, 190–5.

17 See chapter 6 for these accounts.

18 Chas. B. Secord, *The Church*, 11 April 1845. Of course, Secord may have seen giving support to FitzGibbon as a way of also calling attention to his mother's walk.

19 James FitzGibbon's certificate, as reprinted in Elizabeth Thompson, 'Laura Ingersoll Secord,' *Niagara Historical Society Papers* 25 (1912): 8.

20 Laura Secord, *Anglo-American Magazine* [Toronto] 8, no. 5 (1853): 467.

21 See Patricia Jasen, 'Native Lands,' in *Wild Things: Nature, Culture, and Tourism in Ontario 1790–1914* (Toronto: University of Toronto Press, 1995).

22 *Niagara Mail*, 27 March 1861; 3 April 1861.

23 Benson Lossing, *The Pictorial Field Book of the War of 1812* (1869), 421.

24 William F. Coffin, *1812: The War and Its Moral: A Canadian Chronicle* (1864), 148. See, for example, McKenzie's description of Coffin's work: 'his account was a *mélange* of real and imaginative happenings' (*Laura Secord*, 104). However, McKenzie admits that 'people liked Coffin's version,' as the cow 'fitted the pioneer picture perfectly' (105); the cow and Secord have remained in the public's mind, while Coffin and his book have been forgotten.

6: The Lives of the Loyal Pioneers: Historical Societies and Historical Narratives

1 The founding dates for these organizations were as follows: WCHS, 1890; NHS, 1895; OHS, 1897; WHS, 1889; BHS, 1908. There were many other groups, such as the Lundy's Lane Historical Society, formed in 1887, and women's historical organizations, such as the Women's Wentworth Historical Society (WWHS), formed in 1899.

2 For a longer discussion of the context in which these groups were formed, see Gerald Killan, *Preserving Ontario's Heritage: A History of the Ontario Historical Society*, 30–6.

3 Some members of the Kingston organization were Queen's University professors, while the membership list of the WCHS read like a roll-call of

Upper Canadian power and privilege: Jarvis, Powell, Boulton, Robinson, and Strachan.

4 Killan, *Preserving Ontario's Heritage*, 30–4.

5 Carnochan was the president and co-founder of the NHS, while Gilkison and Priddis were long-standing and active members of the BHS and London and Middlesex Historical Society. Gilkison's father, Colonel Jasper Gilkison, was Superintendent of the Six Nations reserve from 1862 to 1891. For a discussion of his tenure, see Sally M. Weaver, 'The Iroquois: The Consolidation of the Grand River Reserve in the Mid-Nineteenth Century, 1847–1875,' in Edward S. Rogers and Donald B. Smith, eds, *Aboriginal Ontario: Historical Perspectives on the First Nations*, 182–211.

6 There are a number of hints in the OHS correspondence as to the financial straits of these women. See for example, Clementina Fessenden to Elizabeth Thompson, acting secretary of the OHS, after Gilkison was pushed off the program (apparently by Agnes Machar) at an OHS meeting held at Queen's University: 'To think after being asked to read a paper, and then with her limited means (she has only what she makes doing fancy work) coming down for nothing' (AO, OHS Correspondence, MU5422, Series C, file 6, 1908, 1903–8, Fessenden to Thompson, n.d.). For Curzon's financial difficulties, see, for example, AO, William Kirby Collection, MS542, Correspondence, reel 1, Curzon to William Kirby, 21 November 1888; also 22 March 1894.

7 Killan, *Preserving Ontario's Heritage*, 34.

8 Ibid., 61. While to some extent they displayed concerns associated with antimodernism, I would argue that characterizing all members of the historical societies as antimodern is an oversimplification, particularly when we consider the influence of gender differences in shaping attitudes towards past and present. For a discussion of antimodernism, see T.J. Jackson Lears, *No Place of Grace*; Ian McKay, *The Quest of the Folk*; Donald A. Wright, 'W.D. Lighthall and David Ross McCord.'

9 James Coyne, 'Presidential Address,' *OHS Annual Report* (1899): 34 (emphasis added).

10 See, for example, Benedict Anderson, 'The Angel of History,' in *Imagined Communities*; Homi K. Bhabha, 'DissemiNation: Time, Narrative, and the Margins of the Modern Nation,' in *Nation and Narration*; Eric Hobsbawm and Terence Ranger, eds, *The Invention of Tradition*.

11 See, for example, John Dearness, 'Presidential Address,' *OHS Annual Report* (1913): 41–7. Dearness was the vice-principal of the London Normal School.

12 James Coyne, 'Presidential Address,' *OHS Annual Report* (1902): 73.

13 For Fessenden's activities, see AO, MS193, NHS Minute Books, reel 15; also Molly Pulver Ungar, 'Trenholme, Clementina (Fessenden),' in *DCB*, vol. xiv: 1008–9.

14 There are many examples of exchanges between the OHS and WCHS and other organizations. In 1908 the WCHS of Ottawa reported that it had corresponded with groups and institutions across Canada and the United States, as well as with Director General Lomba in Montevideo, Uruguay (*OHS Annual Report* (1908–9): 70).

15 John Dearness, 'Presidential Address,' *OHS Annual Report* (1914): 38.

16 Andrew Hunter, 'Secretary's Report,' *OHS Annual Report* (1923): 40. This point has also been made by Carl Berger (see 'Progress and Liberty,' in *The Sense of Power: Studies in the Ideas of Canadian Imperialism 1867–1914*).

17 Carnochan wrote to Boyle that one of the 'boys' stationed in South Africa had just sent her 'some little relics': 'a Kaffir girl's leg bracelet [and] a Boer pass' (AO, MU5422, box 4, 1903–8, file May 1903–4, 16 June 1902). See also the programs of the St Catharines Women's Literary Club for 1914–15 and 1915–16, when papers were presented on India, such as 'Hindu India,' 'Muslim India,' 'British India,' 'Hindu Women,' and 'The Influence of British Women on India' (Brock University Special Collections [hereafter BUSC], Women's Literary Club of St Catharines Collection [hereafter WLC], box 10).

18 While it is true that, as Killan argues in *Preserving Ontario's Heritage*, 83–4, 'goodwill and understanding' and not 'bigotry and dogma' characterized the OHS's stance on French-English relations, its members often compared French colonialism to British as a contrast 'between autocracy with governmental initiative and control ... and democracy and individualism' (Coyne, 'Presidential Address' [1902], 74).

19 Donald H. Akenson, *The Irish in Ontario*, 134.

20 For such a perspective see Norman Knowles, *Inventing the Loyalists*.

21 See, for example, Emma Currie, *The Story of Laura Secord*, 27–30; 'Brief Sketch of a Canadian Pioneer,' *OHS Papers* 6 (1905): 92–4; W.I. Scott, 'A U.E. Loyalist Family,' *OHS Papers* 32 (1937): 140–70. This period also saw a great deal of interest in genealogy in French Canada.

22 Hayden White, 'The Value of Narrativity in the Representation of Reality,' in W.J.T. Mitchell, ed., *On Narrative*, 1–23, especially 19–21.

23 'Brief Sketch of a Canadian Pioneer,' *OHS Papers* 6 (1905): 92–4, especially 93–4. Christianity was often featured as one of Joseph Brant's greatest contributions to his people. See Augusta Gilkison, 'Some Events in the Life of Capt. Joseph Brant Not Generally Noticed,' *OHS Papers* 20 (1923): 90–1.

24 Coyne, 'Presidential Address' (1902), 78–9.

25 Ibid., 74.
26 'Reminiscence of Mrs. White,' *OHS Papers* 7 (1906): 153–7, especially 157. Note that Catherine White's reminiscence was collected in either the 1850s or '60s, when she was seventy-nine, not at the turn of the century.
27 See, for example, Charles and James C. Thomas, 'Reminiscences of the First Settlers in the County of Brant,' *OHS Papers* 12 (1914): 58–71, especially 66.
28 Major Gordon J. Smith, 'Land Tenure in Brant County'; C. Gillen, 'Captain Joseph Brant'; Augusta Gilkison, 'Early Days in Brantford,' in *Some of the Papers Read during the Years 1908–11 at Meetings of the Brant Historical Society* (N.p.: BHS, 1911).
29 C.T. Campbell, 'Pioneer Physicians of London District,' *Transactions of the London and Middlesex Historical Society* 1, Part VIII (1917): n. pag.; also University of Western Ontario, D.B. Weldon Library, Regional Collection, LMHS Correspondence, General Files, box 4, Mrs Haight, 'Life and Work of Amelia Poldon – Pioneer Historian of Norwich,' May 1938.
30 The societies also enjoyed stories of early explorers, and tales of Cartier, Champlain, Mackenzie, La Vérendrye, and others appear frequently in their records. See, for example, the WCHS report, *OHS Annual Report* (1898): 20–3; also the WCHS of Ottawa report, *OHS Annual Report* (1899): 39–42. The Thunder Bay Historical Society conducted research on topics such as the development of resource industries in the North and the spread of Roman Catholic missions.
31 Killan, *Preserving Ontario's Heritage*, 181–90.
32 Dennis Duffy also remarked on this tendency in *Gardens, Covenants, Exiles: Loyalism in the Literature of Upper Canada/Ontario.*
33 John S. Barker, 'A Brief History of David Barker, a United Empire Loyalist,' *OHS Papers* 3 (1901): 168–70, especially 168.
34 'Brief Sketch of a Canadian Pioneer,' *OHS Papers* 6 (1905): 92–4, especially 93.
35 Ibid., 93–4; also Pearl Wilson, 'Irish John Wilson, and Family, Loyalists,' *OHS Papers* 31 (1936): 228–42; A.E. Byerley, 'Pioneers and Pioneers Days of Fergus,' *OHS Papers* 30 (1934): 66–9.
36 Janice Potter-MacKinnon, *While the Women Only Wept*, 158.
37 See, for example, ibid., and Knowles, *Inventing the Loyalists.*
38 Ernest Green, 'Gilbert Tice, U.E.,' *OHS Papers* 21 (1914): 186–97, especially 186–7.
39 Castell Hopkins, *OHS Annual Report* (1910): 11 (AO, MU5424, box 5, file 1). See also Coyne's speech at the dedication of Secord's Lundy's Lane monument in 1901, when he regretted the lack of 'representatives of our

brother Canadians of French origin, who contributed to the defence of the country in the war of 1812' (*OHS Annual Report* [1901]: 58). Secord was often described as having acted as a 'brave Canadian.'

40 Berger, *The Sense of Power*, 96. As M. Brook Taylor has shown in his analysis of the work of nineteenth-century writers such as John Charles Dent, Francis Hincks, and Charles Lindsey, 'national historians were essentially Upper Canadian historians in masquerade' (*Promoters, Patriots, and Partisans: Historiography in Nineteenth-Century Canada*, 231).

41 See Malcolm Chase, 'This Is No Claptrap: This Is Our Heritage,' in Christopher Shaw and Malcolm Chase, eds, *The Imagined Past: History and Nostalgia*; David Cannadine, 'The Context, Performance, and Meaning of Ritual: The British Monarchy and the "Invention of Tradition," c. 1820–1877,' in Hobsbawm and Ranger, eds, *The Invention of Tradition*; and Raphael Samuel, 'Resurrectionism' and 'Heritage,' Parts II and III of *Theatres of Memory*.

42 Take, for example, the case of William Kirby, the Niagara poet and epic novelist, whose family had arrived in Ontario from Britain, but via the United States; Kirby's wife claimed UEL descent. Kirby was also a family friend of Emma Currie and had taught her as a child. See AO, MS542, reel 1, Currie to Kirby, 21 October 1903.

43 Charles Mair, for example, the author of the drama *Tecumseh* and an enthusiastic promoter of Canadian history, had served in the 1870 force sent to quash the Red River Rebellion (Norman Shrive, *Charles Mair: Literary Nationalist*). See also Berger on imperialists' glorification of the War of 1812 as a victory, instead of the defeat of 1783 (*The Sense of Power*, 90–3).

44 See Jonathan F. Vance, *Death So Noble*, 42–3; for monuments to archetypal Loyalists, see Knowles, *Inventing the Loyalists*, 138–9.

45 Hopkins, *OHS Annual Report* (1910): 14. Berger's work has pointed to the romanticism of the UEL tradition, influenced by Francis Parkman's histories of New France and the work of Sir Walter Scott (*The Sense of Power*, 94–5). I agree that romanticism flavoured (although it not dominate) historical societies' narratives of the Loyalists and pioneer life, but romanticism is even more prevalent in the societies' narratives of the War of 1812, especially in the creation of tragic and doomed heroes such as Brock and Tecumseh. To be sure, the distinction is a subtle one.

46 For a discussion of the creation of the myth of Isaac Brock, see Keith Walden, 'Isaac Brock: Man and Myth.' For papers on Brock, see the WCHS report in *OHS Annual Report* (1898): 20–3; also AO, OHS Scrap Albums, MU5438, Series D, box 21, Janet Carnochan, 'Old Niagara' (n.d.), and 'Military Reserve at Niagara,' 28 June 1905. Mary Agnes FitzGibbon spent a great deal

of time during her 1897 tour of England gathering information about and artefacts connected to Brock, including his miniature (AO, WCHS Correspondence, 1890–1915, F 1180, box 1, Series A – Correspondence, FitzGibbon to Sara Mickle, 17, 25, 26 May; 2, 11, 21 June; 18, 19 July 1897).

47 For descriptions of Tecumseh, see William F. Coffin, *1812: The War and Its Moral* (1864), 164–5, 233–7; AO, MU5438, box 19, Janet Carnochan, 'Historical No. 274,' 17 October 1913; and D.B. Read, *The Life and Times of Major-General Sir Isaac Brock, K.B.* (1914), 177–8. For Tecumseh's and Brock's mutual descriptions, see Matilda Edgar, *The Makers of Canada: General Brock* (1904), 246–7.

48 See, for example, Coyne's invocation of a military masculinity that transcended regional, national, ethnic, and racial differences: 'Regulars and militiamen, U.E. Loyalists and natives of the old land, French-Canadians and men of the Six Nations, all shared in the dangers and the glory of the battle of the Beechwoods' ('Unveiling of the Laura Secord Monument, 22 June 1901, at Lundy's Lane,' *OHS Annual Report* [1901]: 57).

49 Colonel Ernest Cruikshank had begun his career as a farmer and militia officer near Welland; he had then been the General Commanding Officer of Military District 13, Calgary, 1909–17. Cruikshank was Vice-president of the Historic Landmarks Association when the group was founded in 1907, a member of the Historic Sites and Monuments Board of Canada and its Chair in 1919, Director of the military historical section of the Department of Militia and Defence, and OHS president during 1920–2. He was noted for his carefully researched, if rather dry, work in Canadian military history. See Killan, *Preserving Ontario's Heritage*, 99–101, 180; also C.J. Taylor, *Negotiating the Past*, 38–41. David Breckenridge Read was a former mayor of Toronto; in addition to his biography of Brock, he published *Rebellion of 1837*, an anti-Mackenzie, pro-Tory study of the rebellion (Killan, *Preserving Ontario's Heritage*, 41).

50 Mary Agnes FitzGibbon, 'An Historic Banner: A Paper Read on February 8th, 1896,' *Transaction No. 1 WCHS* (Toronto: William Briggs, 1896), 9.

51 For papers on the war published by women's organizations and women's groups interested in the War of 1812, see the WCHS report in *OHS Annual Report* (1898): 20–3; and Janet Carnochan, 'Old Niagara' (n.d.), and 'Military Reserve at Niagara' (AO, MU5438, box 21, 28 June 1905). As well, the WWHS purchased the Gage homestead, site of the Battle of Stoney Creek, making that encounter a central focus of their work and obtaining a provincial grant in order to do so. See their reports in the *OHS Papers* from 1899 on, as well as WWHS, 'Ye Olden Tyme Entertainment: Souvenir Book and Program,' 16 April 1900, the program for a fund-raiser for the site.

52 Byerley, 'Pioneers and Pioneers Days,' 66; John S. Barker, 'Reminiscence of Mrs. White, of White's Mills, Near Cobourg, Upper Canada,' *OHS Papers* 7 (1906): 156; Charles and James C. Thomas, 'Reminiscences of the First Settlers,' *OHS Papers* 12 (1914): 61.

53 Ibid.

54 Barker, 'Reminiscence of Mrs. White,' 156; Charles and James C. Thomas, 'Reminiscences of the First Settlers,' 60–1.

55 See, for example, Berger, 'The Loyalist Tradition,' in *The Sense of Power*; Knowles, *Inventing the Loyalists*.

56 Charles and James C. Thomas, 'Reminiscences of the First Settlers,' 67.

57 See, for example, John May, 'Bush Life in the Ottawa Valley Eighty Years Ago,' *OHS Papers* 12 (1914): 153–63.

58 Ibid., 154.

59 Amelia Poldon, 'Women in Pioneer Life,' *OHS Papers* 17 (1919): 25–9.

60 Ibid.

61 For an elaboration of this concept, see Homi K. Bhabha, 'Of Mimicry and Men: The Ambivalence of Colonial Discourse,' in *The Location of Culture*.

62 Catherine F. Lefroy, 'Recollections of Mary Warren Breckenridge, of Clarke Township,' *OHS Papers* 3 (1901): 110–13, especially 111.

63 Wilson, 'Irish John Wilson, and Family, Loyalists,' 237.

64 Lefroy, 'Recollections of Mary Warren Breckenridge, of Clarke Township,' 112–13.

65 I would like to thank Kathryn McPherson for suggesting this insight. For captivity narratives in the Canadian context, see Sarah Carter, *Capturing Women: The Manipulation of Cultural Imagery in Canada's Prairie West*.

66 For a discussion of similar issues in British imperialism, see Antoinette Burton, *Burdens of History: British Feminists, Indian Women, and Imperial Culture, 1865–1915*, 20.

67 Currie, *The Story of Laura Secord*, 21–33.

68 Sarah Curzon, *The Story of Laura Secord 1813* (1898), 6–7.

69 See Gerald M. Craig, *Upper Canada: The Formative Years 1784–1841*, 43, for a discussion of this shift in policy. Ruth McKenzie also argues that Ingersoll did not fulfil his settlement obligations (*Laura Secord*, 29).

70 J.H. Ingersoll, 'The Ancestry of Laura Ingersoll Secord,' *OHS Papers* (1926): 361–3.

71 Ibid.

72 John Price-Brown, *Laura the Undaunted: A Canadian Historical Romance* (1930), 16–17, 180–2.

73 Currie, *The Story of Laura Secord*, 53–4; Price-Brown, *Laura the Undaunted*, 252–5.

74 Curzon, *The Story of Laura Secord 1813*, 39–47.

75 Ernest Cruikshank, *The Fight in the Beechwoods* (1895), 13.

76 See, for example, Blanche Hume, *Laura Secord* (1928), 1. This book was part of Ryerson Press's Canadian history readers series and was endorsed by both the Department of Education and the IODE.

77 Ibid., 15.

78 Curzon, *The Story of Laura Secord 1813*, 13.

79 Cruikshank, *The Fight in the Beechwoods*, 18.

80 Currie, *The Story of Laura Secord*, 52–3. FitzGibbon supposedly took full credit for the victory, ignoring both Secord's and the Kahnawake Mohawks' roles (McKenzie, *Laura Secord*, 66–7). He later became a colonel in the York militia and was rewarded for his role in putting down the 1837 Rebellion with a £1000 grant (ibid., 89–90).

81 FitzGibbon, quoted in Elizabeth Thompson, 'Laura Ingersoll Secord,' *Niagara Historical Society Papers* 25 (1912): 6.

82 Curzon, *The Story of Laura Secord 1813*, 34.

83 Currie, *The Story of Laura Secord*, 71.

84 Thompson, 'Laura Ingersoll Secord,' 3. Balbriggan was a type of fine unbleached knitted cotton used for hosiery.

85 Price-Brown, *Laura the Undaunted*, 87.

86 Ibid., 107–11.

87 Ibid., 114–15.

88 Ibid., 173–80.

89 Ibid., 252.

90 Ibid., 258.

91 Ibid., 260–2.

92 Merrill Denison, 'Laura Secord,' 118. During the 1920s, the success of Secord's commemorators had inspired American author Sabrina Swain to publish *The Story of Laura Secord and Fanny Doyle – Their Zeal, Patriotism and Sacrifices during the Days of the War of 1812* (1928). According to Swain, Doyle was another heroine of 1812, who unfortunately had not received Secord's acclaim (Doyle had fired a cannon at Fort Niagara during an exchange of shots between it and Fort George in November 1812; she had replaced her husband when he was taken prisoner by the British).

93 Denison, 'Laura Secord,' 132.

94 Ibid., 128, 130–1.

95 Ibid., 135–8.

96 Ibid., 140. However, in his negotiations with the American officers, FitzGibbon tells them that he cannot hope to control his 'ferocious' Indians, who 'are in an ugly mood now ... I fear greatly they'll become

unmanageable, and general slaughter will ensure ... Wild Indians are not troops' (ibid., 145).

97 Ibid., 142.

98 Ibid., 143.

99 Ibid., ix.

100 W.S. Wallace, *The Story of Laura Secord* (1932), 3.

101 Ibid., 3–4. Wood, Wallace maintained, was 'one of the chief authorities on Canadian military history,' who had argued in his *Select British Documents of the Canadian War of 1812* (1920) that 'the result would have been the same without her.' Louis L. Babcock was the author of *The War of 1812 on the Niagara Frontier* (1927), whom Wallace quoted as stating that 'the tale told by Mrs. Secord has been enlarged upon as years have passed; and while she may have tried to give warning to the British forces, it seems fairly clear that her good intentions were fruitless.' Finally, Milo M. Quaife, the editor of *The John Askin Papers, Volume* II (1931), had asserted that a letter from Charles Askin to his father 'negatives [*sic*] the claim that the British learned of the impending American attack from Mrs. Laura Secord, whose supposed exploit in conveying the warning has caused her to be lionized by the Canadian people,' and in the index to the volume he ungallantly labels her 'Secord, Mrs. Laura, myth, 3–4.' It is possible that these works did not draw the attention given to Wallace's pamphlet because at least two of them were published in the United States and because their authors' attacks on Secord were made in the context of general histories of 1812, rather than as specific rebuttals of her contribution.

102 Wallace, *The Story of Laura Secord*, 6–16.

103 Ibid., 20.

104 Ibid., 26.

105 Ibid., 19.

106 Ibid., 17–19.

107 Ibid., 13.

108 Cruikshank, *The Fight in the Beechwoods*, 1.

109 Ibid., 13–14, 19.

110 As Donald A. Wright has pointed out, the documents used by Wallace to dispute Secord's claims were 'generated either after the fact, well after the fact, or at some unstated point in time' ('The Importance of Being Sexist; or, The Professionalization of History in English Canada to 1950,' paper presented to the Canadian Historical Association, Memorial University, June 1997, 35). For the imperial organization of knowledge, embodied in both documents and artefacts, see Thomas Richards, *The Imperial Archive: Knowledge and the Fantasy of Empire*.

111 Killan, *Preserving Ontario's Heritage*, 189–98.
112 See also Wright, 'The Importance of Being Sexist.'
113 Ibid.
114 Ibid. And this particular masculinist position was also a racial one, so that other kinds of knowledge and epistemology – those of Native peoples, for example – were suppressed or ignored.
115 'What Laura Secord Did,' *Saturday Night* (1932); reprinted in *Dunnville Weekly Chronicle*, (1935).
116 See, for example, the following articles in the *Niagara Falls Evening Review:* 'As For Us We Stand By Story of Immortal Laura Secord' (2 Dec. 1931); 'Of Course the Story of Laura Secord Is True' (4 Dec. 1931); 'Laura Secord's Key?' (15 Dec. 1931); 'Story of Laura Secord Will Be Told in School-Books, Says Henry' (9 Jan. 1932). My thanks to Karen Dubinsky for these references.

7: Lessons in Loyalty: Children's Texts and Readers

1 Of course, the work done by the historical societies often provided the research base for the texts, and historical society members wrote some of the books.
2 For a discussion of the OHS's problems with shortfalls in government funding, see Gerald Killan, *Preserving Ontario's Heritage*, 211.
3 See Bruce Curtis, 'Schoolbooks and the Myth of Curricular Republicanism: The State and the Curriculum in Canada West,' *Hs-SH* 16, no. 32 (Sept. 1983): 305–29; Oisin Rafferty, 'Balancing the Books: Brokerage Politics and the "*Ontario Readers* Question,"' *Historical Studies in Education* 4, no. 1 (1992): 79–95; and Dennis Duffy, 'Upper Canadian Loyalism: What the Textbooks Tell,' *JoCS* 12, no. 2 (Spring 1977): 17–26. An older study of school texts that is drawn upon in this chapter is Viola Parvin, *Authorization of Textbooks for the Schools of Ontario, 1846–1950*. Although it is a more popular study, Daniel Francis's *National Dreams: Myth, Memory, and Canadian History* discusses the imperialist messages of history textbooks from the 1880s to the post–World War II period. Francis also examines the stereotypes of Aboriginal peoples, although he does not examine representations of Brant and Tecumseh, in chapter 3, 'Your Majesty's Realm: The Myth of the Master Race.'
4 University Women's Club of Port Credit, *The Canadian Indian in Ontario's School Texts: A Study of Social Studies Textbooks Grades 1 through 8*; Garnett McDiarmid and David Pratt, *Teaching Prejudice: A Content Analysis of Social Studies Textbooks Authorized for Use in Ontario*; Pat Staton and Paula Bourne,

'Sex Equity Content in History Textbooks,' *History and Social Science Teacher* 25, no. 1 (Fall 1989): 18–20.

5 See Michael W. Apple and Linda K. Christian-Smith, eds, *The Politics of the Textbook* (1991); and Stephen Heathorn, '"Let us remember that we, too, are English": Constructions of Citizenship and National Identity in English Elementary School Reading Books, 1880–1914,' *Victorian Studies* 39 (Spring 1995): 395–427. Many thanks to Steve Heathorn for directing my attention to Apple's work.

6 See Robert Stamp, *The Schools of Ontario, 1876–1976*, 107–8, 110–12, for the rise of high-school attendance after World War I. However, studies of schooling at the local level find more variation in attendance until the years after World War II. See, for example, Craig Heron, 'The High School and the Household Economy in Working-Class Hamilton, 1890–1940,' *Historical Studies in Education* 7, no. 2 (1995): 217–59.

7 It is, of course, impossible at this date to state if such was the case, given the absence of work on Ontario children's historical memories, yet we should consider such possibilities and not, therefore, dismiss the readers and their authors because they lacked the analytical rigour and sophistication of so-called 'serious' historical scholarship. Such considerations are of little help in seeking to understand the varied dimensions of historical memory. For work in Canada on memories of childhood, see Neil Sutherland, *Growing Up: Childhood in English Canada from the Great War to the Age of Television*; and Norah Lewis, *'I want to join your club': Letters from Rural Children, 1900–1920*.

8 J.N. McIlwraith, *The Children's Study, Canada* (1899), 174, 188.

9 David M. Duncan, *The Story of the Canadian People* (1907), 158

10 McIlwraith, *The Children's Study*, 132; W.J. Robertson, *Public School History of England and Canada* (1892), 209–10; *Ontario Public School History of Canada* (1910), 125.

11 William H. Withrow, *A History of Canada*, 129–30; McIlwraith, *The Children's Study*, 181–5.

12 This was the case in Emily P. Weaver's *A Canadian History for Boys and Girls* (1905), which discussed Pontiac, although she did mention the 'good and faithful' Mohawk Loyalists (106–7, 129). Weaver did tell her readers that whites taken captive by Indians were, 'strange to say ... unwilling' to return to their home society, and that the Aboriginals with whom they lived (who often had married or adopted the whites) were equally reluctant to part with them (108).

13 *Ontario Public School History*, 129–34; Robertson, *Public School History*, 224–5.

14 For a discussion of the erasure of female militancy and the substitution of stoic, self-sacrificing womanhood in South African Boer memory, see Anne

McClintock, *Imperial Leather: Race, Gender and Sexuality in the Colonial Contest*, 378–9.

15 See, for example, *Ontario Public School History*. W.L. Grant also mentions Crawford, Johnson, Machar, and Pickthall, as well as Mance, de La Tour, and Jameson, in his *Ontario High School History of Canada* (1914).

16 J. Frith Jeffers, *History of Canada* (1894), 56.

17 Nellie Spence, *Topical Studies in Canadian History* (1897), 92–3.

18 Withrow, *A History of Canada*, 136.

19 Grant, *Ontario High School History*, 158–9.

20 Weaver, *A Canadian History*, 165–7.

21 The general absence of Molly Brant merits its own study, although she does crop up in some studies, particularly those of the 1980s and '90s. For discussions of Brant, see William Renwick Riddell, 'Was Molly Brant Married?' *OHS Papers* 19 (1922): 147–57; and, for a more contemporary study, Earle Thomas, *The Three Faces of Molly Brant* (1996).

22 Withrow, *A History of Canada*, 148–9. The textbook writers' commemoration of the War of 1812 as the crucible in which 'Canadian' nationalism was forged differs from Jonathan Vance's arguments, in *Death So Noble*, that World War I fulfilled this function.

23 Grant, *Ontario High School History*, 165.

24 Charles G.D. Roberts, *A History of Canada for High Schools and Academies* (1905), 253.

25 McIlwraith, *The Children's Study*, 174.

26 Spence, *Topical Studies*, iii–iv. Her models were Francis Parkman, François-Xavier Garneau, John Charles Dent, and John Charles Bourinot. See also George E. Foster, Minister of Trade and Commerce, to the OHS, *OHS Annual Report* (1914): 45; and John Dearness, OHS president, ibid., 40–3.

27 W.S. Wallace, *A History of the Canadian People* (1930), 118.

28 Ibid., 143.

29 Ibid., 151–2.

30 James Bingay, *A History of Canada for High Schools* (1934), 211.

31 George W. Brown, *Building the Canadian Nation* (1942), 191–2.

32 Edwin C. Guillet and Jessie E. McEwen, *Finding New Homes in Upper Canada* (1938), 35, 52–3.

33 J.E. Wetherell and Charles W. Jeffreys, *Handbook to Nelson's Pictures of Canadian History* (1927), 54.

34 Ibid., 53.

35 Ibid., 54.

36 Wallace, *A History of the Canadian People*, 352–3.

37 G.G. Harris's *Canadian History Workbook*, which accompanied George

Wrong and Chester Martin's *The Story of Canada* (1930), asked students to analyse the causes of the war, the defence of frontiers, the reasons why Tecumseh joined the British, and the war's outcomes. Gilbert Paterson's *The Story of Our People* (1933) recounted the 'stories' of both British and Canadian history, telling students that they were 'inextricably linked.' In this book, the War of 1812 is narrated as an imperial development and receives only a one-page treatment (402).

38 Bingay, *A History of Canada*, 216–17. See also J.E. Middleton's *The Romance of Ontario* (1931), which was part of a series, The Romance of Canada, that focused on individuals to illustrate historical development. Middleton told his readers that Secord overheard the American plot and walked twenty miles to warn FitzGibbon. 'Her information confirmed the rumours which had been brought by Indians, a short time previously, and Lieutenant FitzGibbon made ready for his expected visitors' (77). The narrative was followed by a picture of Secord's Queenston Heights monument, (79).

39 Brown, *Building the Canadian Nation*, 188.

40 Wallace, *A History of the Canadian People*, 148 and 136–7.

41 W.S. Wallace, *A First Book of Canadian History* (1928), 23.

42 Ibid., 55.

43 The absence of Native peoples from these histories is even more ironic if we consider the 1920s efforts of Native leaders such as the Cayuga chief Deskeheh (Levi General) to take the case of Six Nations sovereignty to the League of Nations.

44 See, for example, Connie Brummel Crook, *Laura's Choice: The Story of Laura Secord* (1993); and Susan E. Merritt, 'Laura Ingersoll Secord: Hero of the War of 1812,' in *Her Story: Women from Canada's Past* (1994), 53–62.

45 W.J. Karr, *Explorers, Soldiers, and Statesmen*, ix.

46 Ibid.

47 Ibid.

48 The Ryerson series was endorsed by both the IODE and the Department of Education. For discussions of Canadian publishers and textbook publishing, see the following articles from *JOCS* 30, no. 3 (Fall 1995): Michael A. Peterman and Janet B. Friskney, '"Booming" the Canuck Book: Edward Caswell and the Promotion of Canadian Writing,' 60–90; Sandra Campbell, 'From Romantic History to Communications Theory: Lorne Pierce as Publisher of C.W. Jeffreys and Harold Innis,' 91–116, and David Young, 'The Macmillan Company of Canada in the 1930s,' 117–33.

49 Although it could be argued that this relegation was to a lesser extent than that of Aboriginal peoples, particularly when white women's encounters with Aboriginal peoples were discussed. See, for example, D.J. Dickie, *In*

Pioneer Days: Dent's Canadian History Readers (n.d.). The sketches and characters included 'A Brave Mother,' Mrs Dempsey, who fought off 'drunken Indians' in her home in the Ontario bush (264–5); 'The School-Mistress,' Rachel Martin, a Kentville teacher and poet (258–9); and 'Great-Grandmother's Day,' a description of the work-day of a 'typical' pioneer woman (225–30). For a discussion of how both European women and subaltern peoples might appear 'outside' of historical time, see McClintock, *Imperial Leather*, 40–2.

50 H.E. Marshall, 'The Story of Laura Secord,' in *Our Empire Story* (n.d.), 104–5; C.L. Paddock, 'Canada's Heroine,' in *Golden Stories for Boys and Girls* (1934), 151.

51 Dickie, *In Pioneer Days*, 191; Karr, *Explorers, Soldiers, and Statesmen*, 183; 'The Story of Laura Secord,' in Donald French, ed., *Famous Canadian Stories* (n.d.), 99. And in some it was not clear just who had been the first to overhear. See Mabel Burns McKinley, *Canadian Heroines of Pioneer Days* (1929), 22–3. This book was endorsed by the IODE.

52 Karr, *Explorers, Soldiers, and Statesmen*, 183; Marshall, *Our Empire Story*, 106; Paddock, *Golden Stories*, 152. In this latter story, Secord is a 'brave little wife and mother.'

53 McKinley, *Canadian Heroines*, 25–6.

54 Karr, *Explorers, Soldiers, and Statesmen*, 184.

55 Marshall, *Our Empire Story*, 107; Paddock, *Golden Stories*, 154; French, ed., *Famous Canadian Stories*, 100. Dickie, however, minimized her fear: 'They received her with a war-whoop which awed but did not daunt her. At first they suspected her, but she persuaded one of the chiefs to take her to FitzGibbon, to whom she explained the danger' (*In Pioneer Days*, 191).

56 Karr, 'Tecumseh the War Chief of the Shawnees,' in *Explorers, Soldiers, and Statesmen*, 175–80; Dickie, 'Joseph Brant,' *In Pioneer Days*, 150–4; 'Tecumseh, the Great Indian Leader' and 'Joseph Brant, the Famous Indian Chief,' in French, ed., *Famous Canadian Stories*, 105–10; Hugh S. Eayrs, *Sir Isaac Brock* (1924), 63. This latter biography was part of Macmillan's 'Canadian Men of Action' Series, edited by W.S. Wallace.

57 See Dickie, *In Pioneer Days*.

58 Arthur G. Dorland, *Our Canada* (1949), 158–9.

59 Aileen Garland, *Canada, Our Country* (1961), 53.

60 George W. Brown, Eleanor Harman, and Marsh Jeanneret, *The Story of Canada* (1961), 230–7.

61 Garland, *Canada, Our Country*, 5–9, 12.

62 Donalda Dickie, *The Great Adventure: An Illustrated History of Canada for Young Canadians* (1950), vii.

63 Ibid., 'The Pioneers.'

64 Although these texts were still performing the work of national narration, it
    was a less obvious pedagogical function than in the early 1900s. See, for
    example, Edith Dyell's discussion of differences between the United States
    and Canada, which included the message that slavery had 'never been a
    problem in the latter' and that Upper Canada's first parliament had out-
    lawed the institution (*Canada: The New Nation* [1960], 55).

65 Garland, *Canada, Our Country*, 72–81. These books often tell their readers
    that pioneer women were responsible for every stage of textile and clothing
    production, an assumption that Marjorie Cohen's work has questioned (see
    *Women's Work, Markets, and Economic Development in Nineteenth-Century On-
    tario*).

66 Dyell, *Canada: The New Nation*. Her discussion, which compared Canada
    and the United States, might have been confusing to students, as it spoke of
    the '19th amendment to the constitution.'

67 Brown, Harman, and Jeanneret, *The Story of Canada*, 331–6.

68 J.W. Chafe, *Canada, Your Country* (1950), 141–3; Dyell, *Canada: A New Land*
    (1958), 341–2; Dyell, *Canada: The New Nation*, 47–8; Garland, *Canada, Our
    Country*, 47, 51.

69 Brown, Harman, and Jeanneret, 'Dominion from Sea to Sea,' in *The Story of
    Canada* (1950).

70 See, for example, the cover of Garland's *Canada, Then and Now* (1954),
    which featured a line of men that began with Natives and then included a
    seventeenth-century colonist dressed like a Puritan, a voyageur, Frontenac,
    an eighteenth-century soldier, a surveyor, and a geologist. Garland's
    Canada, Our Country (1961) also features on its cover a painting of a rail-
    road car startling horses pulling a carriage, children in Victorian clothes
    pointing at the sight, a nineteenth-century labouring man carrying a
    barrel, and houses sitting next to a busy trading post in the background. At
    the rear of the picture stand two 'Indians' on a hilltop, wearing blankets
    and eagle feathers in their hair; they are watching the railway being built in
    the valley and the train advancing along the tracks. Dyell's *Canada: The New
    Nation* has a panorama of 'ordinary Canadians' on its cover, including a
    fisherman dressed in a yellow slicker and holding a large fish; a 'school-
    marm' carrying a book and ringing a bell, a farmer with a scythe, a lumber-
    jack, a Victorian bourgeois family (the father with a top hat and waistcoat,
    the mother in a full-skirted dress with jaunty hat and neat gloves, and their
    daughter, her blonde hair in ringlets, wearing a similar outfit but also
    holding a doll), and a Royal Northwest Mounted Police officer.

71 See Donald B. Smith, 'Fred Loft,' paper presented to the Canadian Histori-

cal Association, Brock University, 1996, 2; NA, Elliott Moses Papers, MG30
C169, vol. 2, File 2, Scrapbook 1918–37, 'Indian Teacher Is Resentful:
Denies Red Man Originally Primitive as Stated,' n.d., n.p.; 'Indian Charges
History Is Unfair to His People,' n.d., n.p.; File 3, Scrapbook 1935–52,
'Premier Gets Head-Dress, but Mrs. Hepburn Has Indian Name'; File 4,
Scrapbook 1936–41, 'Tribute Paid to Lieut.-Col. Martin: Former O.C. of
Local Regiment Is Appointed O.P.S.M.T.F. Secretary,' 'Col. O. M. Martin
Spoke at Remembrance Day Service.'

72 Ibid.

73 AO, RG2–243, Ontario Ministry of Education, General Administration and
Correspondence Files, 1950–1, Correspondence and Ms., Box 8, Circular
14, Textbooks, 1951–2, J.R. McCarthy to Mr S.A. Watson, 22 April 1952, no
file number.

74 Ibid., Box 13, Curriculum – Study of Textbooks to Identify Bias, File DA
100, J.R. McCarthy to F.L. Barrett, President of the Canadian Textbooks'
Publishers' Institute, 18 July 1963. See Stamp, *The Schools of Ontario*, 216–17
for a discussion of McCarthy.

75 Ibid., Box 12, Circular 14: Review of all Textbooks Listed in Circular 14,
G.W.C. Nelson, 'A Review of All Textbooks Listed in Circular 14 for the
Purpose of Identifying Bias or Prejudice towards Ethnic Groups with
Particular References to Indians,' June 1970.

76 Apple and Christian-Smith, *The Politics of the Textbook*, 1.

77 See, for example, AO, RG2–243, Ministry of Education, Box 13, Curriculum – Study of Textbooks to Identify Bias, File DA 100, Anne Yarwood,
Voice of Women, Ancaster, to the Minister of Education, 7 January 1972;
ibid., RG 1–143, Box 10, MA 120/13, File: Bias in Textbooks, 1974, Betty
Arawczyk to Thomas Wells, 26 January 1974, and Evelyn E. Ahola, Dr
Carruthers School, to Thomas Wells, 21 January 1974, on sex-role stereotyping in children's readers. While further research is needed in this area,
the letters to the Ministry on the subject of gender bias suggest that the
province was perceived as being particularly laggard in rectifying this
problem in textbooks.

78 AO, RG2–243, Box 13, Curriculum – Study of Textbooks to Identify Bias,
File DA 100, William Mahoney to Thomas Wells, 5 October 1972.

79 Ibid., Wells to Mahoney, 19 October 1972.

80 Ibid., N. Keith Lickers to Eileen McAlear, 1 August, 1974.

81 See, for example, J.L. Granatstein, *Who Killed Canadian History?* and two
thoughtful responses to Granatstein: A.B. McKillop, 'Who Killed Canadian
History? A View from the Trenches,' *CHR* 80, no. 2 (June 1999): 269–99;
and Bryan D. Palmer, 'Of Silences and Trenches: A Dissident View of

Granatstein's Writing,' *CHR* 80, no. 4 (Dec. 1999): 676–86. See also the *Globe and Mail* series 'The Death of History,' 18–22 September 2000. These are only a few of the entries in this debate; similar ones can be found in the United States and Britain.

82 See, for example, 'The Death of History.' As a contributor to a senior-level textbook in Canadian history for high schools, one of the present authors was faced with the issue of 'what to do about Secord.' Her solution was to mention Secord's walk briefly and then to discuss her importance as a symbol (Paul Bennet, Nick Brune, Cornelius Jaenen, and Cecilia Morgan, *Canada: A North American Nation* [1995], 219–20).

8: 'Seeing' the Past: The Monuments and the Candy Company

1 AO, MU5422, OHS Circular, n.t., David Boyle, 16 February 1901.

2 H.V. Nelles, *The Art of Nation-Building*, 267. For literature on such phenomena, see, for example, Thomas Richards, *The Commodity Culture of Victorian England: Advertising and Spectacle, 1851–1914*; Ellen Gruber Garvey, *The Adman in the Parlor: Magazines and the Gendering of Consumer Culture, 1880s–1930s*; and Keith Walden, *Becoming Modern in Toronto: The Industrial Exhibition and the Shaping of a Late Victorian Culture.*

3 The Canadian Historical Exhibition was held at Victoria College in Toronto and displayed artefacts that ranged from Native tools, weapons, and crafts to the furniture, silver, and jewellery of Upper Canada's elite families. While it was sponsored by the Ontario Historical Society, the exhibition owed much of its success to the Women's Historical Society of Toronto. I have considered the Exhibition and the Niagara museum, as well as the Brant County Historical Society's museum, 'Wampum and Waffle-Irons: Gender and National Identities in the Writing of Canadian Popular History, 1880s–1930s,' Paper presented at the Canadian Historical Association, annual meeting, 1996. Other such material and visual presentations of the past included the restoration of historical homes (e.g., Toronto's Colborne Lodge in the 1920s, by the Women's Canadian Historical Society, and the Gage homestead in Stoney Creek, undertaken by the Women's Wentworth Historical Society), and Loyalist monuments in towns such as Belleville or Brantford. As well, Empire Day festivities in the province's schools relied heavily on historical themes and motifs. For Empire Day in Ontario, see Robert Stamp, 'Empire Day in the Schools of Ontario: The Training of Young Imperialists,' *JoCS* 8, no. 3 (Aug. 1973): 32–42. For other monuments, see Norman Knowles, *Inventing the Loyalists*, chap. 6.

4 AO, MU5422, OHS Circular, David Boyle, 16 February 1901.

5 See Ruth McKenzie, *Laura Secord*, 133–4; and Knowles, *Inventing the Loyalists*, 128–31.

6 Marina Warner, *Monuments and Maidens: The Allegory of the Female Form*. See also Kathryn McPherson, 'Carving Out a Past: The Canadian Nurses' Association War Memorial,' *Hs-SH* 19, no. 58 (Nov. 1996): 417–30.

7 AO, MU5422, Box no. 1, File June 1900–May 1903, Third Annual Report of the Monuments and Tablets Committee. The committee's error – that Secord's monument was the first public memorial to a woman – appears to have gone unchallenged.

8 McKenzie, *Laura Secord*, 113.

9 AO, MU5422, Box no. 1, File June 1900–May 1903, Third Annual Report of the Monuments and Tablets Committee, 'Report of Secord Monument Unveiling Ceremony.'

10 Ibid., Strobel to Boyle, 26 June 1901.

11 Ibid., Strobel to Boyle, 4 July and 26 June 1901.

12 Ibid., Strobel to Boyle, 4 July 1901.

13 AO, RG38–3, Niagara Parks Commission Records, General Manager's Office Correspondence, May 1893–1923, Box 29, File 2, 1 January 1907–21 February 1911, Edna Lowrey to John Jackson, 6 January 1910.

14 Ibid., Jackson to Lowrey, 1 February 1910.

15 Ibid., Lowrey to Langmuir, 12 March 1910; Langmuir to Jackson, 19 May 1910; Lowrey to Langmuir, 9 November 1910.

16 Ibid., Lowrey to Langmuir, 7 January 1913.

17 Ibid., 14 August 1913. $4,000–$5,000 were the estimates they had been given by architects.

18 Ibid., 29 September 1913.

19 Ibid., Jackson to Lowrey, 27 November 1913.

20 Ibid., George Ross to Langmuir, 2 August 1909.

21 Ibid., Jackson to Langmuir, 15 September 1909.

22 Ibid., Currie to Jackson, 5 April 1910; also 3 May 1910.

23 Ibid., Jackson to Langmuir, 27 September 1909.

24 Ibid., Currie to Jackson, 18 May 1910.

25 Ibid., Currie to Jackson, 22 July 1910.

26 Ibid., 7 September 1910.

27 Ibid., 28 September 1910. Currie also told Jackson that she was prepared to pay for fencing for the monument.

28 Ibid., Ross to Langmuir, 14 August 1911.

29 Ibid., Langmuir to Ross, 15 August 1911.

30 Ibid., Currie to Langmuir, 11 March 1912.

31 Ibid., Langmuir to Currie, 29 March 1912.

32 Ibid., Currie to Langmuir, 1 April 1912.
33 Ibid., Currie to Langmuir, 24 October 1912.
34 Ibid., Langmuir to Ross, 4 November 1912.
35 Ibid., Ross to Currie, 6 November 1912.
36 Ibid., Ross to Langmuir, 6 November 1912.
37 Ibid., Langmuir to Ross, 8 November 1912.
38 For discussions of this, see Serafina Bathrick, 'The Female Colossus: The Body as Façade and Threshold,' in Jane Gaines and Charlotte Herzog, eds, *Fabrications: Costume and the Female Body*; Warner, *Monuments and Maidens*; and Joy Kasson, *Marble Queens and Captives: Women in Nineteenth-Century American Sculpture.* Many thanks to Kate McPherson for directing me to Bathrick's work.
39 David Glassberg, *American Historical Pageantry: The Uses of Tradition in the Early Twentieth Century*, 4. A few studies have been conducted of specific pageants in Canada. See, for example, Nelles, *The Art of Nation-Building*; and Peter Geller, '"Hudson's Bay Company Indians": Images of Native People and the Red River Pageant, 1920,' in S. Elizabeth Bird, ed., *Dressing in Feathers: The Construction of the Indian in American Popular Culture.*
40 Glassberg, *American Historical Pageantry*, 4.
41 'I.O.D.E. Historical Pageant,' *Saturday Night* (2 July 1927): 12. This pageant is also discussed in Robert Cupido, 'Appropriating the Past; Pageants, Politics, and the Diamond Jubilee of Confederation,' *Journal of the Canadian Historical Association* 9 (1998): 155–86.
42 Ibid., 12.
43 Ibid., 13.
44 '43rd Anniversary of St. Catharines Women's Literary Club,' *St. Catharines Standard* (9 Dec. 1935).
45 Alexander Maitland Stephens, 'Laura Secord,' in *Classroom Plays from Canadian History* (1929); Norman Symonds, with students from King George Senior Public School, Guelph, *Laura and the Lieutenant: A Musical Play* (1976). Stephens's play dramatizes Secord's meeting with FitzGibbon; the extant script from the musical suggests that it told the 'Secord story' from the Battle of Queenston Heights through to Beaver Dams.
46 BUSC, WLC, Box 5, 'Blazing of the Trail,' n.d., 4. Brighty (1876–1941) was a life-long resident of St Catharines. She also lectured on Canadian and local history to various Niagara clubs and schools; two of her booklets, 'A History of the Orphan's Home' and 'A Pilgrimage through the Historical Niagara District,' were published by the Lincoln County Historical Society. She was also the educational secretary of the Lord Tennyson Chapter of the IODE and belonged to the National Council of Women, the OHS, and the UELs. This biographical information is from ibid., Box 3, E. Stevens,

'Mrs. Isabel McComb Brighty,' scrapbook compiled for the St Catharines Women's Literary Club.

47 Ibid., Box 5, 'Blazing of the Trail,' 1–10.

48 Nelles, *The Art of Nation-Building*, 193.

49 Ibid.

50 BUSC, WLC, Box 5, 'Blazing of the Trail,' 4.

51 Ibid., 4–5.

52 Ibid., 7.

53 Ibid., 8.

54 While such a disappearing act should not be surprising, it is worth pointing out that this was unlike the situation at the Quebec pageant of 1908, where Aboriginal peoples played themselves and were also able to present themselves in domestic settings (Nelles, *The Art of Nation-Building*, 179).

55 BUSC, WLC, Box 5, 'Blazing of the Trail,' 8–9.

56 Ibid., Box 3, 'Mrs. Isobel McComb Brighty,' scrapbook compiled for the St Catharines Women's Literary Club, 'Historic Pageant Scored an Extraordinary Success. "Blazing of the Trail" Drew Capacity Audience. Presented by the Girl Guides. Produced under Personal Direction of the Author, Mrs. Brighty,' *St. Catharines Standard*, n.d.

57 *The Cow That Never Was*, CTV Heritage Theatre Production, 1974, narrated by Pierre Berton and written by Lister Sinclair.

58 McKenzie, *Laura Secord*, 119. For a fascinating study of a similar American commercial icon, Aunt Jemima, see M.M. Manring, *Slave in a Box: The Strange Career of Aunt Jemima*.

59 See Casey Mahood, 'Profit Is Sweet, but Laura Secord for Sale,' *Globe and Mail* (18 Sept. 1998): B4; and Barbara Schecter and Marina Jimenez, 'War of 1812 Heroine Laura Secord Heading South,' *National Post* (3 June 1999): A11. In an added layer of irony, the *Post* ran an interview with this author about commemorations of Secord.

60 Laura Secord Candy Company Archives, Scrapbook A, 'For Old Time Sake,' Laura Secord Candy Company advertisement, 6 May 1920.

61 Keith Walden, 'Isaac Brock,' 127.

62 Ibid., 158–65.

63 Laura Secord Candy Company Archives, Scrapbook A, 'Heart to Heart Talk with Our Friends,' Laura Secord Candy Company advertisement, 6 May 1920.

64 Ibid., 'Refinement and Business.'

65 For a study of the representation of white racial identity in Western culture, see Richard Dyer, *White*.

66 Laura Secord Candy Company Archives, 'An Apology,' taken from *The Telegraph* (29 December 1919). In this piece, the Secord company told its

'dear friends' that the demand for the 'old time homemade candies this Christmas was so great that the supply was entirely exhausted in the early evening of December 24th, with the result that all shops had to be closed. We must, therefore, apologize to our friends who were disappointed in not being able to secure their Christmas supply.'

67 Ibid., 'Announcement.'

68 Ibid., Scrapbook A, 'Quality,' 1919–1920[?].

69 Ibid., 'Laura Secord Candy Shop Shares Profits. Frank P. O'Connor Announces First Plan of This Kind in Candy Industry,' *Kingston Whig-Standard* (16 Jan. 1923). The company's official history also states that it offered sick pay, 'an employee program that paid $10 each for the five best suggestions,' and a sales incentive award (Laura Secord Candy Company Archives, 'The Traditions View,' 1).

70 Ibid., Clair Stewart and Bill Cockburn, 'New Laura Secord Box Design,' *RSC* 4, no. 3 (Oct. 1951): 3, 8. *RSC* was the company paper of Rolph-Clark-Stone, the design firm.

71 Ibid.

72 Ibid., 8.

73 For a discussion of the conflation of race, gender, and class in the image of 'the lady,' see Anne McClintock, *Imperial Leather*, 95–100.

74 Laura Secord Candy Company Archives, Scrapbook B, Appendix Four, '"Traditional Quality" Advertisement (1950s),' 213.

75 Ibid., Scrapbook B, 'Sunday Is Mother's Day,' advertisement run 5 May 1965 in a variety of papers across Ontario as well as in Winnipeg and Shawinigan.

76 Ibid., Eaton Centre advertisement, December 1977.

77 Ibid., 13 June 1978.

78 Ibid., 'Press Release: Official Opening of the Niagara Falls Shop,' 30 June 1964.

79 Ibid., 'She Has Famous Ancestor,' *Evening Review* (June n.d., 1964[?]).

80 Ibid., Scrapbook B, 'Press Release: Official Opening of the Niagara Falls Shop.'

81 Ibid., 200th birthday advertisement.

82 For an exploration of the multiple presences and uses of the past, see Raphael Samuel, *Theatres of Memory*.

9: Laura Secord, the Niagara Region, and Historical Tourism

1 BUSC, WLC, Box 11, File 1, 'An Historical Outing,' *St Catharines Standard* (9 July 1904).

2 John F. Sears, *Sacred Places: American Tourist Attractions in the Nineteenth Century*, 5–7.

3 The town of Niagara-on-the-Lake became officially known as such by the early twentieth century, but residents frequently called it by its older name, 'Niagara.'

4 It is difficult – if not impossible – at present to provide quantitative evidence on the number of tourists that came to Niagara and Queenston, especially in the absence of a Chamber of Commerce, but research in the local newspaper, *The Times*, and the NPC records indicates that during the 1890s, area residents began to think of themselves as part of a tourist economy. Niagara-on-the-Lake's population in 1891 was 1,349; Queenston's would have been somewhat smaller. The total township population (including the nearby villages of St David's and Virgil and the resident rural population) was 1,847.

5 George Seibel, *Ontario's Niagara Parks: 100 Years*, 220–9.

6 Many of these summer residences are still standing and occupied; a few homes take up entire blocks opposite the town's golf course. See *The Times* (15 Aug. 1895) for a discussion of their ownership, and also real estate advertisements (24 May 1901). The Chautauqua grounds in Niagara Township (on the western side of town, along the lake) had been the site of a Chautauqua educational and religious gathering, organized independently from the New York circuit, in the 1880s and '90s; the area continued to attract cottagers and tourists to the Chautauqua and Lakeside Hotels, with their beaches, tennis courts, and other forms of recreation. See 'Chautauqua and Lakeside Park Hotel,' *The Times* (28 May 1896); also Sheilagh S. Jameson, *Chautauqua in Canada*, 93.

7 The architecture of Niagara was a particular and continuing attraction of the town. While most of town had been burned by U.S. troops in 1813, it was rebuilt soon after the war.

8 My research in the local papers, *The Times* and its successor, *Niagara Advance*, shows ongoing coverage of the camp every summer, from 1898 until the early 1970s. See, for example, 'With the Boys in Camp,' *The Times* (10 June 1898); 'Commons Alive with Militia,' ibid. (13 June 1913); 'Haldimand Rifles Stage Entertainment at Camp. Indians, in Ancient Costumes, Perform Ceremony of Giving Major Burns Tribal Name,' *Niagara Advance* (19 July 1934); 'Military Camp Employs Chinese Cooks,' ibid. (29 May 1941); '1700 Army Cadets Training at Niagara Military Camp,' ibid. (20 June 1946). Other attractions were the World Boy Scout Jamboree of 1955 and, of course, the development of the Shaw Festival.

9 'Niagara: Concluding Remarks about Our Historical Town,' *The Times*

(14 May 1896); 'Niagara 1886–1896,' ibid. (2 July 1896); 'News about Town and Vicinity,' ibid. (1 July 1898). Local boosterism probably shaped these writings; the town's paper constantly urged its residents to clean up their properties, welcome tourists, and tell their friends and relatives in other places about the delights of Niagara-on-the-Lake and Queenston.

10 'Chautauqua Breezes,' *The Times* (19 Aug. 1898).

11 AO, MU5438, Box 19, Janet Carnochan, 'Old Niagara,' n.p., n.d. Carnochan was a staunch supporter of Gourlay, and, while she believed that unjust treatment had unsettled his mind, she also thought of him as a far-seeing visionary. See (in ibid.) her 'Story of Robert Gourlay, the Banished Briton,' *The Globe* (26 June 1909).

12 Ibid., Janet Carnochan, 'Early History of Canada as Exemplified by Visitors at Niagara,' *Napanee Beaver* (5 June 1908). The paper had been originally read before the Lennox and Addington Historical Society.

13 Ibid., Janet Carnochan, 'Military Reserve at Niagara,' *Napanee Beaver* (28 June 1905). The Dominion government decided not to sell off the land, and the reserve continued to be a popular training camp, bringing in both the troops and the public. The earliest trip appears to have been in June 1895, when 'thirty robust ladies' went to Niagara with Kirby as their guide. They viewed the Forts, St Mark's Anglican Church, and Maria Rye's former home for orphans, which had been located in the town's former jail (BUSC, WLC, Box 7, 'Pilgrimage of the Literary Club,' June 1895).

14 Ibid., Scrapbook 7, Burke-Gaffney to WLC, n.d. For a discussion of American 'pilgrimages' in the post-World War II decades, see Michael Kammen, *Mystic Chords of Memory*, 547; and David W. Lloyd, *Battlefield Tourism: Pilgrimage and the Commemoration of the Great War in Britain, Australia, and Canada, 1919–1939*.

15 WLC, Scrapbook 7, Burke-Gaffney to WLC, n.d.

16 Frank Yeigh, 'A Pilgrimage along the Historic Niagara,' *The Globe* (1 July 1899).

17 Ibid. See also Katherine Reid, 'Footprints of History in the Niagara Peninsula,' *The Globe* (19 Jan. 1907); Isabel B. Macdonald, 'Old Niagara: A Garden of Historical Treasure,' ibid. (21 Nov. 1908); Madeleine Geale, 'From ... Toronto to Chippawa,' *Canadian Home Journal* (Sept. 1897); Anne Woodruff, 'Historic Queenston,' *Toronto Saturday Night*, n.d.; One of the Pilgrims, 'Historic Niagara: Points of a Pleasant Pilgrimage,' 1898. All articles in AO, MU5441, Series D, OHS Scrapbooks, Niagara 2, Box 22.

18 'Something Must be Done,' *The Times* (14 May 1896). The editor concurred, pointing out that many gentlemen who own 'fine residences' were threatening to leave town unless the council put a stop to the animals'

rambles. 'Can it be possible that our citizens would rather have the cows running at random than a yearly influx of tourists?'

19 'What Niagara Needs,' 'Re: Trolley Line,' *The Times* (5 May 1899).

20 'Thoughts by the Wayside,' *The Times* (20 May 1899).

21 See, for example, Rusticus, 'Niagara 1886–1896,' *The Times* (2 July 1896); and 'Niagara. Concluding Remarks about Our Historical Town,' ibid. (14 May 1896). Others were much more enthusiastic about tourism; see, in *The Times*, 'Old Niagara in 1836' (25 March 1898); 'Recollections of Old Niagara' (8 April 1898); 'What Niagara Needs,' by 'An Ex-Councilman' (3 Feb. 1899); and 'No Show for Manufactories' (9 Dec. 1901). Only Captain Beale, in 'To the People of Niagara,' called for more factories to boost growth and keep taxes low (25 Nov. 1898).

22 Ian McKay, *The Quest of the Folk*. See Dona Brown, *Inventing New England: Regional Tourism in the Nineteenth Century*, on the rewriting of Nantucket's history to accord with the themes of simplicity, tradition, and rusticity (108–9).

23 See 'Chautauqua and Lakeside Park Hotel,' *The Times* (28 May 1898); 'As Others See Us,' ibid. (21 June 1901); and F. Winthrop, 'To the Ratepayers of the Town of Niagara,' ibid. (28 Dec. 1900). Winthrop cited tourists' confusion of Niagara-on-the-Lake with Niagara Falls.

24 Ibid. While both private and public tourist promoters did not always state explicitly that they wanted the area to develop as a distinct entity from the Falls, I would argue such a desire was often implicit in discussions that focused on the need to cultivate taste and dignity in Niagara's tourism. This comparison may have been so apparent to contemporaries that there was no need to mention Niagara Falls by name; they may also have wished to avoid stirring up controversy.

25 In the early 1900s, the Niagara and Port Dalhousie Rail Road ran a train from Port Dalhousie (in the north end of St Catharines) to Niagara to serve the town and the area's fruit growers ('Niagara and Port Dalhousie Rail Road,' *The Times* [22 March 1901]).

26 The NPC files include a number of references to controlling the Queenston Heights environment. See AO, RG 38, Series 3–1, Box 17, File 2, John Langmuir, Chairman, to John Jackson, NPC Manager, 7 March 1911; Langmuir to F. H. Lowrey, 29 March 1911; Mr Suess to Jackson, 11 April 1911; Jackson to Mrs Suess, 1 April 1912, 30 April 1912. These letters concerned the lease of the concession stand at the park.

27 For the NPC's work at Victoria Park, see Karen Dubinsky, *'The Second Biggest Disappointment': Honeymooning and Tourism at Niagara Falls*, 92–3, 108–9.

28 See the correspondence in AO, RG 38, Series 3-2, Box 45, File 1-J, 1 April 1931–31 May 1934.

29 Ibid., Series 3–1, Box 30, File 1, Musson to Phillip Ellis, NPC Chair, 18 April 1922.

30 See correspondence in ibid., 15 January 1934 – 30 May 1935.

31 Ronald Way, *Ontario's Niagara Parks: A History*, 173.

32 For historic plaques, see AO, RG 38, Series 3–1, Box 17, File 4, Jackson to A.A. Pinard, Dominion Parks Branch, Department of the Interior, 29 October 1920.

33 Patricia Jasen, *Wild Things*, 40–1.

34 In 1898 the NHS petitioned the Dominion government that Forts Erie, George, and Mississauga be placed under the Commission's protection (AO, 'Report of the Niagara Historical Society, February 1899,' *OHS Report* [1899]: 35).

35 See, for example, AO, RG 38, Series 3-1, Box 30, File 1, T.L. Church, MP, to Charles Stewart, Minister of the Interior, 19 June 1922; Series 3-2, Box 44, File I-H, William Kirby and H. Smith, Niagara Historical Society, to Jackson, 9 December 1929; Box 96, File I-V, F.J. Keenan, Secretary, Niagara-on-the-Lake Golf Club, to Paul Pare, DND, n.d. [early 1950s?]. The NPC refused to take over Fort Mississauga, which is still surrounded by the town's golf course. Navy Hall, used as a residence by the Simcoes in 1792, consists of a wooden structure enclosed in a twentieth-century stone building. Both it and Fort George were taken over by the National and Historic Parks Branch of the Department of Indian and Northern Affairs (presently known as Parks Canada) in 1969.

36 See correspondence in ibid., Box 45, File I-J, 15 January 1934 – 30 May 1935. For a discussion of the NPC's use of relief workers to build the Oakes Theatre, see Dubinsky, 'The Second Biggest Disappointment,' 205.

37 See AO, RG 38, Series 3–2, Box 45, File I-L, W. C. Brennan to Kaumeyer, 30 June 1938; and File I-O, Brennan to Kaumeyer, 25 September 1939. Brennan Paving Company received $1.3 million in NPC contracts during 1937–42 (John C. Best, *Thomas Baker McQuesten: Public Works, Politics, and Imagination*, 177–9).

38 See correspondence between various teachers and the NPC in AO, RG 38, Series 3–2, Box 95, File I-S, September 1945 to March 1948. These letters do not suggest that the teachers and principals were responding to any systematic advertising campaign mounted by the NPC.

39 Way, *Ontario's Niagara Parks*, 253.

40 Ibid., 338. The NPC often cited the fort's location on the golf course as complicating matters. See AO, RG 38, Series 3–3, Box 95, File I-U, Maxim

Gray, Manager, to C.G. Childs, Superintendent of Historic Parks and Sites, 23 April 1952; and Box 96, File I-V, Gray to Kirby, 3 July 1953.

41 AO, RG38, Acc. 17741, vol. 3–5, Mabel Burkholder, 'Little Trips to Interesting Places in Niagara Peninsula,' *Hamilton Spectator* (26 Jan. 1952); Bill Brown, 'They Still Storm the Ramparts at Old Fort George,' *Weekend Magazine* (21 May 1955). But see 'Old Forts Are Phonies, Archeologist Believes,' *Globe* (2 Aug. 1957).

42 AO, RG 38, Series 3–1, Box 29, File 2, 1 January 1907 – 21 February 1911, R.E. Land to James Wilson, 11 March 1908; Wilson to Land, 12 March 1908.

43 Ibid., Wilson to Land, 12 March 1908.

44 Ibid., F. Sheppard to the NPC, n.d.

45 Ibid., Box 61, File 4-G, Correspondence, 1 October 1927 – 31 March 1928, John Jackson to J.R. Bond, 30 September 1931; Bond to Jackson, 30 October 1931.

46 The domestication of the MacFarland house was eagerly seized upon by reporters, whose articles on its opening featured young women exploring the house, carrying out domestic tasks, entertaining one another, and – interestingly – reclining on a four-poster bed. See AO, RG38, Acc. 17741, NPC Scrapbook, Volume 6, 1958–9: 'House of 1800 Opened to Public This Sunday,' *Globe and Mail* (29 May 1959); 'Glimpse into "Good Old Days,"' *St Catharines Standard* (29 May 1959); 'Historical 1800 Home to Be Opened Sunday,' *Niagara Falls Review* (28 May 1959). Other sites of 'historical' interest in the area were recreated by the NPC, such as Fort Erie; the Commission also helped the WWHS with funding for their maintenance of the Stoney Creek battlefield and house.

47 'P.M. to Dedicate Memorial Arch,' *Niagara Advance* (26 May 1938). Mackenzie King also opened the Mackenzie house on this occasion; the paper pointed out there were plaques that showed Mackenzie addressing the 'Commons' one hundred years ago, as well as plaques to the executed Thomas Matthews and Samuel Lount.

48 In this commemoration of the military, the Commission was assisted by the town's apparently warm reception for the summer army camp, which helped to shape the idea of Niagara-on-the-Lake as a long-standing site for the military.

49 AO, RG 38, Acc. 17741, NPC Scrapbook, Volume 1, 2 February 1949 – 8 December 1951, C.N.A. Ireson, 'Brock's Indian Warriors Forgotten,' *Globe* (3 July 1950). See also 'Haldimand Rifles Stage Entertainment at Camp. Indians, in Ancient Costumes, Perform Ceremony of Giving Major Burns Tribal Name,' *Niagara Advance* (19 July 1936).

50 See, for example, Daniel Francis, *The Imaginary Indian*, chap. 5: 'Performing Indians'; and Veronica Strong-Boag and Carole Gerson, *Paddling Her Own Canoe: The Times and Texts of E. Pauline Johnson (Tekahionwake)*.

51 For a brief discussion of Aboriginal peoples' presence in the Niagara area, see Wesley B. Turner, 'Early Settlement,' in Hugh J. Gayler, ed., *Niagara's Changing Landscapes*, 182–3. It would be difficult to know from NPC records and commemorations of this period that Colonel John Butler's Rangers included Senecas, although a number of re-enactments of the last five years have made that point. For a discussion of African Canadians in Niagara, see Michael Power and Nancy Butler, *Slavery and Freedom in Niagara*.

52 AO, RG38, Series 3–3, Box 95, File I-S, J. Lloyd Hughes, Chair, Gerald Noxon, Secretary, 'Niagara Preserved and Restored: A Brief for the Realization of the Historical, Architectural and Cultural Values of the Town of Niagara' (Historical Section of the Niagara Post War Planning Commission, 1945), 4. Kammen points to a similar fascination with 'colonial restoration' in the United States (*Mystic Chords of Memory*, chap. 16: 'The Heritage Imperative: Popularizing, Collecting, and Preserving').

53 AO, RG5, Series A-1, Ministry of Tourism, MB 7, 'Historic Sites – Preservation – NOTL, 1963–71,' Folder 16.6, 'A Submission to the Commissioners' Niagara Region Local Government Review,' Niagara Foundation, n.d. Regional government came to Niagara in 1969.

54 Ibid., 'Historic Sites – Preservation – NOTL, 1963–71,' Folder 16.6, Auld to James Allan, 8 February 1965.

55 Ibid., MB 2, 'Preservation of Historic Sites and Buildings, 1960–1,' Folder 183, Mrs A.C. Temple to Bryan L. Cathcart, 5 August 1960; MB 7, 'Historic Sites – Preservation – NOTL, 1963–71,' Folder 16.6, Kenneth Croft to Auld, 18 August 1965; 'A Vacant Lot ... and History,' *The Telegram* (31 July 1965); MB7, 'Historic Sites – Preservation – NOTL, 1963–71,' Folder 16.6, Ralph Cunningham to John Robarts, 2 August 1965; John Bone to John Robarts, 8 February 1967.

56 See, for example, ibid., Welch to Auld, 6 April 1966, 4 May 1966; Welch to Allan, 29 January 1967; Series A-10, MB 38, 'Proposals – NOTL, 1964–6,' Folder 3.27, Welch to T.C. Clarke, Tourist Industry Development Branch, 28 October 1965. Probably the impending Centennial celebrations helped prompt much of this interest. Certainly, Welch along with many Niagara residents were aware that there might be Centennial funds available.

57 AO, RG5, Series A-1, MB 6, 'Historic Sites – Preservation – Field Pharmacy, NOTL 1964–71,' Folder 15.8, George Voth to Auld, 10 August 1970.

58 Ibid., MB 7, Folder 16.6, McOuat to Deputy Minister of Tourism Guy Moore, 13 December 1963.

59 Ibid., MB 19, 'OHF – General (part B) 1968,' Folder 45.10, E.W. Bertinger to Allan, 23 January 1968; Allan to Auld, 31 January 1968; Allan to Bertinger, 31 January 1968; Auld to Bertinger, 5 February 1968.

60 'Historic Laura Secord House Renovations Near Completion,' *St Catharines Standard* (2 March 1972): 22

61 'Women Honour Laura Secord,' *Niagara Advance* (18 May 1972); BUSC, WLC, Box Two, Scrapbook 7, Joan Phillips, 'A Fresh Look at the Legends Surrounding Heroine's Walk,' *St Catharines Standard*, n.d.; Box Three, 'Memories Scrapbook,' 'A Tribute to Emma Harvey Currie and Laura Ingersoll Secord.'

62 See also clippings from Niagara Falls Public Library Special Collections, Jean Huggins Collection, Box One, File Two: 'Secord Home Open to Public,' *Free Press* (3 June 1972); Zena Cherry, 'After a Fashion: Davis to Open Restored Secord Home,' *Globe and Mail* (2 June 1972); Bruce West, 'Authentic Heroine,' *Globe and Mail* (6 June 1972); 'Historic Laura Secord Homestead to Be Opened,' *Dunnville Chronicle* (10 May 1972). The *Niagara Falls Review*, though, made the connection between history and consumption: 'Old history and new candy will be offered at a price in Laura Secord homestead' (12 May 1972).

63 BUSC, WLC, Scrapbook 7, Burke-Gaffney to Women's Literary Society, n.d.

64 'Women Honour Laura Secord,' *Niagara Advance* (18 May 1972); BUSC, WLC, Scrapbook 7, Women's Literary Society flyer, 'Preview of Laura Secord Homestead,' n.d.

65 Niagara Falls Public Library Special Collections, Jean Huggins Collection, Box One, File Two, 'Davis Urges Saving Cultural Heritage,' *Hamilton Spectator* (3 June 1972); 'Authentic Heroine,' *Globe and Mail* (6 June 1972); 'Ontario Slow to Recognize Cultural Heritage, Davis,' *Evening Tribune* (3 June 1972).

66 Another very important aspect of the area's tourism has been that created by the Shaw Festival.

67 In 1984 Janet Carnochan was recognized by the province as having been a 'remarkable woman' who had made a 'tremendous contribution ... to our history,' as well as having provided 'dedicated service in the educational and religious life of Niagara' (Robert Welch, Minister of Women's Issues, quoted in Carol Alaimo, 'Niagara's Janet Carnochan: History May Have Passed Her By but Ontario Will Finally Honour Her,' *St Catharines Standard* [30 May 1984]). Welch began his praise of Carnochan, though, by stating that 'history may have passed her by' (in what way, Welch did not explain) but that in her day she wrote books, travelled thousands of miles, and rubbed 'shoulders with politicians when women's liberation hadn't yet

been invented.' See also 'Distinguished Pioneer's Work Recognized,' *Niagara Advance* (4 April 1984). The theme of women's liberation being, perhaps, unnecessary for the stalwart women of the past (with a hint that feminists of the present simply lacked backbone) was also addressed by Ruth McKenzie in a public discussion of her book about Secord. McKenzie stated that 'women have played a large part in the establishment of Canada. Pioneer women felt part of a team. There was no need for "Women's Lib," for the women were equal' (quoted in Joan Phillips, 'A Fresh Look at the Legends Surrounding Heroine's Walk,' *St Catharines Standard*, n.d.; clippings from BUSC, WLC, Box 2).

68 See www.npc@niagaraparks.com. The site also mentions Laura Secord's American ancestry and her husband's United Empire Loyalist background.

69 Ibid. The NPC also uses the Secord homestead for other events related to the early nineteenth-century history of the area. In July 1999, for example, the Commission mounted a 'special interactive exhibition on 19th century crime and punishment' at the homestead ('Crime and Punishment,' *Niagara Advance* [3 July 1999], 13).

Epilogue: The Iroquois Presence

1 'Les discours de la fête de Dollard l'ont répété à satiété: l'ennemi d'aujourd'hui, ce n'est plus l'Iroquois mais l'encerclement anglo-saxon et ses effets, la modernisation économique et sociale incontrôlable, la pénétration des capitaux et d'une main-d'œuvre étrangers, la dégradation de la culture nationale, la minorisation du Canada français et les attaques incessantes contre ses institutions' (Patrice Groulx, 'Entre histoire et commémoration: L'Itinéraire Dollard de l'abbé Groulx,' *Les cahiers d'histoire du Québec au xxe siècle* 8 [1997]: 26).

2 'Aussy les Iroquois Gens d'ailleurs si Rusés et si Belliqueux y furent ils trompés comme ils l'avouerent dans la Suite a Mr de Callieres, a qui ils déclarerent qu'ils avoient tenu Conseil pour prendre le fort pendant la Nuit, mais que la garde que l'on y faisoit sans Relâche les avoit empêché d'Executer leur dessein, sur tout ayant déja perdu du monde par le feu que mes deux Jeunes freres et moy, avions fait sur Eux le jour précedent.'

3 Louise Dechêne, *Habitants and Merchants*, 7.

4 José António Brandão, *'Your Fyre Shall Burn No More': Iroquois Policy toward New France and Its Native Allies to 1701*, 123. For a similar argument concerning Iroquois war aims, see Roland Viau, *Enfants du néant et mangeurs d'âmes: Guerre, culture et société en Iroquoisie ancienne.*

5 'Les Iroquois, qui ne pardonnent rien, avaient juré à Madeleine, une

grande haine ... Aussi, ne laissaient-ils jamais, chaque fois qu'ils passaient à Sainte-Anne de la Pérade, de lui donner quelques marques de leur ressentiment' (Eugène Achard, *Les grands noms de l'histoire canadienne* [1946], 58). Likewise, Abbé J.-G. Gélinas wrote of this later Iroquois attack (*En veillant avec les petits de chez nous*, vol. I: 48).

6 Donald G. French, ed., *Famous Canadian Stories Re-told for Boys and Girls* (1931), 79.

7 'On l'aurait traitée comme une bête de somme. On aurait surtout outragé sa pudeur. Plus tard, elle serait devenue la troisième ou la quatrième épouse d'un iroquois: ce qui veut dire un ignoble barbare sans loi et sans conscience. Loin de tout secours religieux et vivant au milieu des pires déchéances, on devient presque une bête' (Laurent Tremblay, o.m.i., *Madeleine de Verchères: Un récit pour le Roi* [1957], 23–4).

8 'les sauvages dont le rôle était de se laisser passer au fil de l'épée sans mot dire ...' (Girard, quoted in Madeleine Charlebois-Dirschauer, *Rodolphe Girard*, 132).

9 Pierre Mariel, *Une héroïne canadienne* (1967): 'Mais richesse et eau-de-feu valent-elles qu'on cède pouce après pouce le territoire des aïeux, qu'on laisse dégénérer les traditions ancestrales, et moquer le Grand Esprit?' (47). Likewise, Helmer Linderholm's trilogy of Swedish children's books places great emphasis on 'de krigiska irokesfolken' (the warlike Iroquois) as they fought their romantic battles against the Europeans (*Ridardna och de röda*; *I de rödas krig*; *Fredens hemliga stig*).

10 'Les Indiens indiquèrent aux explorateurs les routes à suivre, sans deviner qu'ils se préparaient des lendemains tragiques' (Jean Coté, *Madeleine de Verchères* [1995], 37, 60).

11 Richard A. Boning, *Soldier Girl* (1975), 37.

12 NA, Launcelot Cressy Servos Papers, MG30, D247, vol. 3, 'They Laid the Foundation,' 3.

13 Ida M. Davidson, 'Madeline de Vercheres,' in *The Capture of Quebec and Madeline de Vercheres* (1929), 40.

14 Margaret Atwood, *Strange Things*, 48.

15 NA, National Film Archives, W. Galloway's taped interview with Arthur Larente, 3 August 1973.

16 NA, RG84, vol. 1255, H5–7–25, vol. 2, pt. 1, Notations, signed 'H. Pinard, 12 October 1923.'

17 'La couleur, ce sont les Indiens qui la fournissent, et comme ce sont de vrais Indiens, elle n'est pas fausse' (Un Canadien, 'Madeleine de Verchères: Un film des premiers temps de la Nouvelle-France,' *Le Devoir* [11 Dec. 1922]: 2).

18 H.V. Nelles, 'Historical Pageantry and the "Fusion of the Races" at the Tercentenary of Quebec, 1908,' *Hs–SH* 29, no. 58 (Nov. 1996): 412.

19 Morgan Kenney, *Madeleine de Verchères: Héroïne canadienne* (1989).

20 'Ontario Schools Remove Textbook after Mohawk Complains of Racism,' *Montreal Gazette* (12 Dec. 1992): A10.

21 Personal communication from Bonnie Carter, FSL Consultant, Simcoe District Board of Education, 13 February 1998.

22 Quoted in Daniel Richter, *The Ordeal of the Longhouse: The Peoples of the Iroquois League in the Era of European Colonization*, 159.

23 'Terry Fox Top Canadian Hero: Net Poll,' *Globe and Mail* (11 July 1999): A5. However, CBC-TV's series *Canada: A People's History* does not mention Laura Secord. Her absence from the series has been noted disapprovingly by visitors to the series' website: www.cbc.ca/history/. My thanks to Nicole Woodman-Harvey for the website reference.

24 Jane Urquhart, *The Whirlpool* (1986). A dramatic adaption by Brian Quirt of Urquhart's novel, also titled *The Whirlpool*, was produced at Toronto's Tarragon Theatre, 23 February – 2 April 2000.

25 In Klunder's notes, she observes that she is related to Secord through her husband's and her father's families ('Sit Down and Take a Stand,' program for the 8th Annual PEN Benefit, 4 May 1998). Klunder has created other works of art involving Secord, including her painting *Laura Secord's Udderly Patriotic Cow* (which appeared in her exhibit Laura Secord: The Bitter Truth'). This painting was used as a cover for W.H. New, *Land Sliding: Imagining Space, Presence, and Power in Canadian Writing* (1997).

26 I would like to thank Peggy Hooke for bringing Tanglefoot's 'Secord's Warning' to my attention (*The Music in the Wood*, Tanglefoot Media, 1996). The song, sung *a capella* by male singers, speaks of Secord's bravery, not her femininity or domesticity.

27 See, for example, Connie Brummel-Crook, *Laura's Choice: The Story of Laura Secord* (1993); and Susan E. Merritt, *Her Story: Women from Canada's Past* (1994).

28 For a discussion of such narratives, see Mary Louise Pratt, *Imperial Eyes: Travel Writing and Transculturation.* Pratt describes anti-conquest as 'the strategies of representation whereby European bourgeois subjects seek to secure their innocence in the same moment as they assert European bourgeois hegemony' (7).

29 Homi Bhabha, 'Of Mimicry and Man: The Ambivalence of Colonial Discourse,' in *The Location of Culture*, 86.

30 This tendency was most pronounced in narratives of Secord's walk, in which, as we have seen, Native warriors become equated with a predatory

wilderness both before and during the Battle of Beaver Dams. William Coffin, in *1812: The War and Its Moral*, discussed the use of 'the savage' in the war; while he was attempting to defend British alliances with Aboriginals and, to some degree, Native behaviour when faced with the threat of U.S. invasion, nevertheless he demonstrated a clear belief in Natives' innate propensity to violence, with respect to which Tecumseh was an 'honourable' exception (164–5, 233–7). Natives were often described as 'children of the forest,' a description which, in the late nineteenth-century context, underlined both their closeness to nature and their reliance on instinct, not intellect and formal education; this description also reinforced their dependent status within Euro-Canadian society.

31 See Sarah Carter, *Capturing Women*.

32 Carl Benn, '1815 and Beyond,' in *The Iroquois in the War of 1812*.

33 Gerald Killan *Preserving Ontario's Heritage*, 43–4.

34 See, for example, AO, MS 193, vol. 1 (1895–1909), Reel 6, John O. Brant-Sero's speech at a meeting held 17 September 1897, 'Historical Anniversary,' n.d.; Asa R. Hill, 'The Historical Position of the Six Nations,' *OHS Papers* 19 (1922): 103–9; Evelyn H. C. Johnson, 'The Martin Settlement,' in *Some of the Papers Read during the Years 1908–11 at Meetings of the Brant Historical Society* (n.p.: BHS, 1911), 55–64; Johnson, 'Chief John Smoke Johnson,' *OHS Papers* 6 (1905): 7–11.

35 Brant County Museum, Brant Historical Society Records, Minute Book 1, 11 December 1913, 13 March 1914, 3 February 1917, 18 September 1929, 20 May and 10 June 1931, 4 July and 5 October 1933, 20 April 1937.

36 Ibid., 20 March 1935, 21 November 1939, 18 March 1941, 19 November 1947.

37 Ibid., 26 January 1937, 18 March 1941.

38 Ibid., 15 September 1948.

39 NA, MG30 C1, Vols. 1 and 2, 1846–1975.

40 Woodland Cultural and Educational Centre, Brantford, Ethel Brant Monture clipping file. Monture was also a staff member for the Canadian Council of Christians and Jews, an organization she respected 'not only because of its interest in Canadian Indians but because this interest lacks do-gooder overtones of which her people are sensitive and resentful' (Monture clipping file, Monture, 'Red Threads of Continent Society Topic,' n.d). This was the text of a talk she gave to the Etobicoke Historical Society at Montgomery's Inn.

41 Harvey Chalmers II, *West to the Setting Sun* (1965), n.p.

42 Ibid.

43 Ethel Brant Monture, *Canadian Portraits: Brant, Crowfoot, Oronhyatekah,*

Famous Indians (1960). Brant pointed out, for example, that Brant had problems with his oldest son, Isaac; she also included details on the political and social roles of women in both the Iroquois and Blackfoot confederacies (58–60, 86–7).

Bibliography

Abbreviations

ANQ-M   Archives nationales du Québec à Montréal
ANQ-Q   Archives nationales du Québec à Québec
ANQ-TR   Archives nationales du Québec à Trois-Rivières
AO   Archives of Ontario
BHS   Brant Historical Society
BUSC   Brock University Special Collections
CHR   *Canadian Historical Review*
DCB   *Dictionary of Canadian Biography*
Hs-SH   *Histoire sociale – Social History*
JoCS   *Journal of Canadian Studies*
LMHS   London and Middlesex Historical Society
NA   National Archives of Canada
NHS   Niagara Historical Society
NPC   Niagara Parks Commission
OHS   Ontario Historical Society
RHAF   *Revue d'histoire de l'Amérique française*
UEL   United Empire Loyalist
WCHS   Women's Canadian Historical Society
WHS   Wentworth Historical Society
WI   Women's Institute
WLC   Women's Literary Club of St Catharines
WWHS   Women's Wentworth Historical Society

Primary Sources

Manuscript Collections

ANQ-M, Comité du monument Dollard, P3.

ANQ-M, Fonds Béatrice Clément, P43.

ANQ-M, Fonds Marie-Claire Daveluy, P1000/1/115.

ANQ-M, Raisons sociales, TP11.

ANQ-M, Régie du cinéma, E188.

ANQ-Q, Collection des pièces judiciaires et notariales, M67.

ANQ-Q, Fonds George F. Baillairgé, P715.

ANQ-Q, Verchères-Naudière – Procès avec le curé de Batiscan, ZQ27.

ANQ-TR, Fonds de la famille Baillargé [sic], P29.

AO, Kirby Collection, Correspondence 1888–1894, MS542.

AO, Ministry of Tourism, Minister's Correspondence, 1965–73, RG5 Series A.

AO, Niagara Historical Society Minute Books, 1895–1964, MS193.

AO, Niagara Parks Commission Records, General Manager's Office Correspondence, 1893–1960, RG38–3.

AO, Niagara Parks Commission, Scrapbooks, RG38 Acc. 17741.

AO, Ontario Historical Society, Correspondence, Series C, 1898–1926, MU5422.

AO, Ontario Historical Society Scrap Albums, Series D, MU5438 and MU5441.

AO, Ontario Ministry of Education, General Administration and Correspondence Files, 1950–1974, RG 2–243.

AO, Women's Canadian Historical Society of Toronto Records, 1895–1930, F 1180.

Archives de la Chancellerie de Montréal, dossier Cinéma (campagnes de censure), 773.80.

Archives du diocèse de St-Jean-de-Québec, Ref. St.Frs.Xavier, 55.

Archives du Séminaire de Québec, Fond Verreau.

Archives du Séminaire de Trois-Rivières, Fonds Tessier, 0014-Q1–80.

Bibliothèque municipale de Montréal, Salle Gagnon, Concours littéraire Société St-Jean-Baptiste de Montréal, Lot 10, C1.

Bibliothèque municipale de Montréal, Salle Gagnon, Documents divers, Lot 2, C-50.

Bibliothèque municipale de Montréal, Salle Gagnon, Fonds de la ligue des droits de la femme, 0/8, Lot 4.

Bibliothèque nationale du Québec, Fonds Réjean Olivier, MSS-48.

Brant County Historical Museum, Brant Historical Society Records, Minute Books, 1908–1973.

BUSC, Women's Literary Club of St Catharines Collection, 1905–1973.

Centre de recherche Lionel Groulx, Fonds Joseph Gauvreau, P39.

McGill University, Osler Library of the History of Medicine, William Henry Drummond Fonds, P103.

Musée des beaux-arts de Montréal, État de la recherche, Louis-Philippe Hébert, 'Madeleine de Verchères,' 1988.3.

NA, Archives des Colonies, Collection Moreau de St-Méry, MG1.

NA, Archives des Colonies, General correspondence, Canada, MG1 Series C11A, Transcriptions.

NA, Currie Family Papers. MG27 II F5.

NA, Fonds Rodolphe Lemieux, MG27 II D10.

NA, Grey of Howick Papers, MG27 II B2.

NA, Launcelot Cressy Servos Papers, MG30 D247.

NA, National Film Archives, Hye Bossin Collection.

NA, Nouvelle-France, Archives judiciaires, MG8 B4.

NA, Nouvelle-France, Official correspondence, 3rd series, MG8 A1.

NA, Parks Canada, RG84.

NA, Picture Archives, Acc. 1984–4–13654.

National Library of Canada, Kay Pattinson, 'Commander at Fourteen.' (Typescript drama, copyright August 1955.)

Niagara Falls Library Special Collections, Jean Huggins Collection.

Ottawa City Archives, Ottawa Municipal Chapter IODE, MG43.

Queen's University Archives, Lorne Pierce Collection, Blanche Hume Papers.

Secord Company Archives, Don Mills, Ontario, Laura Secord Candy Company Scrapbooks A-C, 1913–1980s.

University of Toronto Archives, George Brown Collection, A86–044/005.

University of Western Ontario, D.B. Weldon Library, Regional Collection, Belden-Peel Papers 1880–1940.

University of Western Ontario, D.B. Weldon Library, Regional Collection, LMHS Correspondence.

Verchères, Hôtel de ville, Dossier Madeleine de Verchères, 300e anniversaire.

Woodland Cultural and Educational Centre, Brantford, Ethel Brant Monture clipping file.

Electronic, Sound, and Film Resources

The Cow That Never Was. Narrated by Pierre Berton. Screenplay by Lister Sinclair. CTV Heritage Theatre Production, 1974.

NA, National Film Archives. W. Galloway's taped interview with Arthur Larente, 3 August 1973.

NA, Sound and Visual Archives. Société Radio-Canada, CAVA 1989–0542, 'Sameditou,' 1989–09–25.
– TV Ontario and Rosebud Films, *Madeleine de Verchères*. Screenplay by Barry Pearson. French version by Marie-Hélène Fontaine. 1981. 24 minutes.
National Library of Canada. Select Phone CD-Rom.
Pellerin, Ginette, dir. *Evangeline's Quest*. National Film Board of Canada, 1996.
Tanglefoot. 'Secord's Warning.' *The Music in the Wood*. Tanglefoot Media, 1996.
www.cbc.ca/history/
www.npc@niagaraparks.com

Newspapers and Periodicals

L'Action française. 1919–26.
Le Devoir. 1912, 1923, 1922.
Globe and Mail. 1998–2000.
Niagara Advance. 1917–74.
Niagara Mail. 1861, 1868.
Nova Francia. 3 (1927–8) and 4 (1929).
Ontario Historical Society Annual Reports. 1898–1934.
Ontario Historical Society Papers. 1901–34.
La Patrie. 1922.
La Presse. 1913, 1922, 1924.
Quarter Latin. 1922.
La Revue de Manon. 1925.
St Catharines Standard. 1935, 1972, 1984.
The Times [Niagara-on-the-Lake]. 1898–1915.

Published Primary Sources

Achard, Eugène. *Les grands noms de l'histoire canadienne*. Montreal: Librairie générale canadienne, 1946.
Adair, E.R. 'Dollard des Ormeaux and the Fight at the Long Sault.' *CHR* 13, no. 2 (June 1932): 121–38.
Anburey, Thomas. *Travels through the Interior Parts of America in a Series of Letters by an Officer*. London: William Lane, 1789.
Angus, Alexander D. *Old Quebec: In the Days before Our Day*. 2nd ed. Montreal: Louis Carrier, 1955.
L'Annaliste. 'M. Rodolphe Girard: L'Homme du jour dans le domaine des lettres.' *Le monde illustré* (7 March 1903).
Armstrong, Teresa Costigan. 'The Heroine of Vercheres.' *Women's Historical Society of Ottawa: Transactions* 5 (1912): 71–9.

'As for Us We Stand by Story of Immortal Laura Secord.' *Niagara Falls Evening Review* (2 Dec. 1931).

Aubert de Gaspé, Philippe. *Mémoires.* Montreal: Fides, 1971 [1866].

Babcock, Louis L. *The War of 1812 on the Niagara Frontier.* Buffalo: n.p., 1927.

Baillairgé, F.-A. *Marie-Madeleine de Verchères et les siens.* Verchères, 1913.

– *Jeunesse et folies.* Verchères, 1925.

Bassett, John M., and A. Roy Petrie. *Laura Secord.* Don Mills, ON: Fitzhenry and Whiteside, 1974.

Bennet, Paul, Nick Brune, Cornelius Jaenen, and Cecilia Morgan. *Canada: A North American Nation.* 2nd ed. Whitby, ON: McGraw-Hill Ryerson Press, 1995.

Bibaud, Maximilien. *Les Machabées canadiens.* Montreal[?]: n.p., 1859.

Bingay, James. *A History of Canada for High Schools.* Toronto: Nelson, 1934.

Biographie universelle ancienne et moderne. Vol. 23. Paris: L.G. Michaud, 1819.

Boissonault, Mme. *L'Huis du passé.* Montreal: n.p., 1924.

Boning, Richard A. *Soldier Girl.* Baldwin, NY: Dexter & Westbrook, 1975.

Bourassa, Henri. *Femmes-hommes ou hommes et femmes? Études à bâtons rompus sur le féminisme.* Montreal: Imprimerie du Devoir, 1925.

Braun, Esther. *A Quebec Sketch Book.* Quebec: Chateau Frontenac, 1925.

Brodeur, Madame Donat. 'Deux héroïnes de la Nouvelle-France.' *Canadian Antiquarian* 3rd series, 5 (1908): 64–72.

Brown, George W. *Building the Canadian Nation.* Toronto: J.M. Dent, 1942.

Brown, George W., Eleanor Harman, and Marsh Jeanneret. *The Story of Canada.* Toronto: Copp Clark, 1950.

– *Canada in North America to 1800.* Toronto: University of Toronto Press, 1961.

– *Canada in North America 1800–1901.* Toronto: University of Toronto Press, 1961.

Bruchési, Jean. 'Madeleine de Verchères et Chicaneau.' *Les cahiers des dix* 11 (1946): 25–51.

Brunet, R. 'Chronique européenne.' *Le monde illustré* 14 (1897–8): 68–70.

Cerbelaud-Salagnac, Georges. *Mademoiselle de Verchères.* Montreal and Paris: Fides, 1958.

Cézembre, Jacques. 'Les romans de la vie: Madeleine de Verchères, la Jeanne Hachette canadienne.' *Dimanche-illustré* (14 Sept. 1930).

Chafe, J.W. *Canada, Your Country.* Toronto: Ryerson Press, 1950.

Chapman, William. *Les Quebecquoises.* Quebec: C. Daveau, 1876.

Charlevoix, P.-F.-X. de. *Histoire et description générale de la Nouvelle France.* Paris: Rollin fils, 1744.

Clio Collective. *Quebec Women: A History.* Trans. Roger Gannon and Rosalind Gill. Toronto: The Women's Press, 1987.

Coffin, William F. *1812: The War and Its Moral: A Canadian Chronicle.* Montreal: n.p., 1864.

Colby, Charles. *Canadian Types of the Old Régime, 1608–1698.* New York: Henry Holt and Co., 1908.

Coté, Jean. *Madeleine de Verchères: L'Intrépide 'Magdelon.'* Outremont: Les Éditions Quebecor, 1995.

Creighton, Luella Bruce. *Canada: The Struggle for Empire.* Toronto: J. M. Dent, 1960.

Crook, Connie Brummel. *Laura's Choice: The Story of Laura Secord.* Winnipeg: Windflower Communications, 1993.

Cruikshank, Ernest. *The Fight in the Beechwoods.* Welland: W.T. Sawle, 1895.

Currie, Emma A. *The Story of Laura Secord and Canadian Reminiscences.* St Catharines: n.p., 1900.

Curzon, Sarah. *The Story of Laura Secord 1813.* Welland: Telegraph Print, 1898.

Dainville, D. [Gustave Bossange]. *Beautés de l'histoire du Canada.* Paris: Bossange frères Libraires, 1821.

Daniel, François. *Histoire des grandes familles françaises.* Montreal: E. Senécal, 1867.

Daveluy, Marie-Claire. *Aux feux de la rampe.* Montreal: Bibliothèque de l'Action française, 1927.

Davidson, Ida M. *The Capture of Quebec and Madeline de Vercheres.* Winnipeg: Manitoba Text Book Bureau, 1929.

Dawson, Rev. Aen. McD. 'The Heroine of Vercheres.' *Canadian Antiquarian and Numismatic Journal* 6 (1878): 142–5.

de Ferron, Thérèse. 'Une héroïne de la Nouvelle-France: Marie-Madeleine de Verchères.' *Revue hebdomadaire* (4 Oct. 1924).

de Kastner, Frédéric. *Héros de la Nouvelle France.* Québec: La Cie d'Imprimerie Commerciale, 1902.

de la Chatre, P. 'L'Héroïne de Verchères.' *Le Nouvelliste des Trois-Rivières* (8 Aug. 1929).

de Roquebrune, Robert. *Les canadiens d'autrefois: Essais.* Montreal: Fides, 1962.

Denison, Merrill. 'Laura Secord.' In *Henry Hudson and Other Plays: Six Plays for the Microphone from the Romance of Canada Series of Radio Plays.* Toronto: Ryerson Press, 1931.

Dickie, D.J. *In Pioneer Days: Dent's Canadian History Readers.* Toronto: J.M. Dent, n.d.

Dickie, D.J., and Helen Palk. *Pages from Canada's Story.* Toronto: J.M. Dent, 1932.

Dickie, Donalda. *Pages from Canada's Story: Selections from the Canadian History Readers.* Toronto: J.M. Dent, 1947.

– *The Great Adventure: An Illustrated History of Canada for Young Canadians.*
Toronto: J.M. Dent, 1950.

Dionne, N.E. 'Une héroïne canadienne.' *La Kermesse: Revue hebdomadaire* 6
(28 Oct. 1892).

Dorland, Arthur. *Our Canada.* Toronto: Copp Clark, 1949.

Doughty, Arthur. *A Daughter of New France: Being a Story of the Life and Times of
Magdeleine de Verchères, 1665–1692.* Ottawa: Mortimer Press, 1916.

Doughty, Arthur, and William Wood. *The King's Book of Quebec.* Ottawa: The
Mortimer Co., 1911.

Douglas, James. 'The Status of Women in New England and New France.'
Queen's Quarterly 19, no. 4 (April-May-June 1912): 359–74.

Drevet, Marie-X. 'Une héroïne de la Nouvelle-France: Marie-Madeleine de
Verchères.' *Le Dauphiné* [Grenoble] 3520 (19 Oct. 1924): 143–4.

Drummond, William Henry. *Phil-o-rum's Canoe and Madeleine Vercheres.* New
York: G.P. Putnam's Sons, 1898.

Du Bois, Mary Constance. 'Captain Madeleine (Wild Flower of Chivalry).' *St
Nicholas Magazine* (June 1928).

Duncan, David M. *The Story of the Canadian People.* Toronto: Morang, 1907.

Dyell, Edith. *Canada: A New Land.* Toronto: W.J. Gage, 1958.

– *Canada: The New Nation.* Toronto: W.J. Gage, 1960.

Eayrs, Hugh S. *Sir Isaac Brock.* Toronto: Macmillan, 1924.

Edgar, Matilda. *The Makers of Canada: General Brock.* Morang, 1904.

Falardeau, Claude. *Des Zéroquois aux Québécois.* Montreal: Les Presses Libres,
1969.

Fidélité à Ville-Marie: Récits et légendes. Montreal: La Société des écrivains
canadiens, 1942.

FitzGibbon, Mary Agnes. 'An Historic Banner: A Paper Read on February 8th,
1896.' *Transaction No. 1 WCHS.* Toronto: William Briggs, 1896.

'Fleur de Lys: Page littéraire empruntée au drame de M. Rodolphe Girard.' *Le
monde illustré* (7 March 1903).

Fréchette, Louis. *La légende d'un peuple.* Trois-Rivières: Écrits des forges, 1989
[1887].

Frémont, J. 'Notice sur Mademoiselle de Verchères.' *Annuaire de l'Institut
canadien de Québec* 12 (1888): 69–72.

French, Donald G., ed. *Famous Canadian Stories Re-told for Boys and Girls.* New ed.
Toronto: McClelland and Stewart, 1931.

– *Famous Canadian Stories: The Romance of Discovery, Exploration and Development.*
Toronto: McClelland and Stewart, 1945.

Gagnon, Philéas. 'Le curé Lefebvre et l'héroïne de Verchères.' *Bulletin de
recherches historiques* 6 (1900): 340–5.

Garland, Aileen. *Canada, Then and Now.* Toronto: Macmillan, 1954.

– *Canada, Our Country.* Toronto: Macmillan, 1961.

Garneau, F.-X. *Histoire du Canada depuis sa découverte jusqu'à nos jours.* 2nd ed. Quebec: John Lovell, 1852.

– *Additions à l'histoire du Canada de F.X. Garneau.* Quebec: n.p., 1864.

– *Histoire du Canada depuis sa découverte jusqu'à nos jours.* 8th ed. Revised and expanded by Hector Garneau. Montreal: Éditions de l'Arbre, 1944.

Gélinas, Abbé J.-G. *En veillant avec les petits de chez nous au foyer: Causeries historiques.* Vol. 1. Montreal: Librairie Granger Frères, 1928 [1915].

Gerbié, Frédéric. *Le Canada et l'immigration française.* Quebec[?]: n.p., 1884.

Gosselin, David. *Tablettes chronologiques et alphabétiques des principaux événements de l'histoire du Canada.* Quebec: J.A. Langlais, 1887.

Grant, George M. *French Canadian Life and Character.* Chicago: A. Belford, 1899.

Grant, Janet. *Madeleine de Verchères.* Toronto: Grolier Limited, 1989.

Grant, W.L. *Ontario High School History of Canada.* Toronto: T. Eaton Co., 1914.

Groulx, Lionel. *Chez nos ancêtres.* 2nd ed. Montreal: Bibliothèque de l'Action française, 1920.

– *Le dossier de Dollard: La valeur des sources, la grandeur du dessein, la grandeur des résultats.* Montreal: L'Imprimerie Populaire, 1932.

– *Notre maître, le passé.* 1st series. 2nd ed. Montreal: Librairie Granger Frères, 1937 [1924].

– *Notre maître, le passé.* 3rd series. Montreal: Librairie Granger Frères, 1944.

– *Mes mémoires.* Vols 1–2. Montreal: Fides, 1970–1.

Guillet, Edwin C., and Jessie E. McEwen. *Finding New Homes in Upper Canada.* Toronto: Thomas Nelson and Sons, 1938.

Harris, G.G. *Canadian History Workbook.* Toronto: Ryerson Press, 1930.

Henri, I.S., arrangement and words. *Madeleine de Verchères.* 1929.

Hodent, M. 'Philippe Hébert: Le maître de la sculpture canadienne.' *La Canadienne* [Paris] 11, no. 9 (Sept. 1913).

Hume, Blanche. *Laura Secord.* Toronto: Ryerson, 1928.

'I.O.D.E. Historical Pageant.' *Saturday Night* (2 July 1927).

Jebb, Richard. *Studies in Colonial Nationalism.* London: Edward Arnold, 1905.

Jeffers, J. Frith. *History of Canada.* Toronto: Canada Publishing Co., 1879 and 1894.

Kames, Lord (Henry Home). *Sketches of the History of Man.* 2nd ed. Edinburgh: William Creech, 1788.

Karr, W.J. *Explorers, Soldiers, and Statesmen: The History of Canada through Biography.* Toronto: J.M. Dent, 1929.

– *Explorers, Soldiers, and Statesmen: The History of Canada through Biography.* Rev. ed. Toronto: J.M. Dent, 1937.

Kenney, Morgan. *Madeleine de Verchères: Héroïne canadienne.* Toronto: D.C. Heath, 1989.

La Potherie, C.-C. Le Roy de. *Histoire de l'Amérique septentrionale.* Paris: Nyon fils, 1722.

Lacoursière, Jacques. 'La véridique histoire de Madeleine de Verchères et son curé ...' *L'Actualité* 1, no. 3 (Nov. 1976).

Lamarche, Jacques. *Madeleine, héroïne de Verchères, seigneuresse de La Pérade.* Montreal: Lidec, 1997.

Lanctot, Gustave. 'Was Dollard the Saviour of New France?' *CHR* 13, no. 2 (June 1932): 138–46.

Larrieu, Albert. *Madeleine de Verchères.* Montreal: Éditions Archambault, n.d.

'Laura Secord.' *Anglo-American Magazine* 8, no. 5 (1853): 467.

'Laura Secord's Key?' *Niagara Falls Evening Review* (15 Dec. 1931).

Laviolette, Guy. *Marie-Madeleine de Verchères: Châtelaine de la Pérade, 1678–1747.* Quebec: Gloires nationales, 1944.

Lefebvre, Marie-Thérèse. *La création musicale des femmes au Québec.* Montreal: Les éditions du remue-ménage, 1991.

LeMoine, J.M. *Les héroïnes de la Nouvelle-France.* Trans. from English. Lowell, MS: Raoul Renault, 1888.

Lessard, Michel. 'Déficit 1642–1992 ou le programme des festivités du 350e de Montréal.' *Croc* 118 (May 1989).

Linderholm, Helmer. *Riddarna och de röda. Madelon* i. Stockholm: Tidens Förlag, 1981.

– *I de rödas krig. Madelon* ii. Stockholm: Tidens Förlag, 1982.

– *Fredens hemliga Stig. Madelon* iii. Stockholm: Tidens Förlag, 1983.

Livesey, Robert. *Footprints in the Snow: The Heroes and Heroines of Canada.* Mississauga: Little Brick Schoolhouse, 1978.

Lossing, Benson. *The Pictorial Field Book of the War of 1812.* New York: n.p., 1869.

Lower, Arthur R.M. *Colony to Nation: A History of Canada.* 4th ed. Toronto: Longmans Canada, 1964 [1946].

Machar, Agnes Maule, and Thomas G. Marquis. *Stories of New France: Being Tales of Adventure and Heroism from the Early History of Canada.* Boston: D. Lothrop Company, 1890.

'Madeleine de Verchères.' *L'Action catholique* (8 Feb. 1923).

'Madeleine de Verchères.' *Le Droit* (19 Feb.–4 March 1936).

Mariel, Pierre. *Une héroïne canadienne.* Paris: André Bonne, 1967.

Marie-Victorin, Frère. *Peuple sans histoire: Fantaisie dramatique en un acte et trois tableaux.* Montreal: Les Frères des Ecoles chrétiennes, 1937.

Marmette, Joseph. *Héroïsme et trahison: Récits canadiens.* Montreal: Librairie Beauchemin, 1930.

Marsh, E[dith]. L. *The Story of Canada.* London: Thomas Nelson and Sons, 1913.

Marshall, H.E. *Our Empire Story.* Edinburgh: T. & A. Constable, n.d.

– *Canada's Story Told to Boys and Girls.* London: T.C. and E.C. Jack, 1920[?].

Masse, Denis. 'Quatre héros légendaires.' *La Presse* (5 Sept. 1992).

McIlwraith, J.N. *The Children's Study, Canada.* Toronto: Wm. Briggs, 1899.

McKenzie, Ruth. *Laura Secord: The Legend and the Lady.* Toronto: McClelland and Stewart, 1971.

McKinley, Mabel Burns. *Canadian Heroines of Pioneer Days.* Toronto: Longmans, Green & Co., 1929.

Merritt, Susan E. *Her Story: Women from Canada's Past.* St Catharines: Vanwell Publishing, 1994.

Middleton, J.E. *The Romance of Ontario.* Toronto: W.J. Gage, 1931.

Miller, J.O. *Brief Biographies Supplementing Canadian History.* Toronto: Copp Clark, 1902.

Monture, Ethel Brant. *Canadian Portraits: Brant, Crowfoot, Oronhyatekah, Famous Indians.* Toronto: Clarke Irwin, 1960.

Morgan, Henry James, ed. *Types of Canadian Women and of Women Who Are or Have Been Connected with Canada.* Vol. 1. Toronto: William Briggs, 1903.

Morgan, Joan Elson. *Castle of Quebec.* Toronto: J.M. Dent, 1949.

Morrison, Grace. *Vignettes d'histoire du Canada, les premières années: Magdelaine de Verchères.* Markham: Fitzhenry & Whiteside, 1989.

Mournaud, Mlle Françoise. *Les Allobroges au Canada (suivi de relation des faits historiques de Mlle Marie-Magdeleine de Verchère).* Blois: J. de Grandpré, 1935.

Munro, William Bennett, ed. *Documents Relating to the Seigniorial Tenure in Canada, 1598–1854.* Toronto: The Champlain Society, 1908.

'Of Course the Story of Laura Secord Is True.' *Niagara Falls Evening Review* (4 Dec. 1931).

Ontario Public School History of Canada. Toronto: Morang, 1910.

'Ontario Schools Remove Textbook after Mohawk Complains of Racism.' *Montreal Gazette* (12 Dec. 1992).

Paddock, C.L. *Golden Stories for Boys and Girls.* Oshawa: Canadian Watchman Press, 1934.

Parkman, Francis. *Count Frontenac and New France under Louis XIV.* Vol. 2. New York: Library of America, 1983 [1877].

Paterson, Gilbert. *The Story of Our People.* Toronto: Ryerson Press, 1933.

Pearson, Lester B. *Mike: The Memoirs of the Right Honourable Lester B. Pearson, Vol. 1, 1897–1948.* Toronto: University of Toronto Press, 1972.

Pepper, Mary Sifton. *Maids and Matrons of New France.* Toronto: George N. Morang & Co., 1902.

Price-Brown, John. *Laura the Undaunted: A Canadian Historical Romance.* Toronto: Ryerson Press, 1930.

Prince Edward Island. Department of Education. *Annual Report.* Examination Papers. 1917–1957.

Programme souvenir 1710–1960: 250e anniversaire, Paroisse Saint-François-Xavier, Verchères, Québec. Saint-Jean: Edition du Richelieu Ltée [1960].

Quaife, Milo M., ed. *The John Askin Papers, Volume II.* Detroit: n.p., 1931.

'Questions.' *Bulletin de recherches historiques* 6 (1900): 160.

Rapport de l'archiviste de la Province de Québec (1927–8).

Raymond, E[thel] T. *Madeleine de Verchères.* Toronto: Ryerson Press, 1929.

Read, D.B. *The Life and Times of Major-General Sir Isaac Brock, K.B.* Toronto: Wm. Briggs, 1914.

Reade, John. *Madeleine de Vercheres.* Toronto: Copp Clark Co., 1890.

Renault, Raoul. 'Une héroïne canadienne.' *La Revue canadienne* 31 (1895): 347.

Richard, Édouard, ed. *Supplement to Dr. Brymner's Report on Canadian Archives by Mr. Édouard Richard (1899).* Ottawa: King's Printer, 1901.

Roberts, Charles G. D. *A History of Canada for High Schools and Academies.* Toronto: Morang, 1905.

Robertson, W. J. *Public Story History of England and Canada.* Toronto: Copp Clark, 1892.

Rocheleau, Corinne. *Françaises d'Amérique: Esquisse historique.* Worcester, MS: La compagnie de publication Belisle, 1915.

Roy, J.-Edmond. 'Madeleine de Verchères.' In Pierre-Georges Roy, *La Famille Tarieu de Lanaudière,* 175–203. Lévis: n.p., 1922.

Roy, Pierre-Georges. 'Madeleine de Verchères, plaideuse.' *Transactions de la Société Royale du Canada,* 3rd series, 15 (1921): 63–72.

– *Les monuments commémoratifs de la Province de Québec.* Québec: Louis-A. Proulx, 1923.

– ed., *Un procès criminel à Québec au dix-septième siècle: Anne Edmond accusée de s'être travestie en homme et d'avoir répandu de fausses nouvelles.* Lévis: Bulletin de recherches historiques, 1904.

Roy, Régis. 'Une vaillante canadienne.' *Le monde illustré* (21 Oct. 1893): 296–7.

Schecter, Barbara, and Marina Jimenez. 'War of 1812 Heroine Laura Secord Heading South.' *National Post* (3 June 1999): A11.

Secord, Chas. B. *The Church* (11 April 1845).

Secord, Laura. *Anglo-American Magazine* 8, no. 5 (1853): 467.

Skelton, Isabel. *The Backwoodswoman.* Toronto: Ryerson Press, 1924.

Some of the Papers Read during the Years 1908–11 at Meetings of the Brant Historical Society. n.p.: BHS, 1911.

Spence, Nellie. *Topical Studies in Canadian History.* Toronto: Chas. J. Musson, 1897.

Stephens, Alexander Maitland. *Classroom Plays from Canadian History.* Toronto: J.M. Dent, 1929.

'Story of Laura Secord Will Be Told in School Books, Says Henry.' *Niagara Falls Evening Review* (9 Jan. 1932).

Sullivan, Alan. 'Madeleine Verchères.' In Ontario Women's Liberal Association, *Hearts of Gold: Being Chronicles of Heroism in Canadian History.* Toronto: Globe Printing Co., 1915.

Sulte, Benjamin. 'Report of the French Secretary.' *The Historical Landmarks Association of Canada, Annual Report* (1915).

Swain, Sabrina. *The Story of Laura Secord and Fanny Doyle – Their Zeal, Patriotism, and Sacrifices during the Days of the War of 1812.* 3rd ed. Buffalo: n.p., 1928.

Symonds, Norman, with students from King George Senior Public School, Guelph. *Laura and the Lieutenant: A Musical Play.* Toronto: E.C. Kerby, 1976.

T.G. 'Magdelon la Canadienne.' *Le Temps* (14 Aug. 1912).

Therriault, Sister Mary Carmel, s.m. *Madeleine de Vercheres.* Boston: Catholic Language Workbooks, 1951.

Thompson, Elizabeth. 'Laura Ingersoll Secord.' *Niagara Historical Society Papers* 25 (1912).

Tremblay, Laurent. o.m.i. *Madeleine de Verchères: Un récit pour le Roi.* Montreal: Rayonnement, 1957.

Tremblay-Matte, Cécile. *La chanson écrite au féminin, 1730–1990: De Madeleine de Verchères à Mitsou.* Laval: Éditions Trois, 1990.

Vachon, André. 'Jarret de Verchères, Marie-Madeleine.' *DCB.* Vol. iii: 308–13.

Vidal, Nicole. *La Nuit des Iroquois.* Paris: Éditions de l'amitié-G.T. Rageot, 1983.

Ville, Léon. *Madeleine de Verchères: Une héroïne canadienne.* Paris: Tolra éditeur, 1928.

Wallace, W.S. *A First Book of Canadian History.* Toronto: Macmillan, 1928.

– *A History of the Canadian People.* Toronto: Copp Clark, 1930.

– *The Story of Laura Secord.* Toronto: Macmillan, 1932.

Weaver, Emily P. *A Canadian History for Boys and Girls.* Toronto: Wm. Briggs, 1905.

Wetherell, J.E., and Charles W. Jefferys. *Handbook to Nelson's Pictures of Canadian History.* Toronto: Thomas Nelson and Sons, 1927.

'What Laura Secord Did.' *Dunnville Weekly Chronicle* (1935).

Withrow, William H. *A History of Canada for the Use of Schools and General Readers.* Toronto: Copp Clark, 1876.

Wood, William, ed. *Select British Documents of the Canadian War of 1812*. Toronto: n.p., 1920.

Wrong, George, and Chester Martin. *The Story of Canada*. Toronto: Ryerson Press, 1930.

Yeigh, Frank. 'A Pilgrimage along the Historic Niagara.' *The Globe* (1 July 1899).

Young, Katherine. *Stories of the Maple Land: Tales of the Early Days of Canada for Children*. Toronto: Copp Clark, 1898.

Secondary Sources

Agulhon, Maurice. *Marianne into Battle: Republican Imagery and Symbolism in France, 1789–1880*. Trans. Janet Lloyd. Cambridge: Cambridge University Press, 1981.

Akenson, Donald H. *The Irish in Ontario: A Study in Rural History*. Montreal: McGill-Queen's University Press, 1984.

Anderson, Benedict. *Imagined Communities: Reflections on the Origin and Spread of Nationalism*. 2nd ed. London: Verso, 1991.

Apple, Michael W., and Linda K. Christian-Smith, eds. *The Politics of the Textbook*. London: Routledge, 1991.

Atwood, Margaret. *Strange Things: The Malevolent North in Canadian Literature*. Oxford: Clarendon Press, 1995.

Bathrick, Serafina. 'The Female Colossus: The Body as Façade and Threshold.' In *Fabrications: Costume and the Female Body*, ed. Jane Gaines and Charlotte Herzog. London: Routledge, 1990.

Benn, Carl. *The Iroquois in the War of 1812*. Toronto: University of Toronto Press, 1998.

Berger, Carl. *The Sense of Power: Studies in the Ideas of Canadian Imperialism 1867–1914*. Toronto: University of Toronto Press, 1970.

– *The Writing of Canadian History: Aspects of English-Canadian Historical Writing, 1900–1970*. Toronto: Oxford University Press, 1976.

– 'The True North Strong and Free.' In *Interpreting Canada's Past*. Vol. 2. *After Confederation*, ed. J.M. Bumsted. Toronto: Oxford University Press, 1986.

Best, John C. *Thomas Baker McQuesten: Public Works, Politics, and Imagination*. Hamilton: Corinth Press, 1991.

Bhabha, Homi K. *The Location of Culture*. London: Routledge, 1994.

– ed. *Nation and Narration*. London: Routledge, 1990.

Billig, Michael. *Banal Nationalism*. London: Sage Publications, 1995.

Blain, Jean. 'La moralité en Nouvelle France: Les phases de la thèse et de l'antithèse.' *RHAF* 27, no. 3 (Dec. 1973): 408–16.

Bodnar, John. *Remaking America: Public Memory, Commemoration, and Patriotism in the Twentieth Century.* Princeton: Princeton University Press, 1992.

Boutilier, Beverly, and Alison Prentice, eds. *Creating Historical Memory: English-Canadian Women and the Work of History.* Vancouver: University of British Columbia Press, 1997.

Brandão, José António. *'Your Fyre Shall Burn No More': Iroquois Policy toward New France and Its Native Allies to 1701.* Lincoln: University of Nebraska Press, 1997.

Brouwer, Ruth Compton. 'Moral Nationalism in Victorian Canada: The Case of Agnes Machar.' *JoCS* 20, no. 1 (Spring 1985): 90–108.

Brown, Dona. *Inventing New England: Regional Tourism in the Nineteenth Century.* Washington, DC: Smithsonian Press, 1995.

Burton, Antoinette. *Burdens of History: British Feminists, Indian Women, and Imperial Culture, 1865–1915.* Chapel Hill: University of North Carolina Press, 1994.

– 'Who Needs the Nation? Interrogating "British" History.' *Journal of Historical Sociology* 10, no. 3 (Sept. 1997): 228–48.

Cadogan, Mary, and Patricia Craig. *You're a Brick, Angela! A New Look at Girls' Fiction from 1839 to 1975.* London: Victor Gollancz, 1976.

Campbell, Sandra. 'From Romantic History to Communications' Theory: Lorne Pierce as Publisher of C.W. Jefferys and Harold Innis.' *JoCS.* 30, no. 3 (Fall 1995): 91–116.

Carter, Sarah. *Capturing Women: The Manipulation of Cultural Imagery in Canada's Prairie West.* Montreal: McGill-Queen's University Press, 1997.

Charlebois-Dirschauer, Madeleine. *Rodolphe Girard (1879–1956): Sa vie, son œuvre.* Montreal: Fides, 1986.

Chevalier, Jacques. 'Myth and Ideology in "Traditional" French Canada: Dollard, the Martyred Warrior.' *Anthropologica.* n.s. 21, 2 (1979): 143–75.

Choquette, Leslie. *Frenchmen into Peasants: Modernity and Tradition in the Peopling of French Canada.* Cambridge: Harvard University Press, 1997.

Coates, Colin M. 'Authority and Illegitimacy in New France: The Burial of Bishop Saint-Vallier and Madeleine de Verchères vs. the Priest of Batiscan.' *Hs-SH.* 22, no. 43 (May 1989): 65–90.

Cohen, Marjorie. *Women's Work, Markets, and Economic Development in Nineteenth-Century Ontario.* Toronto: University of Toronto Press, 1988.

Cohen, William. 'Symbols of Power: Statues in Nineteenth-Century Provincial France.' *Comparative Studies in Society and History* 31 (1989): 491–513.

Confino, Alon. 'Collective Memory and Cultural History: Problems of Method.' *American Historical Review* 102, no. 5 (Dec. 1997): 1386–403.

Cook, Ramsay. *The Maple Leaf Forever: Essays on Nationalism and Politics in Canada.* Toronto: Macmillan, 1971.

Craig, Gerald M. *Upper Canada: The Formative Years 1784–1841.* Toronto: McClelland and Stewart, 1963.

Cupido, Robert. '"Sixty Years of Canadian Progress": The Diamond Jubilee and the Politics of Commemoration.' *Canadian Issues* 20 (1998): 19–33.

Curtis, Bruce. 'Schoolbooks and the Myth of Curricular Republicanism: The State and the Curriculum in Canada West.' *Hs-SH* 16, no. 32 (Sept. 1983): 305–29.

Davis, Natalie Zemon. *Society and Culture in Early Modern France.* Stanford: Stanford University Press, 1975.

– *Women on the Margins.* Cambridge: Harvard University Press, 1995.

Dechêne, Louise. *Habitants and Merchants in Seventeenth-Century Montreal.* Trans. Liana Vardi. Montreal: McGill-Queen's University Press, 1992.

Dekker, Rudolf M., and Lotte C. van de Pol. 'Republican Heroines: Cross-Dressing Women in the French Revolutionary Armies.' *History of European Ideas* 10, no. 3 (1989): 353–63.

Dickinson, J.A. 'Annaotaha et Dollard vus de l'autre côté de la palissade.' *RHAF* 35, no. 2 (1981): 163–78.

– 'La conception populaire de la tenure.' In *Évolution et éclatement du monde rural,* ed. Joseph Goy and Jean-Pierre Wallot, 162–72. Montreal: Presses de l'Université de Montréal, 1986.

Dubinsky, Karen. *'The Second Biggest Disappointment': Honeymooning and Tourism at Niagara Falls.* Toronto: Between the Lines Press, 1999.

Duffy, Dennis. 'Upper Canadian Loyalism: What the Textbooks Tell.' *JoCS.* 12, no. 2 (Spring 1977): 17–26.

– *Gardens, Covenants, Exiles: Loyalism in the Literature of Upper Canada/Ontario.* Toronto: University of Toronto Press, 1982.

Dugaw, Dianne. 'Balladry's Female Warriors: Women, Warfare, and Disguise in the Eighteenth Century.' *Eighteenth-Century Life* 9, no. 2 (Jan. 1985): 1–20.

Dupré, Céline. 'Jarret de Verchères, Pierre.' In *DCB.* Vol. ii: 295–6.

Dyer, Richard. *White.* London: Routledge, 1997.

Edensor, Tim. 'Reading Braveheart: Representing and Contesting Scottish Identity.' *Scottish Affairs* 21 (Autumn 1997): 135–58.

Edwards, Mary Jane. 'Drummond, William Henry.' In *DCB.* Vol. xiii: 284–6.

English, John. *Shadow of Heaven: The Life of Lester Pearson, Volume One: 1897–1948.* London: Vintage, 1989.

Errington, Elizabeth Jane. *Wives and Mothers, School Mistresses and Scullery Maids: Working Women in Upper Canada 1790–1840.* Montreal: McGill-Queen's University Press, 1995.

Francis, Daniel. *The Imaginary Indian: The Image of the Indian in Canadian Culture.* Vancouver: Arsenal Pulp Press, 1992.

– *National Dreams: Myth, Memory, and Canadian History.* Vancouver: Arsenal Pulp Press, 1997.

Fraser, Antonia. *The Warrior Queens.* New York: Alfred A Knopf, 1989.

Frégault, Guy. *Le XVIIIe siècle canadien: Études.* Montreal: Éditions HMH, 1968.

Furuland, Lars, et al. *Ungdomslitteraturen: Historik, kommentarer, texturval.* Stockholm: Rabén & Sjögren, 1994.

Gagnon, Serge. *Le Québec et ses historiens de 1840 à 1920.* Quebec: Presses de l'Université Laval, 1978.

Garber, Marjorie. *Vested Interests: Cross-Dressing and Cultural Anxiety.* New York: Harper Collins, 1993.

Garvey, Ellen Gruber. *The Adman in the Parlor: Magazines and the Gendering of Consumer Culture, 1880s-1930s.* Oxford: Oxford University Press, 1996.

Geller, Peter. '"Hudson's Bay Company Indians": Images of Native People and the Red River Pageant, 1920.' In *Dressing in Feathers: The Construction of the Indian in American Popular Culture,* ed. S. Elizabeth Bird. New York: Westview Press, 1996.

Gelly, Alain, Louise Brunelle-Lavoie, and Corneliu Kirjan. *La passion du patrimoine: La Commission des Biens Culturels du Québec, 1922–1994.* Sillery: Septentrion, 1995.

Gervais, Diane, and Serge Lusignan. 'De Jeanne d'Arc à Madeleine de Verchères: La femme guerrière dans la société d'Ancien Régime.' *RHAF* 53, no. 2 (Automn 1999): 171–205.

Gignac-Pharand, Elvine. 'L'Évolution de la littérature de jeunesse au Canada français.' *Cultures du Canada français* 3 (1986): 5–17.

Gildea, Robert. *The Past in French History.* New Haven: Yale University Press, 1994.

Gillis, John R., ed. *Commemorations: The Politics of National Identity.* Princeton: Princeton University Press, 1994.

Glassberg, David. *American Historical Pageantry: The Uses of Tradition in the Early Twentieth Century.* Chapel Hill: University of North Carolina Press, 1990.

Gordon, Alan. 'Contested Terrain: The Politics of Public Memory in Montreal, 1891–1930.' Ph.D. thesis, Queen's University, 1997.

Granatstein, J.L. *Who Killed Canadian History?* Toronto: Harper Collins, 1998.

Greer, Allan. *The Patriots and the People: The Rebellion of 1837 in Rural Lower Canada.* Toronto: University of Toronto Press, 1993.

– *The People of New France.* Toronto: University of Toronto Press, 1997.

Grewal, Inderpal. *Home and Harem: Nation, Gender, Empire, and the Cultures of Travel.* Durham, NC: Duke University Press, 1996.

Griffiths, Naomi. 'Longfellow's *Evangeline*: The Birth and Acceptance of a Legend.' *Acadiensis* 11, no. 2 (Spring 1982): 28–41.

Groulx, Patrice. 'Entre histoire et commémoration: L'Itinéraire Dollard de l'abbé Groulx.' *Les cahiers d'histoire du Québec au xxe siècle* 8 (1997): 22–35.

– *Pièges de la mémoire: Dollard des Ormeaux, les Amérindiens et nous.* Hull: Asticou, 1998.

Guilbault, Nicole. *Il était cent fois La Corriveau: Anthologie.* Quebec: Nuit blanche, 1995.

Hall, Catherine, Jane Lewis, Keith McClelland, and Jane Rendall. 'Introduction.' *Gender and History: Special Issue on Gender, Nationalisms, and National Identities* 5, no. 2 (Summer 1993): 159–64.

Handler, Richard. 'On Having a Culture: Nationalism and the Preservation of Quebec's *Patrimoine.*' In *Objects and Others: Essays on Museums and Material Culture*, ed. George W. Stocking, Jr. Madison: University of Wisconsin Press, 1985.

Hanna, Martha. 'Iconology and Ideology: Images of Joan of Arc in the Idiom of the *Action française*, 1908–1931.' *French Historical Studies.* 14, no. 2 (Fall 1985): 215–39.

Hathorn, Ramon. *Sarah Bernhardt's Canadian Visits.* Canada House Lecture Series, no. 52. London: Canada House, 1992.

Hayward, Susan. *French National Cinema.* London: Routledge, 1993.

Heathorn, Stephen. '"Let us remember that we, too, are English": Constructions of Citizenship and National Identity in English Elementary School Reading Books, 1880–1914.' *Victorian Studies* 39 (Spring 1995): 395–427.

Heilbrun, Carolyn. *Writing a Woman's Life.* New York: Ballantyne Books, 1988.

Heron, Craig. 'The High School and the Household Economy in Working-Class Hamilton, 1890–1940.' *Historical Studies in Education* 7, no. 2 (1995): 217–59.

Hobsbawm, Eric, and Terence Ranger, eds. *The Invention of Tradition.* Cambridge: Cambridge University Press, 1983.

Hufton, Olwen. *The Prospect before Her: A History of Women in Western Europe.* Vol. 1. *1500–1800.* London: Fontana, 1997.

Hughes-Hallett, Lucy. *Cleopatra: Histories, Dreams and Distortions.* London: Bloomsbury, 1990.

Jameson, Sheilagh S. *Chautauqua in Canada.* Calgary: Glenbow-Alberta Institute, 1979.

Jasen, Patricia. *Wild Things: Nature, Culture, and Tourism in Ontario 1790–1914.* Toronto: University of Toronto Press, 1995.

Jean, Marcel. *Le cinéma québécois.* Montreal: Éditions du Boréal, 1991.

Kammen, Michael. *Mystic Chords of Memory: The Transformation of Tradition in American Culture.* New York: Vintage Books, 1993.

Kasson, Joy. *Marble Queens and Captives: Women in Nineteenth-Century American Sculpture.* New Haven: Yale University Press, 1990.

Killan, Gerald. *Preserving Ontario's Heritage: A History of the Ontario Historical Society.* Ottawa: Ontario Historical Society, 1976.

Klinck, Carl F., et al., eds. *Literary History of Canada: Canadian Literature in English.* 2nd ed. Vol. I. Toronto: University of Toronto Press, 1976.

Knowles, Norman. *Inventing the Loyalists: The Ontario Loyalist Tradition and the Creation of Usable Pasts.* Toronto: University of Toronto Press, 1997.

Krumeich, Gerd. 'Joan of Arc: Between Right and Left.' In *Nationhood and Nationalism in France: From Boulangism to the Great War, 1889–1918,* ed. Robert Tombs. London: Harper Collins Academic, 1991.

Lacasse, Germain. *Histoires des scopes (Le cinéma muet au Québec).* Montreal: Cinématèque québécoise, 1988.

Lears, T.J. Jackson. *No Place of Grace: Antimodernism and the Transformation of American Culture, 1880–1920.* Chicago: University of Chicago Press, 1982.

Lever, Yves. *Histoire générale du cinéma au Québec.* Montreal: Boréal, 1995.

Lévesque, Andrée. *La norme et les déviantes: Des femmes au Québec pendant l'entre-deux-guerres.* Montreal: Les éditions du remue-ménage, 1989.

Lewis, Norah. *'I want to join your club': Letters from Rural Children, 1900–1920.* Kitchener, ON: Wilfrid Laurier University Press, 1996.

Lipsitz, George. *Time Passages: Collective Memory and American Popular Culture.* Minneapolis: University of Minnesota Press, 1990.

Lloyd, David W. *Battlefield Tourism: Pilgrimage and the Commemoration of the Great War in Britain, Australia, and Canada, 1919–1939.* Oxford: Berg, 1998.

Low, Rachael. *The History of the British Film, 1918–1929.* London: George Allen & Unwin, 1971.

Lowenthal, David. *The Past Is a Foreign Country.* Cambridge: Cambridge University Press, 1985.

Lynn, John A. *Giant of the Grand Siècle: The French Army, 1610–1715.* Cambridge: Cambridge University Press, 1997.

Macdonald, Sharon. 'Boadicea: Warrior, Mother and Myth.' In *Images of Women in Peace and War: Cross-Cultural and Historical Perspectives,* ed. Sharon Macdonald, Pat Holden, and Shirley Ardener. Madison: University of Wisconsin Press, 1988.

Manring, M.M. *Slave in a Box: The Strange Career of Aunt Jemima.* Richmond: University Press of Virginia, 1998.

Martin, Denis. *Portraits des héros de la Nouvelle-France: Images d'un culte historique.* LaSalle: Éditions Hurtubise HMH, 1988.

Mathieu, Jacques, and Jacques Lacoursière. *Les mémoires québécoises.* Sainte-Foy: Les Presses de l'Université Laval, 1991.

May, Lary. *Screening Out the Past: The Birth of Mass Culture and the Motion Picture Industry.* Chicago: University of Chicago Press, 1980.

May, Louise Anne. 'Worthy Warriors and Unruly Amazons: Sino-Western Historical Accounts and Imaginative Images of Women in Battle.' Ph.D. thesis, University of British Columbia, 1985.

McClintock, Anne. 'Family Feuds: Gender, Nationalism, and the Family.' *Feminist Review: Nationalisms and National Identities* 44 (Summer 1993): 61–80.

– *Imperial Leather: Race, Gender, and Sexuality in the Colonial Contest.* London: Routledge, 1995.

McDiarmid, Garnett, and David Pratt. *Teaching Prejudice: A Content Analysis of Social Studies Textbooks Authorized for Use in Ontario.* Toronto: Ontario Institute for Studies in Education, 1971.

McKay, Ian. *The Quest of the Folk: Antimodernism and Cultural Selection in Twentieth-Century Nova Scotia.* Montreal: McGill-Queen's University Press, 1994.

McKillop, A.B. 'Who Killed Canadian History? A View from the Trenches.' *CHR* 80, no. 2 (June 1999): 269–99.

McLaughlin, Megan. 'The Woman Warrior: Gender, Warfare and Society in Medieval Europe.' *Women's Studies* 17, nos. 3–4 (Jan. 1990): 193–209.

McPherson, Kathryn. 'Carving Out a Past: The Canadian Nurses' Association War Memorial.' *Hs-SH* 29, no. 58 (Nov. 1996): 417–30.

Messamore, Barbara. 'The Social and Cultural Role of the Governors-General in Canada.' In *Imperial Canada*, ed. C.M. Coates, 78–108. Edinburgh: Centre of Canadian Studies, 1997.

Mills, David. *The Idea of Loyalty in Upper Canada, 1784–1850.* Montreal: McGill-Queen's University Press, 1988.

Morgan, Cecilia. *Public Men and Virtuous Women: The Gendered Languages of Upper Canadian Religion and Politics, 1791–1850.* Toronto: University of Toronto Press, 1996.

Morris, Peter. *Embattled Shadows: A History of Canadian Cinema, 1895–1939.* Montreal: McGill-Queen's University Press, 1978.

Morton, Graeme. 'The Most Efficacious Patriot: The Heritage of William Wallace in Nineteenth-Century Scotland.' *Scottish Historical Review* 77, no. 2 (Oct. 1998): 224–51.

Nelles, H.V. 'Historical Pageantry and the "Fusion of the Races" at the Tercentenary of Quebec, 1908.' *Hs-SH* 29, no. 58 (Nov. 1996): 391–415.

– *The Art of Nation-Building: Pageantry and Spectacle at Quebec's Tercentenary.* Toronto: University of Toronto Press, 1999.

New, W.H. *Land Sliding: Imagining Space, Presence, and Power in Canadian Writing.* Toronto: University of Toronto Press, 1997.

Noel, Jan. 'Women in New France: Further Reflections.' *Atlantis* 8, no. 1 (Fall 1982): 118–24.
– 'New France: Les femmes favorisées.' In *The Neglected Majority: Essays in Canadian Women's History*, ed. Alison Prentice and Susan Mann Trofimenkoff, 18–40. Vol. 2. Toronto: McClelland and Stewart, 1985.
– *Women in New France.* Historical Booklet No. 59. Ottawa: Canadian Historical Association, 1998.
Nora, Pierre. *Realms of Memory: Rethinking the French Past.* 3 vols. Trans. Arthur Goldhammer. New York: Columbia University Press, 1996.
Novick, Peter. *That Noble Dream: The 'Objectivity Question' and the American Historical Profession.* Cambridge: Cambridge University Press, 1988.
Owram, Douglas. 'The Myth of Louis Riel.' *CHR* 63, no. 3 (Sept. 1982): 315–36.
Palmer, Bryan D. 'Of Silences and Trenches: A Dissident View of Granatstein's Writing.' *CHR* 80, no. 4 (Dec. 1999): 676–86.
Parvin, Viola. *Authorization of Textbooks for the Schools of Ontario, 1846–1950.* Toronto: University of Toronto Press, 1965.
Peterman, Michael A., and Janet B. Friskney. '"Booming" the Canuck Book: Edward Caswell and the Promotion of Canadian Writing.' *JoCS* 30, no. 3 (Fall 1995): 60–90.
Pierson, Ruth Roach. *'They're Still Women after All': The Second World War and Canadian Womanhood.* Toronto: McClelland and Stewart, 1986.
Potter-MacKinnon, Janice. *While the Women Only Wept: Loyalist Refugee Women in Eastern Ontario.* Montreal: McGill-Queen's University Press, 1993.
Power, Michael, and Nancy Butler. *Slavery and Freedom in Niagara.* Niagara-on-the-Lake: Niagara Historical Society, 1993.
Pratt, Mary-Louise. *Imperial Eyes: Travel Writing and Transculturation.* London: Routledge, 1992.
Prentice, Alison, et al. *Canadian Women: A History.* Toronto: Harcourt Brace Jovanovich, 1988.
Rafferty, Oisin. 'Balancing the Books: Brokerage Politics and the "*Ontario Readers* Question."' *Historical Studies in Education* 4, no. 1 (1992): 79–95.
Régimbald, Patrice. 'La disciplinarisation de l'histoire au Canada français, 1920–1950.' *RHAF* 51, no. 2 (Autumn 1997): 163–200.
Richards, Thomas. *The Commodity Culture of Victorian England: Advertising and Spectacle, 1851–1914.* Stanford: Stanford University Press, 1990.
– *The Imperial Archive: Knowledge and the Fantasy of Empire.* London: Verso, 1993.
Richter, Daniel. *The Ordeal of the Longhouse: The Peoples of the Iroquois League in the Era of European Colonization.* Chapel Hill: University of North Carolina Press, 1992.

Roby, Yves. *Les Franco-Américains de la Nouvelle-Angleterre, 1776–1930.* Sillery: Septentrion, 1990.

Rosenzweig, Roy. *Eight Hours for What We Will: Workers and Leisure in an Industrial City, 1870–1920.* Cambridge: Cambridge University Press, 1983.

Roy, Fernande. 'Une mise en scène de l'histoire: La fondation de Montréal à travers les siècles.' *RHAF* 46, no. 1 (Summer 1992): 7–36.

Rublack, Ulinka. 'Wench and Maiden: Women, War and the Pictorial Function of the Feminine in German Cities in the Early Modern Period.' *History Workshop Journal* 44 (Autumn 1997): 1–22.

Rudin, Ronald. 'Contested Terrain: Commemorative Celebrations and National Identity in Ireland and Quebec.' In *La Nation dans tous ses états: Le Québec en comparaison,* ed. Gérard Bouchard and Yvan Lamonde, 183–204. Montreal: Harmattan, 1997.

– *Making History in Twentieth-Century Quebec.* Toronto: University of Toronto Press, 1997.

Samuel, Raphael. *Theatres of Memory.* Volume 1. *Past and Present in Contemporary Culture.* London: Verso, 1994.

Sears, John F. *Sacred Places: American Tourist Attractions in the Nineteenth Century.* Oxford: Oxford University Press, 1989.

Seibel, George. *Ontario's Niagara Parks: 100 Years.* Niagara Falls: Niagara Parks Commission, 1985.

Shaw, Christopher, and Malcolm Chase, eds. *The Imagined Past: History and Nostalgia.* Manchester: Manchester University Press, 1989.

Shepherd, George. *Plunder, Profit, and Paroles: A Social History of the War of 1812 in Upper Canada.* Montreal: McGill-Queen's University Press, 1994.

Sherman, Daniel J. 'Monuments, Mourning and Masculinity in France after World War I.' *Gender and History* 8, no. 1 (April 1996): 82–107.

Showalter, Elaine. *Sexual Anarchy: Gender and Culture at the fin de siècle.* Markham, ON: Penguin Books, 1990.

Shrive, Norman. *Charles Mair: Literary Nationalist.* Toronto: University of Toronto Press, 1965.

Smith, Anthony. 'The "Golden Age" and National Renewal.' In *Myths and Nationhood,* ed. Geoffrey Hosking and George Schöpflin. London: Hurst & Company 1997.

Smith, Donald B. 'Fred Loft.' Paper presented to the Canadian Historical Association, Brock University, 1996.

Spectacle, Monument, Memory. Special issue of *Hs-SH* 29, no. 58 (Nov. 1996).

Stamp, Robert. 'Empire Day in the Schools of Ontario: The Training of Young Imperialists.' *JoCS* 8, no. 3 (Aug. 1973): 32–42.

– *The Schools of Ontario, 1876–1976.* Toronto: University of Toronto Press, 1982.

Staton, Pat, and Paula Bourne. 'Sex Equity Content in History Textbooks.' *History and Social Science Teacher* 25, no. 1 (Fall 1989): 18–20.

Strong-Boag, Veronica, and Carole Gerson. *Paddling Her Own Canoe: The Times and Texts of E. Pauline Johnson (Tekahionwake)*. Toronto: University of Toronto Press, 2000.

Sutherland, Neil. *Growing Up: Childhood in English Canada from the Great War to the Age of Television*. Toronto: University of Toronto Press, 1997.

Taylor, C.J. *Negotiating the Past: The Making of Canada's National Historic Parks and Sites*. Montreal: McGill-Queen's University Press, 1990.

Taylor, M. Brooke. *Promoters, Patriots, and Partisans: Historiography in Nineteenth-Century Canada*. Toronto: University of Toronto Press, 1989.

Thomas, Earle. *The Three Faces of Molly Brant*. Kingston, ON: Quarry Press, 1996.

Thompson, Elizabeth. *The Pioneer Woman: A Canadian Character Type*. Montreal: McGill-Queen's University Press, 1991.

Trofimenkoff, Susan Mann. *L'Action française: French Canadian Nationalism in the Twenties*. Toronto: University of Toronto Press, 1975.

– 'Henri Bourassa and "the Woman Question."' In *The Neglected Majority: Essays in Canadian Women's History*, eds. Susan Mann Trofimenkoff and Alison Prentice, 104–15. Toronto: McClelland and Stewart, 1977.

– *The Dream of Nation: A Social and Intellectual History of Quebec*. Toronto: Gage, 1983.

Turner, D. John. 'J.-A. Homier photographe, le pionnier oublié du cinéma québécois.' *24 images* 11 (Dec. 1981): 47–55.

Turner, Wesley B. 'Early Settlement.' In *Niagara's Changing Landscapes*, ed. Hugh J. Gayler, 179–207. Ottawa: Carleton University Press, 1994.

University Women's Club of Port Credit. *The Canadian Indian in Ontario's School Texts: A Study of Social Studies Textbooks Grades 1 through 8*. N.p.: Indian-Eskimo Association of Canada, 1968.

Vance, Jonathan F. *Death So Noble: Memory, Meaning, and the First World War*. Vancouver: UBC Press, 1997.

Véronneau, Pierre. *Montréal: Ville de cinéma*. Montreal: Cinématèque québécoise/Musée du Cinéma, 1992.

Viau, Roland. *Enfants du néant et mangeurs d'âmes: Guerre, culture et société en Iroquoisie ancienne*. Montreal: Boréal, 1997.

Vicinus, Martha. *Independent Women: Work and Community for Single Women, 1850–1920*. Chicago: University of Chicago Press, 1985.

Walden, Keith. 'Isaac Brock: Man and Myth, a Study of the Militia Myth of the War of 1812 in Upper Canada, 1812–1912.' M.A. thesis, Queen's University, 1971.

– *Becoming Modern in Toronto: The Industrial Exhibition and the Shaping of a Late Victorian Culture.* Toronto: University of Toronto Press, 1997.

Walkowitz, Judith. *City of Dreadful Delight: Narratives of Sexual Danger in Late-Victorian London.* Chicago: University of Chicago Press, 1992.

Warner, Marina. *Joan of Arc: The Image of Female Heroism.* New York: Alfred A. Knopf, 1981.

– *Monuments and Maidens: The Allegory of the Female Form.* London: Weidenfeld and Nicholson, 1985.

Way, Ronald. *Ontario's Niagara Parks: A History.* Fort Erie: Niagara Parks Commission, 1946.

Weaver, Sally M. 'The Iroquois: The Consolidation of the Grand River Reserve in the Mid-Nineteenth Century, 1847–1875.' In *Aboriginal Ontario: Historical Perspectives on the First Nations,* ed. Edward S. Rogers and Donald B. Smith, 182–211. Toronto: Dundurn, 1994.

Weber, Eugene. *Peasants into Frenchmen: The Modernization of Rural France, 1870–1914.* Stanford: Stanford University Press, 1976.

Wheelwright, Julie. *Amazons and Military Maids: Women Who Dressed as Men in the Pursuit of Life, Liberty and Happiness.* London: Pandora, 1989.

White, Hayden. 'The Value of Narrativity in the Representation of Reality.' In *On Narrative,* ed. W.J.T. Mitchell. Chicago: University of Chicago Press, 1981.

Winock, Michel. 'Jeanne d'Arc.' In *Les lieux de la mémoire.* Vol. 3. *Les France 3: De l'archive à l'emblème,* ed. Pierre Nora. Paris: Gallimard, 1992. 675–733.

Wright, Donald A. 'The Importance of Being Sexist, or, The Professionalization of History in English Canada to 1950.' Paper presented to the Canadian Historical Association, Memorial University, June 1997.

– 'W.D. Lighthall and David Ross McCord: Antimodernism and English-Canadian Imperialism, 1880s–1918.' *JoCS* 32, no. 2 (Summer 1997): 134–53.

– 'Myth, Memory, Meaning.' *Literary Review of Canada* (Dec. 1998): 25–7.

– 'Gender and the Professionalization of History in English Canada before 1960.' *CHR* 81, no. 1 (March 2000): 29–66.

Young, David. 'The Macmillan Company of Canada in the 1930s.' *JoCS* 30, no. 3 (Fall 1995): 117–33.

Young, Robert. *White Mythologies: Writing History and the West.* London: Routledge, 1990.

Illustration Credits

Louis Brouilly: Iroquois warrior grabs Verchères's scarf, from Guy Laviolette, *Marie-Madeleine de Verchères: Châtelaine de la Pérade, 1678–1747* (Quebec: Gloires nationales, 1944), 6

Canadian War Museum: Verchères recruits for the CWAC, Adam Sherriff Scott, 19750317-100

Colin Coates, author's collection: postcard of the Verchères statue, photographer unknown

Charles Comfort: 'Laura Secord, the woman who made Confederation possible,' from Charles Comfort, *Laura Secord and Confederation*

Éric Daudelin: Lefebvre chases Verchères, photospread in Jacques Lacoursière, 'La véridique histoire de Madeleine de Verchères et son curé,' *L'Actualité* 1, no. 3 (1976): 36–7

Joseph Forte: Iroquois watching the fort, from Richard Boning, *Soldier Girl* (Baldwin, NY: Dexter & Westbrook, 1975), 20

Globe and Mail: 'The ride of Sinclair Stevens,' illustrator Ed Franklin, 23 July 1979

Barbara Klunder: Laura Secord period–style chair

J.B. Lagacé: poster of Verchères lighting the cannon (produced for the textbook Desrosiers and Bertrand, *Histoire du Canada*)

Laura Secord Candy Company: advertisements (figs. 8.3–8.5, 8.10–8.11, 8.15); 'dainty' Secord candy shop; respectable exterior of a Secord candy shop; Secord 'Studio'; pioneer foremother; post-war Laura Secord; Junior Majorette

James McIsaac: Verchères prepares the cannon, from Abbé Lionel Groulx, *Chez nos ancêtres*, 2nd ed. (Montreal: Bibliothèque de l'Action française, 1920), 42

Cecilia Morgan, author's collection: 'She walked bravely up to them,' from

Donald French, ed., *Famous Canadian Stories* (1945); Secord monument, Lundy's Lane; Secord monument, Queenston Heights; candy box panels; Women's Literary Club marker; tourist plaque; Secord homestead, Queenston; Secord homestead candy store

National Archives of Canada: Verchères closing the gates, C.W. Jefferys, C10687; young Verchères, Gerald Hayward, C83513; Verchères welcomes the troops, C.W. Jefferys, C70272; Verchères in 1908 parade, PA24723; Hébert's statuette, photographer William James Topley, PA8975; Verchères bids farewell, Patent and Copyright Office collection, PA28626; Verchères welcomes the French troops, Patent and Copyright Office collection, PA28623; prayer of thanksgiving, Patent and Copyright Office collection, PA28624; restaurant sign, Michel Saint-Jean, PA147537; Secord tells her story to FitzGibbon, C.W. Jefferys, C70253; Sandham illustration from the *Handbook to Nelson's Pictures of Canadian History*, Henry Sandham, C124; Iroquois attack on the fort, Patent and Copyright Office collection, PA28625 (Note: The work of C.W. Jefferys is reproduced with the permission of the C.W. Jefferys Estate, Toronto)

National Library of Canada: the noble, demure Verchères, E.Z. Massicotte, C14354; 'driving a cow before her,' J.R. Skelton, NL22302

Lawrence Smith: illustration from 'Laura Secord,' from Merrill Denison, *Henry Hudson and Other Plays: Six Plays for the Microphone*, Romance of Canada series of radio broadcasts (Toronto: Ryerson Press, 1931)

Société St-Jean Baptiste de Montréal: Verchères referendum poster, Francine Serrand and Jacques Lavallée, private collection of Nicole Chagnon and Paul Brisebois

Index